Special thank yous

We would like to extend special thanks to the following people:

Kirstie Addis, Hilary Armstrong, Elizabeth Bowden, David Carter, Paul Carter, Martin Chapman, Amber Crampton, Jack Doyle, Claudia Dyer, Nicola Frame, Alan Grimwade, Nicola Gardner, Emily Gault, Natalie Goodrick, Ros Mari Grindheim, Alex Hall and Ben Kay at Charterhouse, Verity Hartley, Andy Hayler, Bev Jordan, Janice Leech, Michelle Lyttle, David Mabey, Simon Mather and Iain Barker at AMA, Adam Miller, Angela Newton, Jeffrey Ng, John Rowlands, John Rudkin, Oliver Smith, Emma Sturgess, Lynn Taylor, Mark Taylor, Judi Turner, Stuart Walton, Jenny White, Blânche Williams and Emma Wilmot.

Picture credits

Harry Williams (Bryan Webb), Paul Raeside (Jason Atherton), Marc Miller (Tom Kitchin)

Map credits

Maps designed and produced by Cosmographics, www.cosmographics.co.uk
UK digital database © Cosmographics, 2009
Greater London map © Cosmographics, 2009
North and South London Maps © Collins Bartholomew 2009
West, Central and East London maps © BTA (trading as VisitBritain) 2009
produced by Cosmographics and used with the kind permission of VisitBritain.

Please send updates, queries, menus and wine lists to:
goodfoodguide@which.co.uk or write to:
The Good Food Guide, 2 Marylebone Road, London, NW1 4DF

T

Edited by
T.G. McGee and Ira M. Robinson

The Mega-Urban Regions of Southeast Asia

UBCPress / Vancouver

Printed in Canada on acid-free paper ∞

ISBN 0-7748-0530-7 (hardcover)
ISBN 0-7748-0548-X (paperback)

ISSN 1196-8583

To our respective wives, Lori and Ruth

Canadian Cataloguing in Publication Data

Main entry under title:

The mega-urban regions of Southeast Asia

(Urbanization in Asia, ISSN 1196-8583; 1)
Includes bibliographical references and index.
ISBN 0-7748-0530-7 (bound). – ISBN 0-7748-0548-X (pbk.)

1. Urbanization – Asia, Southeastern. 2. Asia, Southeastern – Social conditions. 3. Metropolitan areas – Asia, Southeastern.
I. McGee, T.G. (Terence Gary) II. Robinson, Ira M. (Ira Miles), 1924-
HT384.A785M43 1995   307.76'4'0959   C95-910497-6

UBC Press gratefully acknowledges the ongoing support to its publishing program from the Canada Council, the Province of British Columbia Cultural Services Branch, and the Department of Communications of the Government of Canada.

Financial contributions to aid publication were made by the UBC Faculty of Applied Science and the UBC Institute of Asian Research.

Set in Stone by George Vaitkunas
Printed and bound in Canada by Friesens
Copy-editor: Camilla Jenkins
Proofreader: Nancy Pollak
Indexer: Annette Lorek

UBC Press
University of British Columbia
6344 Memorial Road
Vancouver, BC V6T 1Z2
(604) 822-3259
Fax: 1-800-668-0821
E-mail: orders@ubcpress.ubc.ca

Contents

Maps and Figures

Figures

Preface

The title of this book perhaps suggests that all of Southeast Asia falls within its subject matter, but in fact it deals only with the largest mega-cities of the ASEAN countries of Thailand, Malaysia, the Philippines, Singapore, and Indonesia. (Brunei Darussalam is not considered.) In the rest of Southeast Asia, however, only one country is already experiencing some of the early symptoms of mega-urbanization, the Republic of Vietnam. This is the subject of ongoing research by McGee (1995). *The Mega-Urban Regions of Southeast Asia* can thus be said to be representative of contemporary mega-urban developments in Southeast Asia as a whole.

ASEAN, the Association of Southeast Asian Nations, was created in 1967. It has a secretariat based in Jakarta and is dedicated to increasing economic and cultural links among its member states. Regular heads of state and ministerial meetings are held. The association is now moving towards the creation of an ASEAN free trade area (AFTA) by 2008.

A distinguishing feature of recent urbanization in the ASEAN countries is the extension of their mega-cities beyond the city and metropolitan boundaries. This process has particularly affected the largest cities but it is also now occurring in the largest secondary ones, such as Chiang Mai in Thailand, Bandung in Indonesia, and Cebu City in the Philippines. Metropolitan regional growth tends to sprawl along major expressways and railroad lines radiating out from the urban cores, and leapfrogs in all directions, putting down new towns, industrial estates, housing projects, and even golf courses in areas hitherto agricultural and rural. In such areas, regions of dense population and mixed land uses are created, in which traditional agriculture is found side by side with modern factories, commercial activities, and suburban development. T.G. McGee has termed these *desakota* zones, drawing on the Bahasa Indonesia words for town and village.

Extended metropolitan development tends to produce an amorphous and amoebic-like spatial form, with no set boundaries or geographic extent and long regional peripheries, their radii sometimes stretching 75 to 100 km from the urban core. The entire territory – comprising the central city, the developments within the transportation corridors, the satellite towns and other projects in the peri-urban fringe, and the outer zones – is emerging as a single, economically integrated 'mega-urban region,' or 'extended metropolitan region.' Within this territory are a large number of individual jurisdictions, both urban and rural, each with its own administrative machinery, laws, and regulations. No single authority is responsible for overall planning or management.

Mega-metropolitan development, fuelled by rapid economic growth and the availability of different transportation technologies, is producing both positive and negative results. On the positive side, there is evidence that household incomes are increasing. As well, employment opportunities abound, especially for young women. Moreover, an increasing proportion of population, housing, and industry and up to 40 per cent of gross national product is located in these regions. These dynamic regions are crucial to the economic health of the countries of which they are part. On the negative side, growth in the outlying parts of the regions is causing environmental deterioration and ecological degradation, conflicting land uses, inadequate housing and service provisions, and exploitation of female factory workers. These serious problems are compounded by a lack of effective land-use and environmental controls and other institutional machinery necessary for managing the new urban complex. In these areas, administrative departments previously responsible for rural policies have not been reorganized to cope with new urban developments.

The ability of ASEAN not only to retain its current position as one of the world's fastest growing regional economies but also to continue improving the quality of life for its citizens may largely depend on how successful all levels of government, working with the world business community and international aid agencies, will be in coping with mega-urban problems while taking advantage of the positive features of the mega-urban regions. This will require new approaches, new policies, and new administrative-governmental arrangements.

Focus on mega-urban regions in the ASEAN context is comparatively new, but such regions have been emerging in developed countries for several decades, generating a large body of research. Some of this experience has relevance to ASEAN, but there is a need to bring together professional experience and research carried out within ASEAN countries. For this reason, several organizations jointly sponsored a major international conference: the Canadian Universities Consortium (CUC), consisting of the Universities of British Columbia, Calgary, York, and Waterloo, the Asian Institute of Technology in Bangkok, Thailand, the Canada-ASEAN Centre in Singapore, and the Asian Institute of Technology-Canadian International Development Agency (AIT-CIDA) Partnership Project. We are particularly grateful to all these organizations for their financial and logistical support.

The conference, entitled 'Managing the Mega-Urban Regions of ASEAN Countries: Policy Challenges and Responses,' was held at the Asian Institute of Technology from 30 November to 3 December 1992. There were 167 registered participants from 12 countries, including public officials (planners, policy advisers, administrators, and politicians), non-governmental organization representatives, private corporate managers, international experts, academics, and researchers. All of the participants were from, or had worked in, ASEAN or other Asian countries. The purpose of the conference was to identify the major problems, opportunities, and challenges facing the mega-urban regions in ASEAN and to make recommendations for appropriate future policy actions and research.

Twenty-six people presented papers during the conference, of whom fifteen either resided, worked, or taught in developing countries at the time. This was in line with the conference objective to present perspectives *from* mega-urban regions in developing countries, and not just *about* the experience of mega-urban regions in developed countries.

The Mega-Urban Regions of Southeast Asia contains a selection of papers from the conference. The book is organized into four parts. The first presents an overview of mega-urbanization. The second explores the processes influencing the growth and features of mega-urban regions. The third offers a series of case studies of the major mega-urban cities of ASEAN. The final part synthesizes the findings of the volume.

Part 1 introduces the themes of the book. In 'Metrofitting the Emerging Mega-Urban Regions of ASEAN: An Overview,' T.G. McGee surveys the nature and extent of mega-urban regions in ASEAN, the processes underlying their emergence, and their positive and negative features, concluding with a call for new metropolitan institutions more adaptable to these large urban regions. The chapter is, in short, a plea for *metrofitting*.

'Mega-Urbanization in ASEAN: New Phenomenon or Transitional Phase to the "Los Angeles World City"?' identifies possible policy responses required of the public, private, parastatal, and volunteer communities in responding to mega-urbanization issues and challenges. In exploring his subject, Douglas Webster adopts a strategic and futuristic approach. Specifically, he identifies different conditions that ASEAN mega-urban regions might experience by the year 2020, depending upon crucial interventions in such important areas as transportation, employment, environment, and social systems.

Part 2 deals with the processes creating mega-urban regions in ASEAN:

economy, population, housing, transportation, environment, and governance and management. In 'Global Interdependence and Urbanization: Planning for the Bangkok Mega-Urban Region,' Mike Douglass explores the new geography of production and consumption in ASEAN countries with three purposes in mind. First, he demonstrates that received theories underlying much urban and regional planning and policy are based on hierarchical models of urban-industrial diffusion and are of decreasing relevance to the emerging economic landscapes in ASEAN. Second, he proposes a 'regional network' concept to describe the opportunities and dynamics of contemporary spatial development processes. Third, he explores the implications of this approach for urban and regional planning and policy. Throughout the paper, Douglass draws upon the experience of Thailand to illustrate the major concepts put forth and the policy directions advocated.

Ira M. Robinson, in 'Emerging Spatial Patterns in ASEAN Mega-Urban Regions: Alternative Strategies,' focuses on the issue of decentralization within metropolitan regions, which most planners and public officials since the 1970s have seen as one of the key solutions to the problems facing mega-cities. (Dispersal of population and economic activity into secondary, provincial, or intermediate cities on a national basis is another favourite solution, which this chapter does not address.) Robinson argues that decentralization per se is no panacea. What is needed is planned or controlled decentralization in the form of polycentric centres and subcentres, each with a concentration of population and employment and a complete set of community services and facilities within the metropolitan region. Indeed, most Asian mega-cities have spatial planning strategies 'on the books' – that is, in their master plans – proposing the development of a polycentric spatial structure for their metropolitan regions. Unfortunately, few such strategies have been implemented. The result is unplanned and uncontrolled decentralization, which is causing more serious problems, especially environmental problems, than those that decentralization was trying to solve in the first place. In short, there has been lots of decentralization but very little polycentricity. Robinson illustrates these points with respect to the Bangkok Metropolitan Region. He concludes with recommendations for achieving polycentred spatial forms in the future.

The two chapters on housing differ in their focus. In 'ASEAN Urban Housing Sector Performance: A Comparative Perspective,' Shlomo Angel and Stephen K. Mayo present preliminary results for the five ASEAN mega-cities – Bangkok, Jakarta, Singapore, Kuala Lumpur, and Manila – from the extensive survey done by the World Bank's Housing Indicators Program of housing conditions in fifty-two major cities throughout the world. The chapter presents a conceptual framework for evaluating the performance of the housing sector. It also provides data comparing housing sector performance in the five ASEAN mega-cities to that of the rest of the world and explains some of the differences among these cities. Finally, the chapter suggests a framework for housing policy reform and research within the region.

'Housing Women Factory Workers in the Northern Corridor of the Bangkok Metropolitan Region,' by Yap Kioe Sheng and Aminur Rahman, focuses on the housing of female workers employed in the factories situated along the so-called northern corridor, located in one of the five 'outlying' provinces undergoing rapid urban development and industrialization within the Bangkok Metropolitan Region. The corridor is a 20 km stretch of land straddling the main north-south highway that connects Bangkok to the northern regions. The chapter reports the results of a study of the housing conditions and housing demand of these factory workers and describes the different arrangements for housing them, including those undertaken by the companies. Pathum Thani, the outlying province under study, is not administratively recognized as an urban area although it is urbanizing rapidly. As a consequence, development is unplanned and the provision of housing is largely left to the informal sector. This results in an inefficient use of land along the highway, traffic congestion, high fuel consumption, air pollution, and long commuting times.

Dealing with the issue of transportation, Peter J. Rimmer's chapter, 'Moving Goods, People, and Information: Putting the ASEAN Mega-Urban Regions in Context,' focuses on the supranational linkages and interactions in goods, people, and information among the ASEAN and Asian countries between 1983 and 1990. This analysis not only serves as an antidote to the excessive concentration of governments on the internal problems of mega-urban regions but also allows us to recognize the emergence of a Southeast Asian development corridor from Chiang Mai to Bali. In turn, this leads to discussion of the prospects for this corridor to coalesce with an East Asian counterpart running from Seoul to Hong Kong.

In 'Gridlock in the Slopopolis: Congestion Management and Sustainable Development,' V. Setty Pendakur argues that the deadly combination of exponential growth of human population and motor vehicles and 'business as usual' methods of congestion management has given the ASEAN mega-cities the unique title of *slopopolis*. The slopopolis is described as the urban form of endless land development without any regard to urban infrastructure provision, environmental quality, or social consequences, driven primarily by profit-generating economic activities with no obligation to provide urban services. Congestion management practices in ASEAN mega-cities, except for Singapore, are currently inappropriate for managing mega-urban regions. The economic growth of the past decade and unsuitable practices of transport demand management have resulted in the drastic reduction of air quality and have serious negative consequences for the economy. The chapter discusses what governments need to do to change urban transport policy in order to emphasize efficiency, equity, and sustainability. Otherwise, current gridlock in the slopopolis will become a 'permanent crawl.'

Shirley A.M. Conover's chapter, 'The Roles and Contributions of the Private Sector in Environmental Management in ASEAN Mega-Urban Regions,' focuses on two aspects of mega-urban regions: the challenges and opportunities facing the ASEAN regions with respect to the environment; and the roles and contributions of the private sector in the rational management of it. Conover notes that the land and resource base required to support each of the regions is much larger than the administrative boundaries of the urban area itself. If the urban centre expands, the resource base must expand along with it. The total environmental management system of any country or other administrative unit, including the ASEAN countries, is defined as a closed chain of six links: the people, their governments, the private sector, the educational system, communications, and non-government organizations. In this system, private-sector organizations have a key role to play in the ASEAN countries both individually and at times collectively. Metro Manila is used as a case study to analyze private-sector roles and contributions to environmental management.

Aprodicio Laquian's chapter, 'The Governance of Mega-Urban Regions,' deals with different approaches to governance that have evolved in the Third World, including ASEAN countries. The approaches differ mainly in terms of the degree of autonomy or centralism in local-central government relations, the functions assumed by each level of government, the level of participation accorded urban citizens, the role of the private sector in urban development, and the areal scope of governmental jurisdictions. Not surprisingly, forms of governance have also been heavily influenced by specific customs, historical circumstances, and other aspects of each country's political culture. Laquian concludes that new models of urban governance must be found if the economic role of the mega-cities is to be enhanced and the quality of life in such cities is to be maintained.

Ellen M. Brennan begins her chapter, 'Developing Management Responses for Mega-Urban Regions,' by rejecting the fairly common claim that size is the major issue behind the problems faced by mega-cities. She proceeds to examine a number of management issues: the need to develop new systems of data collection and management, new methods of environmental and land management, and innovative techniques for funding such institutional arrangements as metropolitan development authorities.

Part 3 presents a set of five case studies of ASEAN mega-urban regions: the Singapore Growth Triangle, comprising the Malaysian island of Johor, Singapore, and the Riau archipelago of Indonesia; Metro Manila in the Philippines; Jabotabek, the urban region centred on Jakarta in Indonesia; the Kuala Lumpur-Klang Valley region in Malaysia; and the Bangkok Metropolitan Region in central Thailand. Each of the chapters discusses the forces involved in expansion of the designated mega-urban region, the problems and challenges facing the region, and the governmental responses to the challenges and opportunities.

Finally, Part 4 analyzes the main elements of the urbanization process in ASEAN countries and suggests the major policies that could be followed to aid this process.

In preparing this volume we have applied two editorial principles. First, the cut-off point for the data presented is 1992, although in a few cases more recent data have been incorporated. Second, we have followed the authors' preferences with respect to the order of family and personal names. This means that only when a name is referred to in several different chapters by several different authors have we imposed a standard form. All dollar figures in the text are in US funds unless otherwise specified.

Acknowledgments

We wish to acknowledge the generous support of several groups and individuals without whose interest and contribution this volume would have been impossible to publish. In particular, we should like to single out the following:

- The Canadian Universities Consortium and its governing board: Dr Robert Page of the University of Calgary; Dr Axel Meisen of the University of British Columbia; Dr James Bater of the University of Waterloo; and Dr David Bell of York University. The CUC was also a major supporter for the conference itself.
- The Canadian-ASEAN Centre, for supporting the conference from which these papers were drawn.
- The Asian Institute of Technology, for various support functions in preparing the manuscript and for its generous assistance in ways too numerous to mention here, both before and during the conference.
- Ms Viwan Louhapatanalert of the CUC-AIT (Bangkok) and Ms Katie Eliot of the University of British Columbia, for their diligent inputting of the edited manuscript; Ms Gisèle Yasmeen of the University of British Columbia, for re-editing and printing the final version for the publisher; Ms Moe Moe Linn, for her assistance with some of the graphics; and Ms Catherine Griffiths, for preparing the list of references for the entire volume as well as several of the maps.
- Specific financial contributions to aid publication were made by the UBC Faculty of Applied Science, the UBC Institute of Asian Research, and the Northwest Consortium for Southeast Asian Studies funded by the Ford Foundation and the Canadian Universities Consortium.

Finally, we would like to express again how grateful we are to the various writers for their original contributions to the conference itself, and later, for their patience and hard work editing their papers for this volume in accordance with our wishes. Needless to say, we take full responsibility for the delay in its publication, and, along with the individual authors, for any possible errors and shortcomings in its contents, views, and interpretations.

Part 1
Overview and Issues

Map 1.1 **The ASEAN states**

1
Metrofitting the Emerging Mega-Urban Regions of ASEAN: An Overview

T. G. McGee

By the year 2020, the countries of ASEAN[1] (Map 1.1) will have become urbanized societies with more than 56 per cent of their population living in urban areas.[2] This will involve the addition of more than 168 million people to the 1990 urban population of 106 million in the thirty-year period between 1990 and 2020. At the same time, the population of ASEAN will grow from 323 million to 498 million. Thus most of the population increase in ASEAN over the next twenty-five years will occur in areas defined as urban. In a similar manner to the developed countries, ASEAN will experience an urban transition. This will involve major changes in the character of ASEAN societies, with the exception of Singapore, and pose many challenges to political leaders, government planners, and the private sector. These groups will need to develop a new outlook that recognizes the inevitability of the urban transition and faces the challenges that urbanization presents.

The issue of how population will be distributed within the urban system is central to the urbanization process in ASEAN. A high proportion of this urban population will be located in the mega-urban regions that already dominate the urban system of each ASEAN society. What follows is a description and analysis of both the emergence of these regions in ASEAN and implications for policy.

The chapter is divided into four main parts. The first presents a picture of urbanized societies in the ASEAN nations of the future. It must be stressed that, as an exercise in 'futurology,' this interpretation rests upon certain assumptions concerning economic growth, technological change, and the development of human resources, and that these could be interrupted for any number of economic or political reasons. Nonetheless, it is a reasonable projection. The second part describes the features of the emergence of mega-urban regions in ASEAN in the period 1960-90. The third delineates the forces that are creating the new spatial order in the ASEAN region. The fourth and final part discusses policy implications.

ASEAN in 2020: A Picture of the ASEAN Community

By 2020, the ASEAN region had moved to become one of the largest and most prosperous of the Asian trading blocs. During much of the period after 1995, the growth of gross domestic product (GDP) for the original six members – Indonesia, Thailand, Malaysia, Singapore, Brunei Darussalam, and the Philippines – continued at between 4 and 7 per cent per annum. For the three additional members – Laos, Cambodia, and Vietnam – rates of GDP growth had been lower but began to accelerate in the period after 2010 to catch up to the original ASEAN six. The region benefited from the opening up of the world trading system, from a less-regulated global financial environment, and particularly from the growth in Southeast Asian demand, as the nine ASEAN countries exhibited rapid growth and became a free trading bloc with a population of close to 690 million.

Structurally, the original six ASEAN countries experienced continuing change. Indonesia, Thailand, Malaysia, and the Philippines demonstrated growth in export-oriented manufacturing in the 1990s and early twenty-first century. Increased local and regional demand within the ASEAN market also led to the production of an increasing volume and variety of consumer goods. Globalization of world trade permitted each of these countries to establish product specialization in goods such as semi-conductors and automobiles and in the aerospace industry. At the same time, agro-processing and the export of raw materials such as timber, oil, gas, and mineral resources still provided an important part of export earnings. Brunei Darussalam, using income from oil and gas revenues, became an important joint venture capital location in the region, relying increasingly on income generated from these sources. While all the countries developed their urban-based service sectors in such areas as banks and finance, insurance, communications, and tourism, Singapore took advantage of its investment in global positioning in the 1980s and 1990s to become a global centre for the region.

Agriculture had changed substantially in the region. Rice growing was carried out mostly by part-time households, and other agriculture was devoted to industrial crops for which there was a continuing global demand: rubber and, increasingly, tropical food crops, particularly fruit. Most fishing activity was carried out in highly specialized, capital-intensive ponds and processing factories.

Economic changes were also reflected in the distribution of employment in 2020. The proportion of people in agriculture had shrunk to only 12 per cent; manufacturing remained steady at 30 per cent; and services had continued to grow. Of course, these patterns showed variations both between and within countries. In Indonesia and the Philippines, the proportion of people engaged in rice growing remained high and a large number of people held lower-order service occupations because of difficulties in creating sufficient employment in urban areas. In Thailand and Malaysia, however, the proportion engaged in agriculture fell to below 10 per cent. In Singapore, higher-order service employment dominated.[3]

These significant changes in the structure of the economy and employment had provided the basis for a substantial increase in household income, which now averaged $6,000 per household at constant 1990 prices. Growth of income had been accompanied by high levels of domestic savings, fostered at least in part by government fiscal measures, and these provided the basis for a rapid increase in ownership of cars, houses, and other durable consumer goods.

By 2020, most people in the ASEAN core region lived in urban areas. Projections of urban population growth made in the early 1990s proved to be underestimates, and close to two-thirds of the population now lived in urban areas, most in the five mega-urban regions: the Bangkok mega-urban region (30 million); the Kuala Lumpur-Klang mega-urban region (6 million); the Singapore Growth Triangle (10 million); the Java mega-urban corridor (100 million); and the Manila mega-urban region (30 million). These five contained almost 66 per cent of the urban population of ASEAN.[4]

The major urban centres had become the nodes for transportation systems linking the region: fast arterial highways, roll-on roll-off ferries, fast train systems, and air transportation. Investments in regional transportation systems had, of course, started in the 1980s. Singapore's dominance as the central node for air traffic had been established by that year, for example, but in the early twenty-first century funds provided by joint ventures between government and private sectors had been used in a major push to create a regional system of fast land transportation. It had greatly facilitated the increased mobility of goods and people. The banks of the Asian region had been more than willing to lend funds for these developments, which assured good returns on investment.

The remaining components of the urban system consisted of secondary cities such as Cebu, Manado, Penang, Chiang Mai, many of which had more than one million people and played an important role in regional interactions at both national and international levels. Finally, there were myriad small towns acting as market and service centres in rural areas. These had not grown greatly in numbers or size.

Thus dominating each ASEAN country was an extended mega-urban region (EMR). During the latter part of the twentieth century, many planners had predicted that the uncontrolled growth of these EMRs and their attendant problems of congestion, environmental deterioration, and service provision would prove to be intractable. Yet the introduction of vigorous urban management, an adequate infrastructure, and mass transit based on electrical rail systems enabled these large urban regions to function effectively, attracting international investment and a large proportion of each country's services. Indeed, each EMR generated a significant proportion of its country's income, in most cases exceeding 60 per cent.

Ecologically, the patterns of land use for the EMRs were rather similar. With the exception of Singapore, all had opted for low-density, spread-out patterns of settlement. In the late 1990s, a major debate had emerged over whether high-density, high-rise housing should dominate, as in Singapore, or low-rise, expanding housing in a spatially expanding city. Although virtually all planners agreed that high-rise commercial development, already well advanced, was the only economically feasible option in the face of inner-city land costs, there was less agreement on low- and middle-income high-rise housing. Rapidly expanding development of housing into the urban peripheries in the 1990s largely usurped this debate, leaving little alternative but to accept a low-rise, physically expanding urban region built around a number of nodal points that included shopping malls, office complexes, and so on. This was very much the Los Angeles model, with one exception. The introduction of a fast, intra-urban transit rail system in the first decade of the twenty-first century presented a viable alternative to the car for commuting travel in most of the EMRs.

The internal land-use patterns of the EMRs reflected these developments. Much of the central urban core was now given over to high-rise office buildings, shopping centres, and government departments. These activities were located in a number of central business districts in what came to be called by developers a city within a city. Typical of such areas were the Sudirman Central Business District (CBD) in Jakarta and the 'city' within Kuala Lumpur.

As these developments occurred, many of the low-income inhabitants moved out to new housing estates close to the industrial estates established on the periphery of the regions. Upper- and middle-income dwellers also lived on the periphery as well as in more expensive estates. Interspersed between new towns, housing estates, and industrial zones were leisure developments: golf courses, entertainment centres, and so on. Within the cores of the cities, some of the older housing had been rehabilitated and gentrified. This process had already begun in Singapore in the 1990s.

This picture of the ASEAN urban world is, of course, only one vision, and it is highly conjectural. Nevertheless, it is almost certain that the ASEAN countries will be predominantly urban by 2020. Why this is so is discussed below.

The Emergence of Extended Metropolitan Regions in ASEAN

Much of the preceding scenario is based on analysis of the trends in ASEAN from 1960 to 1990. In those thirty years, the countries of ASEAN underwent significant economic change. As Figure 1.1 indicates, all the ASEAN countries with the exception of the Philippines experienced annual growth of GDP per capita in excess of 8 per cent per annum in the period 1965-87, which puts them below the Asian newly industrializing countries (NICs) of Taiwan, South Korea, and Hong Kong but considerably in excess of the rest of Asia.

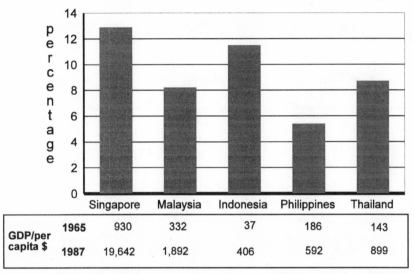

Figure 1.1 **GDP per capita and annual growth rate of ASEAN countries, 1965-87.** Data from World Bank (1990)

Rapid economic growth has produced important changes in the distribution of GDP, and all the countries have seen a decline in agriculture, an increase in industrialization, and a stable contribution from the service sector (Figure 1.2). This rapidly changing structural situation has had a fundamental impact on the social and spatial organization of these societies, particularly on urbanization.

As Figure 1.3 shows, the labour force has shifted considerably from agriculture to manufacturing and services, a trend that is likely to appear even more dramatic when the 1990 round of census data becomes fully available. At least one symptom of change is a more than 10 per cent increase in the level of urbanization in most cases. By 2000, the proportion of urban population will have increased even more, to almost 40 per cent, or about 155 million people (Table 1.1). Clearly, the future of ASEAN is related more and more to the growth of its urban centres.

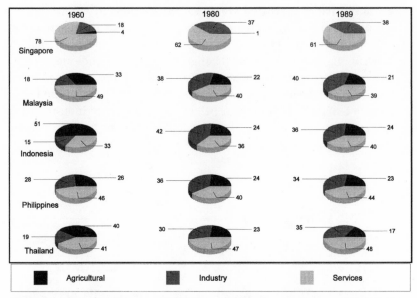

Figure 1.2 **GDP distribution of ASEAN countries by percentage, 1960-88.** Data from World Bank (1990)

There is cause to believe that the figures – derived from the World Bank and based on national definitions of urban – may even be substantially underestimated. Country definitions are often based on politically defined urban areas that 'underbound' the true physical extent of urban settlement. As well, there is considerable evidence that much non-agricultural activity is functionally part of the urban system and therefore the areas in which this activity is located should be included in redefined urban areas. Finally, there are vigorous economic, social, and political processes encouraging the extension of urban areas into their surrounding hinterlands, prompting a need for urban redefinition.

Table 1.1

Urban population change in ASEAN, 1980-2000

	Urban population as % of total population			Average annual urban population growth rate	
	1965	1990	2000	1965-80	1980-8
Singapore	100	100	100	1.6	1.1
Malaysia	26	43	51	4.5	4.9
Indonesia	16	31	40	4.8	4.8
Philippines	32	43	52	4.2	3.7
Thailand	13	22	30	5.1	4.7

Sources: World Bank (1990); United Nations, Department of International Economic and Social Affairs (1991)

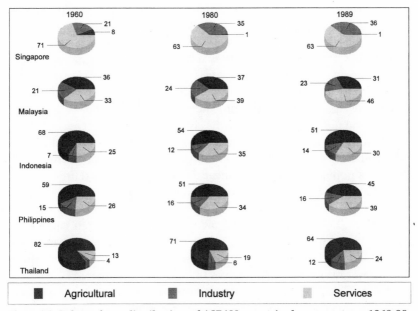

Figure 1.3 **Labour force distribution of ASEAN countries by percentage, 1960-90.**
Data from World Bank (1990)

Elsewhere (Ginsburg, Koppel, and McGee 1991), my colleagues and I have attempted to grapple with these processes, arguing that the distinctive ecological and historical conditions of Asia have led to the evolution of high-density rural areas given over to intensive agriculture (in which rice is a major crop) and in close proximity to the major urban areas. These conditions have created several salient factors. First, substantial pools of labour have emerged which can be tapped by relocating industry.[5] Second, considerable improvements in transportation and communications have greatly increased the accessibility of regions close to the urban core, and in some cases have led to corridor development between two major urban centres. Third, EMRs have proved very attractive to a number of decentralizing activities, including housing, recreation and, in some cases, tourism.

These developments, while superficially appearing to repeat the Western experience of urbanization in the nineteenth and early twentieth centuries, are in fact occurring in a different manner and mix. First, the supposedly clear distinction between rural and urban activities is breaking down much faster than was the case in the West. Second, considerable advances in transportation technology, particularly relatively cheap intermediate technology such as two-stroke motorbikes, greatly facilitate the circulation of commodities, people, and capital, leading to the creation of mega-urban regions. Third, the rapidity of industrialization and economic growth in the ASEAN region has primarily been focused on mega-urban regions, and particularly on the peripheral parts of these regions.

While it is not incorrect to see these processes in terms of the well-established spread of metropolitan areas documented, for instance, by Gottmann (1961) in the United States, in the Asian context the spatial extent, the large *in situ* population, and the extraordinary mixture of agricultural and non-agricultural activities is distinctively different.

Operating in Asia is the emergence of what can be described as region-based urbanization, as opposed to city-based urbanization. Rather than drawing a population from rural areas to a city, region-based urbanization utilizes an *in situ* population in the extended metropolitan region as well as drawing migrants from other rural areas (see Figure 1.4). As Chinese geographer Zhou has put it, 'These are the people who live in villages but work in cities' (Zhou 1991, 97). This is spatially extended urbanization rather than just population concentration, and it raises a significant number of new research and policy issues that need to be explored.

Of course, ASEAN governments are beginning to recognize the importance of this extended urbanization and to redefine existing urban boundaries. Today, three components are often recognized: the city core, which

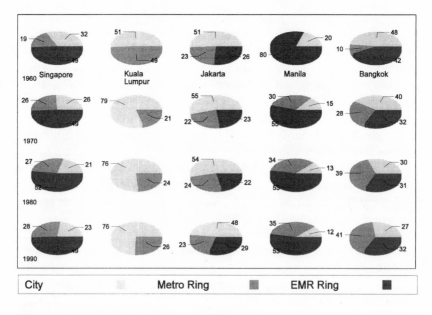

Figure 1.4 **Population distribution of ASEAN EMRs by percentage, 1960-90.** Data from various Southeast Asian Censuses. *Note:* Does not always total 100 per cent, due to rounding.

generally corresponds to the older defined city limits; the metropolitan area, which broadly bounds the most heavily built-up settlements that have expanded from the city core; and the extended metropolitan area, a term now applied to the areas of urban settlement in corridors radiating outwards from the metropolitan area. The term *desakota* refers to this last zone of urbanization, where non-agricultural activity is increasingly mixed with agriculture.

The following section studies the five major EMRs of ASEAN: Bangkok, Kuala Lumpur, Singapore, Jakarta, and Manila. The data base for such an analysis is quite sketchy, relying primarily on census materials, government publications, and secondary sources. The form of the data allows little more than the most cursory of comparisons.

1960-90: An Empirical Analysis

The historical and contemporary patterns of urbanization in Southeast Asia have been documented in many published works and will not be repeated here. While many studies have analyzed the dynamics of urbanization and its impact on the urban systems of Asia, few have focused on the recent evolution of the main urbanizing regions in ASEAN. These emerging urban regions are the primary focus of urbanization in the area, but their relative importance is not clearly understood. Indeed, their appearance is too often portrayed in terms of disaster and problems. I believe that this interpretation can be radically changed if their evolution is better understood.

To legitimize this claim, it is necessary to define the geographical extent of the EMRs as encompassing areas adjacent to presently defined urban areas, for it is here that urbanization is occurring most rapidly. We can see this reflected in the growing proportion of the population engaged in non-agricultural occupations, the growth of industry and services, and the establishment of residential areas, industrial estates, etc. At present, most definitions of the five EMRs involve two main components: the city core and the metropolitan region encompassing adjacent urban settlements.

Tables 1.2 and 1.3 show population data from 1960 to 1990. Table 1.4 also includes more detailed data for 1990. Although the data may seem somewhat confusing, three main trends in the spatial patterns of the population can be identified. First, with the exception of Singapore, the outer rings of the metropolitan area have generally been increasing their proportions of the total population and growing at faster rates than the city cores. This seems to imitate patterns already observed in Western economic activity. The case of Jakarta, which shows a slight variation from this trend, is probably explained by the greater areal extent of the Jakarta Special District. The district has the status of a province in Indonesia and extended boundaries in the area defined as a city. Kuala Lumpur is even more of an anomaly, explained by the creation of the Federal District in 1972, greatly extending its boundaries (see Figure 1.4).

Table 1.2

Population of Southeast Asian cities, metropolitan areas, and EMRs, 1960-90

	1960[a]		1970		1980		1990	
	(thousands)	(%)	(thousands)	(%)	(thousands)	(%)	(thousands)	(%)
Singapore								
City proper	912	32	1,038	26	1,050	21	1,205	23
Metro ring	531	19	1,036	26	1,364	27	1,500	28
EMR ring[b]	1,393	49	1,912	48	2,575	52	2,575	49
Total EMR	2,836	100	3,986	100	4,989	100	5,280	100
Kuala Lumpur								
City proper	316	51	872	79	920	76	1,258	74
Metro ring	311	49	234	21	279	24	442	26
EMR ring	0	0	0	0	0	0	0	0
Total EMR[c]	627	100	1,106	100	1,199	100	1,700	100
Jakarta								
City proper[d]	2,973	51	4,567	55	6,481	54	8,222	48
Metro ring[e]	1,314	23	1,863	22	2,740	24	4,007	23
EMR ring[f]	1,543	26	1,896	23	2,671	22	4,868	29
Total EMR	5,830	100	8,326	100	11,892	100	17,097	100
Manila								
City proper	1,131	20	1,330	15	1,630	13	1,982	12
Metro ring	8	<1	2,637	30	4,270	34	5,947	35
EMR ring[g]	4,471	80	4,909	55	6,658	53	8,962	53
Total EMR	5,610	100	8,876	100	12,558	100	16,891	100
Bangkok								
City proper	1,299	48	1,867	40	2,100	30	2,310	27
Metro ring	278	10	1,318	28	2,715	39	3,566	41
EMR ring[h]	1,157	42	1,503	32	2,124	31	2,646	32
Total EMR	2,734	100	4,688	100	6,939	100	8,522	100

Notes:
a Various census data: 1957, 1960, 1961.
b Malaysia District of Johor Bahru and Indonesia Kapbupaten of Riau.
c Includes Kuala Lumpur district remainder and Klang District.
d Daerah Khusus Indonesia Jakarta
e Kabupaten Bgor
f Bekasi and Tangerang Kabupaten
g Includes provinces: Zambales, Bataan, Pampanga, Bulacan, Rizal Laguana, Batangas, Cavite, Quezon.
h Includes *changwats*: Nonthaburi, Samut Prakan, Nakhon Pathom, Samut Sakhon, Pathum Thani
Sources: Various Southeast Asian censuses (1957-90)

Table 1.3

Increase in population of Southeast Asian cities and metropolitan areas, 1960-80

	1960-70	1970-80	1980-90
Singapore			
City	+14.0	+0.1	+15.0
Other	+95.0	+31.0	+10.0
Metro area	+43.0	+16.0	+12.0
Kuala Lumpur			
City	+176.0	+5.0	+36.7
Other	-25.0	+19.0	+58.4
Metro area	+76.0	+1.0	+41.8
Jakarta			
City	+54.0	+42.0	+26.9
Other	+41.0	+47.0	+46.2
Metro area	+55.0	+43.3	+32.6
Manila			
City	+0.1	+22.0	+21.6
Other	+328.0	+62.0	+39.3
Metro area	+248.0	+148.0	+34.6
Bangkok			
City	+14.0	+12.4	+10.0
Other	+374.0	+106.0	+31.3
Metro area	+101.0	+51.0	+19.5

Sources: Various Southeast Asian censuses (1960-80)

Second, the city cores in general have maintained a substantial share of the metropolitan populations. Only Manila city had dropped below 40 per cent of the metropolitan area population by 1980, and this was certainly due to boundary expansion with the creation of the Manila Metropolitan Authority in the early 1970s. As Tables 1.2 and 1.3 indicate, the city populations continued to grow, with increasing densities and congestion as important consequences.

Third, all the metropolitan areas grew substantially, each exceeding a population of one million and having rates of increase four and five times that of the respective countries. This indicates the growing attraction of urban centres for migrants from throughout the country. The trend has been commented upon in many studies and needs little comment here. The ASEAN metropolitan areas appear to be exhibiting somewhat similar spatial patterns of growth to Western countries. Nonetheless, urbanization is now occurring in a much wider region than was historically the case in Western countries.

Preliminary analysis of the 1990 census data for the EMRs of Bangkok and Jakarta (see Table 1.4) gives more detail. Indeed, at least one of the four *wilayah* (internal administrative units of Jakarta city) actually lost population. As calculations from Table 1.4 show, 66 per cent of growth in the Jakarta EMR occurred in the outer rings and 87 per cent in the case of the Bangkok EMR. In the case of the Manila EMR, 92 per cent of growth occurred in the outer rings.

Table 1.4

Population distribution of Jakarta and Bangkok EMRs by main zones, 1980 and 1990

| | 1980 | | 1990 | | |
	(thousands)	(%)	(thousands)	(%)	% Increase
Jakarta					
City core	6,481	54.0	8,222	48.0	26.8
Metro ring	2,740	24.0	4,007	23.0	46.2
EMR ring	2,671	22.0	4,868	29.0	82.2
Total	11,892	100.0	17,097	100.0	43.7
Bangkok					
City core	2,010	30.0	2,310	27.0	10.0
Metro ring	2,715	39.0	3,566	41.0	31.3
EMR ring	2,214	31.0	2,646	32.0	19.5
Total	6,939	100.0	8,522	100.0	22.8

Sources: Various Southeast Asian censuses (1980-90)

Three broadly emerging patterns of spatial growth can be identified. First is what I will call the expanding city state model, in which the vibrant Singapore city state is expanding its economic activity and leisure needs into the adjacent regions of the Riau archipelago (Indonesia) and Johor state (Malaysia). This growth triangle has become the focus of much attention, raising as it does important issues relating to a 'borderless economy.' How will the various states and private enterprises involved handle this evolving expansion of economic activity across international boundaries? Potentially, such growth offers an encouraging opportunity for Indonesia and southern peninsular Malaysia to benefit from the fast increasing wealth of Singapore.[6]

Second is the case of Kuala Lumpur. The EMR can be compared with Seoul because it is a region of comparatively low population density and has been able to control its growth through a polynucleated pattern of new towns and smaller suburban centres located along the major arterial routes of the city. The establishment of Kuala Lumpur as a Federal District has greatly aided this process of controlled growth and gives the EMR a distinctive quality compared to other ASEAN countries (Aiken 1981; Lee Boon Thong 1992b).

The third model is the high-density EMR exemplified by Jakarta, Manila, and Bangkok. Data collected for Jakarta and Bangkok indicate that from 1980 to 1990 the proportion of population resident in the metropolitan areas and EMRs increased quite dramatically (Table 1.4). Almost 52 per cent of the Jakarta EMR population is now resident outside the city core. In the case of Bangkok, the figure is 73 per cent. Thus it is these outer zones that are of increasing importance to urban growth and development.

In each of the EMRs, large rural populations principally engaged in rice cultivation have occupied the city peripheries, and economic activity has moved into these regions to tap surplus labour pools. This often occurs along major arterial highways, such as the Rangsit highway in Bangkok, and draws labour from surrounding rural areas. This labour is often female, and such employment generally leads to an increase in household incomes (Table 1.5).[7]

Table 1.5

Percentage of women aged 15-34 in non-agricultural occupations

	1971	1980	% Increase
Jakarta			
Metro area	18.77	24.85	33.67
Other	1.08	14.51	1251.17
EMR[a]	13.72	21.89	381.53
Manila			
Metro area	35.87	38.73	7.97
Other[b]	27.84	28.04	0.68
EMR	28.65	29.11	1.41
Bangkok			
Metro area	41.27	46.28	12.16
Other[c]	23.33	39.88	78.54
EMR	28.46	41.71	59.58

Notes:
a Bekasi and Tangerang Kapupaten
b Includes provinces: Bataan, Pampanga, Bulacan, Rizal, Laguna, Batangas, Cavite, Quezon
c Includes *changwats*: Nonthaburi, Samut Prakan, Nakhon Pathom, Samut Sakhon, Pathum Thani
Sources: Various Southeast Asian censuses (1971-80)

Income growth is reflected in the overall dimensions of economic change. As mentioned, the urbanizing regions are responsible for a major proportion of each country's GDP and are the location of much of the direct foreign investment.[8] They are experiencing a decline in agriculture and an increase in non-agricultural activity made up of industrial decentralization and direct industrial start-ups as a result of foreign and local investment. These economic patterns vary from country to country. Singapore is the most advanced, followed by Malaysia and Thailand. In the Jakarta[9] and Manila EMRs, a much more dualistic form of economic growth is occurring, as significant proportions of the population are absorbed into low-income, small-scale economic activity. The changes have been characterized across the ASEAN countries by a powerful increase in industrialization in the 1970s and, more particularly, the 1980s.

Initially, of course, this pattern typified the so-called Asian NICs, such as Hong Kong, Singapore, Korea, and Taiwan. Now it is moving to ASEAN. This is largely due to a boom in direct foreign investment in export-oriented manufacture, most of it from Japan and Asian NICs. Rapid industrialization is therefore highly important in explaining the spatial process. Much investment is in industries that require cheap labour, although the industries are becoming more dependent on skilled labour and higher technology.

Such economic growth creates extraordinary dynamism, changing land use, creating legal and illegal settlement, and causing types of traffic response to proliferate. It would be surprising if it did not create problems such as environmental damage, waste removal, and transportation woes.

At the social level, the urbanizing regions are extraordinarily heterogeneous. Villages with households that still rely upon agriculture for some of their income exist side by side with golf courses, industrial estates, and squatter encampments. The outer regions of the zones exhibit a remarkable mixture of lifestyles and income-earning opportunities.

The Dynamics of Mega-Urbanization: Forces Creating the New Spatial Order in ASEAN

Recognizing the underlying processes of economic, social, and technological change that are accelerating the growth of large urban regions is an important part of understanding the phenomenon. Although they are complex and highly interrelated, for convenience of analysis the processes are divided into three groups: urbanization and the transactional revolution; urbanization and globalization; and urbanization and structural change. Some analysts have distinguished between explicit processes, such as deliberate government policies designed to reduce the size of cities or restructure the urban network, and implicit processes, which occur because of sector investments that are not designed to achieve specific urban results. Government subsidies on food prices are an example. Most of the processes fuelling the growth of large urban centres may be labelled as implicit, and while governments have understood that they will affect urban-rural relations they have not always been clear about consequences. This will be discussed further in the final section of the chapter.

Urbanization and the Transactional Revolution

Central to the processes creating EMRs is a constant series of transactions flowing through national and international space. In a very general way these transactions can be grouped into four categories: (1) people; (2) commodities; (3) capital; and (4) information. Thus commuting is a form of geographic transaction performed by *people,* usually daily; shipping spices from, say, Manado to Rotterdam is a *commodity* transaction; transferring funds from New York to Singapore represents a *capital* flow; and the news program on national television beamed to all parts of a country represents an *information* transaction.

Flows of information and capital are now increasingly less subject to the constraints of space. Thus funds can be moved from New York to Singapore almost instantly through electronic transfer. On the other hand, moving people and commodities still involves a time-distance relationship. Nevertheless, developments in transportation have increasingly collapsed that relationship.[10]

Most planners realize that the implementation of this transactional revolution is emphasizing the process of centralization in the urban systems of their countries. In the case of Thailand, for instance, the proportion of urban population living in the Bangkok EMR has steadily increased over the past few decades (McGee and Greenberg 1992). In Indonesia, the proportion of urban population living in urban areas of more than one million has risen from 32.6 per cent in 1971 to 41.5 per cent in 1990 (Imran 1992). In the Philippines, the proportion of urban population living in the Manila Metropolitan Region has risen from 29.4 per cent in 1970 to 33 per cent in 1990 (McGee and Mathur 1993).

The transactional revolution is also leading to new configurations in the total urban systems of ASEAN countries. Douglass (1984) has shown, for example, how the pattern of transactions has emphasized the emergence of an urban crescent stretching from Medan through Palembang to Jakarta and the north coast urban centres of Java, and on to Ujung Pandang, Manado, and the Kalimantan main urban centres. Firman (1992) shows this corridor developing in Java in an analysis of the 1980-90 census data. In Malaysia, urban growth is occurring in the north-south corridor stretching from Penang through Ipoh to Kuala Lumpur and through to Johor Bahru.

At the level of the urban region centred on one large urban core, the transactional revolution produces a form of urbanization that takes place in leaps and bounds, creating a discontinuous pattern of land use. This is most marked in the urban periphery, where agriculture, industry, leisure activities, and residential developments are juxtaposed. Expansion can occur across water too, as can be observed in the Singapore Growth Triangle.

Of course, other factors are at work besides transactional changes. In part, outward expansion of urban centres is encouraged by increasing land costs and changes in economic activity in the central city. The process is also encouraged by government policies directed towards industrial decentralization away from the congested city cores. The growth of middle-class housing developments and a growing need for recreational space contribute as well. Opportunities for leisure are important for many firms and individuals who move to the outer fringes of these cities, where life is less regulated. These developments are also fuelled by improved information flows, which cut down transportation costs.

Urbanization and Globalization
All the transactional processes described as operating at a national level also operate at the global and subglobal, or regional, levels. These are comparatively well known and the research can be summarized as follows.

The Emergence of the New International Division of Labour (NIDL)
At the global level, industrial activity has either been established in or relocated to some of the developing countries. ASEAN has been a major focus of this investment over the past two decades. The new international division of labour (NIDL) takes advantage of advances in communications, transport, and production technologies, allowing major international investors to identify niches in various locations within a global production system for export. Finding lower labour costs, away from the industrial core economies, is part of the logic of this process. Although establishing export zones is an important part of the NIDL, it is also characterized by the assembly and production of consumer goods in ASEAN countries for a growing domestic market.[11]

The organization of production and marketing has changed significantly to focus on managing the logistics of purchasing, production, and marketing in order to minimize costs and maintain high levels of quality control. During the 1980s, order-cycle times in developing countries were reduced by 400 per cent and 'just-in-time' (JIT) delivery continued to increase. It is estimated that one-quarter of 'logistics costs' are made up by transportation. Of course, this logistical management is made possible by improvements in telecommunications and information systems.[12]

These changes now permit the procurement of raw materials for manufacturing and production of goods and market products at a global level. Developing countries are vigorously competing to be chosen as sites in this global system. This is one reason why export zones such as the semi-conductor assembly zone in Bayan Lepas in Penang State, Malaysia, remain globally competitive even though wages have begun to increase (McGee, Salih, and Young 1991). Thus globalization creates pressure to make the transactional space more efficient.

Thus it is hardly surprising that the majority of international investors, encouraged by various forms of state initiatives (tax holidays, etc.), choose to concentrate their investment in the mega-urban regions of ASEAN. Figures on manufacturing investment in Malaysia in the 1970s, during the first wave of export-oriented industries, show that over 50 per cent of international investment in manufacturing occurred in the Klang Valley-Kuala Lumpur urban region. With 10 per cent of Malaysia's population, this area was responsible for generating some 60 per cent of manufacturing employment (McGee 1978). Data on Indonesia for the 1970s and early 1980s reveal a comparable emphasis.[13] McGee and Greenberg (1992) record similar data for the Bangkok EMR for the 1980s. Thus the operation of the NIDL reinforces a tendency for economic activity to focus on the mega-urban regions.

The Emergence of Global Mega-Urban Regions
A second facet of these accelerating global forces is the establishment of global mega-urban regions, which have become the major nodal points in the movement of capital, people, and commodities. Within the ASEAN region, there is much competition between member countries – Thailand and Singapore compete to act as a major air transportation node, for example – but at present Singapore is certainly emerging as the leading global urban region.

Singapore has aggressively set out to make itself the financial and information centre for the region. One statistic shows how successful this has been: in 1990, Singapore outward and inward international telephone calls were more than the total international calls of Indonesia and Thailand. The Singapore figure increased dramatically in the last four years before 1990 (Singapore 1991c). The advantages of a stable city vigorously following a policy of internationalization undoubtedly helped this development, but government policies that included radical changes in the internal distribution of housing, industry, and recreation have been no less important. Within the ASEAN region, the proximity of the states of Johor, Malaysia, and Riau, Indonesia, has facilitated decentralization of industry, housing, and recreation from Singapore. This process has been encouraged by the governments of Malaysia and Indonesia, which have made substantial investments in infrastructure to expedite it. The emergence of the Singapore Growth Triangle (Singapore,

Johor, and Riau) is an interesting example of how the forces of globalization and structural change are creating a mega-urban region that transcends national boundaries.[14]

The Emergence of Intense Global and Regional Competition
The development of ASEAN mega-urban regions has involved intense global and regional competition between regions for a share of the global market. For instance, almost all the ASEAN mega-urban regions have now built world-class convention centres and world trade centres. In a similar manner, ASEAN mega-urban regions compete to capture a larger proportion of tourist visits, which have accelerated over the past ten years. This involves building telecommunication networks, airports, and road networks to attract visitors. In addition, there is a need to create an aesthetically pleasing built environment that incorporates historical and cultural elements of the city. Singapore's rehabilitation of parts of its old Chinatown, and Kuala Lumpur's riverside 'yuppie market' in the old vegetable and meat market, are examples of the process. Emphasizing the competitive strength of a particular urban region on the global market increasingly involves marketing cities and their urban regions.

Urbanization and Structural Change
The major structural changes in ASEAN economies have been discussed above, but it must be clear that most of the arguments concerning the growth of mega-urbanization rest upon continuing growth and structural change that will see an increasing proportion of a country's population living in urban areas and engaged in non-agricultural occupations.

Policy Implications of the Emergence of EMRs in ASEAN
The argument of this chapter is comparatively simple, namely that the urban systems of most ASEAN countries will be dominated by the large mega-urban regions, or EMRs as they are labelled here. This can be seen as very challenging to ASEAN governments because the macrocephalic process of urbanization raises a central question: How are governments going to reconcile national goals of spatial equity with the unequal distribution of wealth that mega-urban regions appear to cause?

This important strategic issue is further clouded by the popular view that large cities are a drag on development. Five important myths have contributed to this attitude. They need to be defused if mega-urbanization is to be managed effectively.[15]

Myth one is that the large size of cities, or urban regions, is a problem. Undoubtedly their size in terms of population is a major problem for decision makers. The thought of having to provide services to populations that will for the most part be in excess of 20 million by 2020 is indisputably alarming. These are aggregated numbers for large urban regions, however, and they are made up of a very large number of subregions with different responses to needs. The subregions could utilize their own revenue-generating capacity in conjunction with national and provincial governments to provide services and infrastructure.

Myth two, often supported by some international agencies, is that large cities cannot be sustained. It is often argued that the high rates of energy consumption and large volume of non-recyclable waste of developing countries render the large urban regions very difficult to sustain. But such practices impose challenges to develop systems that make use of recycling and that use renewable sources of power such as hydro-electric power. If urban regions were not sustainable we would have witnessed large-scale economic collapse already, and this has not occurred.

Myth three is that large cities are economically parasitic. Implicit in this viewpoint, most provocatively developed by Lipton (1977), is the argument that urban regions are unfairly favoured by terms of trade at the national level. Put simply, regulatory intervention by national government (i.e., food and transportation controls) favours urban regions over rural regions and the former therefore benefit at the expense of rural regions.

While this is certainly true in some cases, it is also correct that the agglomeration economies of urban areas reduce transaction costs, and the greater productivity of the urban regions is far more important in explaining their greater wealth than the transfer of surplus income from rural to urban areas. Certainly the fact that the urban areas of, for example, Indonesia generate between 50 and 60 per cent of the non-gas and oil GDP cannot be explained in terms of rural-urban transfer alone. Indeed, there is an increasing amount of evidence that urban-rural transfers (remittances, government transfers) are well in excess of any surplus transfer developed out of rural-urban transfer. This is particularly the case in Java, where high rates of mobility (circulatory migration) – greatly facilitated by intermediate transportation – permit the transfer to be carried out very regularly.

Myth four is that large cities are characterized by excessive problems of poverty. It cannot be denied that urban regions have ongoing problems of poverty, but it is also true that the household income in these regions is on average four times that of the nation at large. More personal income (admittedly unevenly distributed) can therefore flow over into opportunities for the poor in the informal sector. In fact, the whole issue of urban poverty, including its measurement, needs to be carefully evaluated as part of programs of welfare transfer and so on.

Myth five is that large cities are places of disharmony and poor quality of life. This is a very arguable assertion. Most evidence supports the view the cultural life of nations is primarily articulated in the large cities. They have the major concentration of institutions of higher learning, national theatres, museums, and art galleries. The quality of life is primarily developed at the household level, however, and for most urban dwellers (apart from the hardcore poor) this too is superior to that of rural areas.

It is therefore important to spell out the implications of these extended metropolitan regions for the future of ASEAN urbanization. It can be argued that such zones are catalytic regions for economic growth and that economic growth should be encouraged. It has been suggested, however, that such regions are extraordinarily difficult for planners to handle. The mixture of activities often creates serious environmental, transportation, and infrastructural problems, particularly if such regions are treated with conventional city planning. In a conventional approach, the capital requirements for infrastructure alone seem totally out of reach to most national governments in developing Asia. On the other hand, the very mixed, decentralized, intermediate and small scale of economic organization and the persistence of agriculture in these EMRs offer exciting prospects for recycling, use of alternative energy sources, and so on, which are difficult to introduce into conventional city space. The challenge to planners is to take advantage of the growth feature of these regions, while ameliorating the costly side-effects of growth and the problems of regional inequality that will emerge as the areas grow.

The sustainability of these regions is even more important if one accepts the rather gloomy predictions based on the unilinear model of Western urbanization. As many writers have often observed, if the cities of China and Indonesia alone were to reach the levels of energy consumption of New York or London, the demand on world fossil energy sources would be impossible to fulfil. Similar arguments can be presented with respect to food supplies. Many writers have commented on the likely food demands of large Asian cities and the problem that future growth poses to national food supplies. Increasing food imports is a viable option, but the opportunity to maintain a high level of national food self-sufficiency through increasingly intensive agricultural production in the desakota regions is very attractive. Finally, the extraordinary range of activities in these regions offers many opportunities for employment of able-bodied household members, resulting in increased household income and consumption.

It is, of course, a legitimate question to ask how persistent these EMRs will be. Will the processes of concentration ultimately triumph and lead to a reassertion of the conventional city? For the reasons already cited, particularly those relating to the collapse of time-distance and the mix of transportation technology available, I believe that such regions will be remarkably persistent. Indeed, data becoming available from the 1990 round of censuses support this claim.

This assertion has important implications for planning and policy formation for the regions. There appear to be six priorities for most ASEAN countries, and these I group under the term 'metrofitting.'[16]

First, governments will have to decide the policy priorities to be given to the urban regions. Careful analysis of the geographical extent of the regions and collection of data on population, employment, economic growth, and infrastructure and welfare needs of their populations are necessary. If the regions are as important to economic growth as has been suggested here, then governments will have hard decisions to make about their explicit spatial policies, such as industrial dispersal or regional development. This does not mean that governments should discontinue policies designed to improve the quality of life and economic growth of less-developed regions. Rather, they should carefully reconsider explicit policies designed to force economic activities away from centralizing mega-urban regions.

Second, ASEAN governments will need to develop an integrated approach to the management of these urban regions. At present they are administered by a plethora of administrative units and sectorally responsible departments. As a consequence, the possibility of developing an integrated response to, for example, waste management is very difficult. This is where the package of policies that is part of metrofitting comes into play. These include the following:

- integrated national, regional, and local strategies for national development
- institutional changes including a shift from sectoral management to metropolitan management, involving decentralization of decision making and control
- increased capacity to generate income, particularly from land and property taxes
- human resources at all levels capable of managing urban regions
- adequate policies to deal with environmental problems.

Only by developing the institutional, management, and human resource capacity to manage urban regions can ASEAN governments respond to the many challenges they face in the coming years.

Third, governments will need to improve access in these zones of intense interaction. One can argue that building fast, major arterial routes such as the Shinkansen, the Seoul-Pusan Highway, and the Taipei-Kaoshiung Freeway, was crucial in the development of Japanese, Korean, and Taiwanese mega-urban regions, respectively.[17] In a similar manner, the completion of fast arterial highways between Bangkok and Singapore will change the economic landscape of Thailand, Malaysia, and Singapore. The network of pre-existing feeder roads flows very easily into these fast central transportation routes. Governments should also take every advantage of pre-existing systems such as water routes and encourage flexibility in transportation modes.

Fourth, governments will have to monitor environmental and land-use problems carefully to keep conflict to a minimum. The development of fast systems of data collection is crucial to this activity, as are responsive, decentralized implementing agencies.

Fifth, governments will need to develop policies to cope with the welfare of the inhabitants of the region. Highly flexible labour regimes, varying types of work, and the maximum input of a majority of the households place considerable strains on central social institutions such as the family, as well as on the educational and cultural institutions that characterize these regions.

Finally, it will be necessary to address the activities of the private sector and its role in these regions. It must be clear from the previous discussion that private capital pursuing labour has stimulated developments within an envelope of state and international policy decisions. From the point of view of private capital, the regions are attractive because of cheaper labour, cheaper land, and a more flexible work environment. Here, capital is deployed in an extraordinarily diverse set of ways: capital intensification in chicken rearing; subcontracting of production processes; industrial estates and upper-income housing estates; and so on. The 'planning trick' will be to make these regions continue to attract capital and still avoid the grave social, economic, and environmental problems of rapid growth. But what seems important is that the fundamental features of the regions – flexibility in economic and political organization, facilitative transactive networks, and a constant acceptance of change – be incorporated into the planning process.

I envisage persistent extended metropolitan regions in many ASEAN countries, in which flexibility, mobility, and change are constant elements. The physical planning and design response will involve radical departures from current ways of thinking. For instance, shopping for basic commodities might incorporate elements of the 'periodic markets' traditionally part of such regions. One could extend such thinking to entertainment, education, and virtually any sphere of service activity. The regions are, after all, an amalgam of pre-existing high densities and juxtaposed technology.

Of course, not all ASEAN countries are going to be characterized by identical responses, and therefore policy responses will vary from country to country. But even in the city state of Singapore, it is obvious that urban expansion is at work, extending into the Johor and Riau portions of the

Singapore Growth Triangle. In this case, developments need both national and international planning policy responses. The challenges are daunting, but ASEAN urbanization in the 1990s and beyond requires a new urban-economic agenda. This is the challenge that must be taken up by ASEAN governments in the move towards an increasingly urban-dominated future by the year 2020.

Notes

1 This refers to the six members of ASEAN as of 1992: Thailand, Malaysia, Indonesia, Singapore, the Philippines, and Brunei Darussalam. There is a strong possibility that ASEAN by 2020 will have been enlarged to include Cambodia, Laos, and Vietnam, but this book is concerned only with the first five countries.

2 These estimates are based on projections produced annually by the United Nations, Department of International Economic and Social Affairs (1991). UN predictions are based upon various estimates of rural and urban population relative growth rates. After reviewing Indonesian urban population projections carried out by Gardiner (1990), I find it likely that the UN estimates of urbanization levels may be some 20 million too low in this case because of underestimates of actual urban areas. If this were the case for other ASEAN countries, the urban population would be approximately 300 million by 2020 with a level of urbanization of 61 per cent.

3 I realize that these kinds of employment projections could be substantially out of line, but in both Indonesia and the Philippines there is much greater commitment to food self-sufficiency than in Malaysia or Thailand.

4 Population projections for the five extended metropolitan regions (EMRs) are based on growth rates due to urban expansion and net urban migration that will continue at double the total population growth rate for at least the next fifteen years. This means that urban population growth rates will be 3 to 5 per cent per annum. Singapore will be the exception to this pattern, as it is today. As part of the Singapore Growth Triangle, however, Singapore would benefit from the growth of population and economic activity in its hinterland. See McGee (1989b, 1991) and McGee and Yeung (1993).

5 Unfortunately, I cannot document this assertion for all the EMRs of ASEAN, as this is an ongoing project.

6 See MacLeod and McGee (1992) for a description of these developments. Also see Lee Tsao Yuan (1991).

7 See Greenberg (1992) and Isarankura (1990) for a discussion of these developments in the Bangkok EMR.

8 While we do not have precise figures for all these ASEAN EMRs, data generated for the Bangkok Metropolitan Area (McGee and Greenberg 1992) indicate that in 1988 almost 40 per cent of Thailand's GDP was generated in this region. For Jakarta, the figure was something like 42 per cent in the earlier 1980s. See Douglass (1984) and National Urban Development Strategy Project (1985).

9 For an excellent, up-to-date discussion of the developments see Ida Ayu Indira Dharmapatni (1991).

10 It should be emphasized that travel time sometimes actually increases despite technological innovation. An excellent example is traffic congestion. The Japan International Cooperation Agency published a report in 1988, for instance, claiming that the costs of Bangkok's jammed roads may amount to almost 60 per cent of Bangkok's regional product (cited in *Asiaweek,* 28 February 1990, p. 32).

11 The global dimensions of the process have been described in a number of publications. See, in particular, McGee (1967, 1986) and Ginsburg, Koppel, and McGee (1991).

12 See Kellerman (1993) for an expanded discussion of this point.

13 The data do not include investment in the mining, gas, and oil sector. See National Urban Development Strategy Project (1985) and Hill (1990).

14 Another temporary example is Hong Kong-Guangdong.

15 The next section echoes ideas developed by Hamer (1990), Linn (1983), and Linn and Wetzel (1990).

16 'Metrofitting' is adapted from the term now being used in Singapore for rehabilitation of older buildings, which is called 'retrofitting.' I have simply taken the first letter from the word mega-urban. This term carries the conceptual meaning I need, for it suggests a comprehensive rehabilitation and renewal, which is certainly the case in large urban areas.

17 See McGee and Lin (1993) for examples of this argument.

2
Mega-Urbanization in ASEAN: New Phenomenon or Transitional Phase to the 'Los Angeles World City'?
Douglas Webster

Several large, city-centred regions in ASEAN[1] have developed characteristics associated with extended urban regions or mega-urbanization.[2] The extent to which this is a qualitatively different phenomenon from past urbanization – either in Asia or on other continents – or merely a demographic change in scale is a subject of considerable debate. Similarly controversial is the extent to which the current state of mega-urban regions in Asia, and particularly in ASEAN, is fluid and temporary – associated with rapid industrialization en route to a less dynamic, quasi-stable urban form that will appear distinctively different from the present desakota model[3] – or whether Asian mega-urban regions represent something distinctively different from urbanization in other parts of the world.

This chapter is meant to be speculative, to raise questions and provoke debate. It is hoped that subsequent research and analysis will shed light on some of the questions raised.

The chapter draws from the experience of extended urban areas in ASEAN and in particular the mega-urban areas of Bangkok, Jakarta, and Manila. Second-order urban regions in ASEAN (in terms of population), such as the Singapore Growth Triangle, Kuala Lumpur, and Surabaya may achieve mega-urban status at some point.

Mega-urban regions in ASEAN are likely to grow demographically until about 2030, based on natural population growth of their resident populations and net in-migration (primarily domestic but including net international in-migration). However, *rates* of urbanization are peaking or will peak later in this decade. The downward fall in the rate of urbanization will accelerate after about 2010. Then, absolutely declining populations in rural areas of ASEAN will feed fewer people into urban areas. Additionally, declining natural population growth rates throughout ASEAN will contribute to a pronounced slowing in urbanization rates in the next century. After 2030, population growth of mega-urban regions in ASEAN is likely to be slow. By that time, however, many such regions will be demographically large. For example, Jabotabek – the extended Jakarta-centred urban region – will contain over 30 million people by 2010. The more narrowly defined Jakarta metropolitan region will contain over 17 million people (Culpin Planning 1993).

Mega-urban regions in China and Latin America, however, will be significantly larger than those in ASEAN in the early part of the next century. Depending on spatial definitions used, ASEAN mega-urban regions will be relatively small compared to either Chinese extended urban regions, such as Hong Kong-Shenzhen-Guangzhou or the Shanghai-centred extended urban region, or Latin American urban regions, such as the Mexico City-centred mega-urban region. Thus, although ASEAN mega-urban regions will be large in the next century, they will not be overwhelmingly so compared with other regions throughout the world (United Nations, Department of International Economic and Social Affairs 1991). ASEAN extended urban areas will not be breaking new ground demographically.

In this chapter, I first consider the general nature of mega-urbanization in ASEAN. This is necessary because policies and associated strategic initiatives should vary considerably depending on whether one assumes that future ASEAN mega-urban regions will more or less resemble present systems or not. Second, based primarily on the most likely scenario presented, I suggest some ways to improve human welfare in mega-urban regions in ASEAN.

The Nature of Existing Mega-Urbanization in ASEAN

ASEAN mega-urban regions grow through:[4]
- natural growth of the resident population
- envelopment of surrounding high population density landscapes, including smaller urban centres[5]
- net in-migration from rural areas and, to a lesser extent, net international in-migration.

ASEAN cities are highly dependent on both public and private transportation for the movement of people and the high degree of goods movement associated with manufacturing-based, export-oriented urban economies. As a consequence, ASEAN mega-urban regions generally tend to grow along transportation corridors. Except for higher-order jobs in the formal sector, employment markets tend to be localized within ASEAN mega-urban regions, creating overlapping commuting areas often based around nodes such as industrial parks, shopping centres, educational complexes, government office agglomerations, transportation complexes such as airports, and so on.

Economic activity in mega-urban regions grows physically by leapfrogging over existing rural land use, a process associated with land speculation, access or lack of it, and lack of physical planning controls. These scattered forms of land development, when combined with corridor development, lead to a mixing of urban and rural employment and land-use characteristics in the peripheral areas of mega-urban regions in ASEAN. (As a consequence of the amoeba-like form of the regions, the peripheries are very large.) Because mega-urban regions have tended to develop as sets of more or less self-contained modules, they often resemble an agglomeration of recurring villages, towns, and small cities roughly tied together by the road system, rather than as systems with unique sub-areas or communities displaying specialized functions or roles. The traditional distinction of the planning profession, and of social science disciplines, between rural and urban, becomes very blurred in the case of this emerging urban form.

In summary, current thinking portrays mega-urban regions in ASEAN as sets of interacting and overlapping localized subsystems. Spatial, functional, and informational integration occurs mainly through the role of elite, middle-, and upper middle-income groups. Many people in the system live day to day within relatively confined spatial, informational, and employment subsystems. The middle class and elite, of course, use more of the overall mega-urban system, geographically, functionally, and informationally. Goods movement, too, frequently involves long journeys within the urban region. For many people living in mega-urban regions of ASEAN, however, their daily lives involve relatively bounded geographic areas.

Future Mega-Urban Scenarios

Continuation of the Present Phenomenon

One hypothesis for the future of ASEAN mega-urban regions is that they will resemble present systems in terms of form, function, and other characteristics, at least for the foreseeable future. The rationale for this position is based on a variety of arguments:

(1) The structure of ASEAN urban economies – ersatz (trade-oriented) capitalism and reliance on export-oriented manufacturing based on foreign investment – discourages development of higher-order functions such as research and development, some business services, locally owned manufacturing, etc. Thus, as ASEAN mega-urban regions grow they will tend to replicate existing modules, adding more labour-intensive assembly plants, for example, rather than transforming themselves into something new by adding higher-order, specialized functions that would create more complementarity among different parts of the city region. (Singapore is certainly an exception in this regard in that it has already developed a strong economic reliance on higher-order functions.)

(2) The nature of the rural landscapes and cultures that were enveloped

by mega-urban regions was high density with distinct villages and towns. This has established a structure whereby former free-standing towns, such as Rangsit in the Bangkok area or Bogor in the Jakarta area, tend to continue to define and dominate local activity systems. (Again, Singapore is an exception.)

(3) The nature of Southeast Asian culture, in particular its strong support for family, community, and neighbourhood institutions and forms of organization, will contribute to personal identification with communities within the mega-urban region, encouraging people to identify with certain areas, live near relatives, and seek or create employment within these communities. In other words, physical integration through better transportation and telecommunications infrastructure will not necessarily lead to residential, employment, and social mobility as it has in North American mega-urban regions such as Los Angeles.

(4) Relatively limited road networks will slow in-filling of interstices, creating long corridors, land-use leapfrogging, and other physical patterns that will make it more difficult to integrate physical and functional systems, particularly in terms of efficient transportation. In the Bangkok region, for example, 100 km^2 areas lack any arterial or secondary roads to service their interiors (Archer 1987, 243). Similar conditions, to a somewhat lesser extent, exist in parts of Jakarta and Manila. Associated with this pattern will be a continued mixing of urban and rural activities and land uses in a large percentage of the land area of ASEAN mega-urban regions.

(5) Some believe that current high rates of economic growth in ASEAN will decelerate, slowing the factors that contribute to significant changes in the form of mega-urbanization. That is, to some extent the inexorable movement towards greater integration and complexity will be slowed by a decline in the primary driving force to this end, namely economic growth.

The Transmittal Hypothesis

If ASEAN countries were growing slowly economically and were not undergoing rapid structural and social change, a case could be made that mega-urbanization, as currently manifested, is relatively stable. However, the contrary is true, with the possible exception of Manila. This leads to a second scenario. All evidence points to more integration in ASEAN mega-urban regions, not less. Entropy is not in play; large-scale, integrated, more complex systems are emerging. Systemic integration is occurring spatially, economically, and through informational transformation, in the following ways:

(1) Regional rapid transit systems and, more importantly, freeways, are being constructed or proposed on a large scale in urban regions such as

Bangkok, Jakarta, Singapore, and Kuala Lumpur. These systems are likely to make it easier, in the medium run, for people and goods to move throughout extended urban regions. In the jargon of geographers, such infrastructure contributes to a collapse of space within urban areas. The developing flow patterns are not downtown oriented, as in older North American and European cities, but are based on cross-commuting among a multitude of nodes, as is the case in Los Angeles. (Where, for example, is Bangkok's 'downtown'? Is it the Silom, Ratchada Pisek, Government, China Town, or Victory Monument area? Probably all of the above, plus new suburban and ex-urban nodes that will evolve.)

(2) With economic growth, the role of the urban informal sector is diminishing and will continue to diminish in ASEAN mega-urban regions, creating more homogenous labour markets in terms of wages, stability, and working conditions. The economies of ASEAN mega-urban regions are likely to become less dualistic, not more so. (Future extreme inequity within ASEAN countries is more likely to be between remote rural areas and mega-urban regions, such as northeast Thailand and Bangkok, than within extended urban systems.)

(3) Related to (1) and (2), various communities within the extended urban region are developing comparative advantage complementing other areas of the city and thus making geographic areas in mega-urban regions more interdependent. Large-scale industrial estates are being constructed, partly in response to environmental concerns. Business districts are emerging, as are tourist areas, educational complexes, government areas, high-traffic airports, etc.[6] As the economies of ASEAN urban regions become more complex, more interdependence is developing among various specialized communities within the extended urban area.

(4) With economic growth, environmental awareness, and technological changes, public utility systems, particularly water distribution systems, are likely to become larger. Bangkok, for example, relies less than formerly on individually pumped ground water (which is illegal in the case of new development) and more on large-scale systems. Large-scale systems may be developed to handle newly emerging waste disposal needs, such as disposal of toxic and hazardous wastes. Large-scale sewerage systems will appear in the future.[7] These utility systems contribute to more dense, ordered, and integrated urban development.

(5) The economic structure of most ASEAN urban regions will display an increased reliance on service activity, both business and personal. Business services will tend to be regional, national, or international rather than purely local. The trend towards free trade within the ASEAN community will contribute to this development.

(6) Communications media are becoming more developed and pervasive

in ASEAN mega-urban regions, creating a more cohesive image of these regions in the minds of their residents. People will increasingly associate with the mega-urban region rather than with specific neighbourhoods.

(7) Squatter housing will diminish as a percentage of the total housing stock in ASEAN extended urban areas, again contributing to a more integrated and formal urban system. This is already happening on a significant scale in Bangkok.

The Community or Neighbourhood Hypothesis

Although the first scenario is naïve and the second appears the most likely,[8] a third is possible. This would be based on conscious actions, led by public policy, to create future mega-urban regions that embody economic growth, structural change, and the use of modern technology but include many of the positive features of the locally oriented current mega-urban form, as described in the first scenario.

Whether this is desirable depends on one's values; some advocate it to protect neighbourhoods and avoid the social and psychological alienation often associated with functionally integrated cities in the 10- to 20-million category. Los Angeles, for example, is now viewed as the world city of the future: a generic, technologically driven, futuristic urban region that transcends identification with North or South, with any particular culture, or with any specific level of economic development. Yet many would question whether it represents a desirable urban future.[9] (Of course, it would be a fallacy to assume that certain types of physical form are necessarily associated with patterns of urban behaviour.) As has been argued above, ASEAN mega-urban regions are likely to resemble Los Angeles in form, function, and social characteristics more and more unless conscious efforts are made. Otherwise, technology (particularly the automobile and freeways), demographic scale, modern 'global' lifestyles,[10] and the multinodal spatial structure associated with modern service, high technology, and light manufacturing economies become extremely strong determinants of urban structure and processes.

To make this scenario a reality, public policy and initiatives would need to focus on communities within the mega-urban fabric, enhancing their quality of life. Local services such as water supply, public health, education, recreational facilities, and so on would need to be improved. Less emphasis would be placed on transportation and other linking or flow infrastructure, and costs (primarily in terms of human time) would thus continue to be incurred in moving about the regions.[11] Land-use planning would have to encourage a mix of land uses and functions rather than zoning large contiguous land areas for single uses, as occurs in the West.[12] (In a way, the Chinese shop/house epitomizes this mixing of employment, residence, and recreation within small areas.) Similarly, when squatter areas are cleared, current practices involving large-scale resettlement remote from the current community and employment would have to be rethought.

To some extent, the above dynamics can be seen in cities such as Bangkok. Those having government business in Bangkok now frequently stay in local hotels, such as the Royal Princess or Majestic, in the government area. In the past, they would have stayed in 'centrally located' hotels, in the Silom or Sukhumvit areas. This type of decision by individuals has set off a chain reaction, generating neighbourhood restaurants, and so on. Although such dynamics are probably less powerful than Los Angeles-type mega-urban integration forces, they are in play.

Of course, some functions, such as removal of toxic and hazardous wastes, would be less efficient without large-scale industrial parks, etc. Some inefficiencies would be compensated for by the greater level of self-policing, and sometimes cooperative assistance, within coherent neighbourhoods. Again, Bangkok provides an example. Neighbours are increasingly complaining to authorities over local nuisances such as noise and waste. This scenario could be further facilitated by the development (in cases where they do not exist) and implementation of urban infrastructure technologies that contribute to decentralization: small-scale water supply, waste treatment, and related systems.

Whether this scenario is consistent with economic growth is debatable. Modern manufacturing requires large, one-storey factories for 'just-in-time' systems. Can such factories be dispersed into a variety of neighbourhoods? On the other hand, modern service activities tend to cluster around nodes in urban areas, and interaction among these nodes can be handled to a large degree through effective telecommunication systems.

Summary
The key elements of change in ASEAN mega-urban regions are what can be termed linking features, such as transportation systems, water and sewerage systems, waste disposal systems, and telecommunication systems. (Telecommunications systems are different from the others in that, when fully developed, they reduce the importance of geography uniformly throughout urban regions.) Transportation infrastructure is not a dependent variable in shaping ASEAN cities but a driving or propulsive agent. Land use becomes the dependent variable. The fact that land-use planning systems are so weak in many ASEAN cities, particularly in Bangkok, Manila, and to a lesser extent Jakarta, gives even greater relative importance to linking/flow infrastructure compared to that of cities such as Los Angeles.

The trend is thus towards increased integration of ASEAN mega-urban regions unless a conscious policy effort is made to generate another outcome, such as that portrayed in the community or neighbourhood hypothesis.

Action Priorities

Because ASEAN mega-urban regions are so complex and changing so fast, any attempts to improve conditions and/or mould their future form should be based on strategic planning and management. That is, key points of leverage should be identified and policy, programs, and projects should be focused on these points. Mega-urban regions in ASEAN require strategic action plans as much, or more than, land-use plans. Because ASEAN citizens are familiar with, and accepting of, five-year national plans, it is likely that they would be highly supportive of strategic plans for their extended urban areas.

Although priorities will obviously vary from city to city, certain generalizations can be made. The high-priority actions identified below are based on the second scenario described earlier, namely that ASEAN mega-urban regions are in a state of transition to much more integrated, complex systems. (To a considerable extent, Singapore has already achieved this highly integrated state. As it becomes more closely linked with Johor and Riau, it is likely to become more multinodal and more like Los Angeles.[13]) In my judgment, it is very unlikely that the third scenario will come to pass, given the degree of political and bureaucratic control and will that its implementation would entail and the massive infrastructure programs (particularly for transportation) already being developed, especially in Jakarta and Bangkok. In other words, Los Angelization is already underway. Furthermore, there is no evidence to indicate whether or not the decision makers and citizenry in the ASEAN extended urban regions desire the community approach of the third scenario. High-priority actions recommended for the mega-urban regions are as follows:

(1) Transportation infrastructure represents the key point of leverage in shaping these regions. How crucial the role of transportation infrastructure is depends on whether one is trying to foster urban-region integration or to create a more decentralized structure. The types, networks, and application of transportation initiatives would vary significantly. If integration is the goal, the emphasis would be on creating region-wide transportation infrastructure as quickly as possible to reduce costs of movement. Freeways, controlled-access bus lanes, urban rapid transit systems, commuter rail systems, and high-speed trains within extended urban regions where feasible would all form a part of the infrastructure. If decentralization is the goal, policy makers would want to retain higher costs of

movement and parking to encourage more localized activity systems, commuter patterns, and the like. (The Jakarta airport represents a classic case of transportation infrastructure, which significantly shaped mega-urban form in Jabotabek – the combined form of Jakarta, Bogor, Tangerang, and Bekasi. The proposed new Bangkok airport will result in a local community of 500,000 to 700,000 people between Bangkok and the Eastern Seaboard, a very important shaping influence on the mega-urban form.)

(2) Telecommunications systems should be developed to the greatest extent possible. Because telecommunication services essentially pay for themselves through user charges, there is a strong economic rationale for developing such systems as quickly as possible and no clear economic reason for not doing so.[14] The obvious and very significant positive externality created by telecommunication systems is that verbal, fax, or data transfer messages often substitute for physical journeys. This reduces pressures on overworked transportation systems in mega-urban regions, facilitating efficient movement of goods and people requiring face-to-face contact. The rapid proliferation of mobile telephones in ASEAN cities is a positive indicator in this regard.

(3) Systems of governance need to be developed to coincide geographically with the extent of mega-urbanization and functionally with the needs of these emerging regions. In many cases, the ASEAN mega-urban regions actually cover several provinces. For example, the Bangkok Metropolitan Region includes parts of five provinces and still does not incorporate the full Bangkok EMR.

If meaningful measures are to be taken, particularly on macro issues such as shaping urban form and developing coherent transportation, telecommunication, and utility networks, regional government must encompass the entire mega-urban region. The present problem in ASEAN is that planning regions, such as Jabotabek and the Bangkok EMR cover the urbanized, built-up areas adequately but metropolitan governments, such as those of the Bangkok Metropolitan Region and Jakarta, do not. This results in reasonably sophisticated government for the metropolitan areas, but provincial (in both senses of the word) government for the outlying parts of the mega-urban area. This partially explains why environmental conditions are often poorer on the peripheries of ASEAN cities than in the centre, particularly in terms of toxic waste and potable water quality (United Nations, Economic and Social Commission for Asia and the Pacific 1993b).

(4) If people living in mega-urban regions are to experience improved well-being, urban public-sector officials need considerably more financial resources. (Concomitantly, the training of government officials in ASEAN urban government agencies needs to be upgraded.) Although increased

transfers from national governments would be welcome and desirable in most cases, the most obvious remedy is to levy property taxes more effectively at the mega-urban regional level. Of course, because of the mix of rural and urban land uses on the periphery of such regions, care would have to be taken to avoid creating inequitable taxation. Genuine farmers should not be taxed out of business and driven into the hands of land speculators.

(5) For the purposes of efficiency and equity, it is important that user charges be levied for facilities and services primarily used by the middle and upper classes. Freeways, for example, should be operated as toll roads once they are finished, thus avoiding raising money from the poor to build facilities for the better off.[15] Such policies contribute not only to the goal of equity but also to efficiency, as monies collected can be used to build new facilities and/or maintain existing ones.

In many cases, public infrastructure such as rapid transit systems, controlled-access bus lanes, highways, airport terminals, etc., should be constructed and run as build-operate-transfer (BOT) systems. This method of obtaining high quality urban facilities and infrastructure saves the public sector the cost of borrowing for large capital expenditures, yet the facilities eventually revert to the public sector. Of course, such an approach requires public-sector guidance if expected benefits are to be achieved. Privatization and related systems such as BOT should occur within a systematic framework based on clear goals for the mega-urban region in question.

(6) The mega-urban region should be viewed as a system, and associated set of subsystems, that needs to be managed effectively. Often, the modus operandi of various departments in city governments have not been carefully analyzed for decades. Urban management should be regarded by politicians in ASEAN mega-urban centres as a higher priority than urban planning. Traditional urban planning either did not exist in ASEAN until recently[16] or is ineffective, as in Jakarta. This does not mean that ASEAN mega-urban systems lack order and patterns. On the contrary, they are shaped by transportation systems, pre-existing rural land use and plot patterns, natural features such as shorelines, rivers, and hills, and by prominent human-made features such as canals, religious buildings, and important buildings associated with government and/or royalty.

Important urban subsystems requiring effective management include conventional and hazardous waste collection, local revenue collection, transportation, water supply, human waste disposal, stormwater run-off, education, health, neighbourhood services such as potable water and fire protection, police and security services, and land tenure and registration.

In ASEAN, and indeed worldwide, there is a dearth of training and educational facilities and programs in urban management. (Europe is now starting to establish urban management programs, particularly in the Netherlands.) ASEAN should consider taking the lead in establishing applied training and educational programs in this area. If successful and effective, such services could be marketed worldwide.

(7) Air pollution is a significant problem in almost all ASEAN mega-urban regions. The prime source is vehicles, particularly diesel-powered buses and trucks and motorcycles with two-stroke engines. Human health risks render the problem critical, and appropriate measures should be taken to ensure that vehicle pollution is reduced. Fortunately, unleaded petrol has or is being introduced. Technology exists for much cleaner vehicles, through such measures as catalytic converters. In most cases, however, the measures require legislative action at the national level. Because EMRs are the prime recipients of pollution generated by vehicles, urban politicians need to lobby at the national level to bring about appropriate legislation.

(8) Other urban environmental problems of high concern according to surveys are solid waste collection and the cleanliness of rivers, canals, and ocean frontage (Webster 1992). Urban environmental priorities should be focused in these areas as well as on air pollution.

(9) Generally, the aggregate level of employment created in ASEAN EMRs is not problematic. In fact, cities such as Singapore and Kuala Lumpur are experiencing significant labour shortages. Nevertheless, a 'fitting' problem often exists; job seekers do not know what positions are available except through word of mouth and so do not obtain the best jobs for which they are qualified, while employers do not obtain the quality of employee they are seeking. Given the areal extent of mega-urban regions, it is important that information systems be developed to inform job seekers about employment opportunities. These systems could be based on electronic bulletin boards in selected facilities throughout the EMRs.

(10) Urban-based human resources development, particularly in education and health, needs to be given more emphasis. Because ASEAN urban economies are restructuring every decade or faster, much higher levels of education, particularly in technical fields, must be delivered if this very fast pace of urban economic restructuring is to continue.

Health priorities need to be reordered according to what the United Nations Economic and Social Commission for Asia and the Pacific (ESCAP) calls the new Asian health issues. Health problems in ASEAN mega-urban regions are no longer dominated by Third World health problems such as malnutrition and water-borne bacterial diseases but are characterized by modern urban phenomena such as stress-related disorders, drug and alcohol abuse, accidents, AIDs, heart disease, and cancer.

(11) Improvements in ASEAN mega-urban regions will only occur if the private, public, community-based and non-governmental organizations (CBOs and NGOs), and information sectors are involved in a meaningful way. Although most of the actions proposed above need to be undertaken, or at least coordinated, by the public sector, there is a significant role for the private and voluntary sectors. The media have a very important role to play in helping people to understand mega-urban regions as holistic entities and in encouraging the behavioural, consumption, and attitudinal changes that will improve ASEAN mega-urban regions.

Implications

To plan for ASEAN mega-urban regions comprehensively is probably impossible, particularly in Bangkok and Manila and to a lesser extent in Jakarta. The regions are becoming not so much sets of overlapping modules replicating services and functions as integrated systems with various parts of the system playing different roles according to comparative advantage.[17]

Strategic planning and management are needed to address the challenges of extended urbanization in ASEAN, with a heavy emphasis on management. Strategic planning must be based on monitoring of key indicators in the mega-urban regions. At the same time, various scenarios should be developed, identifying appropriate actions to take when monitoring reveals certain trends or conditions, either within the mega-urban region or in terms of the external environment affecting the region.

Planning based on data sets collected every ten years (as in the case of most national censuses), five-year plans, and other approaches based on out-of-date data and generating out-of-date actions will die. Urban planning will move closer and closer to real time, becoming more and more reliant on computerized data bases and plans. The data bases could be readily updated and the plans would be amenable to sensitivity analysis and revision based on the preferences of social groups, technological change, and so on.

Planners have long agreed that comprehensiveness, optimality, and complete rationality are impossible. The current conventional wisdom regarding planning is reflected in terms such as indicative, guided development, or strategic planning. It appears that many principles of the strategic planning approach will become more important during the turn of millennium in dynamic and technologically advanced city regions such as those of ASEAN. That strategic planning stresses both the external and the internal environment, that it realistically focuses on a few key points of leverage in complex systems, that it recognizes the ability of individuals to get things done ultimately, and that it stresses action over documentation, or plan making, are all characteristics likely to be even more in demand in tomorrow's world. The emerging ASEAN urban world is likely to prefer planners over plan makers, valuing people who can identify strategic actions and the points of leverage to apply those actions, who have the qualities to make ideas become reality.

Future strategic urban planning in ASEAN cities is likely to borrow increasingly from Japanese practice. The Japanese stress practice over theory, refinement of a good idea or approach over conflict among alternatives, and the supreme importance of monitoring. Osaka, Japan, for example, currently monitors key functions of that mega-urban region on the basis of real time (Ex Corporation 1993a, 1993b).

Future urban strategic planning in ASEAN must be dynamic because the rate of change in ASEAN is very rapid. Urban residents are increasingly less patient in waiting for solutions, while many environmental issues require immediate action if irreversibilities are to be avoided. Planning must result in slower time lags between identification of an issue, problem, or opportunity, and action. In fact, ultimately, planning may approach real time and converge with what we now know as management.

A few key priorities should be set and appropriate matching strategies effectively delivered. These should make a difference to the well-being of the population and to the form, character, and function of the region in question. Although the role of transportation, telecommunications, and utilities infrastructure is crucial because of the magnitude and geographic structure of these regions, other initiatives are needed, particularly in the areas of urban environment and human resources development.

The extended urban regions of ASEAN are unlikely to stall or solidify based on their present form, function, and characteristics. This is much more likely to happen in South Asian mega-urban regions such as Calcutta, Bombay, Dhaka, and Karachi, which will probably not restructure through economic forces as rapidly. Because of the nature of ASEAN demographic processes, extended urban regions in ASEAN are also likely to remain in the 10- to 30-million population range during the next century. Current technology is capable of supporting high quality urban environments of such a size, particularly in regions that are relatively affluent and rapidly becoming more so, as is the case in ASEAN nations.

Because the demographic growth of the ASEAN mega-urban regions is falling or will shortly fall, it is essential to act immediately to shape them. There is no time for prolonged planning processes or unnecessary deliberation because urban demographic growth rates are currently near their peak. It is much easier to shape city regions during periods of fast growth, when large increments are being added to the physical, social, and economic structure, than when they are stagnant. Additionally, capital can usually be raised more easily during periods of rapid economic growth.

In summary, emerging mega-urban regions in ASEAN should not be viewed as overwhelming entities soon beyond the control of human institutions. They will not become too large to be planned and managed, nor will they lack financial and human resources to deal with their problems. Nevertheless, realistic, focused actions should be taken as soon as possible. It is important that the ASEAN mega-urban regions be shaped through appropriate institutions, policies, programs, and projects. Lastly, but importantly, the policy target is moving, and future policy should be based on the types of mega-urban regions emerging in ASEAN, not on the entities that exist now.

Notes

1 ASEAN, or the Association of Southeast Asian Nations, consists of Brunei Darussalam, Indonesia, Malaysia, the Philippines, Singapore, and Thailand.

2 Populations of key ASEAN cities are forecast to grow by the year 2000 to 13.7 million in the case of Jakarta, 11.8 million in the case of Manila, and 10.3 million in the case of Bangkok. These are very conservative estimates based on United Nations Department of International Economic and Social Affairs (1991). Other estimates are much higher. For example, Marcussen (1990) estimates that the Jabotabek region will contain 27-30 million people by the year 2000. For further description of the general magnitude of mega-urbanization expected, see Robinson (1991).

3 For a description of the desakota concept, see McGee (1991).

4 For more detail in regard to these processes, see McGee (1989a).

5 Wet rice (padi) growing areas, such as the central region of Thailand, which surrounds Bangkok, have particularly high rural densities. On the other hand, cities surrounded by plantation-based rural landscapes, such as Kuala Lumpur, have much lower surrounding rural densities.

6 Bangkok is currently designing the world's largest airport in terms of passenger traffic capacity. It will be located at Nong Ngu Hao, about 30 km east of central Bangkok.

7 For example, see Unkulvasapaul and Seidel (1991).

8 For those who have observed Jakarta at regular intervals since the early 1970s, the rapid movement of this mega-urban region towards a Los Angeles form is very obvious. In the early 1970s, Jakarta was essentially a set of rural, village-like neighbourhoods. The downtown, in a commercial or retailing sense, was not particularly distinct from the remainder of the city or a small town. Today, the urban region is becoming rapidly integrated as a total system, joined by freeways. Higher-order economic functions and a rapidly growing formal labour market have evolved. In addition to the downtown found along Jalan Tamrin, several high-rise nodes, in the style of the multinodal Los Angeles model, are arising. There is little reason to believe that this trend will not continue. Indeed, it is likely to accelerate.

9 See, for example, 'L.A. Third World City: Multi-Ethnic Melting Pot a Simmering Stew of Despair,' *Arizona Republic*, 18 October 1992. Fragmentation of modern urban society in Western countries is described in Harvey (1989).

10 See Schwartz (1991). Global lifestyles are increasingly being driven by youth. During the period of rapid urbanization until 2030, there will be billions of what Schwartz and other futurists call 'global teenagers.'

11 Such an approach is unlikely to affect goods movement as much as might initially be

thought. Goods can be moved between midnight and 4:30 A.M., when traffic is relatively light, even in ASEAN mega-urban regions.

12 Jane Jacobs has been a strong critic of the role of Western-based land-use planning in creating alienating urban communities. See Jacobs (1961). Scattering industry would create enormous problems in terms of handling hazardous and toxic waste. In some cases, dangerous industries should not be near residential areas at all, creating the need for large amounts of contiguous land zoned for dangerous or heavy industrial use.

13 The fact that the Singapore-based growth triangle has major water bodies separating its various components makes the Los Angeles analogy less appropriate than in the case of other ASEAN cities such as Jakarta, Manila, and Bangkok.

14 For a description of the potent role of telecommunications in contemporary society, see Toffler (1990).

15 For equity reasons, public transport vehicles such as buses should be charged much lower fees per passenger than private vehicles in the case of freeways. Charging user fees will raise the costs of doing business in ASEAN cities, which may be reflected in urban inflation and possibly competitiveness. However, efficiency gains (time, fuel, vehicle depreciation) will probably outweigh any monetary costs.

16 Bangkok, for example, did not have an official urban plan until July 1992.

17 In the past, a city such as Bangkok could be viewed as ten Chiang Mais and Jakarta as several Surabayas; that is, as smaller cities replicating themselves many times within the urban fabric. Alternatively, Chiang Mai would resemble many neighbourhoods in Bangkok. Now new forms are evolving in which mega-urban cities are developing higher-order functions associated with different areas.

Part 2
Processes Creating Mega-Urban Regions in ASEAN

3

Global Interdependence and Urbanization: Planning for the Bangkok Mega-Urban Region

Mike Douglass

Global Interdependence and New Spatial Patterns of Development

Transnationalization and DFI-led Industrialization in Southeast Asia

Urbanization processes and patterns in Asia have dramatically changed since the late 1960s. The literature of three decades ago, which talked of urban involution and suggested that urbanization in Asia was somehow an expression of distorted forces of underdevelopment, seems anachronistic in the 1990s. During the interim, not only has the pace of urbanization accelerated in almost all countries, but much of the impetus of this acceleration has come from industrial growth tied to the world economy. For the market-oriented economies of Southeast Asia these changes have been fundamentally linked to a pronounced shift of direct foreign investment (DFI) by transnational corporations (TNCs) from primary commodity production and trade to export-oriented manufacturing.

The increasing presence of TNCs in the world economy is impressive. Recent studies estimate that in 1990 transnational corporations, which numbered at least 35,000 and had a minimum of 150,000 affiliates throughout the world, accounted for annual investment flows of $225 billion and controlled $4.4 trillion in worldwide sales (United Nations 1992a). The stock of global assets of TNCs increased eightfold between 1960 and 1980, reaching a reported level of $580 billion in 1981 (Stopford and Dunning 1983). By 1990, these assets were estimated at $1.7 trillion, and intra-TNC and TNC-affiliate trade accounted for a minimum of one-third of all world trade (United Nations 1992a). These figures do not account for other forms of indirect control of local enterprises by TNCs through licensing, contracts, and other new forms of non-equity investment (United Nations Centre on Transnational Corporations 1988). When intra-firm trade is combined with another trend, namely, the interlocking of TNCs from different national origins in such key sectors as automobiles, electronics, and construction, the image presented by conventional international trade theory of a world composed of 'national' economies loses much of its substance. TNCs now also outpace even leading governments in research and development expenditures.[1]

Direct foreign investment (DFI) has become the principal vehicle through which the integration of many Asian countries into the international economy is being achieved. While evidence shows that between 1986 and 1990, TNC investments accounted for 74 per cent of all long-term private-sector capital in-flows for more than ninety developing countries, a select number of countries located along the Asian arc of the Pacific Rim have been their principal recipients. Of the $32 billion invested in Asia, Latin America, and Africa in 1990, two-thirds went to East and Southeast Asia.[2]

The primary explanations for transnationalization of capital as the major integrative force in the global economy begin by noting that the rapid emergence of transnational corporations can be seen from an historical perspective. It has coincided with the dawning of the most recent epoch of world capitalist development, beginning in the 1950s and 1960s. This epoch arose initially from the need of US corporations to maintain access to European markets and in response to product cycles that allowed new entrants into markets as technologies become more accessible. The tremendous productive capacity of the Fordist factory system necessitated ever expanding markets, and by the 1960s, major US makers of automobiles, electronics, and home appliances were already dependent upon earning substantial shares of their profits from sales in Europe in order to maintain market shares and oligopolistic market conditions.

By the late 1960s, however, corporations from high-wage countries also began to move abroad in search of cheap labour in a limited number of low-income countries in Latin America and Asia. This process was aided by fundamental changes in political posture and revolutionary advances in technology. Politically, the advent of postcolonial governments, after a decade or so of intense nationalism and anti-Western/Japanese sentiment, provided the territorial basis for stabilizing the political and social relations of production for investment. Competition among these governments has over the years led to increasing hospitality to investors. This has included preferential treatment through such means as lengthened tax holidays and provisioning of key infrastructure and services for investors. It has also entailed legal and regulatory mechanisms to minimize labour militancy and the use of police and military force to maintain civil obedience.

Revolutionary advances in transportation and communications technologies provided the mechanisms to control decision-making processes from a limited number of cities on a global scale. Telecommunications – including the appearance of the now ubiquitous fax machine – and computer technologies allow same-time communications and decision making.

Economic space has shrunk and capital investment can be switched rapidly from production to commerce and finance on a global scale. TNCs in the service sector have become leaders in these areas. Powerful computer-communication networks, owned by single firms or a group of firms, are increasingly becoming the means for international transactions.

The penetration of TNCs into manufacturing activities in Southeast Asian economies is even more impressive. Until the late 1980s, direct foreign investment was principally led by US and European transnational corporations. Since 1986, however, an historically important new trend has been underway as DFI has begun to be dominated not only by Japan but also by the Asian newly industrializing countries (NICs), which for the first time became net exporters of investment capital (United Nations 1992a; Douglass 1991b).

The magnitude of these changes is shown in Table 3.1. For South Korea and Taiwan, the appreciation of their currencies and the removal of government restrictions on outward capital flows underlie accounts showing that out-flows of investment now exceed in-flows. Much of this has been directed towards the US as a means of maintaining access to markets but increasing labour and other costs also lie behind the trend, forcing these countries to target ASEAN nations as sites for offshore labour-intensive manufacturing. This is exemplified by the decision of the Korean affiliate of the shoemaker, Nike, to move its sports shoe production from Korea's southeast coast to Indonesia in 1991. Foreign investment by Korean transnationals had already increased 45-fold between 1970 and 1980, and 30 per cent of their investment in 1982 went to Southeast Asia, mostly in manufacturing activities operated by affiliates of Korea's large industrial groups (Esho 1985). From 1987 to 1989, DFI from Korea increased sixfold and was also more clearly focused on Southeast Asian countries as wages and other costs of production increased at home (Kim and Park 1991).

Taiwan investment in Asia is also growing. Taiwan investors had a declared total of 976 investment cases in Malaysia worth $5 billion and had investments worth $755 million in Indonesia by June 1992. Taiwan-based investments in China were estimated to include 4,000 enterprises amounting to $4 billion (*Far Eastern Economic Review,* 15 October 1992).

For its part, Hong Kong remains the major conduit for international investment into Shanghai and other coastal regions of China. Singapore has also joined the transnationalization process as a proxy for firms wishing to maintain Asian headquarter functions in this modern city-state while tapping the labour pools and lower land costs in Malaysia and Indonesia.

The data in Table 3.1 also show that the recipient countries have different mixes of investment by source country. Whereas Thailand has been

Table 3.1

Japan and Asian NIC direct foreign investment in Southeast Asia 1987-9

	Total direct foreign investment 1987-9							
	Thailand		Philippines		Malaysia		Indonesia	
	($ mill.)	(%)	($ mill.)	(%)	($ mill.)	(%)	($ mill.)	(%)
Japan	7,999	46.9	294	19.4	1,367	30.7	1,348	12.5
Asian NICs	4,420	25.9	504	33.1	1,743	39.2	3,093	28.6
Hong Kong	1,176	6.9	188	12.4	194	4.4	897	8.3
South Korea	295	1.7	21	1.4	80	1.8	692	6.4
Singapore	769	4.5	27	1.8	455	10.2	435	4.0
Taiwan	2,180	12.8	268	17.6	1,013	22.8	1,070	9.9
Other	4,632	27.2	722	47.5	1,338	30.1	6,362	58.9
World total	17,051	100.0	1,520	100.0	4,448	100.0	10,803	100.0

Sources: Far Eastern Economic Review, 16 November 1989; Asian Development Bank (1991)

exceptionally targeted by Japanese investment, Indonesia continues to be dominated by non-Asian sources, primarily US oil and timber investors. Malaysia received more investment from the Asian NICs than from either Japan or the rest of the world, and because of political and social instability the Philippines continues to be relatively neglected by all investors. The reasons for these differences are in many ways based on historical patterns of colonization and development. They also emanate from the political posture of the respective governments, with Thailand being the most unrestrained in terms of regulations on foreign investors and Indonesia being the most ambiguous in terms of both regulation and the involvement of business elites in opening potentially lucrative domestic markets to TNCs.

These differences are likely to become less pronounced in the coming years as DFI from East Asia and Singapore begins to interpenetrate all countries and markets in Southeast Asia and as DFI from the US becomes less prominent. Whatever the trends, the over-riding process is one of continuing transnationalization of production throughout the region. This process necessarily entails changes in spatial patterns of development as well as political, social, and economic restructuring.

The Changing Spatial Order: Five Emerging Patterns

The Polarization of Development

At least five new dimensions of spatial restructuring have resulted from the globalization of urbanization processes. One – the polarization of development in a limited number of urban regions – has been the subject of both ideological and empirical debate for more than three decades. What is new about recent trends is the reassertion of these polarizing processes in countries that were only a decade ago touted as having reached the 'stage of maturity' after which patterns of uneven spatial development were to be attenuated by polarization reversal and 'trickle-down' mechanisms (Douglass 1990). As shown in Table 3.2, the share of population in core regions in Asian countries has increased along with the urbanization process.[3]

Table 3.2

Urbanization and population concentration in core urban regions of selected Asian countries, 1970 and 1980

	GDP per capita	% Urban		Core population (millions)			Core as % of national population		
	1983	1970	1980	1960	1970	1980	1960	1970	1980
Bangladesh	130	9	11	5.1	7.6	10.0	10	11	12
India[a]	260	20	24	12.2	16.6	23.1	3	3	4
China[b]	300	17	21	38.4	45.4	53.4	6	5	5
Sri Lanka	330	22	28	1.0	1.5	3.1	21	21	21
Pakistan	390	25	28	2.1	3.6	5.4	5	5	6
Indonesia[c]	560	17	20	6.7	9.2	13.0	8	8	12
Thailand	820	21	25	2.6	3.7	6.7	10	11	13
Philippines	760	33	36	4.1	6.4	9.6	15	18	20
Malaysia	1,860	29	37	1.0	1.6	2.3	16	19	21
South Korea	2,010	41	57	5.2	8.9	13.3	21	28	36
Taiwan	2,675	62	70	2.2	3.7	5.7	21	25	32
Average	803	28	34	4.2	6.3	9.2	13	15	18

Notes:
a Core areas combine Calcutta, Greater Bombay, and Delhi.
b China core = total population of the 22 cities with more than one million inhabitants (1981)
c Core share for Java only. Years for India and Indonesia: 1961, 1971, 1981; for West Malaysia, 1957, 1970, 1980; for Bangladesh, 1961, 1974, 1981; for Pakistan, 1961, 1972, 1981; for Sri Lanka, 1963, 1971, 1981.
Sources: World Bank (1986); Vining (1986); Asian Development Bank (1986). For Indonesia: Biro Pusat Statistik, 1980 census. Also see Douglass (1990).

Although many factors are related to spatial polarization of development, recent studies showing that it is heightened by an urbanization process linked to extroverted industrialization are consistent with the data presented in Table 3.2 (Mutlu 1990; Smith and London 1990). In this regard, the Korean experience – like that of Japan in the 1980s – reveals that as an advancing economy moves away from domestic labour-intensive production of exports and begins to experience its own processes of transnationalization, processes of uneven spatial development favouring core regions may experience a resurgence. By the end of 1989, Korean TNC investments abroad amounted to more than $1.44 billion, with all indications showing that investment trends would continue to accelerate in the coming years (Kim and Park 1991).

Since the late 1960s, the Seoul and Pusan mega-urban regions have absorbed the bulk of the increase in the national population. The Seoul-Inchon-Kyonggi mega-urban region has also continued to absorb increasing shares of the national population. In 1990, its population reached more than 18 million, and for the first time its share exceeded that of the combined urban and rural populations of the rest of the nation less the population of the Pusan mega-urban region.

The recent surge in the growth of the Seoul mega-urban region is directly related to the transnationalization of Korean corporations, which is being manifested in the offshore movement of labour-intensive manufacturing from the Pusan region and the hypergrowth of international business functions in Seoul (Douglass 1993b). Land prices in Seoul have soared in response to the increasingly intense demand for commercial property and massive speculative land investments that have spun off from high rates of accumulation by Korea's huge corporations, the *chaebol*, which are leading the transnationalization wave. The experience of Korea gives a new dimension to the more general observation that no country in Asia has been able to reverse spatial polarization of population and economic development during the course of industrialization.

The spatial logic of contemporary industrial location and corporate decision making linked to international markets and worldwide systems of production accentuates these trends. This is so for two reasons. First, modern production requires sophisticated transportation and communications systems usually found only in the core regions of medium- and lower-income countries. Second, these regions also provide key amenities – schools, hospitals, sports, and other leisure facilities, and even steady supplies of electricity – which other regions can rarely offer. This is the context in which the formation and expansion of mega-urban regions in Asia must be understood.

The Emergence of Mega-Urban Regions

The second pattern of development is the emergence of mega-urban regions. More than simply the polarization of development in 'mega-cities,' the appearance of mega-urban regions is the outcome of complex economic and technological processes that have allowed for daily commuting and commercial interaction along corridors between core urban centres and into rural and urban hinterlands that extend far beyond the catchment areas of only a few decades ago. Called desakota regions by McGee (1991) and 'extended metropolitan regions' by Ginsburg, Koppel, and McGee (1991), they are complex fields of rural and urban interaction that reach 100 km or more from major urban nodes. As such they defy classification as either rural or urban; yet they are absorbing increasing shares of national populations.

The extreme may be the Seoul mega-urban region, which now accounts for approximately 40 per cent of the population of South Korea. But even in Japan, where Tokyo has been the target of renewed processes of transnationalization-led polarization, the Tokyo mega-urban region now accounts for almost 30 per cent of the national population (Douglass 1992a).

In understanding the structure of mega-urban regions, it is important to note that they are not simply composed of a limited number of trunk roads leading from core urban areas. Nor is spatial interaction necessarily directed towards the larger urban core. It may be nested among subregional clusters of villages, towns, and rural-based enterprises. As EMRs develop, interaction takes place through networks composed of specialized subregions linked to the larger regional sphere by finely grained webs of transactional space. These may involve animal-powered modes of transportation, bicycles, push carts, pedicabs, motorcycles, automobiles, buses, and trucks, all of which move in different patterns at different scales of interaction. At the same time, satellite dishes appear in the less densely settled rural interstices where urban elites make weekend homes. In this emerging ASEAN version of the 'postmodern' landscape, neither centrality nor propinquity is the principal defining characteristic of daily interaction. Such landscapes are as much a product of international economic integration as of localized development impulses.

Conventional planning, organized into separate urban and rural development ministries at the centre and municipal jurisdictions at local levels, is ill equipped to handle the development of these ambiguously rural and urban mega-urban regions. Prevailing concepts for regional development still fix on growth-pole constructs that guide investments to a limited number of large urban nodes. These are assumed to develop the countryside through trickle-down processes of diffusion. These modes and concepts of planning ignore both the complex rural-urban networks, which include industries located in nominally rural areas, and the continuing need to develop agriculture. New planning frameworks and models are needed to manage and take advantage of the potential for development.

World Cities and International Urban Hierarchies
As posited by McGee (1990a), just as there is no single national development context or process, there is no single type of mega-urban region. From an international perspective, one of the major differentiating factors is the position of each region with respect to transnational control and decision making and the international division of labour. At the top of

this hierarchy is a limited number of 'world cities,' such as London, New York, Tokyo and, in the perhaps not-too-distant future, Singapore. These act as command centres and vortices for the accumulation and circulation of global capital (Friedmann 1986; Sassen 1991). Reminiscent of Hymer's (1972) prediction that transnational corporations would produce a hierarchical division of labour over space that would correspond to the vertical division of labour on a world scale under the control of the firms, this pattern of control concentrates high-level decision-making occupations in a few key cities in the most advanced countries.

A second tier of cities, which along the Asian arc of the Pacific Rim is composed principally of the capital cities of market-oriented economies, acts in an intermediary capacity, administering the decisions taken in world cities and their local-level translation into tactics and agreements with governments and other firms, for national-level allocation and switching of investments.

At the lowest level are the cities and rural sites, including export-processing zones, where day-to-day production takes place. Most of these sites are near international seaports, but as international air transport expands – along with the spread of electronics and other sectors producing high value-added, low weight, and low bulk components – even inland cities such as Thailand's northern city of Chiang Mai can be targeted for labour-intensive segments of production in the global factory. Such inland sites are, however, unlikely candidates for either world city or second-tier decision-making and administration centres.

Transborder Regions
Bridging the subnational, national, and international levels is the fourth spatial pattern of development: the formation of transborder regions, urban agglomerations, and mega-urban regions that span national boundaries. The most dramatic examples on the Pacific Rim are to be found along the US-Mexican border, where several transborder cities, such as San Diego and Tijuana, have developed into huge, bi-cultural mega-urban regions (Herzog 1991). Among the principal examples emerging on the Asian arc of the Pacific Rim is the much touted 'Development Triangle' being promoted by the Singapore government and composed of Singapore, Malaysia's southern Johor state, and Indonesian islands in Riau province (Chng 1989). Hong Kong and the Pearl River delta, the Bohai Rim of northeast China and South Korea, and newly proposed transborder regions covering parts of the former Soviet Union, China, Japan, and South Korea are other well-known examples. At a more modest scale, such transborder agglomerations as those expanding across the Thai and Malaysian border provide more evidence of this international phe-

nomenon. Towns bordering Burma, Laos, and Malaysia are identified by the Thai government as key targets for development (National Economic and Social Development Board 1991b).

In a shrinking economic and political world, the emergence of transborder regions is one of the most revealing manifestations of the contradictions between global capital and the nation-state. On the one hand, enterprises seek the free flow of all forms of capital as a means to maximize returns on investments. In this regard, many of the tools developed by TNCs – which range from transfer pricing to the construction of Third World tax havens and indirect control of production through nominally independent local firms – have undermined the integrity of national economies and the nation-state as a political entity. On the other hand, nation-states must be relied on to perpetuate and stabilize the international division of labour that allows capital to, for example, develop consumer markets in one region while exploiting cheap pools of labour in another.

Border regions appear as a means to manage these contradictions. Their raison d'être is simply that they magnify the ways in which borders can be used to inhibit the free flow of labour and also act to separate social and political forces that result in differential costs of production, including environmental regulation, while capital can move freely on either side of the border. They also create ambiguous territorial entities that are neither clearly under the control of their respective nation-states nor completely without legal and institutional frameworks to carry out the normal functions of providing public goods, regulating labour, and dealing with struggles over collective consumption and the built environment.

In Southeast Asia, transborder cities and regions also appear to address many of the ethnic and cultural issues, induced during colonial times, that continue to plague the stability of the nation-state. Thus, in the Growth Triangle, Singapore can continue to pursue its racial policy of maintaining a Chinese state while Malaysia pursues its mirror of this policy by promoting *bumiputra* development – encouraging Malay enterprise and activity. In this context, the government of Singapore intends to sustain the move of the city-state's economy up the ladder towards high technology and the international finance sectors of production and services while adjacent areas of Malaysia and Indonesia provide the Fordist industrial labour and the weekend playgrounds for Singaporean and international elites.

In all of these relations, it is crucial to note that the Growth Triangle, and the division of labour upon which it depends, would not be possible if there were no international boundaries to maintain the socially and politically constructed differences among Singapore, Johor, and the Riau islands of Indonesia. The emergence of transborder regions is thus not

simply an accident of world development. To the contrary, it is fundamental to sustaining the transnationalization processes that characterize
its current phase.

International Networks and Development Corridors

The fifth pattern combines all of the above into an emerging international
network of arterial air, surface, and sea transportation corridors, telecommunications linkages, and decision-making pathways to integrate local
and national development into an increasingly globalized system of production, commerce, finance, and consumption. The continued polarization of development into mega-urban regions, the expansion of selected
port cities and other coastal locations, the blurring of national boundaries
by transborder regions, and the appearance of world cities are subpro-
cesses of this global movement. The basic elements of the Pacific Asia
development network are shown in Map 3.1.

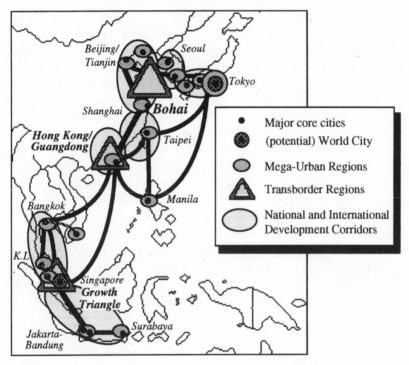

Map 3.1 **Emerging spatial network of development, Pacific Asia**

This network is still embryonic in terms of both its physical infrastructure and its political dimensions, but it is also in many ways developing
faster than the political geography of the region would seem to allow.

Economic relations between China and South Korea have, for example, been strengthened in advance of official political relations, and the integration of the Korean and Chinese economy around a Bohai (Yellow Sea) Rim transborder regional economy is seen as a way not only to take advantage of the division of labour between the two countries but also to promote the development of South Korea's perennially lagging and politically volatile Cholla provinces of the southwest. Similarly, the Singapore-centred development of the transborder Growth Triangle has proceeded rapidly despite the historical reluctance on the part of Indonesia to engage in international programs with the Chinese state of Singapore.

None of these trends is either secure or necessarily benevolent. At the international scale, and contrary to the assertion that the Asian arc of the Pacific Rim is becoming a 'Third World region' standing against a North-South American and a European region, the economic health of Pacific Asia continues to depend upon access to and growth in US and European markets, neither of which is guaranteed in an age of economic recession and potential protectionist reaction to the increasing affluent Japanese, Asian NIC, and ASEAN societies. The Pacific Asian economies remain highly protected and complementarities in production among them are low. The political, social, and economic tensions generated by processes of accelerated urban industrialization also have potentially destabilizing outcomes.

Internally in the countries of Southeast Asia, the surge of foreign investment has already had a number of consequences that promise both economic improvements and increasing social conflict. The 'proto-proletariat' is becoming an 'authentic' proletariat (McGee 1982; Armstrong and McGee 1985) and is found to be composed principally of peasant women brought to the city to work in textile mills, electronics industries, and a host of other industries ranging from shoe production to fine jewellery (Douglass 1993a). If the experience of such countries as South Korea indicates what is to come, the emergence of a wage-based labour force, in situations in which income gaps rise along with urban land prices and housing costs, may generate increasingly militant labour movements if governments do not ensure that economic welfare increases are widely shared (Bello and Rosenfeld 1990).

If the pace of urban industrialization is sufficient to create acute labour shortages, it may bring other cleavages. In both Malaysia and Thailand, the rate of labour absorption has been sufficient to lead analysts to predict that supplies of cheap rural labour will be depleted before the turn of the century. In the case of Thailand, these projections have led to speculation that Laos, Cambodia, and possibly Burma will become significant sources of low-wage workers (Hackenberg and Wangboonsin 1990). In the same light, Malaysia is expect to experience heightening conflict between the politics of pro-*bumiputra* nationalism and the economics of migration from Indonesia into rural estate crop production and urban household servant occupations. In both cases, social cleavages may expand along ethnic lines that, in many ways, parallel class divisions. These processes are already well underway in Japan and South Korea.

In the mega-urban regions of all the market-oriented ASEAN countries, a broad middle class is also emerging from urban industrial growth promoted through foreign investment. The evidence is already clear that this trend has given larger voice to social movements demanding basic political freedoms, better environments, and improved urban infrastructure. At the same time, however, the economic interests of the middle class and elites work to oppose the very measures that would effect these changes: the right of the poor to organize against landed interests, tax increases, zoning, and government use of rights of eminent domain to take private land for the purposes of widening urban roads.

The interim result has been the appearance of fortified condominiums and neighbourhoods, where the lifestyle imitates that of the Western 'mall-based' supermarket aspects of consumerism. This development has been part of an extreme intensification of land-use conflicts, magnifying the already obvious contrasts between opulence and poverty and between encapsulated living spaces and urban environmental deterioration. Nowhere are they more apparent than in Thailand and its emerging mega-urban region of Bangkok.

Spatial Transformations in Thailand

There is no doubt that, beginning in the mid-1980s, Thailand entered a new era of economic development that is highly contingent upon direct foreign investment and worldwide markets for manufactured exports. Exports of textiles, electronic goods, and other labour-intensive manufactured goods accelerated from 1986 onwards and have been the major factor propelling national economic growth. Much of the push for export-oriented industrialization has come from rapid structural changes in the economies of East Asia, resulting in quantum increases in direct foreign investment by those economies into labour-intensive production in ASEAN countries.

As Table 3.1 has shown, during the three years from 1987 to 1989, Thailand was the primary recipient of direct foreign investment among the four 'next generation' manufacturing exporters of Asia (the ASEAN-4 of Thailand, the Philippines, Malaysia, and Indonesia). With approximately three-quarters of this investment coming from Japan and Asian NICs, the $17 billion in direct foreign investment during those years is significant not only as it reflects the high level of investment and rate of

increase but also for what it says about the new position of the Thai economy as a host for labour-intensive export industries being shed from the
higher income economies of Asia.

The very rapid growth of manufactured exports following from direct
foreign investment in Thailand has been accompanied by substantial
increases in employment in manufacturing and related service sectors. As
many as 500,000 jobs may have been directly associated with the growth
of manufactured exports between 1985 and 1989 (Douglass 1990). With
the entire workforce growing by 3.8 million workers over this period, these
figures imply that exports directly absorbed the equivalent of somewhere
between 11 and 17 per cent of the additions to the Thai labour force.

Earlier, this chapter has argued that the transnationalization of capital
and DFI-led industrialization have contributed to the spatial polarization
of development. More than any other Pacific Asian country, Thailand has
been long known for its high spatial concentration of urban population,
urban-based manufacturing and industrial activities, and urban amenities.
The degree of concentration in all these indicators equals or exceeds that
of most other mega-city regions in Asia.

As shown in Table 3.3, population counts substantially underestimate
both the unevenness of spatial development and the level of economic
and social power accruing to national core regions. Thus, although
Bangkok had only about 10 per cent of the national population in 1980, it
accounted for one-quarter of the GDP, 70 per cent of manufacturing
employment, and 100 per cent of national bank headquarters in addition
to very high proportions of energy consumption, information services,
and higher level educational facilities.

Part of the explanation for this is geographical. Few other cities in Asia so
solidly occupy the centre of gravity of the national economy and its links
with the outside world. The only significant challenge to Bangkok is the
Eastern Seaboard, which in fact is part of the emerging Bangkok mega-
urban region.

But geography alone does not explain the high and increasing levels of
regional inequality in Thailand. Many analysts have, for example, pointed
to past government policies that exhibited strong biases towards Bangkok.
These include: heavy taxes on rice; relatively low priority placed on rural
development; explicit and implicit subsidies for import-substitution
industries, which have had a strong attraction to Bangkok; historically
high per capita expenditures on infrastructure development in Bangkok
vis-à-vis other *changwats;* and a high degree of concentration of political
and administrative decision-making functions in the capital city. None of
these aspects taken separately is unique to Thailand; each can be observed
in many other Asian countries (Ruland 1988). But their combination,

Table 3.3

Concentration of population and activities in selected cities of Asia

	Bangkok 1980	Manila 1980	Seoul 1980	Shanghai 1981
Population (millions)	5.2	5.9	8.4	6.1
Ratio to 2nd city	49:1	10:1	3:1	1.1:1
Ratio to 3rd city	59:1	12:1	5:1	1.2:1
Share of nation (%)				
Energy consumed	62	60	n.a.	n.a.
Manufacturing employment	70	73	25	5
Value manufacturing production	>70	70	22	11
Private bank investments	>70	n.a.	64	n.a.
National bank headquarters	100	100	100	n.a.
GDP	27	32	31	7
Motor vehicles	47	47	41	n.a.
Telephone connections	74	75	42	5
Universities	54	34	44	n.a.
University students	92	62	46	7
Doctors	67	n.a.	50	3
Hospital beds	n.a.	41	50	2
GDP per capita: rest of nation	3:1	3:1	2:1	6:1

Source: Bronger (1985)

along with the particular geography of the nation, has fostered a marked polarization of development.

Given the already extreme levels of polarization in Thailand, the jump in regional disparities following the surge in DFI in 1986 and 1987 is all the more striking. Table 3.4 shows trends in per capita gross regional domestic product (GRDP) for the decade 1978-87.[4]

Steadily widening disparities are apparent between the Bangkok Metropolitan Region and all other regions in the nation. The downturn in the economy in the early mid-1980s affected all regions, including Bangkok, but the recent massive injection of direct foreign investment in industry from 1986 overwhelmingly accrued economic advantage to the BMR. Table 3.4 also includes data using the so-called Williamson coefficient (the coefficient of variation weighted by each *changwat*'s share of the national population) to measure regional income inequality.[5] Two major conclusions can be drawn from the table. One is that regional inequalities have been on the increase. The other is that Bangkok continues to be the principal source of this increase. When the Bangkok metropolis (Bangkok and Thonburi) is excluded from the data, the level of inequality falls dramatically. When the larger Bangkok Metropolitan Region is excluded, the coefficient becomes even smaller. In fact, the data show that without the

Table 3.4

Inequalities in the distribution of gross regional domestic product per capita by region, 1978-88

	Gross regional domestic product per capita (Baht thousands)										
	1978	1979	1980	1981	1982	1983	1984	1985	1986	1987	1988
BMR	28.7	35.1	41.3	46.9	49.5	52.2	56.1	55.5	61.4	71.6	87.0
Central	9.5	11.1	13.0	13.3	13.9	14.6	16.1	17.6	17.2	18.7	24.4
East	19.4	21.3	27.4	22.0	23.3	24.0	25.2	27.2	31.0	31.1	35.8
West	14.6	15.1	19.2	20.2	21.2	20.1	21.2	19.1	19.5	19.8	22.5
Northeast	4.2	4.9	6.0	6.6	7.2	8.1	8.0	8.1	7.9	8.3	8.5
Northern	7.5	8.3	9.9	6.4	8.5	8.3	8.2	6.9	7.0	8.0	9.5
South	10.8	12.4	13.7	12.8	13.0	14.4	15.1	13.7	12.9	14.6	20.4
Thailand	11.0	12.6	15.0	12.5	13.4	15.3	14.8	19.0	19.3	20.8	27.6
Weighted coefficient of variation											
All *changwats*	0.84	0.88	0.90	1.04	1.04	1.02	1.07	1.16	1.17	1.25	–
Without Bangkok	0.69	0.70	0.74	0.61	0.59	0.55	0.57	0.93	0.69	0.69	–
Without BMR	0.56	0.57	0.61	0.54	0.51	0.47	0.48	0.53	0.60	0.55	–

Source: Thailand, National Statistical Office, various years

BMR, the level of inequality actually declined in 1986-7.

The increasingly uneven pattern of spatial development has been noted by other researchers. Jitsuchon and Sussangkarn (1990), in detailing the rapid growth of the manufacturing sector during the 1985-8 period, conclude that the combination of industrial boom and faltering agriculture has led unmistakably to widening income disparities, with the largest decline in income shares affecting the poorest 20 per cent of the population. Over the period 1975-6 to 1985-6, the Gini coefficient increased from 0.43 to 0.50, and the increase has been most rapid in recent years.

A second important contributing source of disparity has been the very slow increase in productivity of agricultural labour. This can be set against the fact that the Bangkok Metropolitan Region accounted for 77 per cent, and the BMR plus the Central Region for 89 per cent, of the nation's value added in manufacturing in 1987 (Tamburnlertchai 1990).

With regard to the link between regional inequalities and the international economy, the most revealing example of the role of government in managing spatial inequalities is the implementation of the Board of Investment (BOI) policy to decentralize DFI away from Bangkok. The government had given no attention to industrial decentralization until the Third Plan period, when a 1972 Revolutionary Decree provided special incentives for promoted firms located in designated Investment Promotion Zones (IPZs). The composition and location of IPZs has varied considerably over time. In 1990, the designated sites covered sixty-seven provinces as well as Bangkok and its five surrounding provinces and the

Table 3.5

Distribution of Board of Investment approved investments, 1986-9

| Location | 1986 | | | 1987 | | | 1988 | | | 1989 | | |
	Number	Baht millions	(%)	Number	Baht millions	(%)	Number	Baht millions	(%)	Number	Baht millions	(%)
BMR	208	23,343	67	576	58,582	86	1,007	127,186	63	861	200,301	76
Bangkok	51	5,553	16	113	7,465	11	191	10,672	5	169	85,752	30
Inner ring	99	10,267	29	388	41,579	61	466	53,114	26	365	29,297	10
Outer ring	58	7,523	22	75	9,538	14	350	63,400	31	327	81,752	29
Rest of nation	91	11,515	33	53	9,065	13	455	74,573	37	309	69,252	24
Total	299	34,858	100	629	67,647	100	1,462	201,759	100	1,170	269,553	100

Source: Douglass (1991a)

Laem Chabang Industrial Estate are all IPZs. In 1990, designated sites were located in Bangkok and its five surrounding provinces, the Laem Chaband Industrial Estate, and sixty-seven other provinces. Projects located in the BMR, or Zone 1, were to receive the fewest benefits while those located in Zones 2 (the outer ring of the BMR) and 3 (all other areas) were to receive the most. Projects in Zone 1, for example, were to receive no corporate tax holiday unless they met export or employment targets. Tax reductions and exemptions on imported raw materials were to be granted only to projects located in Zone 3.

Yet despite these policies and incentives, between 1986 and 1989, Zones 1 and 2 accounted for 70 per cent of the total foreign and domestic investment approved by the BOI, with much of the more recent growth in investment occurring in Zone 2, the outer ring of the BMR (Table 3.5).

All data indicate that foreign investment is a leading force in the formation of the Bangkok mega-urban region, particularly along the corridor from Bangkok north to Don Muang airport and beyond to Ayuthaya, where industrial estates have begun to cluster. Investment outside the region continues to be dominated by resource-based industries, such as rubber products in the south and a tomato canning factory in the northeast. Without additional government emphasis on diffusing investment throughout the country, there is little reason to expect that future private investment will significantly improve regional inequalities during the Seventh Plan (Biggs et al. 1990).

Regional inequality in development is also associated with regional differences in the incidence of poverty. In Thailand, the northeast and the south are the two chronically poor regions of the country. The northeast, which is the most populous region of the nation, accounts for 38 per cent of all households at or below the basic needs poverty line in 1988-9. But poverty is also reportedly increasing in rural areas elsewhere. The proportion of the Central Region population classified as poor has increased consistently, from 13 per cent in 1975-6 to almost 16 per cent in 1988-9. In particular, poverty in central villages has grown from 14 to 19 per cent during that period but declined from about 12 per cent in 1980-1 to 6.4 per cent and 8.4 per cent in central sanitary districts and municipalities, respectively.

Population data clearly indicate that Thailand's new economic era has not only heightened uneven spatial development but has also accelerated urbanization and the rural-urban transition. Although in the past the Kingdom had among the lowest levels of urbanization in Asia, reflecting the agrarian nature of its economy and export base, two important factors are now in place to accelerate the transition to an urban-based economy and society. The first is the precipitous drop in the natural population growth rate, which is already having an impact on labour supplies. Thailand Development Research Institute (TDRI) projections show that, for the nation as a whole, the population growth rate will fall from 1.42 per cent per year during 1990-5 to 0.96 per cent per year during the 2005-10 period. The second trend is an expected continuation of high rates of growth in DFI-led urban-based manufacturing and services, which will shift employment out of agriculture and rural areas.

At the same time, a new era in Thai history will commence after 2000 as out-migration from more peripheral regions begins to produce negative rural population growth rates. Although the rates of decline will vary by region, the overall trend will be one of diminishing population and sup-

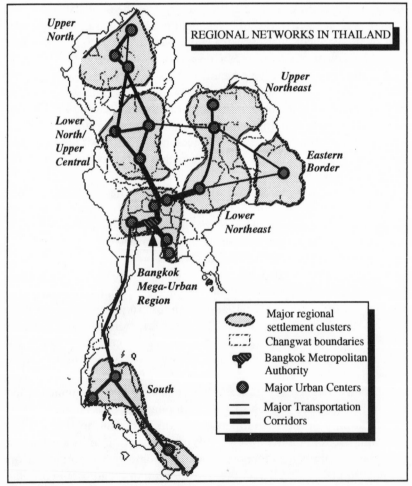

Map 3.2 **Regional networks in Thailand, 1990-2010.** Based on Douglass (1991a)

plies of labour for agriculture and rural employment. Projections indicate that for the entire 1990-2010 period, the rural population will increase by 0.3 million people, but for the years after the turn of the century the rural population will begin to decline. Rural population decline will be offset by accelerating urban population growth, with projections pointing to annual increases of several hundred thousand people to Thailand's urbanizing areas.

By the first quarter of the next century it is possible that Thailand's urban transition will be substantially completed, with as much as 60 to 70 per cent of the national population living in urban regions. The intensive period of spatial restructuring now underway will therefore have a long-lasting impact on the formation of the national urban and regional system. Table 3.6 presents one perspective on this issue. In the table, projected population increases for the 1990-2010 period (Ashakul 1990) are allocated to regions not demarcated by administrative boundaries but on the basis of settlement clusters and regional networks of interaction (Map 3.2). This view is better able to capture the spatial dynamics of development and also reveals more clearly the ways in which population and population changes are spatially configured. The table shows that although all regions will have absolute increases in population, only two, the Bangkok mega-urban region and the south, will increase their share of the national population. For the southern region, the increase will be primarily due to continuing relatively high rates of population growth. The major share of population increase in the Bangkok region will be from migration.

Earlier estimates for the 1986-91 period projected that the BMR would grow by an estimated 200,000 people per year, to reach 9.3 million inhabitants in the latter year (Phisit 1987). But these figures did not account for

Table 3.6

Projected distribution of population in Thailand by region, 1990-2010

	Population (millions)		Growth rate per annum (%)	Total population (millions)	(%) Increase
	1990	2010			
Bangkok mega-urban region	12.2	17.3	1.8	5.1	34.2
Upper North	5.3	6.4	0.9	1.1	7.4
Lower North	7.1	7.9	0.5	0.8	5.4
Northeast	17.3	21.0	1.0	3.7	24.8
Eastern border	2.0	2.5	1.1	0.5	3.4
South	7.5	10.4	1.6	2.9	19.5
Rest of Kingdom	4.2	5.0	0.9	0.8	5.4
Thailand	55.6	70.5	1.2	14.9	100.0

Source: Douglass (1991a)

the expanded growth of the mega-urban region, and even with the assumed slow-down in the population growth of the BMR, this larger region is expected to garner a minimum of one-third of the total population increase for Thailand between 1990 and 2010.

In absolute terms, the extended Bangkok mega-urban region (which includes Ayuthaya, Chachoengsao, Chon Buri, Ratcha Buri, Suphan Buri, and Samut Songkhram, all within a 100 km radius of central Bangkok) will absorb another 5 million people over the next twenty years to reach a population of at least 23 million. Given the concentration of construction, DFI, and economic growth in this region, these projections must be viewed as conservative.

Confirming the theme that mega-urban regional growth involves an intensive mix of rural and urban activities, data on employment in the Bangkok mega-urban region show increasing concentration of manufacturing employment at the periphery of the Bangkok metropolis where agriculture is also going through a transformation away from rice production and towards animal stockyards, higher value-added food and industrial crops, and the production of grass for golf courses.

This mix of intensified agricultural production and industrial decentralization in the region is producing a spatial structure that is much more interwoven than the widely accepted models of node-hinterland hierarchies allow. In countries such as Thailand, with long traditions of sedentary agriculture, dense rural settlement with small-scale producers, and increasingly elaborate local and national transportation systems, spatial development is more characterized by expanding networks of rural-urban linkages that defy simple models of spatial structure. They also present new issues and problems for urban and regional planning and management.

Managing Spatial Transformations and Mega-Urban Regions

The internationalization of regional development underlying the polarization of development and expansion of mega-urban regions in Asia poses a number of dilemmas for policy. At the centre of these is the hypermobility of capital, which has formed global networks of 'flexible accumulation.' These are characterized by rapid spatial and sectoral switching of investments underlying exaggerated booms and busts in local fortunes and a heightened unevenness in spatial development. In the movement of capital, comparative advantage is no longer defined by natural resource endowments or past industrial histories but by social and political processes creating packages of incentives to attract footloose industry. The result has been overt competition for global investment through increasingly generous subsidies and guarantees and regulation of labour and civil society (Douglass 1991b).[6]

The International Dimension of Regional Policy

The imperative to provide incentives for DFI in export-oriented manufacturing necessarily focuses policy on short-term development. Tensions not only exist within and between short- and long-term perspectives but they tend to be magnified as economic growth accelerates (Castells 1989). Thus when governments attempt to attract industries by maintaining low claims on investors through, for example, tax holidays or limited controls on environmental impact, they face chronic financial shortfalls in providing basic urban economic and social infrastructure.[7] In the case of Bangkok, the gap between the demand for and supply of such infrastructure has widened substantially under the massive influx of foreign investment and imperatives to create a commercial centre for global capital.

The consequences of the widening inability to keep pace with economic growth in Thailand are well known. Traffic congestion, environmental degradation, and inadequate community infrastructure are at levels that threaten future economic growth and are hazardous to the health of citizens (Douglass 1993a). The situation is made all the more striking when one learns that the Bangkok Metropolitan Region reportedly received more than 90 per cent of the combined central government, state enterprise, local government, and private-sector infrastructure investments in the municipalities of Thailand during the Sixth Plan period, from 1987 to 1991 (Krongkaew 1991).

The inability to translate short-term gains into long-term sustainability is the major problem facing all cities in Asia and goes far beyond economic considerations to include questions of political and social stability. The forces of change induced by accelerating industrialization – including the emergence of new urban classes with rising expectations for improved welfare and political reform – have brought political turbulence to all of the newly industrializing countries.

Thailand had its own experience with the consequences of these transformations when in April of 1992 a spontaneous social movement challenged the long-standing military dominance of political life. What remains to be seen is whether a new order of political stability that enlarges democratic practices can be constructed along with the industrialization process. If it can, Thailand will provide a model distinctly different from that of the authoritarian regimes which marshalled the East Asian NICs through their early industrialization stages. If it cannot, other countries in Asia and Latin America have shown that the perception of political instability can lead to abandonment by capital and, along with it, severely diminished prospects in the global economy.

The accelerated growth of the Bangkok mega-urban region is exacerbating an already severe set of problems. Environmental deterioration is among the most pressing. Five of Thailand's seven lead smelting plants are found in the Bangkok mega-urban region along with 83 per cent of fluorescent lamp manufacturing plants and between 90 and 97 per cent of the chemical, dry cell battery, paint, pharmaceutical, and textile manufacturing plants (Phantumvanit and Liengcharernsit 1989). The major waterways feeding the city of Bangkok can no longer sustain life. Ground subsidence, widespread flooding, and seepage of saline water into freshwater aquifers pervade a city in which only 2 per cent of the population is connected to the sewer network. Air pollution is more than twice the acceptable level and is officially classified as 'dangerous.' Even the farthest reaches of the region have begun to experience serious environmental degradation. The negative environmental impact on the Chao Phraya River now reaches beyond the ancient city of Ayuthaya (Japan International Cooperation Agency 1990a). As suggested above, water pollution in this part of the region is caused by a combination of intensive animal husbandry and industrial development. On both counts, the downstream consequences for Bangkok are not encouraging.

In Bangkok, intensified land-use conflicts are exacerbating already severe problems of slum formation and inadequate housing. By the mid-1980s, Bangkok had as many as 1,000 slum areas with estimates of the total slum population ranging up to 1.5 million (Kaothien and Rachatatanun 1991; Ard-Am 1991). These slums are often located in areas of constant flooding and are without sewerage or public garbage services. Many are on private land, which has subjected them to increasing evictions and a push of the poor to the outer fringes. In just two years, from 1984 to 1986, at least 15,000 slum and squatter households in Bangkok were either cleared or served eviction notices (Yap 1989, 31). A recent study reveals a net loss of more than 11,000 slum housing units from within a ten-mile radius of the centre from 1984 to 1988 (PADCO-LIF 1990). During the same period, another 21,000 units appeared in areas reaching beyond 30 km from the centre. Alternative low-cost housing projects built by the National Housing Authority have been too expensive for the poorest urban residents. About 70 per cent of the eligible low-cost housing dwellers sold their rights to higher-income families and returned to squatter-slum areas. Evictions for land development have accelerated along with the recent economic boom.

Because much of the work obtained by low-income households is found in the centre of the city, many have abandoned housing made available in the periphery in favour of poor living conditions in the core. The children of these households are particularly susceptible to the dangerous environmental conditions in these central areas. Among the most common dangers is lead poisoning from automobile emissions. In Bangkok, levels of 340 µg per litre have been found in blood samples of children, with levels of 200 µg shown to have haematological effects, including seizures, behavioural changes, mental retardation, irritability, lack of coordination, and clumsiness (United Nations, UNICEF 1990, 28-9).

Government policies have not significantly challenged the forces underlying the displacement of the poor. In supporting private land-development rights they have, to the contrary, abetted them. In the 1980s, policies adopted for slum improvements in Bangkok divided slums into three categories: those qualified for assistance as permanent low-income settlements; those targeted for only temporary upgrading (minimum utilities and government services); and those that would receive no upgrading 'because they are likely to be needed by landowners for redevelopment' (Cheema 1986, 6). As might have been expected, those in the first category were all on government-owned land. Clearly, the government would avoid confronting the broader issue of land concentration and would, instead, yield ever decreasing areas of public space as a means of mediating the conflict between rich and poor in the city.

Land development in the Bangkok mega-urban region is fundamentally driven by Thailand's links to the world economy. The logic of those linkages is being played out in central areas of the region by intensive land conversion from housing and petty services to international commercial and financial uses. The spatial paradox of this change is that as night-time densities decrease with the shift of housing out of the core, daytime densities will skyrocket as huge multistorey office complexes continue to displace small shops and houses.

In zones farther from the centre, suburban housing, agriculture and animal husbandry, large-scale industry, and amenity uses are developing in an often chaotic manner. Particularly in areas that lie outside municipal jurisdictions, a category that includes very large areas of the mega-urban region, much of development is poorly monitored, whether it is the conversion of rice paddy land to the production of golf course grass or the advent of 'disco barge' music wars along once quietly scenic rivers. For the region as a whole, although a host of national planning bodies are involved in land-use decisions, no agency or body coordinates or ameliorates land and resource development activities. Because the mega-urban region does not fit into any recognized administrative entity, the interaction between these activities remains largely invisible in the planning process.

Making them more visible and more central to the national planning process is an important task not only for urban and regional management but also for the continuing prosperity of the Thai economy, given the already severe land and environmental problems facing the mega-urban region and its key role in national development. The government has given explicit recognition to this issue by including the concept of an extended BMR in their Seventh Five-Year Plan (National Economic and Social Development Board 1992; Douglass 1990). According to the Plan, land-use development and regional management are to be coordinated by a newly created Extended BMR Development Committee (EBMRDC) at the national level. Among the initiatives to effect coordination are: special development funds for the region; financial planning coordination among central, provincial, and municipal governments; strengthening of local government financial capacities; encouragement of NGOs to assist in social welfare programs and slum upgrading; and recognition of community organizations as legitimate actors in the provision and maintenance of public goods, utilities, and services.

Whether these intentions will be carried out in practice remains to be seen, but the direction taken is potentially of great significance for improving management of the Bangkok mega-urban region. There is a history in Asia and elsewhere of setting up toothless coordinating bodies with good intentions and lacklustre results. Yet in the current milieu of serious popular and government concern for more effective planning, the EBMRDC may over time increase its potential. The strengthening of local governments and the inclusion of NGOs and community organizations are also much welcomed signs that local participation in the planning process will give greater voice to the many concerns often unheard from above.

National Spatial Development Strategies

As noted at the outset, Asia has no case in which the proportion of the total population living in the national core region has declined. This has not even occurred in South Korea, where exceptionally strong public policies were adopted to decentralize industry. In Thailand, where public policy has been much more open to the working of the market and sectoral development policies have been biased towards Bangkok, there seems to be little room for a 'polarization reversal' in the coming years. Scepticism about the potential for regions outside of the Bangkok area to play a significant role in Thailand's urban transition is underscored by recent trends. There are, for example, few indications that the economic base for urbanization in most provinces – agriculture – is generating the broad-based increases in productivity and income needed to provoke higher levels of demand for urban goods and services. Macro-economic data show that, during the 1980s, value added in major agricultural crops had few gains.[8]

These trends notwithstanding, national planning in Thailand from the mid-1970s to the mid-1980s (the Fourth and Fifth Plans) gamely sought to control the growth of Bangkok and achieve a better balance between rural and urban development (Ashakul and Ashakul 1988). The principal means to accomplish this was to direct investments to a select number of growth poles and lower-order rural centres in each of the major regions. As the foregoing discussion indicates, however, during this period, polarization in the BMR continued and rural-urban disparities remained high.

Although many opportunities to link rural and urban development on a regional scale remained relatively unexplored, the Sixth Plan (1986-91) adopted a much more clearly urban-oriented view of development, which reversed the previous position on limiting the growth of the Bangkok Metropolitan Region. The Eastern Seaboard project involved developing a new port on the eastern seaboard of the Gulf of Thailand (National Economic and Social Development Board 1991b) and garnered the lion's share of investment to spur the growth of regional cities. With the new wave of direct foreign investment pouring into the nation after 1986, reliance on industrial decentralization and urban diffusion models of regional development increased.

Map 3.3 summarizes the national spatial development of the Sixth Plan. Instead of trying to explicitly slow down the growth of Bangkok, policies were directed towards improving urban management through privatization, cost recovery programs, and more stringent 'polluter pays' measures to stem environmental deterioration (Ashakul and Ashakul 1988). As argued in the Sixth Plan, the extended BMR represents the most important economic and employment base in the country, and trying to stem its growth would have severe efficiency costs for the national economy.[9]

Even if investment in Bangkok were to deliver short-term efficiency gains to the Thai national economy, however, it would still be necessary to anticipate longer term regional development needs and potential in a manner that engages all regions and their citizens more positively in the national development process. The Sixth Plan addressed this by continuing past policies that concentrated public investments in a limited number of 'first generation' regional growth centres, namely, Chiang Mai, Khon Kaen, Nakhon Ratchasima, Songkhla/Hat Yai, and Chon Buri, the last of these being the principal target.

The regional policies of the Sixth Plan have been substantially carried over into the current Seventh Plan (1992-6), except that the new plan does not formally recognize the extended Bangkok Metropolitan Region as a geographical entity for government investment. The focus remains on regional growth centres, and investments are to be coordinated through the Ministry of Interior from central to provincial and municipal levels. Local levels of government are to be strengthened to enhance planning and implementation.

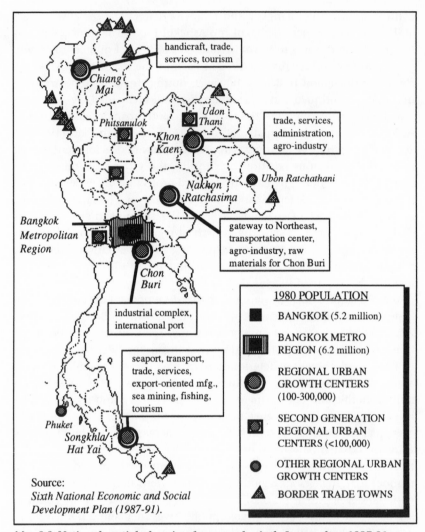

Map 3.3 **National spatial planning framework, sixth 5-year plan, 1987-91**

Success in stimulating regional development through a focus on four or five regional cities has had only limited success over the past decade and more. Whether investments were too modest or institutional frameworks too centralized is a matter of debate, but more substantial limitations exist within the concept itself.[10]

Specifically, the guiding construct for the policy is that of decentralizing industry into various growth poles and diffusing development down a national urban hierarchy. Thus, investments are first made in the largest provincial cities and a second generation of centres is to be targeted at an unspecified time. Within this construct, rural areas will benefit from development impulses cascading down the urban system as the system itself develops and becomes more articulated.

For the most part, however, even the largest provincial cities are too small in comparison to Bangkok to act as 'countermagnets' of growth. The economies of provincial cities are based on trade, agro- and resource-based processing, government spending, and, in some areas, tourism, and they are geographically unlikely candidates for export-oriented industrial loca-tion. Their future depends more on growth and prosperity in their hinter-lands than on footloose manufacturing attracted from Bangkok or abroad. The 'propulsive' effects of the growth centres on their hinterlands are also reported to be very modest.

A Chiang Mai study shows, for example, that investing in municipal services and infrastructure in this city would, by itself, have only a marginal impact on stimulating development of the Northern Region as a whole (Ladavalya and Siripool 1988). In fact, in order of benefit, expendi-tures by Chiang Mai factories accrued greater benefits to Bangkok than to the surrounding hinterland of urban Chiang Mai. The study concluded that 'the countryside cannot provide what is needed in a modern, indus-trializing economy' (p. 54), but it also noted that no concerted effort has been made to develop new business to use what is available in rural areas of the region. Chiang Mai residents apparently felt the same way; they spent most of their money in the city and Bangkok, with 'very little going to nearby rural areas.' Sales of finished products primarily occurred in Chiang Mai City and Bangkok, and 'sales to nearby rural areas are meager' (p.27). A study of Surat Thani produced similar findings (Kung 1986).

These and other studies confirm the need to rethink the urban-centred approach towards rural regional development (Gibb 1984; Grandstaff 1990). Table 3.7 attempts to contribute to this rethinking by contrasting the growth-pole approach with a regional network concept. The table sug-gests that whereas the growth-pole concept has been single-mindedly focused on urban-based manufacturing as the leading sector for regional development, the network concept recognizes the multisectoral nature of development in rural regions and depends more upon regional resource endowments and already existing activities than upon inducements to decentralize industries from core regions. It also challenges the prevailing assumptions that rural industries have a strong affinity to locate in cities by observing that, in fact, bulk-losing processing and agro-industry may be more efficiently located near the fields or along major transport routes, including waterways.[11]

The network concept also draws from research in Asia and elsewhere which shows not only that city size is an inadequate indicator of either

Table 3.7

Growth-pole and regional network models compared

	Growth-pole/centre model	Regional cluster/network model
Basic sector	Urban-based manufacturing; usually focuses on large-scale 'propulsive' industries and 'footloose' production units headquartered outside the region	All sectors, depending on local regional endowments and conditions; emphasis on local small to medium-size regionally based enterprises
Urban system	Hierarchical, centred on a single dominant centre, usually identified by population size and associated with the assumptions of central place theory	Horizontal, composed of a number of centres and their hinterlands, each with own specializations and comparative advantages
Rural-urban relations	Image of diffusion processes moving down the urban hierarchy and outward from the city/town to its rural periphery; rural areas as passive beneficiaries of 'trickle-down' from urban growth	Image of a complex rural-urban field of interaction, with growth stimuli emanating from both rural and urban areas and with the intensity increasing along regional intersettlement transportation corridors
Planning style	Usually top-down via sectoral planning agencies and their field offices; regions have 'misty' boundaries determined by economic interaction	Implies the need for decentralized planning systems, with integration and coordination of multisectoral and rural and urban activities at the local level
Major policy areas	Industrial decentralization incentives: tax holidays, industrial estates, national transportation trunk roads	Agricultural diversification, agro-industry, resource-based manufacturing, urban services, manpower training, local intersettlement transportation networks

Source: Douglass (1991a)

growth potential or local linkages but also that cities of the same size can have very different functions and development profiles (Cohen, English, and Brookfield 1977). Rather than trying to make a single, large city into an omnibus centre for a region, the network concept envisions a clustering of many settlements, each with its own specializations and localized hinterland relationships. It also takes a more even view of rural-urban relations by recognizing that appropriate investments in agriculture can lead to higher levels of per capita income in that sector and, further, that rural prosperity is the source of urban growth in agrarian regions. At the same time, selected investments in region-serving functions in cities can help to raise the economic growth potential of both town and countryside.

Finally, growth-pole and regional network concepts differ in the styles of planning they encourage. In the growth-pole concept, the urban node is the all-important spatial 'actor' and regional boundaries are superfluous to planning. In contrast, the multisectoral nature of the network concept implies a need for the localized capacity to coordinate a large number of inter-related activities. Using existing provincial or district boundaries to signal the level at which coordination and integration of planning is to take place is thus an important aspect of the network approach. As the term 'regional network' suggests, the alternative to dividing the urban system into a hierarchy of regional urban growth centres, second-generation regional urban centres, other regional centres, and border trade towns is to view all cities and towns within a region or subregion as members of a tight network of rural and urban linkages forming a larger, more diversified regional economy that would have greater potential for generating agglomeration economies than would a system that focused on a single major centre in each region.[12]

As mentioned, the approach also rests on the general proposition that provincial towns and non-agricultural activities will advance only to the extent that agricultural productivity and incomes also rise. Thus development of rural 'hinterlands' becomes as important as town-centred or urban investments. Recent studies confirm that the major source of demand for urban goods and services in rural Thailand is rural households (Grandstaff 1990). Researchers working in other ASEAN countries have found that neither trade with outside regions nor demand for farm inputs is as important for urban growth in rural areas as local household expenditures for daily goods and services (Gibb 1984).

In this context, the essential features of an agriculture policy are as follows: intensified cultivation through crop diversification towards higher value-added crops; improved farming techniques through expanded extension services and small-scale cooperatives; irrigation and drainage projects; off-farm infrastructure and marketing development; and production services located in nearby towns. Such development would also promote the growth of agro-processing industries and higher-order urban functions.

With regard to urban development policy to support agricultural development, a key distinction needs to be made between town-serving and region-serving activities and investments. There has been a marked tendency by Asian governments to give heavy emphasis to the former. Thus, once growth centres have been selected for priority, the focus of public works and other planning agencies almost invariably moves to urban problems over physical infrastructure such as piped water, sewage and drainage, electrification, housing and squatter settlements, and higher-order services captured by the urban rather than the regional population. More explicit consideration should be given to infrastructure and functions that directly serve rural development: regional marketing centres and services, rural-urban all-weather roads, grain storage centres for rural cooperatives, agricultural extension offices, headquarters for mobile library and post-offices, and a host of other services using cities as centres of convenient access for rural population.

All of these policy initiatives imply the need for better coordination between rural and urban development policies. This raises the widely discussed topic of decentralization of planning to the *changwat* and perhaps even *amphoe* level as a means of coordinating and spatially integrating the many public-sector activities implemented at local levels.

Efforts to distribute gains from agricultural development broadly among all rural households will also eventually lead to the question of agrarian land reform. A substantial body of theory and research convincingly demonstrates that agricultural development based on small farms is superior to that based on large farms in terms of both growth and equity.

The continuing dominance of growth-pole concepts in regional development thinking has meant that agriculture and rural development as the basis for urbanization remains a neglected topic. Policy initiatives to integrate rural and urban planning at the regional scale would potentially go a long way in generating the type of spatially dispersed urban transition long desired by policy makers. The issue of enhancing local planning institutions, which has received increasing attention in recent years, also deserves closer attention in the search for an institutional means to carry forward the complex, localized development process implied by a multi-sector approach composed of small-scale actors and large-scale domestic and foreign investors. In sum, the network concept points towards a more decentralized system of planning and suggests a diversified approach to regional development that rests on integrating rural and urban development on the local scale.

Conclusions

Managing the future of emerging mega-urban regions has a number of policy dimensions. It is important to recognize that books on urbanization and national development that were the mainstay of urban and regional planning in the Third World two decades ago have lost much of their relevance. Urbanization must be rethought in terms of both the forces generating it and the spatial forms it takes, and urban development is now as much an international as a national act.

From this perspective, policies to manage the Bangkok mega-urban region will require as much attention to international development forces as to internal ones. The major international-local policy dilemma is two-pronged: first, how to continue attracting and keeping globally mobile investments; and, second, how to translate them into sustainable development that closes gaps in urban infrastructure and services, reverses environmental deterioration, and promotes a more equitable and democratic process. Pursuing both these objectives is a formidable challenge, yet if economic growth is not carried out within a strategy that accomplishes the latter, neither objective can be secured.

In this regard, establishing an extended BMR would offer one starting point for strategic planning at a more appropriate spatial scale than allowed by existing administrative and planning frameworks. A second major component of spatial policy concerns the development of towns and regions outside of the Bangkok mega-urban region. Most attention to this policy area has focused on industrial decentralization and growth-pole concepts. The scope for industrial decentralization to be the cutting edge of rural regional development seems, however, particularly limited in the Thai context. There is probably no other country in Asia in which the capital city so clearly occupies the centre of gravity of both the national economy and its links with the outside world as Bangkok does in Thailand.[13]

An alternative approach, which builds upon existing rural-urban networks of interaction, has been proposed as a framework for rethinking the rural regional dimension of national development. In the heady atmosphere of accelerated urban-industrial expansion focusing on the Bangkok mega-urban region, rural-based approaches towards national development have been portrayed as turning the clock back or unnecessarily hindering the forces of economic advancement. Thailand, in fact, has a unique opportunity to provide a new model for urban and regional development that is more appropriate to Southeast Asia than the one generated by the experiences of South Korea or Taiwan. This opportunity derives, in part, from the capacity of the Thai economy to develop along both urban-industrial and rural-agricultural lines of economic growth. Unlike the very densely settled, resource-poor Asian NICs, Thailand has a rich and diversified agricultural base, which is expected to contribute substantially to economic growth well into the future. Agro-industry now accounts for more than half of the industrial GDP for the nation, and the economies of most regions outside of Bangkok depend on agriculture as the basic sector to drive structural transformations, rising incomes, and urbanization. A national strategy of economic growth with poverty reduction that implicitly rests on massive migration to a single metropolitan region will miss manifold opportunities to raise the incomes of rural people where they live.

Such a regional development strategy should not, however, rest on a false pretence that either growth poles or regional networks will stop or even significantly slow down the growth of the Bangkok mega-urban region. As long as this area retains its position in the new geography of global capital, there can be little doubt that it will continue to outpace other regions in the country in both economic and demographic terms. One problem for national planning and management is that the ever increasing demands and needs of Bangkok will continue to dwarf those of other regions and relegate them to secondary status in national planning. If so, the prospects for the future of the nation will rest more and more on the sustainability of Bangkok.

Notes

1 The combined research and development expenditures of the ten largest US TNCs, for example, exceed those of the French and British governments (United Nations 1992a).
2 From 1986 to 1990, ten countries garnered 70 per cent of DFI flow to the so-called less developed countries. Six of those – China, Hong Kong, Malaysia, Singapore, Thailand, and Taiwan – were on the Asian arc of the Pacific Rim (The other four were Argentina, Brazil, Egypt, and Mexico) (United Nations 1992a).
3 In this context, core regions – defined in each case as the largest city plus its adjacent administrative districts or provinces – approximate the areas encompassed by the emerging mega-urban regions.
4 The GRDP data for Thailand has been criticized because of the tendency of respondents in Bangkok to describe branch operations in the provinces as being located in Bangkok.
5 The coefficients are derived from data on the *changwat* level, not from the regional data shown in the table.
6 Of eighty-two policy changes made by thirty-five countries in 1991, eighty were intended to ease the process of foreign investment. Sixty-four new bilateral treaties were signed in 1990-1 to ease DFI, compared to a total of 199 for the entire 1980-90 period (United Nations 1992a).
7 Even if land-use planning can be coordinated in the region, the economics of land development in the Bangkok mega-urban region will continue to depend very much on international economic and political conditions. Many observers feel that, given the small share of international trade in manufactured goods occupied by the Thai economy, Thailand still has many opportunities for export expansion even if world markets continue to contract (Dapice and Flatters 1989). Yet any continuation of recession in the US or Japan coupled with protectionist policies in major consumer countries could dampen future economic growth rates in Thailand.
8 For the years 1984 to 1988, the nominal growth rate in agricultural production was 3.0 per cent per year (Dapice and Flatters 1989). Between 1980 and 1987, the percentage of labour in agriculture in the northeast, which is Thailand's most populous region, declined only marginally, from 86 to 84 per cent, suggesting that incomes remain low and structural change is not underway in that region.
9 Among the better known caveats about this claim are: the inability to measure agglomeration economies and the efficiency trade-offs of alternative spatial development strategies, particularly from a medium-to-long-term perspective; the inability either to cost negative externalities or to allow for the possibility that the negative externalities of the same activity may be lower in one region than another; the likelihood that risk aversion, poor information about opportunities outside of Bangkok, concentration of key government regulatory and planning offices in Bangkok, and the lifestyle preferences of management elites all work towards an overestimation of the economic efficiency of Bangkok by private investors; and the inability to account for the cumulative advantages accruing to Bangkok through biases in public policy. When taken together, these problems cast serious doubt on the capacity of market forces to signal the true level of efficiency of a given city or to initiate countervailing trends towards a more dispersed pattern of development.

10 Krongkaew concludes that public expenditures on regional cities are motivated more by the immediate need to cope with problems than by longer-term strategies and that the government 'tended to invest only as the need became obvious' (1991, 38).

11 There is also a 'hidden' economy of rural regions – household crop and food processing, individual enterprises, cottage industries, petty commodity production, small-scale trade – which remains outside regional planning schemes. Perhaps one-quarter or more of the rural economy is not captured in most GNP accounts or industrial sector data. Studies show that 97 per cent of all enterprises employing fewer than fifty people are individual or family run and are crucial in the expansion of rural employment ('State of Small Scale Industry in Thailand,' *Rudoc News*, January-March 1989, no. 4, p. 1).

12 Each region would consist of networks of towns with uncertain hierarchical relations and development functions related equally to hinterland structures and external relations. Rural transportation routes from village to town and between towns would become development corridors, and these would in many instances be as important as towns and interurban linkages. Many firms in bulk-losing processing and agro-industry would locate near the fields or along these corridors, including waterways, rather than in cities or towns. As they do now, small shops would dot the roadside, but in increasing densities as interaction along these corridors deepens.

13 Seoul, for example, is essentially positioned on the wrong side of Korea vis-à-vis international trade, and much of the credit for the 'countermagnet' development along the southeast coast must be attributed to the awkward location of the capital city.

4
Emerging Spatial Patterns in ASEAN Mega-Urban Regions: Alternative Strategies
Ira M. Robinson

The problems being faced by the mega-cities of Asia, including ASEAN, are legion and generally well known. The literature on the subject is increasing rapidly (Fuchs, Jones, and Pernia 1987; Pernia 1992; and United Nations, Economic and Social Commission for Asia and the Pacific 1993b). Suffice it to say, most of these cities face serious problems of housing, traffic, infrastructure provision, crime, health, poverty, and environmental degradation. So serious and dramatic are these problems that they have become lead stories in such international magazines as *Time* ('Growing, Growing,' 14 September 1992; 'Megacities,' 11 January 1993).

Decentralization or dispersal of people and/or economic activities from the mega-cities has been seen by most researchers, planners, and public officials as one of the most effective ways of relieving or reducing the extreme negative effects of these problems. This objective has had two variants: first, *decentralization* of people and/or economic activities from the urban cores into the peripheral areas and along major transportation corridors radiating from the urban cores *within* the metropolitan region; and second, *dispersal* of people and activities into secondary or provincial cities or other growth centres located *outside* the boundaries of the mega-cities and their metropolitan areas. The first of these is the focus of this chapter.

In most Asian mega-cities, decentralization within their metropolitan regions has taken place in recent decades on a fairly large scale. One measure of this has been the widespread growth of 'metropolitan areas' since the Second World War and the recent emergence of 'extended metropolitan regions' or 'mega-urban regions.' As discussed later, most of this decentralization has occurred mainly as a result of natural market forces rather than government policy.

The underlying theme of this chapter is that decentralization of mega-cities is not sufficient. What is needed, as government policy, is spatial reorganization: the deliberate promotion of a decentralized, polycentred or multinucleated spatial form within metropolitan areas and mega-urban regions. At the same time, governments must continue to try to disperse population and industry into outlying regional, provincial, and secondary cities. While most Asian governments do have spatial planning strategies 'on the books' that aim to achieve a multinucleated spatial pattern within their metropolitan regions, very few have been implemented. Much decentralization has occurred but little polycentricity. As a consequence, the mega-cities and their regions are facing new problems that may be as serious (and perhaps intractable) as those that decentralization was trying to remedy. This chapter discusses these problems and the major reasons for them, using Bangkok as an illustrative case study, and concludes with recommendations for overcoming these deficiencies in the future.

Before turning to these matters, it is valuable to discuss two groups of key terms and concepts used here. The first deals with various types of spatial units used to define urban phenomena. The second refers to the processes of growth in metropolitan regions, which are usually elements of spatial planning strategies

Terms and Concepts

Spatial Units

Urban Place or Urban Area
The delineation of areas as 'urban' (as opposed to 'rural') is often related to administrative, political, historical, or cultural considerations as well as to demographic criteria, and it varies from country to country. In the various national censuses, worldwide, the definition of urban includes one or more of the following criteria: type of local government; number of inhabitants; proportion of population engaged in non-agricultural activities; and classification of localities of a certain size as urban, irrespective of administrative boundaries. Even for census purposes, then, the definition of urban involves a multidimensional approach.

In view of this variability, any comparisons between countries are hard to make. The problem is further compounded by the difficulty of keeping urban definitions constant over time. This is especially so in the case of rapidly growing urban areas, where there is a tendency for urban activity to flow outside of urban administrative boundaries.

City
The term 'city' is essentially a political designation, referring to an urban place governed by some kind of administrative or governmental body, and it has definable boundaries. Related terms are 'core city' or 'central city,' which are generally used when discussing or analyzing the growth of metropolitan areas and their component parts.

The term has no size connotation as such, although normally it is larger than a town or village. (Often this reflects the municipal incorporation laws of the specific country.) 'Supercity' or more commonly, 'mega-city,' are terms generally used to refer to the world's largest cities, but there is no agreement on size. To some, mega-cities are cities with at least one million people (Hoyt and Pickard 1969; Jacobson and Prakesh 1974). Others use a criterion of 5 million or more (Hauser and Gardner 1982). To the United Nations, in its recent publications, mega-cities mean urban agglomerations with 8 million people and over (United Nations, Department of International Economic and Social Affairs 1991). Brennan and Richardson (1989) use the same size criterion. In marked contrast to the previous definitions, the well-known Mega-cities Project defines mega-cities as those with 10 million persons or more.

The mega-city is typically not a 'corporate' city, with legal status and political boundaries. Indeed, it usually contains within its boundaries numerous legally distinct and independent units, each with its own administrative boundaries but with no overall administrative, governmental authority responsible for the entire geographic area. There may, however, be an overall planning body.

Another relevant term in which the word city is used is 'secondary city,' or 'intermediate city,' which is below the metropolis and the mega-city in the urban hierarchy although it has no precise cut-off point for size.

Another relevant and frequently used term when describing, analyzing, or proposing desirable spatial patterns is 'satellite' city or town. A satellite is a smaller city, spatially separate from but functionally dependent on a metropolis.

Since cities are demarcated by purely political boundaries, they are generally considered arbitrary spatial units from a demographic-economic-ecological point of view, especially in rapidly growing urban areas, where there is a tendency for urban activity to overspill corporate boundaries while still remaining functionally part of the original urban area. This can lead to considerable underbounding of the true urban area and therefore to underestimating the number of actual urban residents. To deal with this situation, various countries have adopted new spatial units to reflect these ever larger cities and city-regions. Most of them are not legal entities, but a few are accepted as official statistical units in the census. They are often considered appropriate planning units. Those most commonly used are described below.

Urbanized Area

As cities have spread spatially, the boundary between urban and rural has become increasingly blurred, especially where modern transportation has fostered urban sprawl. The 'urbanized area' could also be defined as the 'built-up area,' where buildings, roads, and other essentially urban land uses predominate and have spread beyond the political boundaries of cities and towns. The census of India uses a spatial unit called a 'standard urbanized area,' which comes close to this concept.

Urban Agglomeration

'Urban agglomeration' is a related term used by the United Nations to identify, estimate, and project the urban population worldwide. The term refers to the population contained within the contours of a contiguous territory inhabited at urban levels without regard to administrative boundaries. It includes the population in a city or town plus suburban fringe lying outside of but adjacent to the boundaries of the core city.

Metropolis, Metropolitan Area, Metropolitan Region

The term 'metropolis' is a general concept and suggests the chief city, though not necessarily the capital, of a country, state, or region. It is often loosely used to refer to any large city. Metropolis is essentially a category, concept, or construct devised by social scientists to order their data, and it is given different contents by different investigators.

The term 'metropolitan area,' or 'metropolitan region,' tends to have a somewhat more precise meaning, conceptually and statistically, and as such is usually so recognized in national censuses. It is generally regarded as comprising a central or core city (that is, the corporate city) and peri-urban/fringe/peripheral jurisdictions plus all surrounding territory closely related to if not actually integrated with the central or core city. The national censuses for the United States and Canada define such areas in terms of total population size and size of the central city, and refer to them as 'statistical metropolitan areas.'

The terms 'metropolis' and 'metropolitan area' have actually been used to describe cities in two distinct senses. First, the older, traditional sense views the metropolis as a major centre of urban activities, a gathering place of people, processes, and ideas, and a centre of political influence on surrounding areas. In the second, newer sense, the metropolitan area has come to mean, as implied above, the city with its suburbs.

These two terms 'metropolis' and 'metropolitan area' imply two ways of interpreting metropolitan problems and in turn two groups of such problems. One group relates to the first, more traditional view of a metropolitan city or centre and includes those problems characteristic of large urban centres in the developing world. The second group relates to the term 'metropolitan area' and includes problems arising from the incongruity between the socio-economic and ecological limits of the metropolitan urbanized area on the one hand and its administrative boundaries on the other. With the urbanized metropolitan area divided among several jurisdictions, the 'traditional' metropolitan problems typically become compounded by a lack of coordinated effort to deal with them. Merging administrative areas and/or creating a new all-purpose, administrative level for the entire metropolitan area are typical solutions proposed.

There are a few examples in Asia – such as Calcutta – of metropolitan authorities having been established to solve this second type of metropolitan problem, but these, like most similar examples in the developed world, are not all-purpose, all-encompassing 'metropolitan governments' with strong budgetary and implementation powers. As such they prove to be ineffective. Metropolitan Toronto, in Canada, is one of the few examples in the world of such an all-embracing metropolitan government.

Delimiting a metropolitan area is a complicated task, in which the difficulties faced in defining boundaries of any geographic or socio-economic unit are compounded by the special complexities, noted above, of metropolitan areas themselves. Most efforts at delimiting metropolitan areas use administrative units as the building blocks.[1]

Megalopolis, Conurbation, Superconurbation, Extended Metropolitan Region, Mega-Urban Region

All of these terms, with some slight variations, mean essentially the same thing. During the early 1960s, researchers and analysts in the developed world were beginning to detect a new phenomenon in the spatial pattern of urbanization: the spatial merging of two or more existing metropolitan areas (or metropolises) located fairly close to one another, typically along major transportation corridors, and their coalescence into a highly urbanized and integrated region with many transportation links between centres and great diffusion of urban and semi-urban activities.

French geographer Jean Gottmann (1961) was perhaps the first person to term this spatial pattern a 'megalopolis,' and identified the Atlantic seaboard of the United States, stretching from Washington, DC, north to Boston, Massachusetts, as the first great megalopolis. Writing in 1964, Hoyt also used the same term, and identified seven such 'great megalopolises,' each with at least 10 million persons, none of them in the developing world.

Almost fifteen years later, Gottmann (1976), was critical of those who would set a figure of 10 million inhabitants as the minimum size of a megalopolis, which is much below the figure of 25 million that he had long advocated and still preferred. He noted that there were at that time six megalopolises over 25 million. Only two of these were in Asia, one in a developing country (Shanghai, China). To these six, he felt that three more cases might soon be added, only one of which was in the developing Third World: the Rio de Janeiro-São Paulo complex in Brazil.

In view of current and expected future population trends (see, for example, United Nations, Economic and Social Commission for Asia and the Pacific 1993a), it is not unreasonable to assume that both Hoyt and Gottmann, if they were writing today on the same subject, would undoubtedly designate a number of additional 'megalopolises' in Asia, including the five ASEAN mega-urban regions that are the focus of this volume.

'Conurbation' means essentially the same thing as megalopolis and is commonly used in Britain to describe its urban growth pattern. It was originally conceived by the biologist-planner Patrick Geddes in the nineteenth century and subsequently used in several of Britain's colonies, including India. Later, it was made popular by Patrick Abercrombie in his plan for the Greater London Conurbation.

The term 'superconurbation' is used simply to describe a giant conurbation or megalopolis with a population of at least 12 million (Brunn and Williams 1983, 8). Two other synonyms used for essentially the same concept are 'supermetropolitan region' (p. 8) and 'interlocking metropolitan region.' The latter is currently used by the Chinese to describe their huge regions such as Nanjing-Shanghai-Hangzhou, Beijing-Tianjin-Tangshan, and Hong Kong-Guangzhou-Macao, whose current populations are 69 million, 25 million, and 25 million respectively (Ginsburg, Koppel, and McGee 1991, 89-111).

The ultimate expression of the merging of large agglomerations will occur when the conurbations/megalopolises join together to form a 'world ecumenopolis,' as described by Doxiadis (Brunn and Williams 1983, ch. 12).

The term 'extended metropolitan region' (EMR) was first used by Terry McGee and his colleagues at a conference in 1988 devoted to the subject and later in a book published with papers from the conference (Ginsburg, Koppel, and McGee 1991). It appears in a number of recent papers, published and unpublished, by McGee and some of his PhD students (e.g., MacLeod and McGee 1992; McGee and Greenberg 1992). The introductory chapters to the EMR book also referred to 'mega-urban regions,' and for the purposes of the conference from which the chapters in this current book were drawn this was the preferred term. Mega-urban regions are described at length in the preface.

Processes of Growth

Decentralization[2]

For the purposes of this chapter, 'decentralization' is defined as growth of the population and/or economic activities occurring on the periphery and fringe areas of the central city or along transportation corridors emanating from the urban core, within a metropolitan area or metropolitan region. Decentralization can result from the expansion of existing industry or population on the periphery of the central city or from the actual movement of new industry and/or people from the central city or elsewhere to the fringe or along a transportation corridor. As a general concept, decentralization is often equated with suburbanization. It can occur in two ways: as low-density, scattered leapfrogging or sprawling residential and/or non-residential developments throughout the periphery and fringe and along the transportation corridors; or as concentrations of population and/or industry in medium- to high-density nucleations in the form of centres or subcentres, including satellites or new towns. The former process of decentralization typically occurs on an unplanned, haphazard, uncontrolled basis, resulting mainly from natural market forces. The latter usually results from deliberate governmental planning and/or control.

Dispersal or Deconcentration

Again for the purposes of this chapter, these terms are defined as the growth of urban population and employment that takes place in secondary cities or growth centres located a good distance beyond the boundaries of the city and metropolitan area. Dispersal, or deconcentration, tend to result from the expansion of existing local firms or opening of new ones in small cities, villages, or towns in the outer regions. Alternatively, the process occurs when firms or people in the central city move outside the metropolitan area to a regional or provincial city, or when an industrial plant locates at or near a natural resource outside urban-metropolitan areas.[3]

A 'countermagnet' is a large growth centre located some distance from the metropolitan area. It is designed to create a counter-weight to the primate city or metropolis. Some Asian governments have enacted policies to control the growth of their largest cities and metropolitan areas in an effort to disperse growth to outlying towns, cities, and regions of their states (see, for example, Rondinelli 1987, 65-6).

Nucleation, Multinucleation, Reconcentration

These terms describe the process of spatial development organized around one or more often high-density clusters or nodes of employment and population. At the intra-regional or metropolitan regional scale, this creates a polynucleated spatial structure, or what Romanos (1978) has called 'decentralized concentration' and is the opposite of a sprawling, spreading, scattered pattern. Such a process can also be viewed at the national, interregional scale and involves the movement of people and/or firms from a metropolitan area, or from a small village or rural area in a non-metropolitan region, to a regional city, national city, secondary city, or provincial city, creating a countermagnet on a national scale. Dispersal, like decentralization, can occur as a result of natural market forces or planned government intervention in the form of a national dispersal policy.

Spatial Pattern, Structure, Form, Model
These terms describe an existing or proposed spatial distribution or redistribution, location, and density of population and/or economic activities and settlements in a given geographic area. The spatial pattern can be viewed inter-regionally (as in the spatial distribution of dispersed population, economic activities, or settlements within a national territory), or intra-regionally (within a metropolitan area or metropolitan region). For a metropolitan region, three basic spatial models can be identified:

(1) A monocentric, or concentric, city form was the traditional and historically prevalent pattern in the metropolitan areas of the developed and developing worlds until the Second World War. In this model, the large majority of the metropolitan area's population and employment is centralized in the urban core or central business district of the metropolis.

(2) The second model is a spread-out and sprawling pattern of homes, industrial plants, office complexes, golf courses, and retail trade shops in scattered and non-contiguous locations throughout the periphery and fringe of the metropolitan area or metropolitan region and along major highways and railroad lines radiating from the central cores. The dominant trend in the post-Second World War years in both developed and developing countries, this spatial pattern results from unplanned and uncontrolled decentralization of the population and/or industry. Most extended metropolitan regions or mega-urban regions follow this pattern.

(3) A polycentric or multinucleated spatial form also results from decentralization of population and/or industry, but comprises several interdependent, diversified, and relatively self-contained centres, cities, and towns within a metropolitan area or region. Its underlying principle is the close integration of residences and places of work in centres and subcentres, each developed around and near a transportation node and containing a mixture of retail, commercial, light manufacturing, and relatively dense residential areas. This pattern usually results from conscious governmental planning and/or control and is not a common occurrence in either developing or developed countries.

Figure 4.1 depicts these three spatial models within metropolitan regions and the inter-regional dispersal model referred to earlier.

Advantages and Disadvantages of the Spatial Models
Until the end of the Second World War, most metropolitan areas in both developed and developing countries resembled the monocentric spatial

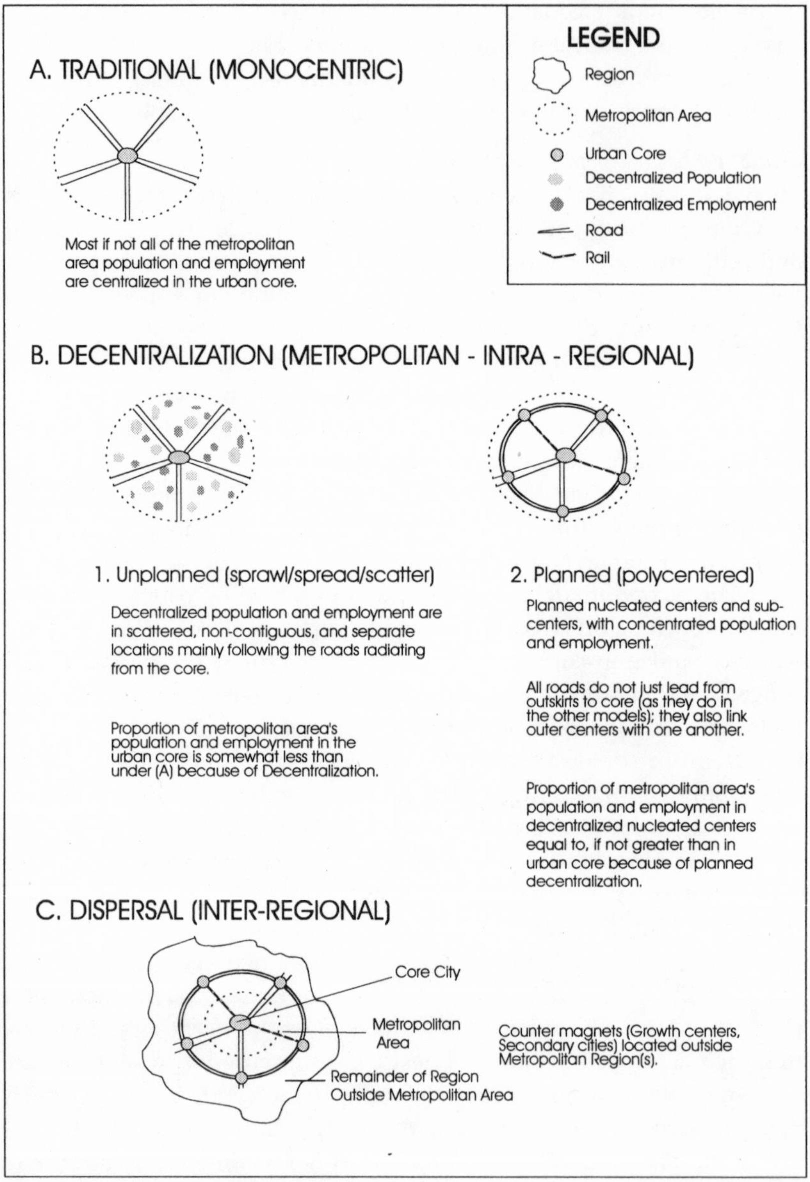

A. TRADITIONAL (MONOCENTRIC)

Most if not all of the metropolitan area population and employment are centralized in the urban core.

LEGEND

- Region
- Metropolitan Area
- ○ Urban Core
- Decentralized Population
- Decentralized Employment
- — Road
- ⌒ Rail

B. DECENTRALIZATION (METROPOLITAN - INTRA - REGIONAL)

1. Unplanned (sprawl/spread/scatter)

Decentralized population and employment are in scattered, non-contiguous, and separate locations mainly following the roads radiating from the core.

Proportion of metropolitan area's population and employment in the urban core is somewhat less than under (A) because of Decentralization.

2. Planned (polycentered)

Planned nucleated centers and sub-centers, with concentrated population and employment.

All roads do not just lead from outskirts to core (as they do in the other models); they also link outer centers with one another.

Proportion of metropolitan area's population and employment in decentralized nucleated centers equal to, if not greater than in urban core because of planned decentralization.

C. DISPERSAL (INTER-REGIONAL)

Core City

Metropolitan Area

Remainder of Region Outside Metropolitan Area

Counter magnets (Growth centers, Secondary cities) located outside Metropolitan Region(s).

Figure 4.1 **Alternative spatial models**

form, with its characteristic high-density single centre – the core city – in which most of the metropolitan area's population and employment were centralized. Right after the war, and increasingly since, an enormous amount of decentralization has occurred, breaking down the monocentric pattern. Both people and industries have settled in areas outside the core city, many relocating from the central city. Most of this decentralization has taken place in the form of the second spatial model, the spread-out, sprawling, scattered form. The third model has emerged only to a limited extent.

Most researchers generally agree that the major disadvantage of the monocentric spatial pattern is its high congestion costs at the centre (see, for example, Richardson 1988; Gordon, Richardson, and Wong 1986; Gordon, Kumar, and Richardson 1989; Erickson 1986). There is also general agreement about the disadvantages of the sprawling spatial model and the advantages of the polycentric form. However, there appears to be some disagreement over what constitutes the latter model. A number of researchers claim that in the post-Second World War years the spatial pattern of many large cities has been transformed from a monocentric to a polycentric structure (see, for example, Richardson 1988, 1989a, 1990; Frisbie and Kasarda 1988), including some in the Third World (see, for example, Dowall and Treffeisen 1991; Richardson 1989a, 1989b). Other researchers, the present one included, strongly disagree with this contention – Bourne (1989, 1991) on the basis of his empirical analysis of trends in the Canadian urban system, and I on the basis of current research. It appears that some researchers have erroneously equated decentralization with polycentricity.

This disagreement is epitomized in the analogy used by Frisbie and Kasarda (1988, 645) in which metropolitan areas that conform to the monocentric model are portrayed as 'fried eggs,' with single, uniform cores surrounded by uniform suburban rings, and metropolitan areas with a polycentric pattern as 'scrambled eggs,' with little structure or internal organization. I would change the analogies slightly. Although I agree with the analogy of the monocentric area as 'fried eggs,' I would portray the sprawling, leapfrogging pattern as 'scrambled eggs' and the polycentric spatial pattern as a 'plateful of poached eggs,' where the various poached eggs represent nucleations and are located – that is, deliberately planned – in key locations within the metropolitan region, represented by the whole plate.

As noted above, most researchers and planners agree that the sprawling pattern has several disadvantages in comparison with the polycentric form. It

- overutilizes existing infrastructure heavily concentrated in city cores and extends social services provision and urban infrastructure (water, sewers, and roads) into the periphery, thereby increasing social service and infrastructure costs
- requires long commutes to work, living, and recreational areas, discourages

provision of public transit by increasing reliance on the automobile, and thus generates high consumption of non-renewable petroleum energy and high levels of airborne pollutants
- imposes personal costs and inconveniences on certain groups in the population by requiring them to purchase second cars or make inconvenient adjustments in scheduling domestic responsibilities and isolates household members – often women and children – without access to a car
- uses urban land and services inefficiently
- has a negative impact on local environmental and ecological systems, including, among other effects, causing loss of agricultural and other non-urban lands
- makes it very difficult to develop a system of local government and thus a sense of community among the residents of the metropolitan region because of the scattered low-density pattern of population distribution.

By contrast, the polycentric or multinucleated pattern, according to many planners and researchers (Gordon, Kumar, and Richardson 1989; Haines 1986; Owens 1986; Richardson 1989a, 1990; Robinson 1985; Romanos 1978; and Van Til 1979), brings many specific advantages:
- Decentralization of jobs to other subcentres within a polynucleated metropolitan spatial structure can relieve congestion costs at the centre without sacrificing the benefits of metropolitan-wide agglomeration economies.
- A polynucleated cluster of cities creates large markets and offers a flexible structure for expansion.
- It is considered the most energy efficient of the various spatial patterns because the reduced spatial separation between urban functions – that is, the clustering of residences, industries, office complexes, and recreation facilities within the same geographic area – makes multipurpose trips feasible, thereby reducing commuting and generally encouraging the development of public transit and the resulting transport and energy savings.
- It preserves natural resources, the environment, and agricultural lands by concentrating development in a few selected locations.
- By making use of existing public infrastructure and minimizing the need for new utilities and services, it lowers infrastructure costs.
- Each of the relatively compact centres can develop its own form of local government, thus making it possible to achieve a sense of community among the residences.

Aware of the disadvantages of the spread-out model and, by contrast, the distinct advantages of the polynucleated structure, many Asian megacities, including those in ASEAN, have promoted polynucleated metropolitan-regional spatial pattern as one of the objectives in their master plans. Unfortunately, as we shall see in the next section, these plans have generally been unsuccessful.

Past and Present Spatial Planning Strategies and the Relationship to Current Trends: The Case of Bangkok

As noted by Richardson (1989b), all very large cities, whether in developed or developing countries, sooner or later have to face the problem of spatial reorganization and, more specifically, of the need to decentralize both population and economic activities into a polycentric metropolitan or metropolitan regional urban form to replace their existing monocentric or concentric pattern.[4] A monocentric or concentric city with a single downtown area, where most of the jobs are located, eventually breaks down as a viable and efficient production unit under the burden of rising congestion costs.

This problem is even more severe in the mega-cities of the developing countries for two reasons. First, the degree and extent of their primacy (in terms of population, employment, and other indicators) is greater than that of their counterparts in developed countries. Second, the proportion of central city land devoted to roads is much smaller than in developed countries – in Bangkok, for example, it is only 8 per cent compared to an average of 20 to 30 per cent in developed countries – and at the same time there is chronic underinvestment in the transportation system.

In recognition of the advantages of polycentricity,[5] most Asian mega-cities have adopted spatial planning strategies aimed at developing a decentralized polycentric form in their metropolitan regions. These are usually incorporated in their master plans. Unfortunately, as described by Richardson and others, they have not been implemented, for several reasons. The form and types of public intervention have often impeded an efficient process of polycentred development, as planners have ignored pricing information conveyed by the private land and estate markets. Population projections in the master plans were far off the mark, and in general the plans were too rigid and inflexible to meet changing conditions. Finally, there has sometimes been too much reliance on the private sector, or else the political will to act has not been sufficient to overcome the opposition of special interests.

Based on a review of the experiences of a number of Asian mega-cities (Calcutta, Delhi, Bombay, Madras, Dhaka, Seoul, Manila, Jakarta, and Bangkok), this writer must reluctantly come to the same conclusion.[6] Since space here does not permit a review of all the mega-cities surveyed, this conclusion will be illustrated by recounting the experience of one ASEAN mega-city, Bangkok.

Bangkok's Regional Spatial Structure

Before proceeding to a discussion of Bangkok's experience with its spatial planning strategy, it will be helpful to describe briefly this mega-city's regional governmental/administrative spatial structure, which consists of four levels (see Map 4.1).

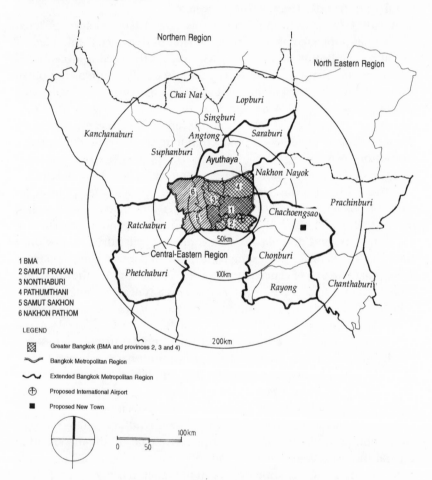

Map 4.1 **Bangkok's regional/governmental administrative spatial structure**

(1) The Bangkok Metropolitan Administration (BMA), an area of 1,565.2 km² (604 sq. mi.) legally and administratively defined as a single municipality and created in 1972 from the amalgamation of the former *changwats* of Phra Nakhan ('old Bangkok') and Thonburi. Within this area, known also as the Bangkok metropolis, the distance from the Bangkok city centre is approximately 30 km and the 1990 population was almost 6 million.

Although the initials BMA are often erroneously thought to mean Bangkok Metropolitan Area, the area of jurisdiction of the Bangkok Metropolitan Administration is less than the actual metropolitan area. While the first general plan for Bangkok was produced in 1960, it was not until July 1992 that the plan for this area was finally given formal approval.

(2) The Greater Bangkok Area (GBA) covers an area of 4,717 km^2 (1,821 sq. mi.) and contains the BMA and the three adjoining *changwats* of Nonthaburi, Pathum Thani, and Samut Prakan. It is not a legally or administratively defined area and is comparable to the metropolitan area of Bangkok. Around 7.25 million people, or 84 per cent of the total Bangkok Metropolitan Region (BMR) population, live in this area, and it is generally viewed as the urban portion of the BMR. As such, many of the problems associated with rapid development within the BMR have occurred in the GBA and will continue to do so in the immediate future, but there is no 'official' approved plan for this area.

(3) The Bangkok Metropolitan Region (BMR), covering an area of 7,758 km^2 (2,995 sq. mi.), is located in south-central Thailand adjacent to the Gulf of Thailand. It includes the BMA and the five contiguous *changwats* (Samut Sakhon, Nakhon Pathom, Nonthaburi, Pathum Thani, and Samut Prakan); or looking at it differently, it comprises the GBA, plus Samut Sakhon and Nakhon Pathom. Within the BMR, the distance from the Bangkok city centre is approximately 50 km. The total population in the region in 1990 was 8.6 million. This area has no legal or administrative authority responsible for its planning, management, or development.

(4) The Extended Bangkok Metropolitan Region (EBMR) is variously defined by different researchers and planners. The Thailand Development and Research Institute (TDRI) defines it as extending beyond the BMR to the north, to Ayuthaya and Saraburi; to the east, to Chonburi, Cha-choengsao, and Rayong; and to the west, to Ratchaburi and Phetchaburi. A somewhat larger region defined in a recent study for the National Economic and Social Development Board (NESDB) includes a population of over 15 million persons in an area of over 59,000 km^2 (or 23,000 sq. mi.). The Seventh Plan defines this extended region slightly differently. Within the EBMR, the radius from the city centre is approximately 100 to 150 km. The NESDB has recommended establishing a development committee, at the highest levels of government, to supervise the overall planning, management, and development of this extended region.

Bangkok's Spatial Plans
Bangkok is considered the most primate city in the developing world. One writer has termed it the 'world's pre-eminent "primate city"' while another

has referred to it as the 'beau ideal of a primate city.'[7] Consequently, historically it has been extremely monocentric in spatial form. It is not surprising, therefore, that since the early 1960s planners, both those involved in the various national development plans and those directly responsible for planning Bangkok, have consistently advocated a decentralized polycentric spatial form for the Greater Bangkok Area. But, as we shall see, they achieved a lot of decentralization but little, if any, polycentricity.

The NESDB was established in 1959 and put in charge of the First National Economic and Social Development Plan for Thailand. In 1960, it employed a consulting firm to produce the first master plan for Bangkok. The consultant first used the Greater Bangkok Area (also referred to as the Greater Bangkok Metropolitan Area), comprising more than 3,000 km^2, as a reference area.[8] This is probably why the plan was dubbed the Greater Bangkok Plan. It ended up, however, producing a thirty-year land-use plan for an area of 460 km^2 and a target population of only 4.5 million. Limiting the population to that number proved to be wishful thinking as the city never developed the way the plan intended. It was never officially adopted and had a negligible impact on the development forces at work, remaining mainly symbolic in value (Kammeier 1984, 29).

In 1962, the Department of Town and Country Planning (DTCP) was established within the Ministry of Interior and charged with, among other responsibilities, periodically updating and revising the Greater Bangkok Plan. The first revision of the plan, issued in 1971, adjusted the aforementioned target population upwards and recommended several other changes. At the same time, the City Planning Division of the then Bangkok Municipality prepared its own updated version of the Greater Bangkok Plan, proposing different land-use patterns and transportation networks. However, neither the alternative plan nor any of the subsequent revisions ever reached the status of a legally binding document until July 1992, when, finally, the Bangkok master plan was given official approval!

The next major step in Bangkok's spatial planning process was the drafting by the DTCP of the second revision, based on the target year 2000. This version, known as the Greater Bangkok Plan 2000, was also prepared in conjunction with the objectives of Thailand's Fourth National Development Plan (1977-81). That plan deviated markedly from its predecessors in that it emphasized the desirability of a polycentric pattern of development, in contrast to all previous plans, which were based on a monocentric form and had assumed continuing centralization. Unfortunately, the Greater Bangkok Plan 2000 shared the fate of its predecessors; at best it was regarded as a guideline and had a negligible impact on private-sector investments.

The Fourth National Development Plan outlined several measures for decelerating and controlling the spatial pattern of Bangkok's growth. By this time, the old *changwats* of Phra Nakhan and Thonburi had amalgamated to form the BMA. Two of the measures proposed were:

(1) An urban development plan for various communities in the suburbs and on the outskirts of Bangkok would be formulated in accordance with the polycentric concept. Each centre in this concept would maintain its self-sufficient socio-economic activities, including infrastructural services and other public facilities.

(2) An international deep seaport would be constructed elsewhere to help alleviate the congestion of Bangkok. In addition, three development corridors emanating from Bangkok would be developed towards the outskirts of the Greater Bangkok Region: one to the north, and two to the southeast.

In a discussion of the philosophy and approach of the Fourth Plan, Dr. Phisit Pakkasem (1987), secretary-general of the NESDB, noted that Bangkok planners had been attracted to the concept of polycentred development as an alternative to the uncontrolled sprawl pattern. He then claimed that almost all government programs and policy statements concerned with Bangkok's future generally support this planning strategy for the capital city. As evidence of this, he pointed to three examples of satellites then being built on the periphery of the Greater Bangkok Area: (1) Nava Nakorn, being constructed along the northern corridor about 50 km north of Bangkok with public- and private-sector participation and planned to accommodate around 100,000 people; (2) the planned new town of Bang Phli to be built by the National Housing Authority along the southeastern corridor, about 40 km from Bangkok; and (3) the Eastern Seaboard subregion, comprising the three provinces of Chonburi, Chachoengsao, and Rayong.

Phisit was perhaps premature in his optimistic outlook. Nava Nakorn since its inception has not attracted any public-sector support but has essentially developed as a large private industrial estate, not a 'new town' in the true meaning of that term. As of 1990, some 54,000 workers were employed in the industrial estate, but only 30,000 people lived there. Likewise, the new town of Bang Phli by the same date was a long way from reaching its population target. Finally, as Phisit himself acknowledged, the development activities and projects of the Eastern Seaboard were not well integrated into the overall pattern of development, and no institutional mechanism has been established to coordinate the agencies whose investment decisions affect this subregion. Subsequent national plans have continued to emphasize development of the region.

Emphasizing that 'the major development issue is how to slow down Bangkok's population growth and lessen its economic dominance,' the

Fifth Plan (1982-6) was critical of past policy and planning efforts (National Economic and Social Development Board 1982). To overcome these deficiencies, it outlined a comprehensive strategy for Bangkok's development in the form of a 'Structural Plan for the Development of the Bangkok Metropolis and Vicinity Towns.' The basic aim was to decentralize economic activity and thereby diffuse growth from the capital city to the five surrounding towns of Samut Prakan, Pathum Thani, Nonthaburi, Nakhon Pathom, and Samut Sakhon, located in the five adjoining *changwats* of the same names.

The plan proposed that these outlying areas be developed as planned communities with a high degree of self-sufficiency, thereby ensuring that residents would not need to commute to Bangkok for employment or lower-level services but only periodically for special cultural or entertainment facilities. It also intended that the agricultural land in and around the five towns would be preserved, and in order to prevent the urbanized parts of Bangkok from spreading farther, a green belt would be designated around the current boundary of the city (the Bangkok Metropolitan Administration). Thus, the Fifth Plan, through the 'Structural Plan,' continued to advocate multinucleated or polycentric metropolitan regional development for Bangkok.

Another key spatial component of the Fifth Plan was the decision to develop the Eastern Seaboard subregion into a major location for basic industries. In the words of the plan, 'the Eastern Seaboard sub-region will serve as a potent employment generator and accords well with the policy to *decentralize Bangkok and diffuse growth to the regions in a systematic manner* ... [and] effectively absorb the flow of migrant labor which would otherwise have been directed toward Bangkok' [emphasis added].

According to the summary of the Sixth Plan (1987-91), controlling the growth of the Bangkok metropolis remained an important national goal (National Economic and Social Development Board 1987). Unfortunately, implementation of this strategy, as in the past, would rely mainly on physical planning methods, primarily land-use controls, and zoning regulations, which have proved in other countries in similar circumstances not to be as effective as non-spatial, non-physical policies. Moreover, despite the very clear statement of the objective to control Bangkok's growth, a considerable amount of investment in large-scale infrastructure projects was still being planned for the capital city. Needless to say, this counteracted the efforts of the government's explicit decentralization policy. Judging from the Sixth Plan, it would seem that the government's Eastern Seaboard strategy would finally be getting off the ground after a decade of discussions about it. The government now seemed to be determined to go ahead with the several elements of its development.

In preparation for the Seventh Plan, the NESDB commissioned several studies from the TDRI and other consultants on urban policy, and later published them together (1991c). An important finding in the TDRI research was that the effects of Bangkok's urbanization were no longer limited to the five outlying provinces. Growth of the Bangkok Metropolitan Region (BMR) is spreading beyond these nearby areas into the EBMR, which is the equivalent of what we are calling, in this volume, a mega-urban region. It is of interest to note that when the Seventh Plan was finally published, the EBMR did not extend as far east as Ratchaburi and Phetchaburi or as far north as Lopburi (see Chapter 16). A recent consultant study for NESDB went even slightly further than the TDRI and included all the provinces in the Western and Eastern Regions and portions of the Upper Central Region in the EBMR, terming this area the Chao Phraya multipolis (Lemon Group, Industrial Consultants 1993).

Map 4.2 shows the extent to which Bangkok's built-up area has extended beyond the BMR into the surrounding provinces to the west, the north, and especially the east. National Statistical Office and NESDB projections show that population and economic growth in the EBMR will increase rapidly throughout the period of the Seventh Plan. The population of the EBMR is expected to grow from 12 million in 1990 to 17 million in the year 2010 and increase its share of the total population during this period from 21.5 to 24.3 per cent (National Economic and Social Development Board 1991c). The region defined by the Lemon Group consultants as the Chao Phraya multipolis had a 1990 population of a little over 15 million and is projected to reach 21.2 million by 2010 (Lemon Group, Industrial Consultants 1993, Interim Report, Sector study 2, Table 58).

Unplanned Decentralization and Its Consequences
During the last two decades, extensive decentralization has occurred in the Bangkok area, seemingly independently of the various plans advocating a decentralized, polycentric pattern. Population growth has taken place in the outer parts of the BMR, that is, in the five provinces surrounding the BMA. Indeed, the subregion beyond the BMR boundaries that together with the BMR has been termed the Extended Bangkok Metropolitan Region has been experiencing rapid growth as well (see Table 4.1). Likewise, manufacturing establishments have been decentralizing to the five provinces surrounding Bangkok (although not at the same rate as population) with their relative share of establishments in the BMR rising while that of Bangkok proper has been declining (Lee Kyu Sik 1988, 12-14).

The physical decentralization of Bangkok was remarkable during the last several decades. The Bangkok urban area expanded from roughly 470

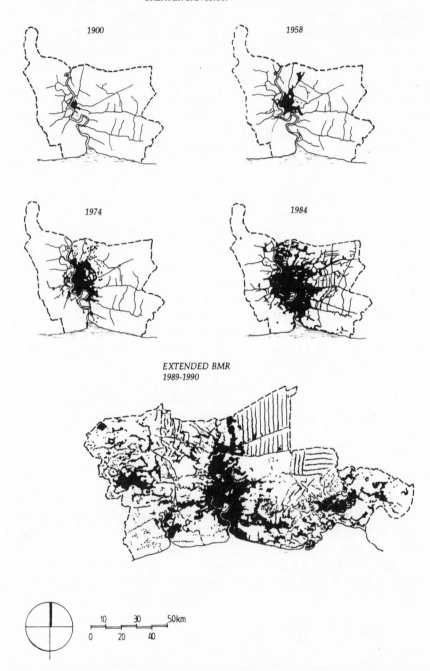

Map 4.2 **Growth of a built-up area: Greater Bangkok, 1900-90**

Table 4.1

Population of the Bangkok regional spatial structure, 1970-2010

	1970	1980	1990	Annual growth rate (%), 1970-90	2010[i]
City[a]	3.185[h]	4.815	5.882	3.12	7.827
Metropolitan ring[b]	.619	.886	1.345	3.96	2.393
Metropolitan area[c]	3.804	5.701	7.227	3.26	10.220
Outer fringe[d]	.884	1.133	1.363	2.19	2.164
Metropolitan region[e]	4.688	6.834	8.590	3.07	12.384
Extended region[f]	2.774	3.503	4.199	2.09	5.909
Mega-urban region[g]	7.462	10.417	12.789	2.73	18.293

Notes:

a Bangkok Metropolitan Administration

b Nonthaburi and Samut Prakan *changwats*

c Greater Bangkok (a) + (b)

d Pathum Thani, Samut Sakhon, and Nakhon Pathom *changwats*.

e Bangkok Metropolitan Region (c) + (d)

f As defined by Thailand Development and Research Institute for the Seventh Plan. Includes the *changwats* of Phetchaburi and Ratchaburi to the west, Ayuthaya and Saraburi to the north, and Chachoengsao, Chonburi, and Rayong to the east

g (e) + (f)

h Figures are in millions

i Projected

Sources: 1970 data: Thailand, National Statistical Office (1971); 1980 data: Thailand, National Statistical Office (1980); 1990 data and 2010 projections: Lemon Group, Industrial Consultants (1993)

km^2 in 1974 to an estimated 1,100 km^2 in 1988 (Setchell 1991, 5). (Map 4.2 shows the growth of Bangkok's built-up area over the years.) Further, if we look at where urban land use has been developed, spatially, we find that during the 1974-84 period, a little more than 45 per cent of land converted to urban uses was at a distance of 11 to 20 km from the city centre, while during the 1984-8 period approximately the same percentage of land converted to urban uses (45.4 per cent) was at a distance of greater than 30 km from the city centre (p. 5).

The bulk of the decentralization has been occurring in the form of 'ribbon development' along the three major transport corridors leading out of the urban core to the southwest, southeast, and north. In addition, it has involved conversion of paddy lands; encroachment on agricultural land; and leapfrogging types of development in the fringe areas, leaving large tracts of unused land in between. Without any public intervention to speak of in the form of either restrictions or incentives – other than opening up new areas through road construction – the conversion of rice fields into urban uses takes place whenever the private owner decides to subdivide land. Access to individual lots is typically provided by long and disjointed dirt roads built by the private developers along the boundaries of elongated agricultural lots. Subsequently, individual houses and all types of smaller and larger private housing estates emerge, mixed with commercial and industrial land uses.

Most of the privately built secondary and tertiary road network consists of narrow, winding, unconnected streets and cul-de-sacs. Secondary roads, which generally serve to link main arterials with local lanes (*soi*), are all but absent from many parts of Bangkok in both the urban core and the outer peripheries because responsibility for planning and building them has been relegated to the private sector. With no great incentive to do anything, private developers have largely failed to provide an adequate secondary road system. The result is a series of 'superblocks,' which in large areas are bounded by main roads and arterials with little or no internal road network to distribute traffic efficiently or provide access within the blocks. This leaves much of the land within the superblock unusable and tends to concentrate the traffic on the relatively few, already overloaded main thoroughfares.

The industrial and urban growth in the outer parts of the region and along the major transportation corridors has taken place without adequate provision of public transit and roads, and this has led to traffic congestion even in these suburban areas. The decentralized but not polycentric growth pattern aggravates congestion because it produces: (1) huge volumes of daily trips from home to work between the sprawling suburbs and the growing employment centres in the inner city, and vice versa, from the city centre to the factories in the suburbs; and (2) a fragmented configuration of the road network. Both these conditions are largely the result of the unplanned and uncontrolled conversion of fringe land into urban land uses.

In large part, this decentralized growth was more a result of market forces than of either explicit government spatial policies or the plans of the DTCP. Lower land prices on the periphery, construction and/or improvement of roads, and expressways opening up new areas for development all facilitated the trend. It is nonetheless a fact that the trend was being reinforced by policy, since many Board of Investment incentives to agro-processing and export-oriented industries were given, in this and earlier periods, to firms now located in the outlying areas or to new firms considering locating there, although these decisions do not appear to have been part of any approved plan.

In the absence of environmental infrastructure, effective land-use planning, and pollution controls in the outlying provinces of the BMR, the rapid, haphazard, and sprawling low-density developments not only result in high infrastructure costs but also bring about environmental deterioration and ecological degradation. Poor drainage and severe flooding are typical throughout Bangkok but especially in the outlying parts of the BMR. Conflicts over water supply are common because of high demand from the growing mixture of land uses. Most developers and industrialists attempt to fulfil their need by pumping underground water. The resulting increase in land subsidence and contamination of underground aquifers could have been predicted. Absence of adequate drainage and sewerage facilities and pollution controls has led to severe water and solid waste pollution. The NESDB has noted that land development in these outlying areas is proceeding at a pace and pattern that exceed the environment's natural carrying capacity and the supply of available resources (1991c).

In recognition of the problem, the government promulgated a new Groundwater Act in 1985, which mandated that well pumping be phased out in the BMR by 1998, but thus far there is no evidence that the regulation is being followed.

Perhaps no clearer indictment of what has been occurring in outlying areas of the BMR could have been made than the statement by NESDB in one of its reports for the Seventh Plan, which stated, 'It appears that it will be necessary to suspend some of these activities or to control resource allocation for both economic and environmental reasons' (p. 42). While the Board does not say so directly, it implies that the very growth that has given the BMR, and the nation, its healthy economy has had social and environmental consequences and costs which, if uncontrolled, may discourage and thus slow down growth in the not too distant future.

The Northern Corridor, an Example
The existing pattern of urban development in the BMR has largely followed a radial pattern based on major roads. These radials, which lead to the north, southeast, and southwest, provide access to Bangkok, its port, airport, and other industrial centres and land transportation to neighbouring countries. Physical development has taken the form of a 'ribbon' or 'corridor,' with buildings and land uses located along and adjacent to the major radials. One such is the northern corridor, of which the major north-south highway connecting Bangkok to the Central and Northern Regions is the spine, extending approximately 20 km in Pathum Thani *changwat.*

The northern corridor is dominated by industries located along both sides of the highway. In 1990, the corridor had 373 industrial units, employing a total of almost 68,000 workers. This represented an increase of over 27,000 workers, or almost 70 per cent, since 1980 (Iqbal 1990, 39).

Almost 80 per cent of the workers in 1990 were young females, most of whom migrated from rural Thailand, attracted by the steady employment and high wages (Iqbal 1990, 40 and Table 4.10). Anchored at the corridor's northern end is Nava Nakorn, a privately owned and developed industrial estate with a total area of 6,000 rai (one rai = 1,600 m^2). As noted earlier, Nava Nakorn was originally intended as a new town but has become basically a private industrial estate with a total of 180 factories, a combined investment of Baht 16,080 million, and employment of almost 54,000 workers, or around 80 per cent of the total corridor workers (Asian Institute of Technology, Urban Planning Workshop 1991).

The intensive industrial development along the highway has generated a mixture of residential and other uses, including conversion of agricultural lands to urban uses. These residential, commercial, and industrial developments have often left large parcels of land unused, partly from the lack of secondary and feeder roads, partly from land speculation by absentee owners, and partly from the absence of any government controls over residential or industrial land use. The northern corridor is located in two provincial districts without any responsible local authority or powers.

As a consequence of the intensive industrial development and adjoining non-industrial uses, there is a heavy mixture of highway traffic with local traffic. The stretch of highway immediately north of Bangkok has a traffic load of almost 83,000 vehicles per day, making it one of the heaviest used highways in Asia (McGee and Greenberg 1992). The bulk of this traffic consists of trucks coming from and going to the various factories along the highway and carrying products from the north to Bangkok and vice versa.

The outlying areas of the Bangkok Metropolitan Region, especially the province of Pathum Thani (where the northern corridor is located), are undergoing changes according to Isarankura (1990) that epitomize the characteristics of McGee's desakota zones.[9]

The Extended Bangkok Metropolitan Region
Similar problems to those in the outer parts of the BMR and along its highways are already occurring in areas outside the Bangkok Metropolitan Region, in the EBMR. As noted in the NESDB Final Report, developments in this extended area mirror those within the five outlying provinces of the BMR. Urban development is primarily located along major highways and roads, and orderly and more efficient development patterns are handicapped by a lack of secondary infrastructure such as distributor roads, piped water, and sewerage systems.

A TDRI researcher recently challenged the State Railway of Thailand to boost its role as a mover of people between Bangkok and the Eastern Seaboard. He argued that current capacity must be increased to at least

175,000 daily in the next decades and strongly recommended that high-speed rail projects should be seriously considered for the region. Also, a huge increase in freight traffic between Bangkok and the Eastern Seaboard is expected because Thai exports and imports will shift by the year 2001 from Bangkok port to the new port of Laem Chabang in the Eastern Seaboard, and most of this must be handled by train. In March of 1993, a German Engineering company, AEG, announced that it was seeking to build a 160 kmh, 200 km-long rail link between Bangkok and the industrial zones in the Eastern Seaboard (*Bangkok Post Weekly Review*, 19 March 1993, p. 11).

Two recent government announcements about future developments in the Bangkok region make the concept of the Extended Bangkok Metropolitan Region even more of a reality and, most significantly, will further aggravate the likely problems unless proper planning and management actions are taken immediately. The first was the announcement of detailed plans for a new international airport to be located at Nong Ngu Hao in Samut Prakan *changwat* (*Bangkok Post Weekly Review*, 19 March 1993, p. 20). Through Dr. Phisit Pakkasem, the government announced that this will become Thailand's major airport, replacing Don Muang, and will ultimately accommodate up to 80 million passengers a year, making it one of the world's five largest in the next century. It is expected that the new airport will serve as a centre for air transport links between China and Europe. It is also expected to be a new magnet for development of nearby high-value manufacturing firms, hotels, office buildings, and other economic activities.

The city of Chachoengsao will serve as the support town for the new airport, instead of Bangkok, because the capital is already overcrowded. Chachoengsao will also provide more convenient access to other Thai regions such as Saraburi and Nakhon Ratchasima. This will call for a new communications network, including roads and an electric train to Samut Prakan to support the airport. Since the announcement, the government subcommittee set up to oversee the development of the new airport has announced that an electric train will be built, on elevated tracks, primarily on government land, connecting the Don Muang and Nong Ngu Hao airports and thus allowing passengers to travel between them without having to pass through the traffic-congested capital city (*Bangkok Post Weekly Review*, 14 May 1993, p. 4).

Up to one million people are expected to be involved in activities related to the airport's construction, 600,000 of them directly. Construction will take about six years and will necessitate the relocation of some 1,500 families. Dr. Phisit emphasized that development of the airport would not affect the surrounding environment, which is presently largely farmland, because most of the land in the province has been acquired in an organized pattern by golf course, factory, and land developers. Nevertheless, he admitted that a new land-use plan will have to be prepared and regulations drawn up to reserve green areas and control land development and construction efficiently.

The second major proposed government development that will profoundly affect the EBMR is a plan to move all government offices out of Bangkok to a new town to be built in the eastern region of Chachoengsao *changwat*. The town will be built on 650,000 rai of degraded state forest land, thereby eliminating the need for land expropriation, and will require investment estimated at Baht 240 million. The site is 120 km from Bangkok, about mid-point between the city of Chachoengsao and Cambodia's border. The proposed population is 60,000 in the first stage, another 30,000 in the second stage, and a final 50,000 in the third stage. The maximum population is planned not to exceed one million (*Bangkok Post Weekly Review,* 21 May 1993, p. 4). The cabinet authorized the DTCP to draw up a master plan for the new town, which was expected to take eight to ten months (*Bangkok Post*, 20 October 1993, 1).

The announcement has received considerable press coverage, some of it controversial. Some people have argued that instead of building a completely new town, it would be better to enlarge the city of Chachoengsao, since it already had the advantage of being designated as a decentralized administration subcentre and the support town for the new international airport. Besides, it would be less costly than building a new town from scratch.[10]

It is clear that the combination of history and current development trends, plus the proposed new projects will push the direction of Bangkok's growth and development towards the east. The centre of Bangkok has traditionally been on the east bank of the Chao Phraya, the three easternmost BMR provinces have been experiencing the fastest rates of growth since 1970 (see Table 4.1), and the Eastern Seaboard continues to be developed. At one time, however, it was anticipated that growth would be primarily towards the north and south.

All of these developments, underway and expected, point up the need for immediate preliminary planning, including an overall strategic plan covering the entire extended Bangkok region as delimited by TDRI and the Lemon Group. As well, some form of government agency or high-level government committee should be established to coordinate, plan, and manage these developments.

There are now more than fifty national and local agencies and state enterprises involved in the planning and implementation of urban development policies, programs, and projects in the Extended Bangkok

Metropolitan Region (Setchell 1991). No single agency is responsible for policy making, planning, coordination, and implementation for the metropolitan region as a whole. To help remedy this situation, the TDRI, in its report to the NESDB on the Seventh Plan, recommended establishment of the Extended Bangkok Metropolitan Region Development Committee (EBMRDC), a new institutional arrangement for the EBMR covering the BMR, Eastern Seaboard, and part of the Upper Central Region. The committee would build upon but supersede the BMR Development Committee (BMRDC), which was established in 1986. Membership of the committee, like that of the BMRDC, would include those at the highest policy level: the prime minister acting as chairperson, and all the relevant deputy prime ministers.

In the view of the TDRI, the EBMRDC would be concerned with planning the integrated development of the EBMR, coordinating the various agencies with responsibilities related to the development of the region, and evaluating major infrastructure projects (including privatized projects) to make sure they are socio-economically beneficial, do not duplicate each other, and are consistent with desired development directions. As of 1994, the proposal had not been adopted.[11] However, the recent announcements of expected future developments in the eastern provinces, noted above, make the establishment of such a coordinating mechanism even more urgent.

Conclusions

The growing metropolitan areas and emerging mega-urban regions in ASEAN provide economies of scale and agglomeration economies that are conducive to diversified and rapid economic development, allowing these huge urban areas to absorb large numbers of people in new jobs and permitting governments to construct modern social and physical infrastructure and other facilities that require a large population in order to operate efficiently. These metropolitan regional areas now play crucial roles in the national economic development of their respective countries. With proper planning and management, the mega-urban regions, including the EBMR, can continue to play a vital role in the economic health of their national countries and at the same time maintain – and hopefully improve – the quality of life of their residents.

Most mega-cities in Asia, including those in ASEAN countries, have been experiencing decentralization of population and economic activities into the peripheries and suburbs in their metropolitan areas and along major highways and railroad lines. More recently, the process has moved even further out, to the so-called 'desakota zones,' to form extended metropolitan regions or mega-urban regions.

In the main, this decentralized growth has been unplanned and uncontrolled. As demonstrated by Bangkok, the resulting problems may be more serious than those that decentralization tried to solve. They include: sprawl, conflicting land uses, long commuting times, high infrastructure costs, high energy consumption, environmental deterioration and ecological degradation, and encroachment on valuable estuarine resources and agricultural lands. In short, this review clearly shows that decentralization per se is no panacea for the problems faced by the mega-cities.

Growth in the outer areas of the mega-urban regions, and especially in the desakota zones, poses both challenges and opportunities. The desakota zones have without doubt represented areas of new economic opportunity, new jobs, and increased income, especially for young female workers. At the same time, these areas are experiencing serious social and environmental problems. If a rigid master plan and accompanying land-use controls were implemented, however, they would slow down economic growth. This dilemma represents a clear challenge to the planners and other public officials in Asia who are responsible for these regions. They need to make their planning and management tools not only strong enough to prevent ecological and environmental deterioration and the other negative consequences that accompany settlement of these fringe areas but also flexible enough to permit the areas to develop in a healthy and socially responsible manner.

Some of the critical problems facing mega-urban regions can only be handled at the mega-urban scale. This involves, in particular, the encouragement and development of a polycentric spatial structure. Certain environmental problems, especially air pollution and water supply, involve external diseconomies by their very nature and can only be adequately dealt with by managing the entire airshed and watershed. In short, such problems cannot be dealt with at the level of spatially disaggregated neighbourhoods or projects.

A polycentric spatial pattern would avoid many of the problems of unplanned decentralization. Most mega-cities have spatial planning strategies aimed at promoting such patterns but have been unsuccessful for the most part in achieving them, in part because of: (1) lack of financial resources to build either the required infrastructure in outlying centres and subcentres or a truly self-contained new city or satellite town; (2) lack of adequate land-use and environmental controls and regulations in the outlying areas; (3) lack of strategic planning and management, including too great a reliance on physical planning measures and not enough consideration of non-spatial (economic, social, environmental) policies; and (4) lack of adequate and appropriate governmental/administrative machinery in the outlying areas for dealing with rapid growth and its resulting problems.

One of the major reasons for the discrepancies between formulated objectives and real-world trends and developments in the ASEAN countries is the absence of an adequate data-collection system. This has three aspects:

(1) No data-monitoring system other than the decadal census is in place to detect population and economic changes in the outer zones of the mega-urban regions (especially in the desakotas) quickly and to make planning and development adjustments accordingly.

(2) Most of the new growth in these regions has been occurring in their outer zones, usually in areas outside urban boundaries and officially classified as rural or semi-rural. In reality, the new growth results from developments and projects that are urban or urban-like in character, but the national censuses and other data-collection programs do not recognize this.

(3) The statistical geographic units used by the various national censuses and other data-collection programs and by planners are either too small (the areas are underbounded) or too large (encompassing both urban and rural areas). In the latter case, they prevent the pinpointing and identification of the smaller subregions, centres, and subcentres within the mega-urban regions. If national censuses collected and analyzed their data for these regions on the basis of small spatial units, these could then be used in two ways: either to construct larger units compatible over time, in an aggregative manner; or to remove data covering annexed areas from a city's population in order to approximate the city as it was earlier. Such data would allow, first, definition for analytical purposes of larger statistical areas, including in particular the mega-urban regions. Second, and most importantly, the data would provide the necessary sub-metropolitan geographic information for these mega-urban regions, given the objective of developing a polycentric structure and the existence of multiple political and governmental jurisdictions within so many mega-cities and mega-regions.

Policy Implications and Recommendations

Rather than attempt to stop or even slow the growth of the growing metropolitan areas and emerging mega-urban regions, governments should try to manage their growth more efficiently and effectively while strengthening the secondary cities and towns in the outer regions. Efforts should be made to ensure that growth within these large urban areas results in greater integration rather than separation of activities and land uses, specifically by encouraging, promoting, and assisting in the development of nucleated clusters of population and employment around existing or new centres and subcentres and/or along transport corridors within the metropolitan region. A polynucleated spatial structure has been shown to have distinct social, economic, and environmental advantages over the monocentric and spread/sprawl spatial patterns.

An effort should be made to develop sufficient financial resources, adequate and appropriate land-use and environmental controls, and administrative machinery appropriate to the growth pattern of the area.

At the mega-urban scale, single coordinating bodies or agencies should be established with functions similar to those planned for the EBMRDC. Using small-unit data collection and analysis and monitoring a set of key statistical indicators, such agencies would be able to detect early on any critical changes and convey them to the lower-level urban units. They would also alter original strategies accordingly, evaluate the impact of government and other investment decisions on labour force composition, employment, income, land uses, and environment, especially in the desakota zones, and, most importantly, help to plan and implement the development of a metropolitan-wide polycentric spatial structure. Mega-urban coordinating agencies such as these should not implement projects or programs and should in no way be in competition with existing agencies that provide services and build facilities or are in the business of regulation.

At the urban scale, villages, towns, and rural areas now experiencing urban or urban-like activities but still officially classified as rural or semi-rural should receive the status of 'formal' urban municipalities and be empowered with the land-use controls and other responsibilities normally assigned to such urban areas. They should also be given the appropriate staff to carry out these duties and responsibilities.

Government planners should carefully select the centres and subcentres for future growth and the location of any future satellite towns or new cities within the polycentred spatial structure. It is essential, for example, that the existing or new centres selected as 'countermagnets' be far enough away that they can develop an independent existence and not be swallowed up by the expanding central city and at the same time close enough that residents can easily commute to the mega-city for specialized services and facilities.

Experience indicates that the spatial organization of metropolitan regions can change only if a wide variety of economic, social, and physical planning policies and instruments is employed in conjunction with appropriate sectoral policies. It is essential that the plans, policies, programs, and projects for developing the centres, subcentres, new cities, and satellite towns be coordinated with infrastructure and transportation plans and projects, especially with respect to secondary road systems. In particular, it is vital that a strategic planning and management approach be adopted in setting goals and choosing projects and programs to implement, stressing both external and internal environment, and that key points of leverage for applying actions are identified.

Finally, efforts should be made to convince national and international agencies responsible for collecting, analyzing, and publishing censuses and related data on towns, villages, cities, metropolitan areas, and megacities to create new spatial systems of data collection and analysis.

Notes

1 A pioneering attempt to outline the problems of metropolitan delimitation and to delimit actual metropolitan areas on an international basis, based on administrative units, was the work in the late 1950s of a group of researchers led by Kingsley Davis in the Institute of International Studies at the University of California, Berkeley, and financed by the Ford Foundation. The researchers applied uniform criteria to areas containing more than 100,000 inhabitants and delimited boundaries for some 720 areas of a total of 1,046 metropolitan areas in the world. The researchers' results culminated in a small volume (International Urban Research 1959), which provides a list of the world's then-metropolitan areas classified by continent and country, showing the total population of each area, including the population of each metropolitan area's 'principal city' (the equivalent of the 'core city' or 'central city'). The populations listed were for the latest national census before the year 1955 – usually 1950 – plus the researchers' own estimates for 1955.

2 By 'decentralization,' I am referring to spatial decentralization: the 'breaking up' or decentralizing of population and/or economic activities from the centralized urban core or city. I am not discussing the decentralization or devolution of governmental functions or decision making, though the former may ultimately result in the latter and vice versa.

3 Experience has shown that both decentralization and dispersal, when they occur as a result of market forces, usually do not produce widespread relocation of higher-order activities – e.g., finance, insurance, research and development, the arts – which generally require face-to-face contacts despite new technologies such as computer conferencing and thus prefer to remain in the urban cores.

4 Nevertheless, as previously noted, I differ with Richardson over what constitutes a polynucleated spatial structure and the extent to which the developing world's megacities are indeed achieving that objective.

5 Theoretical perspectives on the conditions necessary for the emergence of multinucleated cities are described in Odlund (1978) and Brotchie et al. (1985).

6 This conclusion is based on a review of: Richardson (1984, 1989a, 1989b, 1990), Brennan and Richardson (1989), a series of reports on individual mega-cities prepared by the Population Policy Section of the United Nations Population Division under the guidance of Dr. Ellen Brennan, the master plans for individual mega-cities where available, and my own research undertaken with master's degree students at the Asian Institute of Technology.

7 Douglass (1990), in a study for the Thailand Development and Research Institute, found that Thailand had the highest 'primacy index' by far than any of the twelve Asian countries he studied: slightly over twice as large as the next ranked country.

8 This area consists of: (1) the Bangkok Metropolitan Administration; and (2) urban parts of the neighbouring *changwats* of Nonthaburi and Samut Prakan. It did not, however, at first include the urbanized area that has spilled over into the corridor along the main north-south highway, stretching from Bangkok centre to northern Thailand. Recent studies include this *changwat* (Pathum Thani), the BMA, Nonthaburi, and Samut Prakan in the Greater Bangkok Area.

9   Isarankura (1990) identified the following characteristics: (1) a mixture of land uses and economic activities – non-agricultural as well as agricultural – in areas previously primarily agricultural; (2) an increase in household income from non-agricultural activities; (3) an increase in off-farm, non-agricultural employment, especially for women; (4) a variety of employment sources and locations for individual members of farm households; and (5) extreme fluidity and mobility of the population, made possible by relatively cheap forms of transport such as two-stroke motorcycles, buses, and trucks, allowing relatively quick movement over long distances. Iqbal (1990) verified these changes in a former, predominantly agricultural, district in Pathum Thani, resulting from the impact of the northern corridor.

10 The British learned these lessons from their first round of new towns, which were all built 'from scratch' on undeveloped, vacant land. This led planners to shift their approach in the subsequent round of development to expand existing towns and villages into 'new towns.'

11 The fact that Utis Kaothien doesn't mention the EBMRDC in his chapter on the Bangkok Metropolitan Region seems to bear out the validity of that prediction.

5

ASEAN Urban Housing Sector Performance: A Comparative Perspective

Shlomo Angel and Stephen K. Mayo

The challenges facing housing policy makers in ASEAN cities and towns are twofold: to ensure that the housing sector makes a productive contribution towards macro-economic performance; and to ensure that economic development is translated into significant improvement in housing conditions for all. In general, housing conditions in ASEAN cities, and indeed the performance of the housing sector as a whole in ASEAN cities and towns, are not lagging behind those of cities and towns in countries at similar levels of economic development. For a number of specific housing indicators, housing-sector performance appears to be improving with the high rates of economic growth in the region over the past decade.

This statement need not surprise anyone. What might be surprising, however, is that underperformance of the housing sector in ASEAN cities is probably at least as much the result of inappropriate policies as it is of the poverty and demographic pressures in the region. This suggests the high stakes involved in policy reform in ASEAN cities and the potential payoff to a more systematic approach to collecting and using data on housing-sector performance.

The objectives of this chapter are: (1) to provide a general framework for evaluating the performance of the housing sector; (2) to provide data comparing housing-sector performance in five ASEAN capitals (Jakarta, Singapore, Kuala Lumpur, Bangkok, and Manila) to that of the rest of the world; (3) to explain some of the differences in performance among these ASEAN cities; and (4) to suggest a framework for housing-policy reform and research within the region.

This study is the outgrowth of the Housing Indicators Program, which began in 1990 as a follow-up to the *Global Strategy for Shelter to the Year 2000*, prepared by the United Nations Centre for Human Settlements (UNCHS) and subsequently unanimously endorsed by the United Nations General Assembly in 1988 (United Nations Centre for Human Settlements 1987). The *Global Strategy for Shelter* called on governments to shift their housing policies and programs from a reliance on direct production of housing and direct control of housing prices and rents towards enabling policies aimed at facilitating the role of the private sector – both formal and informal and including community organizations and NGOs – in the provision and financing of housing. This shift was believed necessary in order to improve not only the performance of the sector per se but also its potential contribution to wider social and economic goals. There has been widespread recognition that such a shift will require more and better data on the performance of the housing sector and better policy-oriented analysis of such data.

To address these goals, the Housing Indicators Program was begun in 1990 as a joint undertaking of UNCHS and the World Bank, with four major objectives:

(1) to provide a comprehensive conceptual and analytical framework for monitoring the performance of the housing sector

(2) to create a set of practical tools for measuring the performance of the housing sector using quantitative, policy-sensitive indicators and to test these tools in a broad range of countries

(3) to provide important new empirical information on the high stakes for societies and economies of policy making in the housing sector

(4) to initiate new institutional frameworks that will be more appropriate for managing the housing sector and for formulating and implementing future housing policies, in the light of new research findings.

The main steps taken by the program to date have been: to devise an analytical framework for measuring housing-sector performance; to test a broad range of indicators in an extensive survey of housing indicators in a principal city in each of fifty-two countries; to study two national housing sectors in greater detail (Hungary and the Philippines) with a view to addressing specific policy issues; to analyze the data obtained from the survey; and to focus on a set of key indicators that could be collected and disseminated globally on a regular basis.

Emphasis in the survey has been on collecting data in a cost-effective way, relying primarily on secondary data and expert interviews rather than on original data collection. Quality control was addressed through a series of regional meetings between country-based consultants and program staff. In the case of ASEAN data, country-based consultants were recruited in each city. The consultants met us in Bangkok in November 1991 to discuss methodological problems and to examine the data. Corrections of the data continued and were virtually complete by January 1993.

The Conceptual Framework

The analytical framework used by the survey for evaluating housing-sector performance relies on both a normative and a positive view of the sector. The *Global Strategy for Shelter* recognizes that in recent years, market relations have been observed in the housing sector at all levels and in all segments, from the most meagre squatter settlements to highly regulated rent-controlled apartments. Even in centrally planned and formerly centrally planned economies, housing is viewed increasingly as a commodity with an exchange value rather than as a good to be produced and allocated outside of the marketplace. In turn, it is believed that the housing sector is driven by a variety of market forces and that these forces exert powerful influences throughout all parts of the sector despite the existence of apparently distinctive sub-markets.

Recognition of the pervasiveness of market forces has led to the view that even though responsible housing policy must be sufficiently differentiated to deal with particular sub-markets such as high-rise condominiums, public housing rentals, and squatter settlements, it is still useful to look at the sector as a single market. Trends in one part of a housing market will, over time, be closely linked to those in other parts of the market. Policies designed to affect only the low-, middle-, or high-income sub-markets will almost inevitably affect the performance of the others.

Prices, and thus housing affordability by different income groups, are determined in the market by demand and supply factors. Housing demand is determined by demographic conditions, such as the rate of urbanization and new household formation, as well as by macro-economic conditions affecting household incomes. It is also influenced by the availability of housing finance and by government fiscal policies such as taxation and subsidies, and particularly subsidies targeted to the poor.

Housing supply is affected by the availability of resource inputs, such as residential land, infrastructure, and construction materials. It is also affected by the organization of the construction industry, the availability of skilled and productive construction labour, and the dependence on imports. Both the demand and the supply of housing are affected by the regulatory, institutional, and policy environment.

Housing policies and housing outcomes may in turn affect broader socio-economic conditions, such as the infant mortality rate, the rate of inflation, the household savings rate, manufacturing wage and productivity levels, capital formation, the balance of payments, and the government budget deficit.

Although largely private housing markets produce most of the housing in developing countries, this does not necessarily mean that they are either efficient or equitable. Nor does it mean that they completely satisfy all housing needs or help attain broader development goals. Housing-sector policies must be based on a positive view of how the sector actually works in a given context and with specific notions of how it could work better.

To develop a normative view of the housing sector, one must look at how the sector performs from a number of different perspectives. The five most important perspectives are those of housing consumers, housing producers, housing finance institutions, local governments, and central governments.[1]

Each of these perspectives focuses on different qualitative norms. The desired outcomes, while neither universally attainable nor entirely compatible, may be expected to exert an influence both on the behaviour of the key actors and on the way that they perceive the efficacy and responsiveness of government policies and programs. These desired outcomes are as follows:

(1) *Housing consumers.* Everyone is housed, with a separate unit for every household. Housing does not take up an undue portion of household income. House prices are not subject to undue variability. Living space is adequate. Structures are safe and provide adequate protection from the elements, fire, and natural disasters. Services and amenities are available and reliable. Location provides good access to employment. Tenure is secure and protected by due process of law. Households may freely choose among different housing options and tenures (owning versus renting). Finance is available to smooth expenses over time and allow households to save and invest. Adequate information is available to ensure efficient choice.

(2) *Housing producers.* Adequate supply of residential land is available at reasonable prices. Infrastructure networks are adequate and do not hold back residential development. Building materials and equipment and sufficient skilled labour are available at reasonable prices. Entry of new firms into the residential construction sector is not impeded. The residential construction sector is not discriminated against by special tariffs or controls. Adequate financing is available. Housing production and investment can respond to changes in demand without undue delay. Contracts are enforceable. Regulations concerning land development, land use, building, land tenure, taxation, or special programs are well defined and predictable, and government application of these is efficient, timely, and uniform. Adequate information exists to enable producers to forecast housing demand with reasonable certainty. Rates of return on all types of housing investment, including rental housing, are sufficient to maintain incentives for investment.

(3) *Housing finance institutions.* Housing finance institutions are permitted to compete for deposits on equal terms with other financial institutions. The role of directed credit is minimized. Housing finance institutions are not forced to compete unfairly with subsidized finance. Lending is at positive, real interest rates with a sufficient margin to maintain insti-

tutional health. There are sufficient deposits of an appropriate term structure for long-term mortgage lending. Mortgage-lending instruments are permitted that are in demand by households and provide adequate protection for the institution. Systems of property rights, tenure security, and foreclosure are such that the financial interests of lenders can be protected. Appropriate institutions exist to protect financial institutions against undue mortgage-lending risk.

(4) *Local governments.* Housing and associated infrastructures are of adequate quality to maintain public health, safety standards, and environmental quality. Infrastructure networks and services are extended in a timely fashion to all communities. The location of new communities is in close proximity to existing main networks. Land use is productive and efficient. Sufficient land can be obtained for laying infrastructure networks and providing local amenities and public services. Housing provides a major source of municipal revenues for building and maintaining infrastructure services and neighbourhood amenities.

(5) *Central governments.* Adequate, affordable housing is available to all. Targeted subsidies are available to assist households that cannot afford minimum housing. Housing-sector policy is integrated into national social and economic planning. Housing-sector performance is monitored regularly. The housing sector contributes towards broad social and economic objectives: alleviating poverty; controlling inflation; generating household savings and mobilizing household productive resources; generating employment and income growth; enabling social and spatial mobility; increasing productivity; generating investment growth; accumulating national wealth; reducing the balance of payments deficit; reducing the government budget deficit; developing the financial system; and protecting the environment.

While the above list may be incomplete, it does provide a broad normative view of a well-functioning housing sector from the perspectives of its key actors. Needless to say, these perspectives are not necessarily mutually consistent. What benefits one may damage another. Rent control, for example, may benefit families already housed but prevent further investment in rental housing and discriminate against new residents. Reducing house prices may benefit housing seekers but lower the asset value of those owning houses. Land supply may be increased at the expense of environmental amenities. Stronger foreclosure laws may increase mortgage financing for all at the expense of evictions for some. Resolving these seemingly incompatible interests is one of the most fundamental tasks of an effective housing policy.

The Housing Indicators Program has taken the conceptual framework and the norms for a well-functioning housing sector as the basis for gener-

ating a comprehensive set of indicators to measure housing-sector performance. Indicators were designed to cover housing supply, in terms of the
cost and availability of key inputs such as land, infrastructure, building
materials, industrial organization, and the regulatory environment; housing demand, in terms of demographic variables, finance, and subsidies;
and housing outcomes, in terms of prices, quantities, and the qualitative
features of the housing stock. All key norms for a well-functioning housing sector were translated, as far as possible, into quantitative indicators.
These were then tested and collected in the survey. It is important to note
that the framework calls for collection of data not only on housing outcomes but also on factors conditioning those outcomes, such as the legal,
regulatory, institutional, and policy frameworks and the variables indicative of the broader economic climate within which the sector functions.

The Context of ASEAN Housing Markets

Demographic Aspects

Relative to other regions of the world, ASEAN countries offer an interesting mix of levels of urbanization, city size, urban growth rates, and rates
of household formation. Singapore is 100 per cent urban. Thailand, at the
other end of the scale, is only 23 per cent urban, largely due to its expansion of agricultural land through encroachment into forested areas over
the past thirty years. Its level of urbanization is thus much lower than that
expected for the level of economic development. Indonesia is 31 per cent
urbanized, and Malaysia and the Philippines are 43 per cent urbanized,
more in line with their levels of economic development. While Kuala
Lumpur and Singapore are relatively small cities, with urban populations
of 1.23 million and 2.69 million respectively in 1990, Bangkok (6.02 million), Manila (7.93 million), and Jakarta (8.22 million) are among the
largest urban agglomerations in the world.

Singapore's urban growth rate is low, 2.2 per cent per annum, because it
lacks rural-urban migration. Growth rates of the primate cities in the
other four ASEAN countries are high and quite similar: 3.8 per cent per
annum in the Philippines, 4.6 per cent in Thailand, 4.9 per cent in
Malaysia, and 5.1 per cent in Indonesia for the 1980-90 period.[2]
Household formation rates in the ASEAN capitals are closer to one
another than urban growth rates, with higher than expected rates in
Singapore (3.3 per cent per annum) and lower than expected rates in the
other capitals (3.6 per cent in Manila, 4.2 per cent in Bangkok, 3.5 per
cent in Kuala Lumpur, and 4.1 per cent in Jakarta). These differences may
indeed be due to housing availability.[3] Despite the high rates of urban
growth, homelessness appears to be low. In Singapore, Manila, and Bangkok,
it is below the global median of 0.71 per 1,000, at 0.10, 0.12, and 0.34

respectively. In Jakarta and Kuala Lumpur, it is significantly higher, at 3.3 and 4.1 respectively. The overall number of homeless people in the five ASEAN capitals in 1990 appears to have been of the order of 35,000.

Economic Growth and Inflation
Except for the Philippines, which had a very slow growth of GDP per capita – averaging 0.9 per cent per annum during the 1980-90 decade – the other four ASEAN countries have grown very rapidly, far exceeding the global average of 3.2 per cent per annum during this period. Thailand led with 7.6 per cent per annum, followed by Singapore (6.4 per cent), Indonesia (5.5 per cent), and Malaysia (5.2 per cent). Discrepancies in development among these countries have remained quite large, with GDP per capita roughly in inverse proportion to the size of countries. By 1990, it was by far the highest in Singapore ($10,450), followed by Malaysia ($2,160), Thailand ($1,220), the Philippines ($710), and Indonesia ($500). Inflation was kept very much at bay in Singapore and Malaysia, averaging 1.5 per cent per annum during the decade, followed by Thailand with 3.2 per cent. Indonesia experienced considerably higher inflation (8.3 per cent), while the Philippines suffered from high inflation (14.8 per cent).[4]

Finance
The financial stability of the economies of the ASEAN region increased modestly in Malaysia, Thailand, and the Philippines in recent years, growing more rapidly in Singapore and most rapidly in Indonesia. Between 1984 and 1989, for example, the ratio of M2 (money supply) to GDP, a widely used measure of financial stability, increased by 18 per cent in Malaysia, 17.4 per cent in Thailand, and 14.8 per cent in the Philippines. It increased by 37.7 per cent in Singapore and by a significant 76.9 per cent in Indonesia. Levels of financial stability roughly follow levels of economic development, with Singapore leading the region (0.93), followed by Malaysia (0.68), and Thailand (0.67). Indonesia, with a ratio of 0.35, has now surpassed the Philippines, at 0.31. Prime interest rates were typically high. In 1990, prime rates were 5.1 per cent above the long-term inflation rate in the Philippines (19.9 per cent), 6 per cent above it in Malaysia (7.5 per cent), 6.2 per cent above it in Singapore (7.7 per cent), 11.6 per cent above it in Thailand (14.8 per cent), and 13.6 per cent above it in Indonesia (8.5 per cent).

The Policy Context
Policies affecting housing-sector performance include indirect ones such as monetary, fiscal, and trade policy and direct ones such as those concerning infrastructure development and the regulatory framework within

which the housing sector operates. Among the most important of these latter policies are those influencing land use and building regulations, rent control, competition in the building and housing development industry, housing finance, and the administration of property rights.

Singapore stands alone among the ASEAN countries as a city-state without a rural hinterland. Housing policy and housing production are highly centralized in the public sector, which manages 79 per cent of the housing stock. Housing is financed through forced savings in a provident fund and is produced with a moderate level of public subsidy: 5.5 per cent of the government budget. Land acquisition by government is common and efficient, and planning and building regulations are strict and universally enforced. Most housing is built in the form of high-rise towers in large, planned housing estates, resulting in a lower than average urban density of 4,680 persons per km^2.

Malaysia is next to Singapore in the strictness of its planning controls and complexity of its regulatory environment. Following the British town and country planning tradition, attention is paid to orderly development and to the allocation of substantial amounts of residential land to community facilities. Saleable land in Kuala Lumpur, for example, constitutes only 45 per cent of gross land in residential subdivisions, compared to a global median of 66.5 per cent. Construction time is the longest in the region, twenty-four months, compared to a global median of 9.5 months. And while the public sector manages only 19.4 per cent of the housing stock, industrial concentration is extremely high: five development companies account for 75 per cent of all housing production.

Jakarta, Bangkok, and Manila share a similar policy context. Regulation of the housing sector is not strict and is virtually impossible to implement universally, with the result that all three cities have a substantial informal housing sector. Public-sector involvement in housing production is higher in Manila (29.5 per cent), lower in Bangkok (10.5 per cent), and virtually non-existent in Jakarta (1.8 per cent). Housing subsidies are a very small part of the government budget: 1.4 per cent in Manila, 1.1 per cent in Jakarta, and 0.3 per cent in Bangkok. All three cities have focused their attention on improving slum infrastructure, Jakarta leading the way with its massive Kampung Improvement Program. Only Manila has followed up such improvements by granting land tenure to squatters, a program that is still operating today.

Key Indicators of Housing-sector Performance

All of the elements of the ASEAN housing context described above bear on the way in which the housing sector performs in ASEAN cities, although their effects are likely to differ considerably from place to place. This section compares and contrasts a number of key housing-sector outcomes for the five ASEAN capitals that have been part of the Housing Indicators Program and discusses reasons for differences between housing-sector performance in ASEAN cities and cities in other regions.

The key indicators discussed here are a subset of those examined by the Housing Indicators Program. They have been chosen because they capture some of the most salient and policy-relevant dimensions of housing-sector performance. It should be noted here that any such international comparison should always be interpreted cautiously, not only because of common problems of definition and measurement but because differences in outcome may not be easily interpreted on the basis of simple notions of whether a higher or lower value of an indicator is 'better.' If the average ratio of house price to income in one country is higher than that in another, for example, then the relative degree of wealth held in the form of housing assets will be higher in the former country but affordability and access to home ownership by current tenants will be higher in the latter country. Which level of the indicator is better, let alone optimal, depends on a number of technical and normative judgments, and opinions on the matter may also differ among different groups.

In the analysis presented below, emphasis is placed first on examining 'descriptive norms' for each indicator – values of the indicator that appear to be 'typical' for similar countries, with deviations from typical values interpreted in a diagnostic sense. That is, if values for one or more indicators are considerably different from those for similar countries, then questions may be raised about either the sources of the deviation (e.g., economic, cultural, or policy differences) or its welfare implications.

The indicators examined in this study were divided into five main groups, as listed below, but only the results of the analysis for indicators 1, 3, 5, 8, and 9 are presented here.[5]

Price indicators
Indicator 1: The house price to income ratio
Indicator 2: The rent to income ratio

Quantity indicators
Indicator 3: Housing production
Indicator 4: Housing investment

Quality indicators
Indicator 5: Floor area per person
Indicator 6: Permanent structures
Indicator 7: Unauthorized housing

Demand-side indicators
Indicator 8: The housing credit portfolio

Supply-side indicators
Indicator 9: The land development multiplier
Indicator 10: Infrastructure expenditures per capita

The significance of each of the five indicators discussed, its distribution across different levels of economic development and across geographical regions, its value for each of the ASEAN capitals, and the preliminary analysis of the results of the survey are given below. For each of the indicators, a table is presented indicating the median reported value for five different GNP per capita groups and for the five major ASEAN cities under discussion.[6]

Price Indicators

The two key indicators of housing price examined in the study – housing price and rent – are each normalized by income. Each is a gross measure of affordability of housing[7] but also conveys other information on the state of the housing market. Data on housing prices, for example, convey information on wealth held in the form of housing and thus on the potential base for property taxation. Deviations of either measure from norms convey information on potential distortions, which may be indicative of a variety of dysfunctional aspects of housing markets. Indicator 1, the house price to income ratio, is defined as the ratio of the median free-market price of a dwelling unit and the median household income.

Significance
If there is a single indicator that conveys the greatest amount of information on the overall performance of housing markets, it is the house price to income ratio. It is obviously a key measure of housing affordability. When housing prices are high relative to incomes, other things being equal, a smaller fraction of the population will be able to purchase housing. As importantly, however, this indicator provides crucial insights into several housing market dysfunctions, suggestive of a variety of policy failures. When the indicator is abnormally high, for example, it is generally a sign that the housing supply system is restricted in its ability to satisfy effective demand for housing, a feature of many housing delivery systems in both market and centrally planned economies. In such cases, it is often found that housing quality and space are depressed below levels that are typical of countries with well-functioning and responsive housing delivery systems. When the indicator is abnormally low, it may indicate widespread insecurity of tenure, leading to reduced willingness of the population to invest in housing and to lower than necessary housing quality.

Findings

The median reported house price to income ratio for global regions is 4.16 (Table 5.1), and ranges from a low of 1.0 to a high of 6.95. Reported ratios of house price to income are particularly high in countries that have restricted private property rights and give a prominent role to the public sector in the ownership of land and housing. Other countries with particularly high house price to income ratios are those with high construction costs and land prices, caused in part by tight regulatory environments affecting land use and housing construction with policies such as agricultural green belts. The house price to income ratio is indicative of the general level of excess demand in housing markets and is, based on preliminary analyses, associated with reduced housing consumption (especially alternative measures of crowding and dwelling space) and with rates of home ownership.

Table 5.1

House price to income ratio, 1900

	House price/income	ASEAN cities	House price/income
Sub-Saharan Africa	1.00	Jakarta	3.46
South Asia	6.95	Singapore	3.59
East Asia	4.15	Kuala Lumpur	4.25
Latin America	3.06	Bangkok	4.15
Europe, Middle East, and North Africa	5.03	Manila	2.56
Industrialized nations	4.70		
Global mean	4.16		

House price to income ratios in ASEAN countries are not excessive in global terms, varying between a low of 2.56 in Manila to a high of 4.25 in Kuala Lumpur. Bangkok has experienced a rapid rise in land prices and consequently in house prices during the late 1980s, which pushed the ratio from one similar to Manila's to its present value. The reverse has occurred in Kuala Lumpur, where the ratio fell from near 7.0 in the mid-1980s to its present value of 4.25. Low construction costs, corresponding to low-quality urban housing, and low land costs both contribute to the low ratio for Manila.

Interestingly enough, a related indicator, down market penetration, further elucidates the affordability dimension. This indicator measures the ratio between the cheapest housing unit produced in substantial quantities by the private sector without subsidies and median income. This value is very high for Singapore – 13.82 – where the private sector still concentrates on luxury housing. It is lower than the house price to income ratio for the other ASEAN capitals: not much lower in Kuala Lumpur (3.4) but significantly lower in Bangkok (1.7) despite high land and construction costs. This demonstrates that in Bangkok the private sector has penetrated further down market (Angel and Chuated 1990; Foo 1992a, 1992b), considerably further than the global median for this indicator, which is 2.76. Although the values for this indicator in Jakarta and Manila are less reliable, they suggest that in all ASEAN capitals except Singapore, the formal private sector, rather than the informal sector, already provides housing for families with below-median incomes.

One way to interpret variation in the house price to income ratio is based on the fact that it is by definition equal to the rent to income ratio multiplied by a capitalization rate. Research (e.g., Malpezzi and Mayo 1987) has found that the ratio of rent to income across countries first increases with GNP per capita and then decreases. If capitalization rates for rents were constant across countries, variation in the house price to income ratio would be expected to mirror exactly variation in the rent to income ratio, increasing with GNP per capita and then decreasing. As indicated below, rents in Sub-Saharan Africa are systematically lower than those in other regions, and rents in the lower-income ASEAN cities are lower than in the higher-income ones. By itself, this suggests that the house price to income ratio would also be lower in Sub-Saharan Africa than in other regions and lower in Jakarta and Manila than in Bangkok, Kuala Lumpur, and Singapore, as the data suggest.

It should be noted, however, that even when the ratio is low, it is not strictly a measure of access to home ownership. This is because many African cities are characterized by 'compound housing,' with many rooms often built around a central courtyard, each room occupied by a single family. Thus, were prices of 'houses' made up of multiple dwelling units to be considered, ratios of house price to income would rise by a factor equal to the average number of dwellings per structure (often from four to seven). Home ownership in the ASEAN cities is equal to or higher than the global median of 48 per cent but does not correlate at all with low house price to income ratios. Indeed, it is the lowest in Manila (48 per cent), where the ratio is the lowest, and highest in Singapore (90.2 per cent), where the ratio is the second lowest. In the other cities, it is again unrelated to the house price to income ratio: 67.5 per cent in Bangkok, 58.6 per cent in Kuala Lumpur, and 55.8 per cent in Jakarta.

This ratio can be expected to increase at least slightly with continued economic growth, leading to accumulation of wealth and serving as a potential source of revenue for residential infrastructure expansion. It could also be expected to increase if tenure security were increased in

ASEAN squatter settlements as a result of improved land registration systems and explicit programs to legitimize insecure tenure. These would provide incentive to invest in property improvements and offer improved expectations about the longevity of property. Collateralizing this source of wealth could, moreover, contribute both to the expansion of the financial system and to the ability of households to finance either further improvements in housing or other activities such as small business expansion.

Quantity Indicators
The two quantity indicators examined in the study, housing production and housing investment, are both linked to the broader economy through real and financial linkages. Indicator 3, housing production, is defined as the total number of housing units produced in the last year for which statistics are available per 1,000 population in both the formal and informal sectors.

Significance
This indicator is a measure of the overall level of housing construction activity, and has been the subject of relatively long-standing data collection in both developing and developed countries. Statistical coverage, however, is far from universal, and it is poor for developing countries. For the fifty-two countries included in the survey, production data were reported for only twenty-nine in the *Global Report on Human Settlements* (United Nations Centre for Human Settlements 1987). The report contained data for only twelve of the thirty-five developing countries covered by the survey, often considerably out of date.

The indicator represents one measure of the importance of the housing sector to the broader economy, but in combination with other data it is also important as a measure of the ability of the housing delivery system to keep pace with increasing demand. As a measure of the volume of construction, it is closely related to the level of employment in residential construction, use of intermediate inputs, and, through multiplier effects, to the overall level of economic activity.[8] Housing production can also be normalized by the size of the housing stock to give a rate of expansion of the stock, which can in turn be compared with the rate of household formation, thereby indicating whether or not housing production is keeping pace with demographic change.

Housing production relative to the population depends on some basic demographic characteristics of the population, particularly on household size. A higher rate of production of housing units relative to population will be required to accommodate a population with small households than one with large households. Production, however, also depends on

supply and demand factors, which depend on a number of housing policies, such as the availability of housing finance, the availability and price of
land and construction, and the flexibility of land and building regulations.

Findings

Housing production (Table 5.2) per 1,000 population has a median of 6.40
for the sample of fifty-two cities in the survey. With the exception of the
low-income countries, where production is lowest, production per 1,000
population falls modestly, though systematically, with increasing income.
Among regions, rates of production are highest in East Asia (7.16 per
thousand) and lowest in Sub-Saharan Africa (3.42 per thousand). When
an alternative measure of housing production is examined – the percentage rate of change of the housing stock – the trends are qualitatively identical to those for production per 1,000 but are more pronounced.
Comparisons of the rate of production, as a per cent of the housing stock,
with the rate of household formation indicate a vast difference in the ability of housing markets to cope with emerging housing demand. In all
nine countries reporting household formation rates lower than 1 per cent,
the rate of change in the housing stock is above the household formation
rate. By contrast, in countries reporting household formation rates above
3 per cent, fifteen of twenty-one (85 per cent) report that the housing
stock is expanding less rapidly than the household formation rate.

Table 5.2

Housing production, 1990

	House production*	ASEAN cities	House production*
Sub-Saharan Africa	3.42	Jakarta	7.10
South Asia	6.05	Singapore	6.40
East Asia	7.16	Kuala Lumpur	8.60
Latin America	6.01	Bangkok	15.80
Europe, Middle East,		Manila	5.70
and North Africa	6.55		
Industrialized nations	6.12		
Global mean	6.40		

*Units per 1000 population

Except for Manila, which has been subject to a very slow rate of economic growth, all other ASEAN capitals have housing production rates
that exceed the global median of 6.4 per 1,000. Housing production in
Bangkok in 1990 reached an all-time peak and was the highest recorded in
the fifty-two-city sample. Production in Bangkok and Kuala Lumpur out-
paced rates of new household formation, while it lagged behind them in

Manila, Jakarta, and Singapore. The ratio of housing stock growth to new household formation in Bangkok was 1.75; in Kuala Lumpur, 1.25; in Manila, 0.86; in Jakarta, 0.85; and in Singapore, 0.83.

It is somewhat surprising that Singapore, with the slowest rate of population growth, the highest level of economic development, and the highest rate of housing investment, produced new housing at a slower rate than its new household formation compared with other ASEAN capitals. This is most likely a short-term phenomenon. Despite the short-term lags in production, coupled with the slowly decreasing household size, the number of dwelling units in Singapore has kept pace with household formation. Households per dwelling unit are currently 1.01 in Bangkok and are only slightly higher (1.03) in Kuala Lumpur. Higher levels of overcrowding are present in Manila and Jakarta, where this indicator measures 1.10 and 1.14 respectively. Indeed, it is in Manila and Jakarta that housing production must accelerate to meet latent demand.

Quality Indicators
Of the three housing quality indicators examined in this study, floor area per person and permanent structures are indicative of physical housing conditions, whereas unauthorized housing is indicative of the legal status of housing. Indicator 5, floor area per person, is defined as the median usable living space per person (in m^2) over the last year of available statistics.

Significance
This indicator measures the adequacy of living space in dwellings. A low value for the indicator is a sign of overcrowding. Floor area per person is the outcome, to a considerable degree, of market forces, of the interplay of supply and demand for housing. Supply and demand are in turn shaped by a variety of policies. Alternative measures of overcrowding have been the subject of data collection and reporting in international statistical compendia. The two most common of these are persons per room and households per dwelling unit, each of which was included among the data collected during the first phase of the Housing Indicators Program.

Floor area per person and persons per room are highly variable among countries and highly related to each other; either would be an acceptable measure of the adequacy of living space. Based on analysis conducted in the Housing Indicators Program, however, the former has been shown to be the more precise and policy-sensitive measure of the two. The number of households per dwelling unit is only weakly related to the other two measures of crowding, does not vary nearly as much as the other measures among countries, and is subject not only to variation according to cultural preferences but also according to varying definitions of 'household' among countries.

Findings

The median reported floor area per person is 14.4 m^2, with a global range from 4 to 69 m^2 (Table 5.3). Floor area per person increases consistently with economic development, from about 6 m^2 per person in low-income countries to 35 m^2 per person in high-income countries. Sub-Saharan Africa and South Asia have the smallest floor area per person, and industrialized countries have the largest.

Table 5.3

Floor area per person, 1990

	Floor area/ person (m^2)	ASEAN cities	Floor area/ person (m^2)
Sub-Saharan Africa	7.0	Jakarta	10.2
South Asia	7.1	Singapore	20.0
East Asia	13.4	Kuala Lumpur	12.0
Latin America	15.3	Bangkok	16.5
Europe, Middle East, and North Africa	14.5	Manila	12.0
Industrialized nations	31.9		
Global mean	14.4		

Notwithstanding these patterns, there is still considerable variation among countries with similar incomes, much of which appears to be attributable to policy differences influencing land prices and construction costs. Among mid-high and high-income countries, for example, those having the smallest floor area per person also have the highest land prices and construction costs. Preliminary multivariate analyses indicate that more than 80 per cent of the variation in this indicator can be accounted for with reference to three variables: GNP per capita, construction costs, and land costs. Both construction and land costs are, in turn, highly influenced by a variety of policies.

It is significant to note, however, that floor area per person increases only slightly with GNP per capita or with median household incomes. Singapore, which has five times the median household income of Jakarta ($9,984 compared with $1,975) has only twice the floor area per person (20 m^2 compared with 10.2 m^2). Most of the improvement in housing conditions is qualitative, which this indicator unfortunately fails to measure. Kuala Lumpur and Manila report the same floor area per person, 12 m^2, while the median income in Kuala Lumpur is more than twice that in

Manila ($6,540 compared with $3,060). Bangkok reports a higher floor area per person than Kuala Lumpur – 16.5 m^2 – despite a lower median income ($4,132), similar construction costs, and higher land prices. Bangkok appears less overcrowded than Tokyo – which has 15.8 m^2 per person – where incomes are more than nine times higher ($38,230 compared with $4,132). As explained above, this is largely the result of exorbitant construction costs ($2,604 per m^2 in Tokyo compared with $156 in Bangkok) and record high land prices ($2,980 per m^2 of serviced land on the urban fringe of Tokyo, compared with $149 in Bangkok).

Demand-Side Indicators
A variety of factors influencing the demand for housing are essentially beyond the realm of policy, particularly incomes and demographic pressures. Other factors affecting demand are, however, capable of being directly affected by policy. These include the provision of housing finance, the legal framework regarding property rights, and the provision of housing subsidies. While all these factors have been the subject of data collection and analysis in the Housing Indicators Program, the focus here is on finance, specifically on a proxy measure for the availability of credit for housing finance: indicator 8, the housing credit portfolio. This indicator, in addition, measures the prominence of the housing finance system in the overall financial system and is thus of relevance at both the macroeconomic and the household level. It is defined as the ratio of total mortgage loans to all outstanding loans in both commercial and government financial institutions.

Significance
The housing credit portfolio (Table 5.4) is a measure of the relative size of the housing finance sector and its ability to provide households with the funds necessary to purchase housing. When housing credit forms only a small part of total credit, it is quite likely that the finance institutions face legal or institutional constraints that make it difficult for them to meet the demand for housing finance, resulting in shortage of mortgage financing for large segments of the urban population. The depth and strength of the housing credit portfolio are key elements in a well-functioning housing sector. Adequate financing is required to smooth housing consumption over time for consumers and to enable efficient land development and construction for producers.

This indicator is intended both to provide a proxy for access to housing finance by potential buyers of housing and to convey a sense of the importance of the housing finance system to the overall financial system. An alternative measure of access to finance was evaluated during the first

Table 5.4

Housing credit portfolio, 1900

	Housing credit (%)	ASEAN cities	Housing credit (%)
Sub-Saharan Africa	6.0	Jakarta	3.5
South Asia	3.0	Singapore	15.0
East Asia	6.0	Kuala Lumpur	22.0
Latin America	20.0	Bangkok	7.0
Europe, Middle East,		Manila	7.0
and North Africa	10.0		
Industrialized nations	25.0		
Global mean	15.0		

phase of the Housing Indicators Program, the credit to value ratio, which measures the share of annual investment in housing, financed by long-term formal credit. This indicator was, however, found to be less well related to a number of qualitative and quantitative housing outcomes than was the housing credit portfolio.

Despite the relevance of such data to an evaluation of either housing or financial policy, data on neither the housing credit portfolio nor the credit to value ratio have been regularly collected or published in statistical compendia of the housing sector.

Findings

The median reported value of the housing credit portfolio is 15 per cent, with a range of 1 to 50 per cent. Housing credit, as a proportion of the financial assets of a country's banking system, generally increases with economic development. Only 3 per cent of outstanding credit in the low-income countries is held in the form of housing loans, while the corresponding figure in high-income countries is 27 per cent. Variations within and among regions in the housing credit portfolio are considerable, reflecting a variety of market, institutional, and policy influences.

The prominence of housing loans in a country's banking system depends in part on institutional development in the sector. In preliminary analyses, the proportional allocation of assets towards housing loans is strongly influenced by an index that measures the depth of institutional development of housing finance after taking account of the level of economic development and the urban growth rate. Latin America, which has a rich set of financial institutions to deal with housing finance, has an unusually high share of the assets of its banking systems allocated to housing loans, with the median reported to be 21 per cent. Centrally planned economies, which have had neither market-based lending for housing nor market-oriented housing finance institutions, have smaller than expected portions of their financial assets invested in mortgage portfolios.

The housing credit portfolio varies widely among ASEAN cities. Singapore's portfolio is equal to the global median (15.0 per cent), and only Kuala Lumpur exceeds it (with 22.0 per cent). Jakarta, Manila, and Bangkok have lower than median rates (3.3, 7.0, and 7.0 respectively). But while the housing finance system in Jakarta is largely restricted to public institutions, which lend at highly subsidized interest rates (10 per cent below prime), the housing finance system in Bangkok has been growing since the mid-1980s at rates approaching 30 per cent per annum. The private sector has moved into mortgage lending and is presently providing loans at positive interest rates (0.8 per cent above prime). Lending in Kuala Lumpur is also at market rates (1.5 per cent above prime), while in Singapore it is managed by the public sector and is given at negative interest rates (1.7 per cent below prime but 0.5 per cent above the deposit rate).

The effectiveness of mortgage lending is strongly influenced by government regulation of financial institutions and by the strength of foreclosure proceedings. Where foreclosure is lax and slow, as in Jakarta and Manila, percentages of loans in arrears are high, reaching as high as 26 per cent in Manila. In Kuala Lumpur, where the foreclosure system is efficient, on the other hand, loans in arrears are as low as 10 per cent. Fear of arrears and defaults discourages financial intermediaries from lending to low-income people, particularly for housing, which is usually a non-recurrent loan.

The rapid growth of the housing credit portfolio in Bangkok has helped to increase housing production by increasing demand, but it has been able to do so only because housing supply in Bangkok is highly elastic. The same effect has not occurred in Malaysia in the mid-1980s, where supply-side obstacles have blocked the positive effects of injecting new housing finance and instead resulted in higher prices (Mayo et al. 1989).

Supply-Side Indicators

The performance of the housing delivery system depends critically on the performance of a number of different input markets (e.g., land, labour, and building materials) and on a public sector that provides both complementary services such as residential infrastructure and an appropriate and enabling regulatory environment. The Housing Indicators Program has examined indicators of each of these, but here we shall only discuss one. Indicator 9, the land development multiplier, is defined as the average ratio between the median land price of a developed plot at the urban fringe in a typical subdivision and the median price of raw, undeveloped land in an area currently being developed. It is capable of indicating both the efficiency of residential land markets and the adequacy of public provision of infrastructure.

Significance

The land development multiplier measures the premium for providing infrastructure *and* converting raw land to residential use on the urban fringe. It reflects in part the extent to which windfall profits exist in developing land for housing as the result of bottlenecks in infrastructure provision. It is thus an indirect measure not only of the availability of infrastructure but also of the complexity of the development process. It also measures indirectly the existence of monopolistic practices in residential land development. A high value for this indicator is often a sign of shortages of urbanized land for housing.

The indicator is an indirect measure of the supply of infrastructure for residential development. When adequate budgets are available for extending urban infrastructure, the land development multiplier should not be exceedingly large. Low levels of infrastructure expenditures result in land-supply bottlenecks and thus in higher prices for land and housing. They are also associated with inadequate provision of residential amenities, such as water, sewerage, drainage, and electricity, and in subsequent traffic congestion, all of which have a direct effect on the quality of housing.

An additional indicator for which data were also collected during the first phase of the Housing Indicators Program was the land conversion multiplier, which measures the premium associated with converting land from rural to urban use by obtaining the necessary zoning and planning permits. This indicator measures the extent to which regulations restricting urban development increase land costs by restricting land supply.

While this land conversion indicator was found, during the first phase of the Housing Indicators Program, to require a great deal of care in its construction and interpretation, it was also found to be a revealing and powerful measure of the overall performance of urban land markets.

Findings

The median reported value of the land development multiplier is 3.30, with a range from 1.1 to 20 (Table 5.5). The indicator generally declines with increasing economic development, suggesting that provision of serviced land is more responsive to demand in better-off countries. Even values of this indicator in its mid-range appear to indicate that premiums associated with the provision of serviced urban land are considerably higher than the actual cost of land servicing. The indicator reaches its highest values in Sub-Saharan Africa, where demographic pressures of housing demand are great and infrastructure investment and housing production lag demand. It is lowest in industrialized countries, where demand is relatively quiescent and infrastructure supply systems are responsive to market forces. Within regions, there is considerable variability in the land development multiplier, in several instances by a factor of six or seven. This appears likely to result from differences in demand pressures on land development, in infrastructure shortfalls, in infrastructure standards, and in regulatory impediments to land development.

Table 5.5

Land development multiplier

	Land development multiplier	ASEAN cities	Land development multiplier
Sub-Saharan Africa	6.63	Jakarta	2.20
South Asia	2.00	Singapore	1.30
East Asia	2.59	Kuala Lumpur	4.30
Latin America	3.44	Bangkok	2.60
Europe, Middle East, and North Africa	5.50	Manila	6.70
Industrialized nations	2.40		
Global mean	3.30		

The land development multiplier is especially high in Manila, at 6.70: 'Developed but vacant land was thus so scarce in Metro Manila that new and most remote sites could be sold for prices about two-thirds of those estimated for most of the metropolitan area.' (Strassmann, Blunt, and Tomas 1992, 8). It is also above the median in Kuala Lumpur, at 4.30, largely due to the difficulties of servicing land because of high standards and complex permit procedures. In Bangkok, where regulation is relatively smooth, it is much lower, at 2.60. It is also low in Jakarta (2.20) for similar reasons. For quite different reasons, however, it is lowest in Singapore (1.30), where the land-development process is predictable and market prices for public land acquisition are determined by the courts.

In Singapore, the premium associated with land development is very close to the cost of providing infrastructure. Where artificial shortages exist, as in Manila, profits from developing land far outweigh the cost of infrastructure provision. They should indeed act as a signal to develop more land, a signal that presently runs counter to new regulations restricting the transformation of agricultural land to urban use, which means that speculators owning large tracts of urban land have no particular incentive to release it for residential development.

A Framework for Policy Reform in ASEAN Cities
The picture that emerges of the housing sector in the ASEAN capitals is mixed. Singapore and Bangkok both have a strong and vibrant housing sector, but while the former is centrally managed by the public sector, the

latter is a prime example of minimal regulation of the private sector. All ASEAN countries except the Philippines have grown rapidly during the past decade, and growth has often translated into better housing-sector performance. Major differences in overall performance are discernible between the two weaker economies of Indonesia and the Philippines and the stronger economies of Singapore, Malaysia, and Thailand.

Preliminary analysis of the indicator data does not yet yield strong views on housing-policy recommendations for the ASEAN capitals. It is not clear, for example, whether Singapore's accomplishments in the sector have merited the high levels of savings, investment, and government attention required. Key performance indicators in Singapore are not surprisingly different from other countries on the same level of economic development. Thailand's housing sector has progressed rapidly, perhaps too rapidly, and at the expense of environmental amenities. Low levels of infrastructure provision and lack of public commitment to tax property and to alienate land for infrastructure and public services have resulted in housing of good quality but almost non-existent public goods associated with it, in terms of open space, mobility, clean air, drainage, and sewerage. In Malaysia, on the other hand, with a more developed tradition of planning and control of residential development, supply has been highly inelastic and unresponsive to demand and regulations have impeded development.

The path towards improved housing conditions in the region must be informed by an understanding of why the housing sector is performing as it is, and strategies for reform must attack the underlying causes of underperformance rather than simply deal with the symptoms. Underperformance of the housing sector in the ASEAN capitals is the product of both poverty and deliberate government policies. While the analysis of comparative performance presented here has begun to suggest some common themes in the region's poor housing-sector performance, it is clear that a good deal more research must be done to lay the foundation for national strategies for the sector.

The *Global Strategy for Shelter to the Year 2000* outlined a new approach to housing-sector policy that the countries of the region would do well to consider. This approach has also been suggested by the World Bank in a recently published housing policy paper entitled *Housing: Enabling Markets to Work* (World Bank 1993). That document stresses the important connections between housing and the broader economy and emphasizes that not only do macro-economic policies influence the performance of the housing sector in important ways but housing-sector policies can also have an important macro-economic impact.

The connection between macro-economic performance and housing-sector performance is seen clearly in the ASEAN capitals. Many, if not most, of the indicators of performance examined here are clearly related to levels of GNP per capita. With higher incomes and economic development in the region, it would be expected that housing conditions would surpass those of other regions. Thus it is clear that the major objectives for those concerned with housing conditions and housing-sector performance should be to support efforts to accelerate economic growth in the region and to ensure that housing policies are such that increased resources are translated as effectively as possible into improvements in housing-sector performance.

To ensure that housing policies are effective in translating resources into improved performance, enabling strategies should be devised to address three broad areas: stimulating effective housing demand, facilitating housing supply, and changing the institutional framework for managing the housing sector as a whole. As discussed in the World Bank housing policy paper, concern with these areas gives rise to seven key elements of an enabling strategy, to be evaluated in each country. Effective demand for housing can be increased through policies having to do with housing finance, property rights development, and targeted subsidies. Supply can be facilitated through policies having to do with infrastructure investment and maintenance, rationalizing the legal and regulatory framework, and ensuring that the building industry is competitive and efficient. Finally, the institutional framework for the housing sector can be improved by promoting institutional relationships that can manage the housing sector as a whole, paying attention to the interdependence of macro-economic and housing-sector policy and giving voice to all of the key participants in the housing sector. Although this chapter must stop short of examining in detail the applicability of each of these policy elements to the ASEAN countries, it has suggested that a number of the housing problems specific to the region are likely to be ameliorated by a more systematic attempt to design and implement such enabling strategies.

Notes

1 Other actors may be important in different institutional settings. Among the most important are non-government and community-based organizations, state-owned enterprises, and firms involved in real-estate brokerage. A more detailed breakdown will also need to take into account the different perspectives of specific government agencies, such as the land department or the fire department, and of various agents in the formal and informal housing delivery system.
2 Data for the year 1990 from World Bank (1992a), Table 31, pp. 278-9.
3 Preliminary data for 1990 are from the Extensive Survey of the Housing Indicators Program, as of November 1992. The data are being checked for accuracy and are subject to revision. Data presented without a source in the following sections are from the same source.

4 Data for 1990 from World Bank (1992a).
5 Interested readers may obtain data on the indicators not discussed in this chapter by contacting the authors.
6 The tables are based on data processed as of November 1992 and are subject to change.
7 The use of the house price to income ratio and the rent to income ratio as indicators of affordability presents many problems. They do not control for changes in the quality of the housing stock over time. In addition, the relationship between median home prices and median income does not account for actual financial constraints faced by home buyers. Further, the measures do not control for the impact of expected appreciation on housing cost increases. The median home price to median income measure ignores other components of housing costs, including mortgage interest rates and down payments, both of which fundamentally determine monthly payments. It also fails to control for locational variations in median income. See Linnemann and Megbolugbe (1992, 371). Moreover, the medians by themselves do not necessarily account for housing affordability by the lowest income groups, although regularities have been observed in several markets linking affordability across the income distribution to median incomes. These measures are, however, useful as diagnostic indications of possible affordability problems.
8 In several developed countries, where nearly all housing is formally built, data on housing starts, an alternative 'activity indicator,' are easily collected and are used extensively in both popular discussions of the state of the housing sector and sophisticated macroeconomic modelling efforts. In countries with an important informal housing sector, where much of the housing construction activity is officially unrecorded, housing starts data are difficult to collect, but housing completions can be ascertained using either sample surveys or aerial photography.

6

Housing Women Factory Workers in the Northern Corridor of the Bangkok Metropolitan Region

Yap Kioe Sheng and Aminur Rahman

The topic of housing for women factory workers in the northern corridor of the Bangkok Metropolitan Region is situated at the convergence of three distinct issues: housing for migrant workers, housing for women, and housing in desakota regions. Migrant workers are usually temporary migrants who move to a new location for purely economic reasons and intend to return home once they have saved sufficient money. They have a limited willingness to pay for housing and therefore often live in poor conditions. Women are seen either as daughters (who should live with their parents) or as wives (who should live with their husbands) and housing is therefore rarely available specifically for single women. However, women are likely to make more and different demands on housing than do men with regard to security, privacy, services, and so on, and their housing needs are thus more difficult to meet. Desakota regions are urbanizing areas along major corridors in the periphery of the city characterized by a mixture of agricultural and non-agricultural land uses. Because the regions are often not recognized as urban areas from an administrative point of view, they often lack the necessary urban infrastructure, including housing.

The province of Pathum Thani, which forms the northern part of the Bangkok Metropolitan Region, is such a desakota area. It is an extension of the Bangkok metropolitan area, about 50 km from the centre of Bangkok, and contains the northern corridor of Bangkok. The region is experiencing rapidly dwindling agriculture and rapid industrialization by often high-technology industries employing thousands of workers, a majority of them young women from the rural areas. This chapter discusses the housing conditions and housing demand of these women factory workers.[1]

The Bangkok Metropolitan Region

Since 1986, Thailand has experienced unprecedented economic growth, which has transformed the country from an agricultural into an industrial economy. In 1986, agriculture, fisheries, and forestry products accounted for 41 per cent of the total value of exports, and manufactured products accounted for 55 per cent. In 1991, manufactured goods formed 75 per cent of all exports, and basic agricultural, fishery, and forestry products accounted for 21 per cent. Over the past years, the real gross domestic product (GDP) has risen by an average of over 11 per cent per year in absolute terms (*Far Eastern Economic Review,* 20 August 1992, p. 44).

This development had several causes. First, the depreciation of the baht improved the competitiveness of Thai exports. Second, Thailand benefited from a rapid increase in foreign investments from Japan, South Korea, Taiwan, Hong Kong, and Singapore in response to sharply rising prices of the currencies and labour in those countries. Third, investors were attracted by the low wages, low taxes and tax concessions for foreign investors, lenient regulations, and stable economic and political system. Moreover, Thai workers have a reputation for diligence, dexterity, and trainability (*Bangkok Post,* 15 October 1991).

The national economic growth of the past years is concentrated in and around Bangkok. Within the Bangkok Metropolitan Region, the annual growth of manufacturing establishments in the period 1985-7 was the highest in Samut Prakan and Pathum Thani: 10.0 and 13.6 per cent respectively (Lee Kyu Sik 1988, 3). These two provinces, to the southeast and north of Bangkok (see Map 6.1), have evolved as major new economic growth centres with large-scale manufacturing plants creating the majority of the new employment opportunities. Pathum Thani has 43.2 per cent of the manufacturing employment in the Bangkok Metropolitan Region, the second highest after Samut Prakan (Iqbal 1990, 6). As a result, the average GDP per capita in Greater Bangkok reached Baht 96,000 ($3,780) in 1989, while it was Baht 32,000 for Thailand as a whole and just under Baht 12,000 in the northeast, where 37 per cent of Thailand's population lives.

Economic development has been accompanied by a rapid urbanization of the fringes of Bangkok, which now extend far beyond the provincial boundaries of the Bangkok Metropolitan Administration into the adjacent provinces of Nonthaburi, Pathum Thani, Samut Prakan, Samut Sakhon, and Nakhon Pathom, this entire area constituting the Bangkok Metropolitan Region (Map 6.1). The 1990 census estimates the population of Bangkok proper – the area under the jurisdiction of the Bangkok Metropolitan Administration (BMA) – at 1.3 million households or 5.876 million persons.

Industrial and urban development is occurring mainly along the highways leading north, southeast, and southwest, because these corridors have access to Bangkok, its port, its airport, and other industrial centres.

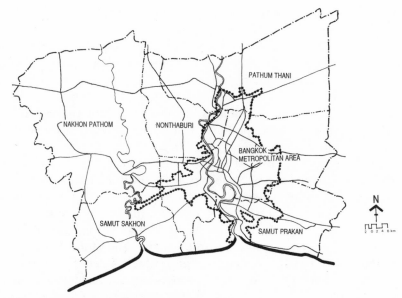

Map 6.1 **Bangkok Metropolitan Region**

Development is the aggregate outcome of location decisions of individual firms in response to operations of the land market and other markets rather than to explicit spatial policies such as DTCP plans or incentive schemes of the Board of Investment (Lee Kyu Sik 1988, 3). However, most of these areas have no piped water supply, no sewerage system, no solid waste collection, and only limited transport services and housing, and they are often outside the jurisdiction of any municipal authority.

Pathum Thani

According to unpublished results of the 1990 population census, Pathum Thani had 412,407 inhabitants, of whom only 14,359 lived in a municipal area: Pathum Thani town. Employment in Pathum Thani increased from 97,000 in 1960 to 167,000 in 1980 and 236,000 in 1984 (Dowall and Kritayanavaj 1987, 8.8). One-third of the 765 factories in Pathum Thani province and 108 of the 154 large factories (more than 200 workers and more than Baht 100 million capital) are located in the district of Klong Luang. The majority of the factory workers in Pathum Thani (64.2 per cent) are also employed in Klong Luang district (Iqbal 1990, 7).

Pathum Thani, and in particular Klong Luang district, attracts many industrial companies, since land is still relatively inexpensive and access to Bangkok is ensured by the highway from Bangkok to the north and northeast. Pathum Thani now has three industrial estates promoted by the Board of Investment, with a total area of 7,000 rai and an investment of Baht 1,979 million at the end of 1990 (*Bangkok Post* 1991, 65). There are another four industrial estates north of Pathum Thani, in the provinces of Ayuthaya and Saraburi. As mentioned in Chapter 4, the most important industrial estate in Pathum Thani is the privately owned and developed Nava Nakorn Industrial Estate, located at the northern tip of the northern corridor (Map 6.2). Originally intended as a new town, Nava Nakorn now has 180 factories with a combined investment of Baht 16,050 million employing almost 54,000 persons. It holds a long waiting list of new applicants, mostly from foreign countries.

A 1990 survey of registered industries indicated that 281 factories in Klong Luang employed 63,712 workers, while the district had only 63,932 inhabitants. Since 1980, the number of factories increased by 113 per cent and the workforce increased by 66 per cent. In 1990, the garment and weaving industry was the largest sector, with forty factories, followed by the electric appliances industry, with thirty-two. The garment and weaving industry had 23,517 workers (36.9 per cent of the industrial workforce in Klong Luang), and the electric appliances industry had 9,645 workers, or 15.4 per cent of the industrial workforce (Iqbal 1990, 24-5).

Incomplete data about the gender of the workforce in the northern corridor show that out of a partial workforce of 39,838, about 75 per cent were women. Six sectors had a majority of women in the labour force: garments (95.7 per cent), leather (92.1 per cent), instruments (86.1 per cent), shoes (80.5 per cent), appliances (80.0 per cent), and weaving (74.9 per cent) (Iqbal 1990, 27-8). The presence of a large female workforce in the industry in Pathum Thani and Klong Luang is only to some extent reflected in the population figures for the area. In 1989, Klong Luang had a population of 63,932: 32,957 women and 31,217 men. The sex ratio was 94.7 (Iqbal 1990, 6). The preliminary data of the 1990 census indicate that the sex ratio in the district of Klong Luang was 86.3, while that for the 15-24 age group was 69.3; for those living in collective housing like dormitories, the sex ratio was 36.3 for Klong Luang.

The literature gives various reasons for the preference of factories to recruit (young) women. It is often assumed that factories hire women because they are considered more willing than men to accept the low wages and poor working conditions that characterize employment in the factories. In fact, they may be more militant than men. There are also indications that factories simply follow a stereotype that women are more patient and nimble and therefore more suitable to do delicate work (Narayanan and Kimura 1992, 141-8; Porpora, Lim, and Prommas 1989, 283-8; Porpora, Lim, and Prommas 1992, 149-53). In the survey conducted by the authors, factory managers expressed a preference for unmarried women workers because they are more reliable, since they do

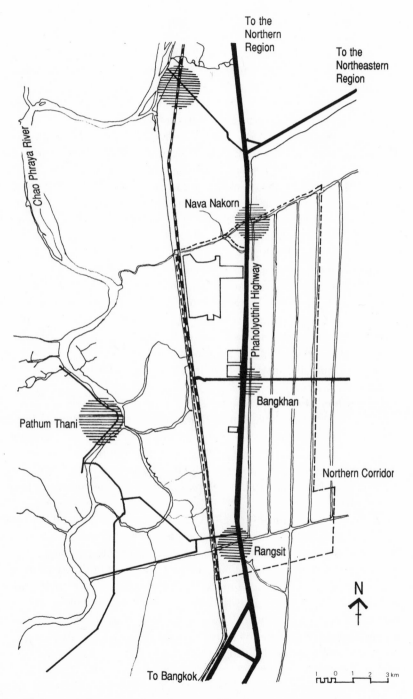

Map 6.2 **Strategic location of northern corridor.** Based on Foo (1992b)

not have to look after their husbands and children and are not expected to become pregnant.

The demand for young women by the industry can only be met because of a large migration to Bangkok of young women. The sex ratio of migrants to Bangkok has changed in recent years from a male-dominated flow to a 3:2 preponderance of women. Migration by women to urban areas is particularly high among young adults. Although many women migrate to Bangkok with no assured employment, very few remain unemployed and those unable to find work probably return home (Arnold and Piampiti 1984, 149-57). Research among textile factory workers showed that the primary motivation to migrate to Bangkok was the desire to save money and help with family support. The sense of filial obligation seemed stronger among women than among men, and women accordingly remit a higher portion of their wages to their parents than do men (Porpora, Lim, and Prommas 1989, 278-83).

Most women intend to return home after a certain time, but a large proportion does not know what the length of stay in Bangkok will be. If everything goes well and the woman can adjust to the different lifestyle in the city, she may spend considerable time in Bangkok and even make it her permanent home. If not, she will return to her place of origin (Arnold and Piampiti 1984, 150-1). The implication is, however, that she will not be prepared to make any long-term investment in housing.

Industrialists' Housing Options

The large number of workers in Pathum Thani needs to be housed, but the province has only two urban centres: Rangsit and Pathum Thani town. The former was until recently a predominantly commercial area; the latter, the provincial capital and the only municipal area of the province, is located away from industrial development, on the other side of the Chao Phraya river.

Because housing conditions affect the health and thereby the productivity of the workers, a factory may have an interest in providing housing to its workforce. A factory may build housing inside the factory compound or buy or rent housing outside the compound but close to the factory. If the factory does not provide housing for its workers or if workers do not like to live in company housing, the workers will have to find their own accommodation and this will result in a demand for inexpensive rental rooms and apartments in and around the factory. Workers may not be able to find suitable housing nearby, however, and will have to travel longer distances. Because public transport is limited, the companies will provide buses to make sure that workers arrive in time for work and to minimize absenteeism. Given the high number of factories within a relatively small area and the large number of workers, commuting by company bus will contribute greatly to the already serious traffic congestion on the highway. So, industrialists appear to have a number of options.

Dormitories on the Factory Compound

When the first factories were established in Pathum Thani, the area was not yet urbanized and companies were able to purchase large plots of land. One company in the Bangkhan area of Klong Luang bought its land in 1970 for Baht 180,000 per rai; it estimates the current land price at Baht 6 million per rai. Apart from the factory complex, the company built six blocks of dormitories: four three-storey wooden dormitories with twenty-six rooms each over two floors, one double-storey wooden dormitory with ten rooms per floor, and one three-storey concrete dormitory with thirteen rooms per floor. The rooms are about 45 m² each.

The four three-storey buildings are occupied by an average of four women per room; the other two dormitories are occupied two or three men per room. The occupants of several rooms share bathing and toilet facilities located on the same floor. The workers do not pay for their accommodation and can select their own roommates. They are not allowed to cook in the room. The factory has a cafeteria with a telephone booth and recreation facilities such as sport fields. Water and electricity supply for the workers is free; cleaners employed by the company service the rooms.

Only 618 out of the 1,095 workers in this factory (56 per cent) live in the dormitories. Women workers seem to be more inclined than the men to live in the factory housing. While 70 per cent of the workforce are women, they form 75 per cent of the occupants of the dormitories. With two or three persons per room, the dormitories for men also appear to be underoccupied. Among ten workers interviewed, however, two were married to co-workers but lived in separate dormitories since there are no married quarters (Changani 1976, 24).

The advantage of on-site dormitory housing for the factory is the short distance between residence and workplace, resulting in greater punctuality, lower levels of absenteeism, greater control by the factory of the workers, and the possibility to engage the workers in overtime and shift work. Disadvantages are the investments in buildings and land and the cost and problems of managing dormitories for a large number of persons (Changani 1976, 54).

Housing outside the Factory Compound but inside the Estate

The more recently established factories are mainly situated in industrial estates, where all the necessary infrastructure is available but land is more expensive. Housing is not allowed inside the factory compound. The Nava Nakorn Industrial Estate has allocated 837 rai of its land for public- and private-sector housing.

In 1982, the National Housing Authority bought 20 rai of land in the estate for low-income rental housing. Since then, it has constructed four blocks of five-storey walk-up apartment buildings with a total of 756 rental units, while two new blocks with 324 units for sale at prices between Baht 300,000 and Baht 400,000 per unit have just been completed. Each unit consists of one multipurpose room with an attached toilet/bathroom and a balcony. The floor area per unit is about 25 m^2 (7.2 x 3.5 m). The official rents of the rental units range from Baht 700 to Baht 850 per month excluding water (about Baht 70 per month) and electricity (about Baht 100 per month). The Nava Nakorn Industrial Estate is responsible for cleaning the estate, while the National Housing Authority collects the rent and carries out the maintenance. About thirty factories rent approximately 400 units for their workers on a permanent basis, while about 300 units are rented to individuals and households.

Two private companies have constructed rowhouses, townhouses, shophouses, and semi-detached houses in the Nava Nakorn estate. The houses were obviously intended for middle- and high-income households whose income earners would be employed in the estate, but such people prefer and can afford to live outside the estate and many of the units have been rented or bought by house groups of factory workers. The shortage of inexpensive housing in the estate seems to be so serious that the owners (or main renters) of the houses have built temporary structures behind the houses for rent to factory workers. The Nava Nakorn Industrial Estate estimates that some 30,000 people live in Nava Nakorn, but due to the housing shortage, factories also rent or buy housing outside the estate.

Company Rental Housing outside the Estate

In the past few years, developers have started to build large numbers of shophouses and some low-cost condominiums in the Klong Luang district. In his study of low-cost condominiums in the northern corridor, Foo identified six such condominiums (those with units costing less than Baht 300,000) in the area between Nava Nakorn Industrial Estate and Rangsit town. All units had a single multipurpose room, a toilet/bathroom, and a balcony. The room sizes ranged from 23 m^2 to 36 m^2. The condominiums are usually five-storey walk-up buildings, and prices range from Baht 250,000 to Baht 450,000 per unit depending on location and floor level. Few low-income households seem to be willing or able to buy this type of housing. In many condominium buildings, however, some units are occupied by employees of a company that rents several units or even one or more floors. The units are shared by groups of four to six workers.

Similar situations can be found in shophouses and other residential buildings. Sometimes, the factory company rents a building, including its management, as a dormitory. The manager is either the owner of the building or a separate company. Units of 15-18 m² in such buildings cost about Baht 1,500 to Baht 1,800 per month. The company pays the rent for the workers or the workers pay Baht 50 to Baht 100 to the company for the accommodation. Three to four workers share one room.

A company usually rents accommodation only for those persons working in shifts. Company buses can bring the night-shift workers to certain drop-off points, but the workers would not be able to go home, as there is no public transport at that time. For such workers, the companies have dormitories in and around Rangsit. Since company policy dictates that workers can only do shifts for seven to ten days per month, the dormitories may have different occupants at different times. In many factories, only a part of the workforce works in shifts. They are usually the unskilled daily labourers with low salaries, and they are responsible for the most simple parts of the production process: assembly, packing, and so on. Skilled workers tend to be older, to have permanent contracts, and to have higher base salaries. They are less inclined to do overtime or shift work because they have higher incomes and work more regular hours. Because they are older, they are more likely to be married and to have children, and they therefore do not like to spend the night in a factory dormitory. They take the bus home in the afternoon.

Bussing

Some companies do not consider it their responsibility to provide accommodation to their workforce. The management of these companies stated that it was too cumbersome and costly to manage dormitories. Because there is insufficient public transport, they run a fleet of buses to bring the workers in the morning from certain points in the region to the factory and to bring them back in the afternoon. The buses usually cover not only the province of Pathum Thani but also Bangkok, Nonthaburi, and Ayuthaya. The buses leave from several places in Bangkok (such as Victory Monument, Lard Prao) at 6:15 or 6:30 in the morning and drive on the highway to pick up the workers who wait along the road. They also bring the middle-level staff living in Bangkok. Small buses and pick-up trucks bring the workers from within Pathum Thani and from Ayuthaya. Every day between 2:30 and 6:30 P.M., an average of 325 buses with a seating capacity of sixty persons each leave the main gate of the Nava Nakorn Industrial Estate.

One of the companies in Nava Nakorn Industrial Estate surveyed for this study has 1,200 workers and 200 administrative and other staff. It rents ten buses with a seating capacity of sixty persons for the day-shift workers: four buses for Bangkok, three for Pathum Thani, two for Ayuthaya, and one for Nonthaburi. The buses from Bangkok leave at 5:30 in the morning and reach Nava Nakorn at 7:30; they leave Nava Nakorn at 5:00 P.M. and complete their trip at 7:30 in the evening. The company also has ten pick-up trucks with a capacity of thirty persons for day-shift workers. The trucks go twice a day to eight destinations within Pathum Thani. Finally, there are four buses/pick-up trucks with thirty-person capacity which shuttle between the factory and the two company houses in Nava Nakorn and Rangsit three times a day for the morning-, evening-, and night-shift workers. The company spends Baht 34,600 per day on transportation: Baht 15,000 for ten buses, Baht 10,000 for ten pick-up trucks, and Baht 9,600 for four buses/pick-up trucks. In other words, it spends Baht 25 per day per worker on transportation and rents one bus for each fifty-eight workers.

Factory Workers' Housing Options

Workers who are not provided with housing by the factory or do not want to live in factory dormitories have to find their own housing. Two categories of women workers can be distinguished: unmarried and married. The young, unmarried women workers, who have often recently arrived from up-country, have two considerations when they decide where to live: cost and proximity to work. The women want to spend as little as possible on housing in order to save as much as possible. Living near the factory keeps transportation cost to a minimum and makes it easier to do overtime and shift work. For married women, the family is an additional consideration.

A survey of low-income housing opportunities in the Bangkhan area of Pathum Thani (Sheikh 1991) found a wide range of rental housing types. These included rooms (housing units in which occupants share water supply, toilet, and bathroom facilities with occupants of other units) and apartments (self-contained units with own bathroom/toilet and water supply) in both wooden and concrete structures (Angel and Amtapunth 1987, 4.12). Many of the structures are situated in informal land subdivisions consisting of unfilled plots serviced by paved or unpaved raised roads, well water, and electricity supply. Informal subdivisions utilize a loophole in the law that exempts a subdivision with nine plots or less from adherence to the minimum requirements for land subdivisions. In this way, it is possible for the subdivider to provide a minimum level of infrastructure (Angel and Pornchokchai 1987, 4.6-7).

The rental rooms are often constructed by a factory employee who has bought and occupied a plot of land in the subdivision. When such workers discover the high demand for low-cost accommodation, they construct eight to twelve rooms in a row, with their own room(s) as the first unit. Many such structures are single storey; others have two or more. The owner, who usually lives in the same or an adjacent building, often rents the rooms to workers employed in the same factory.

The availability of transport services to and from the factory determines to a large extent where workers can live. The two main forms of transport are company buses and public buses. All factories are located right on the highway or in an industrial estate; the best location for housing is therefore also along or immediately off the highway. The company and public buses pass on the highway and the worker can walk to the highway or take a motorcycle-taxi for Baht 3 per trip. Research in the Bangkhan area showed that workers like to stay as close as possible to the highway to avoid having to pay for the motorcycle. If workers live farther away from the bus route (as will usually be the case if they live in Bangkok itself), they will need to take public transport to reach the collection point of the company bus and this increases their transportation cost and travel time.

Rental Rooms and Apartments in Concrete Structures

The concrete structures usually have two floors and eight to sixteen units. Rents in the Bangkhan area ranged from Baht 800 per month for units in very simple buildings to Baht 1,200 for apartments in quite luxurious buildings. Rooms in the luxurious concrete structures were originally intended for factory workers but are now almost exclusively occupied by those students of Thammasat and Bangkok University who can afford such rents. The units have floor areas ranging from 12 (3 m x 4 m) to 40 m^2. All units have separate electricity meters and occupants pay about Baht 50 to Baht 100 per month for electricity. The cost of water depends on the number of occupants in the room but usually amounts to Baht 50 to 100 per month per room. The average income of factory workers in the concrete buildings was Baht 4,250 per month.

Rental Rooms in Wooden Structures

Units in the wooden structures have floor areas of 9 (3 m x 3 m) to 15 (2.5 m x 6 m) m^2. Most wooden buildings are single-storey structures found in the informal subdivisions and in slum and squatter areas. Rooms in the wooden structures cost Baht 500 to 600 per month excluding services. Water and electricity charges depend on the number of persons in the room, but average charges are Baht 50 to Baht 100 per month per room. Water comes from a deep well, while the toilet is a soakpit. Almost all occupants are factory workers; many are young women (with an average age of twenty-two) who share the room and rent with their friends from the factory or with their husbands or boyfriends. Occupants' income is Baht 2,750 per person per month. The workers take the company bus at the highway to go to work.

Slums and Squatter Settlements

In February 1991, the governor of the National Housing Authority proposed to 'make it mandatory for investors to provide housing for workers employed in new factories to be set up in economic zones and private industrial estates' (*Bangkok Post,* 26 February 1991). In her opinion, investors should be required to build workers' housing as part of investment in new factories to prevent slums from springing up in new economic zones, since factories and slums usually exist side by side. It is unclear if the governor included the informal subdivisions in her definition of slums. Identification of slums by the National Housing Authority is based on aerial photographs and the wooden structures in informal subdivisions may look like a slum settlement on an aerial photograph.

A survey by the National Housing Authority in 1988 identified 1,442 informal settlements with a population of 1.1 million in the Bangkok Metropolitan Region (Bangkok, Nonthaburi, Samut Prakan, and Pathum Thani). Slum dwellers represent about 14 per cent of the total population of these four provinces. Although Bangkok still has the highest number of informal settlements (1,032) and slum dwellers (852,500 persons), there was a marked shift of informal settlements from Bangkok to the surrounding provinces between 1984 and 1988. In 1984, Bangkok had 1,113 informal settlements, Samut Prakan 144, Nonthaburi 54, and Pathum Thani 25. In 1988, the number of informal settlements in Bangkok had decreased to 1,049, while in Samut Prakan, Nonthaburi, and Pathum Thani, the numbers had increased to 278, 93, and 44 respectively. In 1988, the informal settlements in Pathum Thani housed some 25,000 persons (Yap 1992, 31-48).

Within the informal settlements, there is definitely rental housing: wooden structures with several rooms occupied by unrelated groups of single factory workers. However, this study did not find evidence that factory workers have developed informal settlements in Pathum Thani on a large scale. Small surveys of slums and squatter settlements in the Bangkhan area showed that this type of housing is mainly occupied by extended families, whereas the factory workers are predominantly young, unmarried women. A daughter, son, or daughter- or son-in-law of a family in a slum may work in a nearby factory, but the head of household is not employed in the industrial sector. The average monthly income of a household in a slum or squatter settlement is higher than that of a factory worker (Baht 7,000 and Baht 4,500 respectively), but per capita incomes are lower in the slums and squatter areas.

Low-Cost Condominiums, Shophouses, and Public Housing
In the past few years, the private sector has gradually moved its housing development activities into areas of Pathum Thani. In Rangsit, and even as far north as Bangkhan, it is building low-cost condominiums. Although some factory workers could afford this kind of housing (in particular working couples with double salaries), there is no evidence that they buy it. However, 40 per cent of the households occupying units in the condominiums consisted of unrelated members; among the renters, the figure was 45.5 per cent. About half of such households were students and the other half were workers, many of them production process workers in the manufacturing industry. The average income of the non-student renters was Baht 4,431 per month; the average rent for the units was Baht 1,421 per month. The study does not make clear who the owners or primary renters of the condominium units are, but they are likely to be factories in the northern corridor that use the units to house their workers. Some shophouse owners, on the other hand, subdivide their property and rent it directly to workers and students in the Klong Luang area.

As explained earlier, the National Housing Authority has four blocks of rental apartments inside the Nava Nakorn Industrial Estate. The occupancy rate in the estate is 100 per cent and there is a long waiting list because the turnover is very slow, about ten to fifteen units per year. Subletting and sharing accommodation are officially not allowed, but they appear to be common practice. In fact, intermediaries seem to have a hold on many, if not most, of the units in the estate and they sublet these to factories and individuals or families for an average rent of Baht 2,000 per unit or Baht 500 per person. The units are occupied by either families or groups of four to six young factory workers who share the rent.

Housing Conditions and Housing Demand
The authors conducted a survey among 261 women working in large factories in the Klong Luang District of Pathum Thani. The women, who had an average age of 25.1, came from all regions of Thailand: 33.2 per cent from the Northeast, 30.9 per cent from the Central Region (including 11.1 per cent from Ayuthaya), 15.4 per cent from the North, and 15.4 per cent from the Bangkok Metropolitan Region (11.9 per cent from Pathum Thani and 3.5 per cent from Bangkok); and the remainder from the South and the East. Of all respondents, 100 women (38.3 per cent) lived in housing provided by the factory and 161 (61.7 per cent) had made their own housing arrangements.

Many women said that they wanted housing at low cost and near to their place of work. In this respect, they all liked company housing. It was usually rent free, and if the dormitory was not near to the factory, a company bus would take them to work. Nonetheless, the major problem of factory housing was that the women could not receive relatives and friends and that if they were married, they could not live with their families. The majority of women in the survey were single (68.6 per cent); the rest were either married (28.7 per cent) or widowed, separated, or divorced (2.7 per cent). Only fourteen women who were married or had been married lived in factory housing, whereas 48.0 per cent of all single women (eighty-six) lived in factory housing.

The women in factory housing were slightly younger (23.3 years) than those in their own housing (26.3 years); they had a lower monthly income (Baht 4,277 versus Baht 4,814); they had arrived more recently in 'Bangkok' (3.7 years versus 5.6 years); and they had not worked in the factory as long (2.5 years versus 3.3 years). Even so, it appears that neither income nor time spent in 'Bangkok' or in the factory were as important as the fact that there was no factory housing for married couples.

The majority of the women (72.2 per cent) were permanently employed by the company; the others were daily labourers, although some had been working with the factory for a long time. The average income of the permanently employed, including overtime and shift work, was Baht 4,755 per month and that of the daily labourers was Baht 4,059 per month. The base salary of the daily labourers was much lower than that of the permanently employed (Baht 3,280 versus Baht 4,083 per month), but they did more overtime and shift work (Baht 778 versus Baht 672 per month). Many daily labourers (54.9 per cent) lived in factory housing and thus could do overtime work. Only 33.2 per cent of the permanently employed lived in factory housing. Companies are said to avoid having large numbers of permanently employed workers living in one place, as it facilitates unionization. They do not run that risk with daily labourers, who can be dismissed more easily (Fairclough 1992, 22).

All factory housing was located in the province of Pathum Thani, but women workers who did not have company-provided housing lived in four provinces: Pathum Thani (61.1 per cent), Bangkok (21.7 per cent), Ayuthaya (15.3 per cent), and Nonthaburi (1.9 per cent). One-way commuting times ranged from less than five minutes to more than two hours. Workers living in factory housing had an average commuting time of 15 minutes. Workers who had their own housing arrangements had to spend much more time: those living in Pathum Thani spent on average 30 minutes, those in Ayuthaya 45 minutes, those in Bangkok 81 minutes, and those in Nonthaburi 107 minutes. Commuting times to Bangkok and Nonthaburi are long because company buses will bring the workers only to selected places in the city or the province, and the workers often have to take one or more public buses to reach home.

The quality of the factory housing is good. Almost all women lived in concrete structures. Only three women lived in factory housing made of concrete and wood, in older dormitories constructed more than ten years ago by the companies in the factory compound. The housing conditions of the women who did not live on factory housing were more varied: 42.5 per cent lived in wooden structures, 35.0 per cent in concrete structures, and 21.9 per cent in structures of wood and concrete. One respondent said she lived in housing made of secondhand materials.

Not all factory housing was rent free; half of the workers paid a small rent to the company. The average rent paid for factory housing was Baht 75 per month. The rents paid by the women who did not live in company housing varied widely, from Baht 500 to Baht 4,000 per month. The average monthly rents were Baht 590 for a room in a wooden structure, Baht 673 for a room in a structure of wood and concrete, and Baht 728 for a room in a concrete structure.

A study on housing conditions of industrial workers conducted in 1976 among factories in Pathum Thani and Samut Prakan showed that women workers living in dormitories were generally satisfied with the accommodation; it was cheap and near the work place, which allowed them to do overtime work and thereby earn more money. The satisfaction was, however, higher among women who had come from the rural areas. Women from Bangkok were generally looking for alternative housing, while others were not (Changani 1976, 45-51). In 1976, unlike today, there may not have been any suitable alternative housing in these areas.

Conclusions

According to McGee (1989b, 15), desakota regions like Pathum Thani are cheap labour reservoirs waiting to be tapped by state, international, and capital investment because of insufficient employment in agriculture for the growing population. Industry provides alternative employment, in particular for women, who can no longer find an income in agriculture. While some conditions in Pathum Thani may be conducive for industrial development – less expensive land and lack of regulations – it does not seem to have had a sufficiently large labour reserve waiting to be tapped. The majority of the women workers (88.1 per cent) do not originate from the province. If the desakota region is extended to include not only Pathum Thani but the entire Central Region as well, 42.8 per cent of the workers originate from this region; but this may stretch the concept of desakota too far.

McGee (p. 17) points out that the desakota regions are characterized by a great mobility of the population, made possible by cheap means of transportation such as motorcycles, pick-up trucks, and buses. The implication seems to be that the industrial sector can draw workers from among a large population in a vast desakota region because cheap transport is available. Housing would not be an issue and is therefore largely ignored. Workers can live at home and take cheap means of transport to the factory, while other members of their household work the land or are employed in other non-agricultural sectors.

This is true for Pathum Thani only to a limited extent. Only 36.5 per cent of the workers originate from Pathum Thani, Bangkok, or Ayuthaya, and they may live at home. All others need to find accommodation; they create an additional demand for housing, of a specific type in a particular location. Buses, pick-up trucks, and motorcycles make it possible for factory workers to work in Pathum Thani and to live anywhere from Bangkok to Ayuthaya, but in practice they can only live in a narrow strip along the highway, the northern corridor. Otherwise, they have to rely on public transport to reach the company bus stop, increasing costs and travel time. Moreover, the river and canals severely limit accessibility to the east and west of Pathum Thani.

Housing in the factory compound is no longer a feasible option due to the increasing land prices and the relatively high management costs. Moreover, there is a rapid increase in 100 per cent foreign-owned firms, which may prefer to keep their investments in property to a minimum in order to maintain mobility. New companies only provide housing to workers who cannot return home after the night shift. Many factory workers find accommodation in rental rooms in informal land subdivisions. Such usually small subdivisions are developed along the highway, a suitable location for the workers but an extremely inefficient form of land use.

The only means of transport available for the workers housed in this extended strip of land between Bangkok and Ayuthaya is the bus. Because it is important for factories that workers arrive on time, the companies have to rent a large fleet of buses to bring workers to the factory. Given the distance and the traffic congestion, commuting times of up to two hours per day are normal and the buses make a considerable contribution to the traffic congestion on the highway and in Bangkok.

The first and not surprising conclusion of this study is that lack of planning of the rapid urban development in the fringe areas of the Bangkok Metropolitan Region has caused considerable waste of resources. Land is developed inefficiently, employment is created without due consideration for worker housing, and the resulting large-scale commuting over long distances generates traffic congestion, high fuel consumption, and air pollution. The unplanned development is partly due to a lack of recognition that such corridors are urban areas and partly to a lack of administrative control.

The second conclusion is that the specific housing demand by companies and factory workers is insufficiently met by either the public or the private sector. This becomes clear from the extent of unofficial rents and subletting in the estate of the National Housing Authority in Nava Nakorn. Companies would obviously prefer their workforce to live near the factory or at least in easily accessible locations. They want to rent buildings, or floors or units in buildings, to house parts of their workforce. The workers want housing at low rents near the factory. The type of housing that both the companies and the workers prefer are rental rooms or apartments where groups of three to six workers can be housed.

Currently, the main supplier of inexpensive rental rooms and apartments is the informal private sector, but the supply is limited, the quality sometimes poor, and the small informal subdivisions along the highway make efficient land use problematic. The formal private sector supplies shophouses and condominiums intended for middle-class purchasers but the shortage of worker housing means that the shophouses are converted into dormitories and condominium units are rented out to workers. It seems that an increased supply of rental housing within Pathum Thani and within the context of a proper planning of the area could result in a more efficient use of resources.

Note

1 This study of housing for women factory workers in Pathum Thani is part of a larger study on low-income rental and rent-free housing in Bangkok funded by the International Development Research Centre (IDRC) of Canada (Yap, De Wandeler, and Khanaiklang, in preparation). The data for the larger study on factory workers' housing were collected in two stages: by students of the Division of Human Settlements Development at the Asian Institute of Technology during the first months of 1991 (Sheikh 1991), and by Aminur Rahman for his MSc thesis during May-June and October-November 1992. Rahman's study was funded by Canadian International Development Agency (CIDA).

The information on women workers is based on a preliminary interpretation of Rahman's findings. Sampling and data collection for the study were seriously affected by an extreme reluctance on the part of the company managers to cooperate: in May and June 1992, workers in several factories in Nava Nakorn were on strike; in October 1992, non-governmental organizations were active in Pathum Thani trying to unionize factory workers. The authors would like to thank the management and workers of the companies that allowed surveyors in their compounds and housing for their cooperation.

7
Moving Goods, People, and Information: Putting the ASEAN Mega-Urban Regions in Context
Peter J. Rimmer

'The development of expanded metropolitanized zones of settlement and economic activity has been made possible by a transportation revolution over the last thirty years or so that is fundamentally "low-tech" rather than "high-tech"' (Ginsburg 1991a, 37).

By the year 2000, ASEAN will have an estimated population of 338 million, 34 per cent of whom will be in urban areas. By then, there will be six centres with populations in excess of 2 million: the larger metropolitan centres of Jakarta, Manila, Bangkok, and Singapore, together with Surabaya and Medan (Table 7.1). If the boundaries of ASEAN are extended to encompass Vietnam and Burma, both Ho Chi Minh City and Yangon would be included.

Paradoxically, Kuala Lumpur is excluded from this list. Such an anomaly highlights the inadequacy of concentrating on ASEAN mega-cities; the agglomerations defined by the United Nations in its *Prospects for World Urbanization 1988* are underbounded and omit significant urban populations (United Nations, Department of International Economic and Social Affairs 1989). This problem has prompted Ginsburg, Koppel, and McGee (1991) to shift to the concept of mega-urban regions, which are much larger spatially and have greater populations. They comprise central cities, their 'fringe areas ... exurbs, satellite towns, and extensive intervening areas of dense population and intensive traditional agricultural uses' (Ginsburg 1991b, xiii).

Following McGee (1991), five mega-urban regions have been identified in ASEAN. Three different categories can be recognized:
(1) the high-density variant typified by Jabotabek, Metro Manila, and the Extended Bangkok Metropolitan Region
(2) the low-density type characterized by the Klang Valley (covering the Kuala Lumpur conurbation, Shah Alam, and Klang), in which growth has occurred through a polynucleated pattern of small towns and smaller suburban centres located on major arterial roads

(3)   the cross-border variant exemplified by Singapore, in which the
dominant node spreads its economic and social activities into adjacent areas with differing factor costs.

Table 7.1

**Urban agglomerations with populations of 2 million or more, 1985, and
average growth rate, 1970-2000**

World rank in 1985	Agglomeration	Population (millions)			Average annual growth rate (%)	
		1970	1985	2000	1970-85	1985-2000
19	Jakarta	4.32	7.79	13.23	3.93	3.53
22	Metro Manila	3.53	7.09	11.48	4.65	3.21
26	Bangkok	3.11	5.86	10.26	4.22	3.73
64	Ho Chi Minh	2.00	2.78	4.42	2.20	3.09
67	Yangon	1.43	2.71	4.45	4.26	3.31
79	Singapore	1.56	2.56	2.95	3.30	0.95
85	Surabaya	1.47	2.32	3.67	3.04	3.06
98	Medan	0.61	2.05	5.36	8.08	6.41

Source: United Nations (1989)

As secondary and intermediate cities in ASEAN are not well developed,
these mega-urban regions dominate their respective urban hierarchies.
The conventional reaction of Western-trained planners to the dominance
and growth of mega-urban regions in ASEAN is to curb their expansion
and funnel rural migration and industrialization to secondary and intermediate cities. As these small towns are unlikely to be able to absorb such
massive rural-urban shifts, the unconventional wisdom is that planning
should be directed towards making these 'engines of growth' work more
efficiently. Much effort, therefore, has been devoted to identifying the differing internal conditions under which these mega-urban regions have
emerged in ASEAN. Their creation has been attributed by McGee (1991, 5)
to the 'considerable advances in transportation technology, particularly in
relatively cheap intermediate transportation technology such as two-
stroke motorbikes, [which] greatly facilitate the circulation of commodities, people and capital.' His archetypal mega-urban region, however, is a
closed spatial system (McGee 1991, 6). No international connections are
shown. Yet these are crucial to the positioning and development of the
urban cores and new settlement forms.

An alternative approach is to suggest that the causes, character, and significance of the ASEAN mega-urban regions can best be understood by
analyzing them as network hubs in terms of their transnational linkages
and flows, and by considering how the associated land transportation system
generates a new extended urban form, the development corridor (Figure

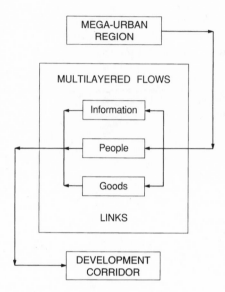

Figure 7.1 **Multilayered flows**

7.1). This proposition is examined here by considering key changes in the international spatial economy since the end of the Pacific War. Then the contemporary international network of nodes and links and traffic flows determining bilateral relationships are analyzed. Particular attention is focused on problems and challenges of the existing transportation and communications system, and current government and private-sector responses are discussed. In considering policy options to provide 'reliable, safe, cost-effective and environmentally sensitive transport services to foster economic development and community wellbeing,' it is necessary to highlight the transitory nature of mega-urban regions (Black and Rimmer 1992, 1). As the nature of the international economy changes, the regions will develop into Ginsburg's 'vast multimetropolitan region of urbanization linking a series of very large cities and metro areas' (1991a, 27) and, in the longer term, into development corridors straddling international borders.

The International Spatial Economy
The ASEAN mega-urban regions are essentially containers of capital accumulation and economic power. They are best understood as international network hubs embedded in a competitive Asian-Pacific urban hierarchy focused on Tokyo. In turn, Tokyo is now linked into a global superstructure, on a par with London and New York. These transformations have been the product of rapid economic growth and the closer economic inte-

gration of Pacific Asia since the Second World War, driven by foreign capital and industrialization.

The development of mega-urban regions has mirrored different stages of national economic restructuring in a 'flying geese' pattern. Tokyo took off first, followed by Seoul, Taipei, Hong Kong, and then Singapore, with the other ASEAN representatives coming after: Bangkok, Jakarta, Kuala Lumpur, and Manila (Table 7.2). The strength of trade, capital, and labour flows with their Northeast Asian counterparts has defined the ASEAN mega-regions rather than interactions within ASEAN, a function of their relative lack of specialization on particular activities. Before discussing the contemporary pattern of these relationships, this chapter considers the nature of major postwar urban changes that have determined this pattern of functional specialization in the East Asian Pacific Rim.

Table 7.2

Evolution of mega-urban regions and dominant economic policies

	1950s	1960s	1970s	1980s	1990s
Tokyo	EOI[a] light	EOI heavy	TI[b]	Global economy	Global economy
Seoul, Taipei Hong Kong, Singapore	Import substitution	EOI light	EOI heavy	TI	Global economy
Bangkok, Jakarta, Kuala Lumpur, Manila		Import substitution	EOI light	EOI heavy	TI

Notes:
a EOI = export oriented industrialization
b TI = technological intensification

Flying Geese
During the early 1960s, the impetus of Tokyo's growth stemmed from the in-flow of American capital and technology. Emphasizing the need to use space more efficiently, it led to redefinition of Tokyo's core and movement of production to suburban industrial estates. Population followed, and the new areas were linked to the core by commuter railways and freeways. As Tokyo was never a major chemical and heavy manufacturing centre, large Japanese corporations financed by the banks spread their industrial activities – iron and steel, oil and petrochemicals – along the Pacific Coastal Belt. This transportation corridor was refashioned by parallel public investments in transportation and communications infrastructure, including

US-designed expressways. From 1964, the Shinkansen has provided its spine and demonstrated to Japanese and foreigners alike a new dimension of time and space. It brought Tokyo and Osaka together in the Tokaido megalopolis.

Simultaneously, spatial restructuring was also occurring in what are now ASEAN capital cities, but in a rather distorted way. Limited private investment in import-replacement production was buttressed by heavy and increasing employment in the public service. Despite considerable public investment in provincial roads, rural production and employment grew slowly. A rural exodus led to the explosion of capital-city populations which overwhelmed the existing transportation and communications infrastructure.

During the 1970s, another phase of spatial restructuring was triggered by new technologies, including wide-bodied aircraft, container ships, and telecommunications. By dramatically reducing the costs of moving goods, people, and information, locational opportunities within what is now Pacific Asia were redefined. Following the liberalization of capital, these opportunities were recognized by major Japanese corporations, which developed their activities on a global scale. They shifted their chemical and heavy industry primarily to Northeast Asia and expanded exports of electrical goods, machinery, and motor vehicles from Japan. While Tokyo absorbed high-tech industries on its periphery, the cores of both Seoul and Taipei were redefined as service centres following the move of production to designated industrial estates and of population to housing estates. Freeways and commuter railways were built to enable workers and residents to keep in contact with the core. Most new chemical and heavy industries, however, went to coastal areas, which were linked to the capitals by interurban expressways.

In Singapore, port development proceeded apace, but the other ASEAN economies pursued agricultural and rural-based strategies with an emphasis on exporting primary produce. Apart from port improvements directed to the development of trunk roads and to railway upgrading to support an import-substitution, industrialization program, there was little investment in transportation and communications infrastructure within the capital cities.

During the 1980s, Tokyo became more fully integrated into international transportation and communications networks, and large-scale changes in land use occurred in response to its newfound status as a global economic centre and to domestic demands. Using their own surplus funds derived from stock and share dealings, large corporations rationalized their portfolios and invested in new areas such as finance and distribution, which made use of advances in information technology. In the process, 'advanced' urban space became a prime source of capital accumulation. Corporations restructured Tokyo's port areas and redeveloped land occupied by obsolete industrial activities to accommodate the leading edges of Japan's emerging information society. The government's policy of using private enterprise and deregulation to stimulate domestic demand and so overcome trade friction with the US helped confirm Tokyo as an international financial and ideas-processing centre and reinforced its urban sprawl. Without the political clout of New York and London, Tokyo is heavily dependent on advances in transportation and telecommunications (electronics and computers) to enhance its position as a network hub.

Mirroring Japan's Tokaido megalopolis, transportation corridors are emerging between Seoul-Pusan and Taipei-Kaoshiung to accommodate functional specialization, and the expressway spines are about to be paralleled by high-speed railways. Following Tokyo's experience, the business hearts of Seoul and Taipei are acquiring important producer services: finance, insurance, and real estate. Their commercial development reflects the shift of industrial investment to provincial locations and offshore, especially to ASEAN, following labour shortages and the loss of preferential tariffs in the US.

This wave of industrial investment from the Tokyo-Seoul-Taipei triangle to ASEAN has been heavily biased towards the environs of capital cities. These cities have become focal points for international transportation and communications networks, reinforcing the pattern. Due to the rapid growth of individual economies within the Asia-Pacific region, mega-cities have evolved into mega-urban regions. Increasingly, transportation and communications planning ideas and concepts have been imported from Japan (Rimmer 1986a).

Existing International Networks and Flows

Asia's leading mega-regions have positioned themselves and competed against each other to become regional network hubs. Not only do commodities and passengers flow through nodes and over links but so do ideas and innovations. In analyzing the flows, it is important to recognize that goods, people, and information are exchanged between firms and households on a spatial network of nodes and links. In this analysis, nodes are mega-urban regions comprising firms and households with goods production and consumption, travel propensities, and information capacities (i.e., universities and research centres).

Following Kobayashi and Okada (1989), a trilevel structural arrangement is envisaged to accommodate interdependent movements of goods, people, and information on a global network. It incorporates:

- low-speed goods transportation to accommodate commercial transactions increasingly dispersed because of the decreasing costs of transportation and computerized production control
- high-speed passenger transportation to cover the movements of individuals necessary for transferring structurally complex information – knowledge – in face-to-face contacts
- telecommunications networks for the transmission of uncomplicated information.

In exchanging standardized information, personal contacts can be replaced by telecommunications. While there is some scope for technological substitution between transportation and telecommunications, research suggests that the new media will increase rather than reduce the need for face-to-face contact. When information is complex, face-to-face contact is necessary for negotiations and transmission of new knowledge. Thus, travel is still essential to promote cooperation among workers and more advanced research and development activities.

Accessibility is a key concept because it determines the potential of each emerging mega-urban region to generate goods, people, and information. Also, it reflects the decreasing friction of distance in telecommunications and the persisting friction in movements of goods and people. Network structure within a mega-urban region is an important determinant of the regional division of labour. With the highest accessibility, the core is the prime location for business people handling both structurally complex and uncomplicated information. Due to the spread of telecommunications, the flow of standardized information at peripheral locations has increased. Thus, workers can be decentralized, and face-to-face contact can be replaced by the transmission of data and information.

All three networks (movement of goods, people, and information) have equal intensity of interaction. They can be tapered, however, to suggest differences among mega-urban regions. In Tokyo, for example, the telecommunications network is outstripping the growth of both high- and low-speed transportation networks – the result of opposition from environmental groups. In Seoul, Taipei, Hong Kong, and Singapore, the dominant level is high-speed transportation. In the other ASEAN mega-urban regions, the crucial level is low-speed transportation. These generalizations are borne out by an examination of flows through existing container shipping, air passenger, and telecommunications networks.

Container Shipping
Between 1983 and 1990, ASEAN container ports serving the five mega-urban regions – Singapore, Bangkok, Manila, Port Klang (Kuala Lumpur), and Tanjung Priok (Jakarta) – experienced a marked increase in through-

put. By 1990, they were handling over 8 million containers. Although
Hong Kong, Kaohsiung and Keelung in Taiwan, and Pusan in Korea handled 13 million containers among them, the ASEAN total was in excess of
the four leading Japanese ports and five leading west coast North
American ports, which both handled 7 million (Robinson 1991). The
global significance of ASEAN ports was compounded by their incorporation into a hub and feeder network, which focused containers and shipping capacity on a smaller number of highly efficient ports (Map 7.1). This
arrangement has allowed ship operators to maximize economies of scale
by linking Western Europe, Northeast Asia, and North America with very
large mother ships of up to 4,000 TEUs (transport equipment units).

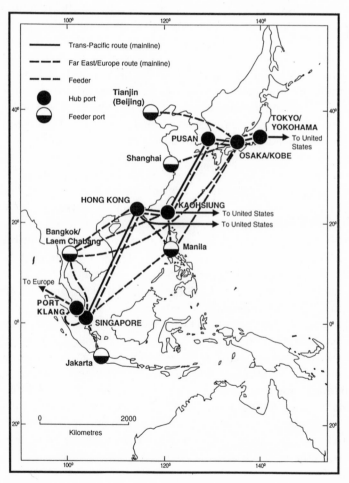

Map 7.1 **Short-sea and deep-sea shipping services, Pacific Asia, 1980s.** Based on
Robinson (1991)

Rapid growth in Northeast Asia and the generation of massive flows of containerized cargo have given rise to giant mainline hubs in Japan, Korea, Taiwan, and Hong Kong (Map 7.2). While ASEAN has emerged as an industrializing region, Singapore has become the world's leading container port and largest ASEAN trans-shipment port. Hong Kong and Kaohsiung, however, continue to serve as trans-shipment hubs for ASEAN feeder cargoes, especially on trans-Pacific routes. Bangkok and Manila, Tanjung Priok, and Port Klang serve almost entirely national traffic, assisted by the third-level ports of Penang and Tanjung Perak (Surabaya).

Within the ASEAN mega-urban regions, much effort is being made to provide links between port-to-port containerization and other domestic modes of transportation. This has been necessary to enable multimodal transport operators such as American President Line, Sea Land, and NYK to meet the demand of business corporations for an integrated transportation system, just-in-time delivery, and rationalization of inventory and production controls. Links between container ports, airports, and telecommunications have to be considered because sea-air systems using containers are being developed and a premium is being placed on innovative, electronic information systems aimed at shorter transit times and accurate identification of cargoes in transit (Rimmer 1991a).

Airports

The Asia-Pacific route network and its links to other parts of the world are shaped and dictated by demand, bilateral air agreements between governments, and increases in the size of aircrafts and the distances they can fly. By 1989, a north-south, high-density air traffic corridor ran from Tokyo to Taipei, Hong Kong, Singapore, and Jakarta (Map 7.3). Reinforcing this pattern is a distribution system that relies heavily on major network hubs for international flights – Tokyo, Hong Kong, Bangkok, and Singapore – which has emerged from the development of non-stop routes.

Analyses of air-passenger movements between 1983 and 1990 highlight the boom in the ASEAN travel market, which has strained airlines and air terminals. This has been created by greater business travel stemming from the internationalization of economic activity and from numbers of international tourists. In the process, Singapore and Bangkok have become the main ASEAN airline hubs, providing transit services for a multitude of carriers between the Asia-Pacific region and the Middle East and Africa (Table 7.3). Kuala Lumpur, Manila, and Jakarta serve primarily national traffic although international traffic is increasing.

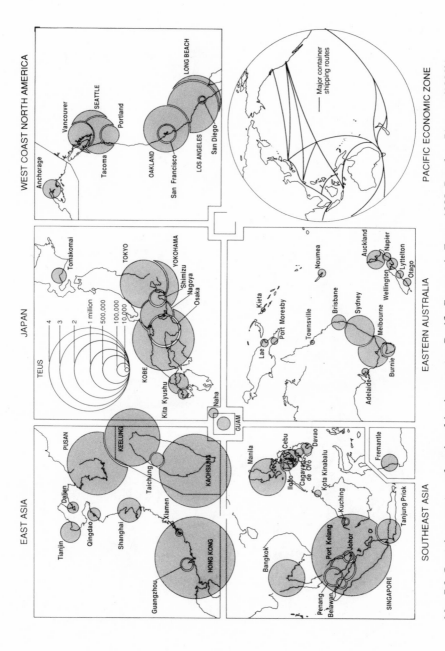

Map 7.2 Container ports and major shipping routes, Pacific Economic Zone, 1988. Based on Rimmer (1990b)

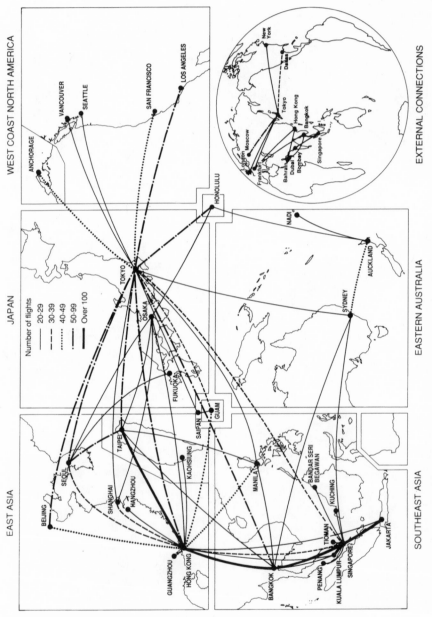

Map 7.3 **Non-stop air passenger flights, Pacific Economic Zone, August 1989. Based on Rimmer (1990b)**

Table 7.3

Comparison of air passenger movements at major airports, 1983 and 1990

	Jakarta 1983	Jakarta 1990	Singapore 1983	Singapore 1990	Kuala Lumpur 1983	Kuala Lumpur 1990	Bangkok 1983	Bangkok 1990	Manila 1983	Manila 1990
Passengers (thousands)										
Southeast Asia	335	685	1,503	2,440	711	1,138	520	973	282	331
East Asia	–	56	581	1,269	87	268	714	1,744	655	982
South Asia	2	1	160	305	24	58	207	364	42	19
Middle East	–	70	28	24	1	38	56	175	81	181
Europe	–	93	313	587	51	125	283	646	67	76
North America	–	–	28	101	–	–	3	38	73	176
Oceania	10	29	321	731	61	118	42	197	128	101
Africa	–	–	–	35	–	–	–	–	–	–
Total	347	933	2,934	5,492	935	1,746	1,825	4,137	1,328	1,866
Percentage										
Southeast Asia	96.4	73.3	51.2	44.4	76.0	65.1	28.5	23.5	20.5	17.8
East Asia	–	6.1	19.8	23.1	9.3	15.3	39.1	42.1	47.7	56.6
South Asia	0.6	0.1	5.4	5.5	2.5	3.3	11.3	8.8	3.0	1.0
Middle East	–	7.5	1.0	0.5	0.1	2.2	3.1	4.2	5.9	9.7
Europe	3.0	9.9	10.6	10.7	5.5	7.2	15.5	15.6	4.9	4.1
North America	–	–	1.0	1.9	–	–	0.2	0.9	8.6	9.4
Oceania	–	3.1	11.0	13.3	6.5	6.8	2.3	4.8	9.4	5.4
Africa	–	–	–	0.6	–	–	–	–	–	–
Total	100	100	100	100	100	100	100	100	100	100

Note: rounding errors
Sources: Derived from International Civil Aviation Organization (1984, 1991)

Telecommunications

The explosion in international telephone calls during the 1980s saturated the capacity of satellites and microwaves and gave rise to a new growth network of fibre-optic cables (Map 7.4). Although satellites and microwaves will continue to be used, the new network will cater to the expansion business services, including the next generation of fax, high-definition television, international video conferencing, and value-added services for financial transactions and computer-aided design (Rimmer 1991c, 14). In telecommunications there is much rivalry between Bangkok and Singapore, the latter having the edge (Table 7.4).

Table 7.4

Bangkok, Singapore, and their major telecommunication correspondents, 1990

	Bangkok		Singapore	
Destination	Outgoing MiTT millions	Market share (%)	Outgoing MiTT millions	Market share (%)
Indonesia	–	–	20.5	13.5
Malaysia	4.9	11.5	–	–
Philipines	–	–	4.1	2.7
Singapore	6.0	14.1	–	–
Thailand	–	–	7.1	4.7
Hong Kong	5.6	13.2	19.4	12.8
Japan	6.4	15.0	19.7	13.0
Taiwan	2.6	6.1	10.6	7.0
India	–	–	6.9	4.5
United States	5.7	13.4	19.7	13.0
Italy	1.1	2.5	–	–
United Kingdom	2.4	5.6	10.3	6.8
West Germany	1.3	3.0	–	–
Australia	1.1	2.5	10.2	6.7
Sub-total	37.1	86.9	128.5	84.7
Others	5.4	13.1	23.3	15.3
Total	42.5	100.0	151.8	100.0

Note: MiTT is Minutes of Telecommunication Traffic. Data are for international public voice circulation only. Bangkok data exclude traffic to Cambodia, Laos, and Vietnam; Singapore data exclude Malaysia. Some rounding errors.
Source: Derived from Staple (1990)

Current Problems and Challenges

The boom in demand for transportation, telecommunications, and tourism – the triple T – has exposed the inadequacies of existing internal infrastructure. These problems are not universal, as ASEAN member states possess a very good network of all-weather roads from villages to market

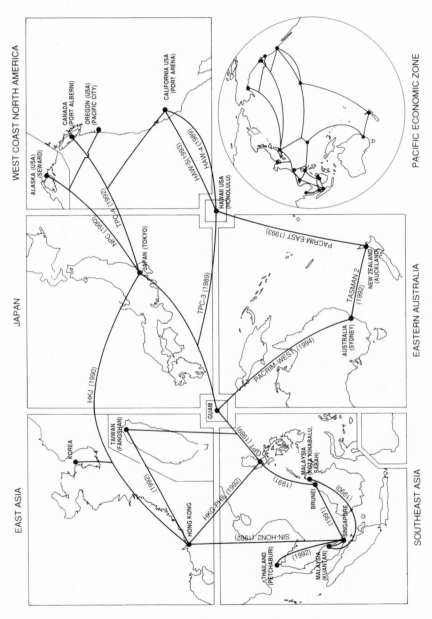

Map 7.4 Network of fibre-optic cables and dates of completion, Pacific Economic Zone. Based on Rimmer (1990b)

towns and from there to the main port cities (Leinbach 1989). Goods and people can move quickly and cheaply, almost on demand, to and from these towns and cities. Although there is scope for marginal improvements, accessibility outside the wet season is not a problem at this level. The main difficulties are concentrated in mega-urban regions other than Singapore: traffic congestion, road accidents, environmental pollution (including air quality, noise, and visual intrusion), overloaded public transport, poor conditions for pedestrians and cyclists, and lack of money to improve those conditions (Thomson 1983). Quite simply, the demand for transportation services has been outstripped by the cost of supplying them. Unless appropriate measures are taken, overtaxed facilities will curb growth and aggravate locational stress (Rimmer and Cho 1989).

Already, the ASEAN mega-urban regions have been subject to a series of country-by-country surveys highlighting problems of traffic law violation and inadequate organizational and financial arrangements for maintaining and operating transport (see, for example, Asian Development Bank 1992; Akatsuka, Kunishima, and Kitauchi 1989; Kitauchi and Akatsuka 1989; Leinbach and Chia 1989; and Rimmer 1986a, 1986b). Rather than summarizing the contents of these surveys region by region, this chapter examines infrastructure requirements.

Table 7.5 shows that transportation infrastructural requirements are considerable for Jabotabek, the Bangkok EMR, Metro Manila, and, to a lesser extent, the Klang Valley. Although measures to construct ring roads and freeways, boost public transport, and speed traffic have accommodated a huge increase in vehicle flows, the problems caused by a lack of planning are now becoming apparent, as are the costs of overcoming delays. The difficulties seem most acute for peak-hour passenger flows because freeways allow heavy, vehicular traffic to bypass the city core. Nevertheless, the freeway systems are still poorly linked and not yet well integrated with areas of industrial development and international airports. No mega-urban region has a mass rapid-transit system with direct access to the airport (though a link is proposed in Singapore).

Most parts of the interurban road system are still inadequate to cope with the number and weight of trucks now engaged in goods movement. The costs of constructing a network to heavy-vehicle standards are very high. Ports are clogged and improvements to coastal general-cargo shipping and inland waterway transportation have been slow. Rail has shifted its emphasis from passengers to freight but improvements in infrastructure, productivity, and quality of service have been too slow to achieve any significant shift from an overburdened road network.

With the boom in tourism, many of the regional airlines are experiencing seat-capacity problems. Buoyant tourism demand, particularly from

Table 7.5

Infrastructural requirements in ASEAN's mega-urban regions

	Greater Bangkok	Jabotabek	Klang Valley	Greater Singapore	Metro Manila
Road	Infrastructure rehabilitation, upgrading, and maintenance	Infrastructure (increased capacity) upgrading and maintenance	Trunk road extensions	Expressways	Infrastructure (main interurban) upgrading and maintenance
Railway	Minor improvements to rail network		Freight and container traffic priority	Mass rapid transit system	New investment not economically justified
Inland waterways	Dredging justified				
Coastal shipping		Rehabilitation and expansion of Tanjung Priok			
Ports	Port improvements at Laem Chabang			Development of Port of Singapore (Tanjong Pagar Container Terminal), Port of Johor and Free Trade Zone	Development of Manila International Containers Terminal
Aviation				Development of Changi Airport (third terminal planned)	Improve Don Muang Airport
Telecommunications				Electronic data interchange	

Sources: Derived from Akatsuka, Kunishima, and Kitauchi (1989); Leinbach and Chia Lin Sien (1989); Mitsui Research Institute (1989); National Economic Social Development Board (1991c)

Northeast Asia, is causing frequent delays and flight cancellations. In the long term, further airport development is required to handle the anticipated influx. Outside Singapore, telecommunications growth has been constrained by delays in the installation of basic telephone facilities.

Current Responses

Responses to transportation problems in ASEAN mega-urban regions involve incremental, low-cost solutions: extensive bus priorities, traffic management and constraint, and selective road improvements. Only in a few instances have freeways and rapid mass transit been justified (Thomson 1983). Since the early 1980s, the prospect of rich-city solutions – freeways, multistorey carparks, rapid transit, and sophisticated control systems – has been heightened by ideas on privatization and deregulation fashioned by the new right in Britain. ASEAN has adopted these concepts, persuaded by the World Bank, the Asian Development Bank, bilateral aid donors, and private bankers (Rimmer 1988, 1990, 1991b; Rimmer, Osman, and Dick 1989). The debate in ASEAN, however, has been devoid of right-wing and left-wing ideology. Essentially, the decisions to restructure transportation and to supply infrastructure and services are the pragmatic reactions of politicians and bureaucrats to the problems of state-owned transportation and infrastructure enterprises. As these enterprises account for a substantial part of investment in ASEAN mega-urban regions, their efficient operation is crucial to sustaining economic growth and improving industrial competitiveness. In many cases, however, their management has been perceived as grossly inefficient, inadequately accountable, and a drain on scarce government resources because subsidies, transfers, and net lending outstrip revenue.

Invariably, the argument is that most state-owned enterprises should be sold to private interests. But privatization is not the only, nor necessarily the most effective, approach. A range of ownership and management options is available for reshaping and reforming state enterprises and improving their efficiency to achieve better financial results and service delivery. In discussing them, a distinction has to be made between state-owned transportation enterprises operating fleets – such as airlines, ships, and trucks and other road transport vehicles, sometimes in competition with private operators – and state-owned transportation infrastructure enterprises operating airports, seaports, and road and rail terminals and providing road and rail infrastructure. Although liberalization of bilateral airline agreements and fare-setting arrangements and privatization of national airlines has been a feature of ASEAN, attention here is restricted to the provision of transportation infrastructure. It has more important policy implications for shaping urban development than do fleet operations.

Most infrastructure in ASEAN, with the exception of roads, is provided by state enterprises. Questions have been raised about the adequacy of infrastructure supplied by these organizations and its efficiency in meeting society's economic, social, and environmental goals at the lowest cost to national resources. Not only are operational and strategic shortcomings and ill-conceived social objectives evident among state-owned fleet operators but investments in ASEAN infrastructure, as instanced by airports, have a high degree of monopoly. This makes it difficult to provide incentives for management and to evaluate performance.

Three different approaches have been used in ASEAN mega-urban regions to improve the efficiency of state-owned infrastructural enterprises, the central issue being the extent to which they can operate at arms' length from government control (Figure 7.2). Each approach is illustrated by brief reference to case studies.

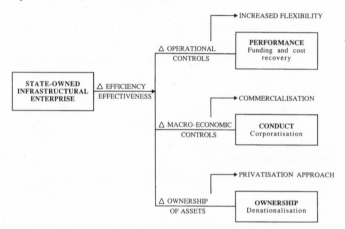

Figure 7.2 **Improving the efficiency of state-owned infrastructure enterprises.** Based on Rimmer, Osman, and Dick (1989, 175)

(1) The increased flexibility approach maintains state ownership and macro-economic controls over borrowing but removes controls over day-to-day management of staffing, pricing, investment, and assets. It has been followed by the Thai government in using the build-operate-transfer (BOT) model to construct Bangkok's 30 km $880 million Second Expressway Project with Japan's Kumagai Gumi Group. The latter receives an agreed percentage of revenue from toll collections.

(2) The commercialization approach maintains state ownership but removes strategic controls over borrowing. This has been used by the State Railway of Thailand in leasing intercity trains to private operators through a competitive bidding process as a means of improving its sales and marketing skills, passenger services, and depleted revenues.

(3) The privatization approach involves the sale of the state's assets to the private sector. The Port of Singapore Authority has privatized some parts of cargo handling and ancillary support activities; 50 per cent of berths have been leased to shipping agents.

It is unclear how many state-owned infrastructural enterprises in ASEAN could operate in a fully competitive environment or could meet the needs of full commercialization. Nonetheless, most could adopt the increased flexibility approach.

The extension of the BOT model is problematic. Although it can be used for infrastructure that generates enough revenue to cover project risks, it is inapplicable for projects with public welfare purposes that do not. Although incentives have been granted to the private sector, ASEAN governments have been reluctant to share the risks. Even supposedly feasible projects, such as Bangkok's proposed Skytrain, have proceeded slowly because of delays in mobilizing bidding support. Most big privatization transportation and telecommunications infrastructure projects in ASEAN mega-urban regions have experienced political problems. Although increased flexibility and commercialization of state-owned enterprises may be preferable to privately controlled organizations, these matters can only be resolved case by case.

Certainly privatization has not provided the new right's 'universal fix' for the task of providing infrastructure. The imminent demise of enthusiasm for privatization and the limitations of the incremental, low-cost solution suggest that the time is ripe for directional planning (Thomson 1983). Given unspecified but rising population, car ownership, and travel demands, this approach seeks to identify the structural and policy choices of strategic significance some twenty or thirty years hence. A directional plan for the year 2020, for instance, would provide the framework for fixed land-use, five- to ten-year design plans: the rolling program of specific projects such as new road alignments, new distributor roads, road widening, railway/tramway alignments, traffic management schemes, and parking controls.

Policy Choices

Generally, planners include a 'do-minimum' option, though no one could seriously entertain that for ASEAN mega-urban regions. A more cautious strategy is to identify and ease immediate bottlenecks with low-cost, high-yielding investments aimed at making better use of existing infrastructure and other facilities. Such measures include traffic management, road widening, limited paving in squatter areas, construction of short link roads, and improvements to public transportation enterprises. There is always a risk, however, that this World Bank-inspired strategy may be

inappropriate for the optimum long term because of distortions in production and consumption.

If the aim is to achieve long-run modal and spatial shifts, large, non-
marginal investments in transportation systems are required – new roads,
railways, and tramways – as are management measures aimed at encouraging a balance between private and public transportation. Whether this
costly, high-risk strategy is used to achieve developmental rewards or
mixed with the bottleneck approach, it is essential to identify the likely
urban form and accessibility patterns (functions of land use, population
distribution, and the transportation system).

Another approach to transportation development stems from the likely
coalescence of mega-urban regions into national megalopolises, in each
case by incorporating the next largest city in a way similar to the binodal
spatial economies of Tokyo-Osaka, Seoul-Pusan, and Taipei-Kaohsiung.
Heavy investments in major transportation links, such as expressways and
electrified railways, could generate ASEAN parallels: Bangkok-Chiang Mai,
Jakarta-Surabaya, and Kuala Lumpur-Penang. Even these megalopolitan
structures are likely to be transitory, later to be incorporated into international corridors of urban settlement.

Looking further ahead, we should be able to identify where development
corridors will emerge within the Asia-Pacific region (Rimmer 1991c). As
shown in Map 7.5, three corridors are recognized within the region: the
Japan corridor (Sapporo to Kitakyushu); the East Asian corridor (Seoul to
Hong Kong); and the Southeast Asian corridor (Chiang Mai to Bali). Attention
here is restricted to the Southeast Asian development corridor, leaving
Metro Manila as an isolated mega-urban region. Although this may be
contentious, the corridor provides an appropriate spatial framework for ask-
ing the right long-term questions. As it is often difficult to prioritize key
spatial components (such as telecommunications or railways), this framework counters any short-term strategy of 'muddling' through. Emphasizing
that investment in nodes takes precedence over investment in link infrastructure, seaports and airports need to be discussed before examining landbridges.
This priority underlines that the contiguity of various places is becoming
less important as ASEAN becomes more 'node intensive' (Batten 1990)

Seaports

During the 1990s, sea cargo within the Pacific region is expected to
increase at an annual rate of 3.7 per cent. Container shipping, however, is
likely to outstrip this rate; the proportion of general cargo, including
industrial products, is likely to increase from 16.6 per cent of shipping services in 1985 to 27.7 per cent in the year 2000. Given that potential
demand will be influenced by the supply of further multimodal services

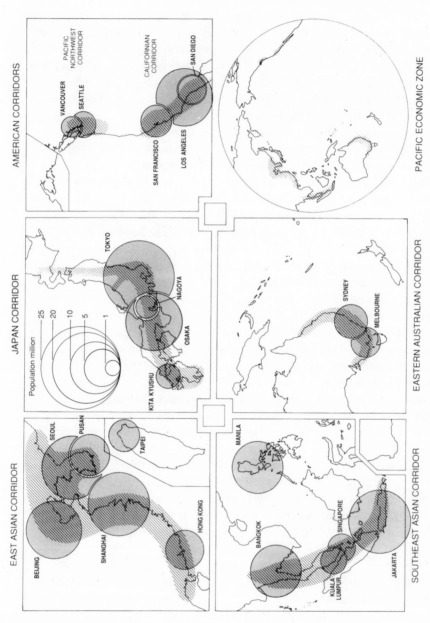

Map 7.5 **Population in the Pacific Economic Zone, 2000.** Based on Rimmer (1990b)

offering total cost reduction, just-in-time delivery, and simplified procedures, the stress will be on larger and faster container ships, specialized terminals, and information tracking systems.[1]

Port growth in ASEAN mega-urban regions will probably continue, given the ability of their dynamic economies to deliver large numbers of containers to and from their own major consumption markets and the region's expanding production bases. The competitive position of Singapore port will be compounded by its favoured location and attractiveness in a network of shipping connections. Already, its ongoing construction program anticipates an annual increase of one million TEUs. By 2030, it will have a throughput of 36 million TEUs. Besides offering an efficient and cost-effective port service, Singapore will seek to sustain its competitive advantage over Hong Kong by developing its associated producer services in finance, insurance, and trading.

The fortunes of other major ports – Bangkok, Manila, Port Klang, and Tanjung Priok – will depend on their potential to capture and manage regional productive capability and locational attractiveness. According to Robinson (1991), they are likely to enjoy continued rapid growth due to strong flows of foreign investment, particularly from Japan and Taiwan. They will also benefit from finance for port development provided by multilateral aid agencies. These funds will also assist the deconcentration of container facilities within the Southeast Asian development corridor. All of these trends will be helped or hampered by a growing commitment to the privatization of container terminals, often in joint ventures with overseas companies, and further deregulation of maritime controls in Indonesia, Malaysia, the Philippines, and Thailand, a reflection of trends within their national economies. These developments may result in Thailand's new port of Laem Chabang attracting mainline services.[2]

Airports

The number of scheduled passengers carried in the Asia-Pacific region is expected to increase from 87 million in 1990 to 189 million in the year 2000. The region's share of the world passenger market is calculated to grow from 31 per cent in 1990 to 51 per cent in 2010.[3] Although airlines are likely to respond with larger aircraft, 85 per cent of the extra load will require additional flights. More aircraft will necessitate larger airports and further route development.

Most of the strain in ASEAN will be centred on Bangkok and Singapore, which are the hubs for European and trans-Pacific routes. Only the planned extensions at Singapore's Changi Airport will be able to cope with the projected growth in demand. Bangkok's Don Muang airport terminal is likely to reach full capacity in this decade, and a $2.5 billion airport is planned for Nong Ngu Hau by the year 2000. Although Kuala Lumpur's Subang will be able to relieve the major hubs, there are plans to open a new airport in Kuala Lumpur by 1998. Governments are also being pressed to expand current hubs by investing in additional runways and terminals. As airports are acknowledged revenue earners, much will depend on the determination of government to resolve these difficulties and also on repealing restrictive aviation policies.

By 2040, air passenger numbers are likely to be three times those of 2000. The removal of airports from congested inner-city areas to peripheral locations within 50 to 80 km of existing urban areas has not provided a lasting solution. A new air system is therefore being considered (Hoyt 1990). It will be based on a set of superhubs handling new classes of aircraft that offer shorter travel times. As shown in Map 7.6, these vast airports will be located between 160 and 800 km from existing population centres in the Southeast Asian development corridor.

The new airports could become the focus of specialized production in high-technology electronics. Domestic links will be provided by tilt-wing and tilt-rotor aircraft and by high-speed train links. Reflecting the existing lines in Japan and those planned in Korea and Taiwan, the prospect of a high-speed route between Bangkok and Kuala Lumpur (and possibly between Jakarta and Surabaya) has been raised. These developments will support the 'global bridges' provided by air transportation and telecommunications. Efforts will also be made to improve landbridges for container movements.

Landbridges

Both Malaysia and Thailand have floated schemes to obviate the need for transhipment through Singapore. Provided that custom clearance procedures were streamlined and new rolling stock and motive power purchased, a landbridge could be established between Malaysia's Kelang Container Terminal and the Bangkok Container Terminal at Bangsue railway yard, which is run jointly by the State Railway of Thailand and the American President Line. Although the original scheme for building the Kra Canal between the Andaman Sea and the Gulf of Thailand was too grandiose, there is a new project to develop a landbridge in this area. This Southern Seaboard project aims to divert European traffic from Singapore and develop an industrial area away from Bangkok. Details of the project are still sketchy, and possible connections with Penang and Medan in a northern triangle remain unspecified (National Economic and Social Development Board 1991b). Yet the prospect of joint public and private participation is an example of what may happen within development corridors as firms seek to capitalize on strategic locations between core areas

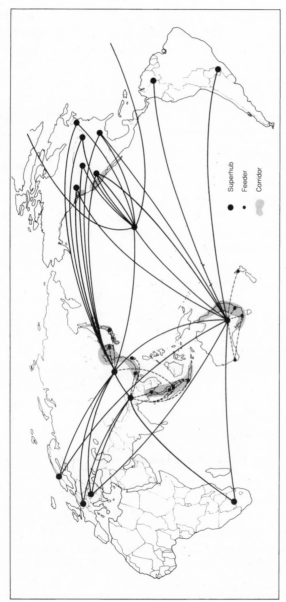

Map 7.6 An abstract view of a future hub air network. Based on Hoyt (1990)

Superhub

Feeder

Corridor

and to exploit their competitive economic advantage within the global economy in terms of labour and natural resources.

Following current European, North American, and Japanese practice, combined industrial and international tourist activities would be centred on a multimodal landbridge (National Economic and Social Development Board 1991b). As shown in Figure 7.3, connections would be forged with existing transhipment hubs and international processing centres along a transportation spine provided by road, rail, pipeline, and optic fibre. The port would import components and materials and export processed products; the airport would export high-value, low-weight finished products and handle inbound and outbound tourists; and an earth satellite station would transmit and receive information. The various components of the transportation structure would facilitate the growth of economic activity in an industrial park associated with the port, in aquaculture and seafood processing for export markets, in a light industrial park and high-tech value-added complex specializing in electronics, electrical machinery, and processed metal products, and in associated training and international research institutes (i.e., soft infrastructure). International tourist resorts would provide an attractive urban environment to draw skilled labour to the new industrial clusters.

If economic growth is to be sustained, industrial and tourist activities must be compatible and the environmental impact minimized. Should these activities proceed, they would consolidate the Southeast Asian development corridor.

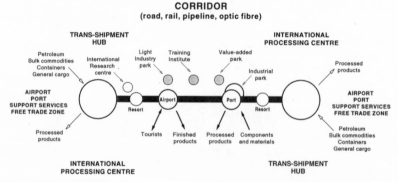

Figure 7.3 **Probable developments around a port-airport-satellite complex.**
Based on National Economic and Social Development Board (1991b)

Conclusions

Changes in the relative status of ASEAN mega-urban regions reflect their acquired role in national and international economies. Their future prospects will be strongly influenced by the nodality, density, and efficiency of the international transportation and communications infra-structure linking them to the rest of the world (Batten 1990). They will also be affected by the global exchange of goods and services, people, and information, including financial transactions. The capacity to exploit the economies inherent in the multilayered network will depend on the ability of firms to capture the collective knowledge permeating across them.

Within this multilayered network, global corporations interact with smaller, cooperating production and distribution units. They are able to reap economies of scale from the global marketing network through nodes, while small production and distribution units in ASEAN employ local labour and capture little pockets of demand. No longer are global corporations confined to the port cities linking intra- and intercontinental transportation systems (Andersson 1990). There are a growing number of locations with potential for good profit within the multilayered networks. They offer opportunities for entrepreneurs to spread their activities and, in the process, to create and consolidate development corridors.

By the year 2040, development corridors in Southeast and East Asia should not be dissimilar to the banana-shaped, macro-economic corridor being formed in Europe, which extends across national borders from southern England to northern Italy. As the Japanese, East Asian, and Southeast Asian development corridors will attract the most investment in infrastructure and research and development, it is possible they will coalesce into a Pacific-Asia corridor running from Vladivostok to Bali. The ensuing likelihood of worsening congestion and accelerated urban sprawl raises important issues: how the quality of urban life in the corridor could be improved; and how conditions necessary for environmental and economic sustainability can be created. Much will depend on integrating planning for land use, transportation, and the environment.

Notes

The assistance of Barbara Banks and Deog-an Lee is appreciated. The figures were drawn in the Cartographic Section, Research School of Pacific Studies, Australian National University.

1   The Japanese Ministry of Transport is supporting the development of a super-speed con-tainership, the techno-super liner. As this 100 m vessel can travel at double the speed of conventional container ships, it could, in theory, bypass the major load centres and favour the development of local ports (Mitsui Research Institute 1989).

2   Container cargo volume in Thailand is forecast to increase from 1.09 million TEUs in 1991 to 1.83 million in 2001 (National Economic and Social Development Board 1991c, I.1.15). The current capacity of Klong Toey wharves at Bangkok port is estimated at 900,000 TEUs per year, while Laem Chabang is forecast to handle 1 million TEUs in 2001.

3   The Asia-Oceania-North America route will have 26 million passengers in the year 2000 and intra-Asia-Oceania will generate 70 million (Mitsui Research Institute 1989, II.4).

8
Gridlock in the Slopopolis: Congestion Management and Sustainable Development[1]
V. Setty Pendakur

Global Context

Economic Growth

Asia is undoubtedly the most dynamic region in the world today. Notwithstanding the disparities in economic performance of individual countries, the GNP growth in the region as a whole averaged nearly 7 per cent annually during the 1980s. In contrast, world GNP growth was around 3 per cent per annum, and it was less than 2 per cent for developing countries (Midgeley 1991). Table 8.1 shows the annual real per capita GDP growth rates, forecast by the World Bank, for different regions of the world. The real GDP growth in Asia was more than twice that in the high-income countries and is expected to continue at a comparatively high rate during the next decade. The expected 1992 GDP growth rates for Asian countries forecast by the Asian Development Bank vary from a low of 3.2 per cent in the Philippines to a high of 8.4 per cent in Malaysia.

Table 8.1

Real per capita GDP growth rate, 1980-2000		
	1980-90 (%)	1990-2000 (%)
All high-income countries	2.4	2.1
All developing countries	1.2	2.9
Sub-Sahara Africa	−0.9	0.3
Eastern Europe	0.9	1.6
East Asia	6.3	5.7
South Asia	3.1	3.1

Source: World Bank (1990)

Not all Asian countries are necessarily cash poor. Table 8.2 shows the foreign currency reserves of the top fifteen countries in the world in 1991. Several Asian countries have large reserves of foreign currency. In general, these reserves should enable them to continue to sustain their high economic growth rates and a high degree of modernization of their economies, at least in the short term.

Table 8.2

Foreign currency reserves, 1991 (US$ billions)

Japan	72	Australia	17	Hong Kong	14
USA	67	Thailand	17	Malaysia	10
Singapore	28	Canada	16	Indonesia	9
Taiwan	18	South Korea	14	Philippines	3

Source: International Monetary Fund

The growth outlook in the 1990s is more favourable for developing countries in Asia than for those in other regions. Forecasts by the World Bank indicate that per capita incomes in South Asia may continue to grow at 3.2 per cent per year for the next decade. Per capita income in the developing countries of East Asia is projected to grow at 5.1 per cent, leading to a 65 per cent rise in average incomes by the year 2000 (World Bank 1990).

The impressive economic performance of Asia, combined with population growth, is causing the region to grapple with extremely rapid rates of urbanization. Already, more than half of the world's urban population increase occurs in Asia and most of this growth is occurring in low-income countries (Midgeley 1991).

Asia today provides contradictory images of demography and development. Some of the world's most prosperous countries, with large capital surpluses and high rates of economic growth – Japan, Korea, Taiwan, Singapore, and Hong Kong – are in Asia. At the same time, 66 per cent of the world's poor live in five countries of Asia: Bangladesh, China, India, Indonesia, and Pakistan (Pendakur 1986).

Except for Japan and the newly industrialized countries (NICs) of Hong Kong, South Korea, Singapore, and Taiwan, Asian countries are poor in terms of capital and technology. They also require massive new investments in the transportation sector of their mega-cities to cater to the ever expanding scale and complexity of mega-city living. The extent to which Asian cities can meet the challenges of urbanization and contribute to macro-economic performance will depend on the efficiency of the transportation systems on which the economic activities depend.

Vehicle emissions are increasingly being recognized as the dominant cause of localized air pollution and health problems. And the pressing demand for motorized forms of personal mobility in Asian cities is generating pressures on the road network, resulting in congestion and creating unmanageable degradation of air quality. The intrinsic development of the urban transportation sector and its response to the pace, scale, and nature of urbanization and economic development in the 1990s will critically influence the quality of living and public health in all cities in the next two decades.

Urbanization

Population growth rates in the developing countries have slowed down somewhat, from a peak of 2.5 per cent per year in the 1970s to about 1.8 per cent in 1991. Even so, the expected urban growth, in absolute numbers, is staggering. By the year 2000, the total global population is expected to reach 6.3 billion, of which 5.0 billion (79 per cent) will be in the developing countries. Of these 5.0 billion people, 2.3 billion (37 per cent) will be living in urban areas (United Nations, Department of International Economic and Social Affairs 1991).

Cities in the low-income countries are fast reaching or even surpassing the ranks of the world's largest cities. This trend breaks the historical connection between city size and levels of economic development and/or political power. The major force behind urbanization is no longer industrialization. Fifty-eight of the world's hundred largest metropolitan areas are now in the developing countries. Nine of them are in China and another nine in India, despite the fact that almost 80 per cent of the population in these countries is still rural. Of the thirty-three metropolitan areas with populations of more than 5 million, twenty-two were in the developing countries in 1990 (Camp 1991).

Large cities in developing countries are growing much faster than those in the industrialized countries ever have. London took 130 years to grow from one million to 8 million, whereas it took Los Angeles fifty years, Bangkok forty-six years, and Mexico City only twenty-seven years. The mega-cities of developing countries are growing at exponential rates.

Cities in the industrialized countries have been growing by 0.8 per cent per year during the past decade, a rate that is likely to decline in the coming decade. Cities in the developing countries have been growing at 3.6 per cent a year, a rate they will maintain through the 1990s. At this rate, their populations will double in less than twenty years. By the year 2000, the urban population of the developing countries will be almost double the size of that in the industrialized world (United Nations, Department of International Economic and Social Affairs 1991).

Asia's population was estimated to be 2.9 billion in 1990, about half the global population (United Nations, Department of International Economic and Social Affairs 1991). The vast majority of Asians are concentrated in the sixteen low-income countries, with GNP per capita below $550 in 1990. This group of countries also contains the majority of the region's – and the world's – urban population and the majority of cities with populations over one million (World Bank 1990).

The urban population in Asia is estimated to increase by 420 million during the next ten years from 1.2 to 1.6 billion. This means that the urban share of the population would increase from 39 per cent in 1990 to

46 per cent by the year 2000. By then, there will be thirteen mega-cities in Asia, with a combined population of 179 million. The majority of these will be in the low-income countries (United Nations, Department of International Economic and Social Affairs 1991).

Mexico City was the largest city in the world in 1990, with a population of 20 million people. Of the twenty largest cities in the world in 1990, only five were in the industrialized countries: Tokyo (18 million), New York (16 million), Los Angeles (12 million), Paris (9 million), and Osaka (9 million). The remaining fifteen were in the developing countries: Mexico, Sao Paulo, Shanghai, Buenos Aires, Calcutta, Rio de Janeiro, Beijing, Bombay, Delhi, Jakarta, Seoul, Cairo, Manila, Moscow, and Tianjin. Table 8.3 shows how this order will change by the year 2000. Of the twenty largest cities of the world by then, only three will be in the industrialized countries. In the global context, cities like Mexico, Shanghai, and Calcutta will dwarf those in Europe such as London and Paris (United Nations, Department of International Economic and Social Affairs 1991).

Table 8.3

The twenty largest cities, 2000

	City	Population (millions)	World rank
Industrialized	Tokyo	19	2
countries	New York	17	4
	Los Angeles	14	10
Developing countries			
Latin America	Mexico City	25	1
	Sao Paulo	22	3
	Buenos Aires	13	11
	Rio de Janeiro	13	13
Africa	Cairo	12	16
Asia	Shanghai	17	5
	Calcutta	16	6
	Bombay	15	7
	Beijing	14	8
	Jakarta	14	9
	Delhi	13	12
	Seoul	13	14
	Tianjin	13	15
	Karachi	12	17
	Manila	12	18
	Bangkok	10	19
	Istanbul	10	20

Source: United Nations, Department of International Social and Economic Affairs (1991)

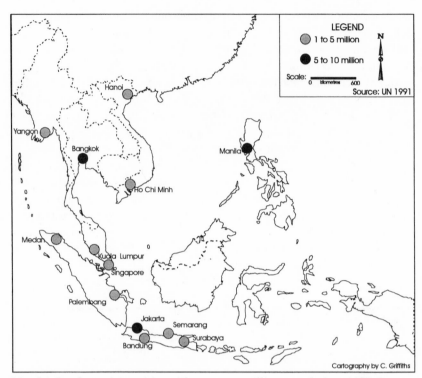

Map 8.1 **Southeast Asian cities with over one million population, 1990.** Data from United Nations, DIESA (1991)

Southeast Asia has several primate mega-cities, such as Jakarta, Manila, and Bangkok. Kuala Lumpur is primate but not a mega-city. There were ten cities of 1 to 5 million people and three of more than 5 million in 1990 (Map 8.1). Map 8.2 shows the expected urban growth by the year 2000, based on UN studies. Jakarta, Manila, and Bangkok are expected to grow beyond 10 million people each, whereas population for the other ten cities will remain at 1 to 5 million.

The features of contemporary urbanization in the developing countries differ markedly from those of historical experience. Whereas urbanization in the industrialized countries took many decades, permitting the gradual emergence of economic, social, and political institutions to deal with the problems of transformation, the process in the developing countries is far more rapid, and is taking place against a background of high population growth, lower incomes, and fewer opportunities for international migration (Pendakur 1986). This transformation also involves an enormous number of people. Between 1950 and 1990, the urban areas of developing countries absorbed 1.2 billion new people (United Nations, Department of International Economic and Social Affairs 1991). Urbanization in the

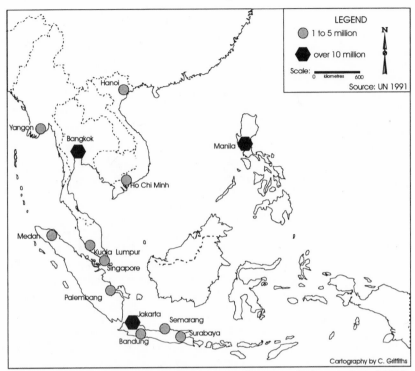

Map 8.2 **Southeast Asian cities with over one million population, projected 2000.**
Data from United Nations, DIESA (1991)

developing countries is characterized by: (1) rapid population growth; (2) strictly controlled international immigration and barriers to immigration (unlike in the European Community); (3) dominance of a very small number of cities; (4) decreasing and/or stable costs of transportation and communications up to 1970 and geometric increases in those costs since then; and (5) a heavy burden from transportation costs on balance of payments since 1975 (Pendakur 1986). The high rates of urban population growth have resulted from larger absolute population movements to cities as well as natural increases within the cities. These growth rates are expected to remain relatively high, at least for the next two decades.

The Urban Poor

World population has grown faster and to higher numbers than Malthus would have ever imagined, but so have incomes. Although higher incomes have left the impression of betterment of average welfare, their distribution continues to be skewed in favour of the wealthy and upper middle class in most developing countries. This mismatch between population and incomes leaves many of the world's people in a vicious cycle of poverty. If we can correct this mismatch, we may yet evade the doom that Malthus saw as inevitable (Clausen 1984).

Of the more than one billion people in the low-income countries of Asia, about 50 per cent live in absolute poverty (Pendakur 1986). The number of urban poor is increasing despite all the measures to alleviate poverty. On a global scale, the number of urban poor households is expected to increase from 34 per cent in 1976 to 57 per cent in 2000 (World Bank 1990, 1992a).

In 1985, Asia had the vast majority, 72 per cent, of the world's poor. Some 700 million people in Asia had annual incomes below $370 per capita. The incidence of poverty is higher in South Asia (51 per cent) than in East Asia (20 per cent).

World Development Report 1990 set out what might be achieved in reducing poverty through expanded provision of social services for the poor coupled with growth scenarios that make productive use of labour. Under these assumptions and within the context of relatively favourable conditions for the global economy, the report estimated that Asia's share of the world's poor would decline from 72 per cent in 1985 to 53 per cent in 2000 (World Bank 1990). However, revised estimates indicate that poverty will continue to persist and that the poor will face even more severe environmental degradation. Asia's share of the world's poor is likely to be around two-thirds by the year 2000 (World Bank 1992a).

The slums and shanty towns of mega-cities in the developing countries are growing at twice the rate of the cities themselves. In parts of Latin America, these communities are known as *callampas,* or mushrooms, because they seem to grow up almost overnight. In some cases, the bulk of the urban population is in the slums: 67 per cent in Calcutta, 42 per cent in Mexico City, and 46 per cent in Bombay (Camp 1991).

Urban Living Standards

Air quality in Asian mega-cities is dismally low. According to 1991 World Health Organization (WHO) studies, 66 per cent of the world's urban population (1.52 billion) had polluted air, another 8 per cent had marginal air quality, and only 26 per cent (0.6 billion) had acceptable air quality. Asia's smokiest cities were Bangkok, Beijing, Delhi, Calcutta, and Tehran (World Health Organization 1991).

The Population Crisis Committee (PCC) has measured the quality of living in 100 largest metropolitan cities with more than 2 million people. Thirty-five of these cities were in Asia (Camp 1991). The livability index consists of the following components, each category having equal weight: public safety; food costs; living space; housing standards; communications; education; public health; peace and quiet; traffic flow; air quality and pollution. While there may be some disagreement as to the relative weight of each component of the index, the methodology is reasonably scientific in assessing a very complex question. Three components are important to transportation planners: ambient noise levels; traffic flow (average peak-hour traffic speeds in kmh); and air quality (air pollution measured in levels of suspended particulate matter, sulphur dioxide, and nitrogen oxide exceeding health thresholds defined by the WHO).

Table 8.4 shows the urban living standards of Southeast Asian cities. Although they do reasonably well in terms of ozone levels, many of them vastly exceeded the WHO standards for suspended particulate matter (SPM) and sulphur dioxide (SO_2). Being exposed to these levels of SPM, SO_2, and carbon monoxide (CO) emissions has serious consequences for public health. The immediate impact is to increase geometrically the incidence of cancers of the respiratory organs and to make more people susceptible to common respiratory diseases such as asthma, bronchitis, and emphysema.

Table 8.4

Urban living standards of Southeast Asian cities, 1990

	Population[a] (millions)	Levels of ambient noise[b]	Traffic flow at peak hour	Clean air[c]
Jakarta	9	6	16	173 days SPM
Manila	9	4	7	24 days SO_2
Bangkok	7	7	13	97 days SPM
Ho Chi Minh	3	7	20	–
Singapore	3	2	37	45 µg/m³ NO_2
Surabaya	3	8	17	–
Bandung	2	4	15	–

Notes:
a 1989 population, differs slightly from UN forecasts
b Subjective rating 1-10; noisiest 1 = > 90 dBA, 10 = < 60 dBa
c Number of days exceeding WHO standards
Source: Camp (1991)

Asian Mega-Cities

Asian mega-cities are dominant in social, political, and economic terms. Thirty to 60 per cent of the national GDP is produced in these cities single-handedly. They have been growing at very high rates, doubling their populations every fifteen to twenty years, primarily because of migration. Their economic capacity to absorb more people is substantially less than the vast number of people migrating into them. They have the nation's highest incidence of poverty and absolute poverty (Pendakur 1992). They also have unhealthy housing and environmental sanitation conditions for large portions of their populations (Camp 1991).

They also have the most severe traffic congestion and environmental problems. Vehicle ownership and growth rates are very high, due mainly to the concentration of wealth in the mega-cities compared to the rest of the country. Table 8.5 shows automobile ownership rates for several countries. Southeast Asian countries already have a substantially high level of motorization, both car and motorcycle, and motorization is likely to continue growing at very high rates. It is also likely that nearly 50 per cent of the country's private vehicles will be in the mega-cities.

Table 8.5

Persons per vehicle, 1991

United States	1.3	Taiwan	7.8	India	298.0
Canada	1.7	Malaysia	9.0	Pakistan	424.5
Australia	1.8	Hong Kong	18.0	China	638.6
New Zealand	1.9	Thailand	20.0	Bangladesh	707.5
Japan	2.3	South Korea	21.0		
Singapore	6.8	Indonesia	21.3		

Source: United Nations (1993b)

Congestion Management and Air Quality

Urban transportation planning methods in Asian mega-cities cater to motor vehicles as much as possible. Motor-vehicle use is heavily subsidized. It is only recently that some of the world's mega-cities are waking up to the fact that controlling automobile use and reducing air pollution is both economically efficient and ecologically sound. For example, the 12 million people spread over 17,000 km^2 of Los Angeles use their 8 million cars extensively. These automobiles and 31,000 businesses spew out 1,130 tons of noxious gases into the atmosphere every day. It is only since 1990 that governments are beginning to take action to curb the area's addiction to the single-occupancy car.

The general political and economic strategy in Asia is to build more highways and freeways and to launch mega-projects – highway and light rapid transit/mass rapid transit (LRT/MRT) – generally with the use of international aid and/or borrowing. The exceptions to this general rule are Hong Kong and Singapore. There is no strong effort, either technically or politically, to reduce single-occupancy automobile use in heavily congested corridors except in Singapore (Pendakur 1992).

The urban transportation systems in Southeast Asia are characterized by: heavily congested city centres; crawl rates of 2 to 10 kmh; the presence of 30 to 60 per cent of the country's motor vehicles; a 6 to 20 per cent annual increase in car ownership; a 10 to 30 per cent annual increase in motorcycles; significant air pollution now and no relief in sight; a very small proportion of total trips made by private car but the direction of almost all capital and maintenance expenditures towards these trips; a substantial proportion of total trips made by transit but little attention to transit priority systems; and a still substantial number of non-motorized trips but accommodation for them beginning in only a few countries while others restrict or ban them (Pendakur 1992).

Some of the worst traffic flow conditions in the world are in Asia. The crawl rates vary from 1 to 20 kmh during the peak hours, and the peak hour itself can last all day. The crawl rates in the worst bottlenecks in Asia were recently identified: Bangkok, Rama 9 and Asoke-Dindaeg roads, 1.2 kmh; Tokyo, Kyoshu Kaido station, Shinjuku station, 4 kmh; Kuala Lumpur, Jl Ampang, 8 kmh; Singapore, Johor Baru causeway, 8 kmh; Manila, Edsa, 10 kmh; Karachi, Nizamabad and Saddar, 10 kmh; and Hong Kong, Cross Harbour Tunnel, 12 kmh (*Asiaweek,* 28 February 1992).

Bangkok

Bangkok, Mexico City, and Lagos have the world's worst levels of traffic congestion, crawl rates, and air quality. They are characterized by governments and technical bureaucracies that cater to the ownership and use of the private car. By any transportation planning and congestion management standards, the worst conditions exist here.

Bangkok has 15 per cent of Thailand's population and 50 per cent of Thailand's motor vehicles. It produces 50 per cent of Thailand's GDP and its GDP grew at 9 to 15 per cent during 1986-91. Per capita income in the city is 315 per cent of Thailand's average. Bangkok is primate in all aspects. Its human population is growing at an annual rate of 2 per cent and the motor-vehicle population is growing at 15 per cent annually (cars 12 per cent and motorcycles 18 per cent). Peak-hour average traffic flow for the Central Business District (CBD) is 6 to 10 kmh and the worst crawl rates are at 1 to 2 kmh (see Table 8.6). Between 500 and 550 new cars are added to Bangkok's car population every day. It is not unusual for a trip of 40 km, from the airport to the CBD, to take anywhere from one to three hours, even with a limited-access toll freeway.

Table 8.6 shows the details of current urban transport demand management techniques used in Bangkok. Massive urban transport investments are being made in Bangkok. An LRT/MRT system nearly 100 km long and consisting of three different route systems has been approved and is expected to be completed in ten years. Massive new freeway systems are under construction. All this, when completed, is supposed to bring the situation to normal. The total bill for mass transit and freeway systems is estimated at $15 billion. There is great deal of effort to create new supply but no effort at all to manage demand.

Table 8.6

Bangkok's urban transportation status

| | Millions of motor vehicles | | | | Growth rate (%) |
	1978	1983	1988	1991	1978-88
Private car	0.25	0.41	0.79	1.11	12
Motorcycle	0.15	0.39	0.77	1.27	18
Other	0.10	0.14	0.20	0.24	6
Total	0.50	0.94	1.76	2.62	

Peak hour traffic flow	Speed
Average for central area	18 kmh
Average for CBD	6-10 kmh
Worst crawl rate	1-2 kmh
Worst condition, Rama 9 & Asoke	1.2 kmh
Suburban crawl, airport to Rangsit	7 kmh

Traffic management demand	Response
Traffic restraint	None
Vehicle ownership restraint	None
Mode shift measures (car to bus)	None
Building additional highways	Under construction
Existing toll highway	Cheap tolls
MRT/LRT system	Several proposed
Area licensing schemes	Rejected

Many Bangkok car owners use leaded gasoline, and 70 per cent of the air pollution is derived from motor vehicles. Carbon monoxide (CO), suspended particulate matter (SPM), and ozone (O_3) levels are very high and far exceed WHO standards. It has been estimated that an eight-hour exposure at street level to Bangkok's air, such as that experienced by street vendors, pedestrians, and traffic police, is equivalent to smoking nine cigarettes a day. A recent study showed that among the 1,758 Bangkok Metropolitan Traffic Police, 753 suffer from a variety of respiratory diseases, including asthma and lung cancer, and from other illnesses, such as conjunctivitis. And 420 of these have been suffering from these diseases for more than five years (Pendakur 1992).

Bangkok's environmental problems are serious and set to become worse in every aspect. SPM in the air ranges two to four times the WHO acceptable maximums, CO is 50 per cent above the standard, and lead is double. Greenhouse gas emissions are far above the average for a country of Thailand's level of economic development. Although per capita emissions of carbon dioxide (CO_2) and methane (CH_4) and use of chlorofluorocarbons (CFCs) are lower than in the industrialized countries, when compared on the basis of emissions measured against GNP, Thailand outranks many other developing and industrialized countries (Panayatou and Phantumvanit 1991).

The Thai government has not responded constructively to these critical environmental threats. In July 1991, duties and taxes on cars and motorcycles were reduced drastically in the guise of competition. Duties on cars went down from 300 to 112 per cent and on motorcycles from 180 to 60 per cent. The immediate impact of this policy in Bangkok will first be a massive increase in the number of motorcycles and then a significant increase in car ownership. The government is also embarking on major new freeways and LRT/MRT systems. These may take five to fifteen years to become operational. In the meantime, degradation of air quality continues.

Kuala Lumpur

Kuala Lumpur is not a mega-city in the quantitative sense but is a powerful primate city. Its population of 1.7 million is only 9 per cent of Malaysia's population but has 34 per cent of the national GDP. During 1986-91, Kuala Lumpur's GDP grew at 7 to 12 per cent annually.

Table 8.7 shows motorization in Kuala Lumpur. The city has 50 per cent of Malaysia's motor vehicles. The already high motor-vehicle population is expected to grow at 18 to 30 per cent per annum during the next ten years: private cars at 18 to 25 per cent and motorcycles at 15 to 30 per cent. If the current planning method of handling private motor vehicles for peak-hour traffic continues, then Kuala Lumpur will require massive new investments in transportation infrastructure, not necessarily assuring either better traffic flow or better air quality. The table shows the traffic flow conditions in Kuala Lumpur. The worst crawl rates are at 3 to 8 kmh and peak-hour traffic flow within the CBD is fairly good at 28 kmh. The government has invested massively during past fifteen years in highway and freeway construction in the city. There is no demand management but fairly good supply management. In the last year alone, traffic volumes are estimated to have increased by 20 per cent. There are proposals to build LRT/MRT systems but none to restrain single-occupancy car travel during the peak hours.

Haze is an annual occurrence in Kuala Lumpur. Although haze is not caused exclusively by motor vehicles, they are a major source of the SPM in the air. There are 2.8 million motor vehicles and they release 3,700 tons of SPM per year (based on 1989 figures). Visibility is greatly reduced and breathing is frequently much impaired. On 10 October 1991, the Malaysian meteorological service measurements of air pollution in Kuala Lumpur indicated 570 µg of SPM per m^3 of air, five times the safe threshold set by the WHO. Visibility in Kuala Lumpur had been reduced to 300 m. The

Table 8.7

Kuala Lumpur's urban transportation status

	Millions of motor vehicles		Growth rate (%)	
	Malaysia 1990	Kuala Lumpur 1990	1985-90	1990-2000
Private car	1.8	0.9	400	18-25 / year
Motorcycle	0.2	0.2		15-30 / year
Other	0.5	0.3		
Total	2.8	1.4		

Peak hour traffic flow	*Speed*
Average for central area	28 kmh
Average for CBD	15 kmh
Worst crawl rate	5-8 kmh
Worst condition,	
Jalan Ampang	3-6 kmh
Suburban crawl	35-50 kmh

Traffic management demand	*Response*
Traffic restraint	None
Vehicle ownership restraint	None
Mode shift measures (car to bus)	Some
Building additional highways	Proposed
Existing toll highway	None
MRT/LRT system	Several proposed
Area licensing schemes	
(proposed 1978 and 1983)	Rejected

government also reported a 5 to 10 per cent increase in the incidence of asthma, conjunctivitis, and other diseases.

Some of the smog is produced by motor vehicles, some by industry, and some by open burning in the plantations. These three sources release 25,000 tons of SPM per year, based on 1989 figures. Depending upon climate and atmospheric inversions, 25 to 40 per cent of the air pollution in Kuala Lumpur is caused by motor vehicles (*Asiaweek*, 25 October 1991). In 1990, Kuala Lumpur's 1.4 million vehicles released 4,000 tons of particulates into the atmosphere, and industries and open burning another 21,000 tons (*Far Eastern Economic Review*, 14 November 1991).

Singapore

All over the world as incomes increase, households invest in higher mobility. This is evidenced by the extraordinarily high rate of increase in private cars and motorcycles in Asia. Even though only a small number of households in this region can now afford to own a motor vehicle, as incomes increase, this will change.

Singapore has the highest taxes on automobile ownership and peak-hour use in the world. A medium-sized car in Singapore costs 2.5 times that in Manila, 3.0 times that in Jakarta, and 4.0 times that in Bangkok. Yet even in Singapore, there is a consistent and steady increase in car ownership. During 1980-90, real per capita incomes in Singapore increased at a rate much higher than in other countries. Consistent with this, there was a gradual and steady increase of 66 per cent in car ownership over the period.

Singapore is one of the few countries in the world with a strict area licensing scheme (ALS), requiring all peak-hour car users destined for the CBD to pay a heavy entry fee. The ALS system was instituted in 1975 and has been operating successfully ever since. It is based on the simple principle that car users have to pay the total cost of using the car and that no subsidies, direct or indirect, are to be given. In simple terms, this means very high road taxes, licences, insurance, entry fees to restricted areas, and parking costs. Concurrently, the government has expanded the bus system vastly and recently built a 44 km MRT system at a cost of $3 billion. It has also accepted strict population planning for cars as a policy principle. All the policy tools are economic in nature. The total population of cars and their growth rate is controlled simply by heavy taxes for ownership and use.

In 1990, a system of bidding or tendering was instituted for the eligibility certificate required to buy a car. This certificate now costs about $7,000 to $10,000. The taxes on six-year-old cars are very high, high enough to make it uneconomical to keep a car for more than seven years. Driving this particular tax is the fact that most old cars are heavy polluters. In addition, construction of a single-car commercial parking space is taxed at $5,000. If someone then wants to use the space during the peak hour, a monthly ALS fee of about $60 applies. The ALS fee is not applicable to car pools with three or more people. Several studies have shown that the measures used in the Singapore ALS are easy to understand, easy to enforce, and effective in reducing the peak-hour car use (Pendakur 1989; Pendakur, Behbehani, and Armstrong-Wright 1984). They are complemented by an excellent and reasonably priced bus and MRT system, which is necessary as a feasible and affordable alternative for the displaced automobile users.

Recently, Singapore has introduced the new concept of the weekend car. This car cannot be used from 7:00 A.M. to 6:00 P.M., Monday to Friday, or from 7:00 A.M. to 2:00 P.M. on Saturdays, except if those days are public holidays. The purpose is to enable car use for social purposes but to cut down on peak-hour, single-occupancy, work-related use.

Immediately after the introduction of the ALS system, there was a substantial reduction in single-occupancy cars and a major shift to transit. In the first few months of operation, private-car use during the peak hours decreased from 48 to 27 per cent. Private-car use decreased as far as peak-hour use is concerned, from 17 per cent in 1980 to 14 per cent in 1990, even though incomes increased. The ALS system has succeeded beyond the original expectations only because the government has been doggedly persistent in its policy of taming the automobile (Pendakur 1992).

Singapore has now embarked seriously on the feasibility of introducing electronic road pricing (ERP). Vehicles would be fitted with electronic devices that registered on electronic collection systems installed in roads. Motorists would then be charged a per kilometre or per mile rate on high usage roads. Studies are being conducted now and ERP is expected to be operational soon (Public Works Department 1991).

Urban Transport Policy and Planning

In large mega-cities such as Bangkok and Tokyo, urban travel has become the worst ordeal of the day. Investment and regulatory policy responses in the Southeast Asian cities, notably excepting Singapore, have hitherto been feeble and have focused primarily on facilitating automobile use, although some cities have made efforts to increase the capacity of transit systems and also to build new LRT/MRT systems.

Even some not-so-comprehensive schemes have been successful in increasing the efficiency of traffic flow. In April 1992, Jakarta traffic police began requiring cars using all major routes during the morning peak hours to carry at least three people. They implemented this plan zealously. The results: cars were moving at 80 kmh and buses cut travel time by some 40 per cent. Since this plan had no basis in law, however, it became undone in June 1992, when courts ruled it illegal (*Asiaweek*, 26 June 1992).

Tokyo provides some interesting lessons. Japan is the richest, most technologically sophisticated country in the world today and has the highest capital surplus. One-third of all Japanese companies and employees are in Tokyo. In the service sector, 50 per cent of all Japanese employment is in Tokyo. Each day, close to 4 million people commute to Tokyo. Greater Tokyo has 10 per cent of Japan's land and 32 per cent of the population. The result is enormous cost, congestion, and fatigue ('Tokyo or Bust,' *Far Eastern Economic Review*, 19 September 1991). The bullet trains, once regarded as a deluxe conveyance, have become another commuting hell for the white-collar Tokyoite. Overcrowding is defined officially as when a rail car is packed to 200 per cent of capacity, when 'bodies are firmly pressed together but you still have enough elbow room to read a magazine.' At 250 to 300 per cent, 'you cannot move your hands.' Recently, Tokyo administration proudly announced that rush hour crowding on the trains had dropped to a mere 200 to 240 per cent of capacity.

It is interesting to consider the work trip time lengths in Tokyo. Seventy per cent of people spend more than forty-five minutes, one way, for work trips; 50 per cent take more than an hour each way. The work day is thus extended to ten or twelve hours. It is no wonder that many Japanese workers would rather stay in capsule hotels overnight than go home for the evening. In poorer countries, the consequences are even more serious. In Bangkok, even where employers provide special employees-only buses, people leave home at 6:00 A.M. and return home at 7:00 P.M. If employee transportation is not provided, the situation is worse (Pendakur 1992).

What are the social, environmental, and economic consequences of this kind of urban living? Can these cities sustain it for any length of time without a total collapse of the system? The social consequences of dislocation, fatigue, and long hours are well documented. The consequences of environmental degradation for public health have also been well documented by several organizations, including the United Nations (United Nations Environment Program 1988; Camp 1991). Submissions to the United Nations Conference on Environment and Development in Rio de Janeiro in June 1992 showed that in one year, Bangkok traffic jams cost an estimated $1 billion in extra fuel burned and work time lost. This does not include the environmental cost of additional air pollution (*Asiaweek,* 28 February 1992). If these cities are to sustain themselves and survive, a new policy regime must focus on including all the costs and benefits – economic, social, and environmental – of choice of transportation mode. This regime must be structured to be flexible and dynamic over time. Efforts should be directed towards building efficiency, equity, and sustainability.

The highest priority should be assigned to people, emphasizing feet first, pedal next, and motor maybe, without sacrificing the focus on an economic and efficient movement of people. Solutions to the congestion problem should focus on assigning appropriate roles for the private car and high-occupancy vehicles during the peak hours and at the same time preserving the right to own and enjoy the use of the car. The primary requisite for developing sustainable urban transport in the mega-cities is to construct dynamic complementary investment and regulatory policies that are economically efficient, ecologically sustainable, and socially equitable. This requires a careful, systematic, and dynamic balancing of the three components, all of which include externalities.

An economically efficient and sustainable urban transport system demands major changes to currently practised analytical methods and to the structure of the political economy applicable to urban transport. It requires that:

- macro-economic costs include sector costs and social costs
- all subsidies – direct, indirect, and cross-sector transfers – be calculated

and balanced against benefits to the environment and to human beings

- public and private costs be calculated and costs recovered from all bene-ficiaries
- user costs be directly related to questions of the equity, costs, and bene-fits relating to economic and environmental sectors
- minimum average mobility and time savings be accomplished.

This last point requires establishing thresholds for time savings as part of public policy.

An efficient and sustainable system requires that analysis and policy measures should:

- establish air quality thresholds for all pollutants (specifically for CO, CO_2, SPM, SO_2, NO_2, and O_3 at least) by all transport vehicles and users, temporally and otherwise
- establish clearly defined environment energy policies that require mini-mum use and maximum conservation and reduce dependency for imported petro fuels
- establish noise thresholds temporally and otherwise for all vehicles and users
- define safety thresholds for both life and property
- avoid permitting social dislocation, degradation, and dysfunction in the interest of maximizing time efficiency of transportation.

Such a system also requires that governments devise broader strategies designed to:

- set clear limits to costs and cost recovery in terms of the ability of the poor to pay for transportation
- permit access to employment by the poor and give high priority to the transportation modes they use
- give substantial priority to non-polluting and less polluting modes such as non-motorized transport and high-occupancy vehicles
- significantly improve non-transportation solutions such as reducing trip lengths by coordinating housing and job locations
- spread system costs and benefits equitably.

This new thinking demands a complete overhaul of the currently used analytical and intellectual bases of transportation policy and planning, which have been in vogue since the late 1950s. These methods have become obsolete as new knowledge has accumulated with respect to pollutants, pollution, public health, costs, and consequences. If the pol-icy and planning system is not drastically overhauled soon, it will be the end of the road.

Note

Valuable research information and documents provided by Richard Scurfield and Peter Midgeley of the World Bank are gratefully acknowledged. Haizi Xu of the School of Community and Regional Planning, University of British Columbia, assisted the author in the analysis and the graphics of this paper and his assistance is very much appreciated.

1 Bangkok traffic exemplifies the term gridlock. Slopopolis is a sloppy metropolis. It is defined as an endless array of subdivision and use of land purely for corporate and individual profit and pleasure without any relevance to or the consideration of community consequences or community benefits. The slopopolis is a metropolis in which private land uses neither pay for nor account for community facilities, social and physical infrastructure, or degradation of air and water quality, but it is also an economically thriving metropolis.

9

The Roles and Contributions of the Private Sector in Environmental Management in ASEAN Mega-Urban Regions

Shirley A.M. Conover

The ASEAN countries are both blessed and cursed with three of the world's largest mega-urban regions: Bangkok, Jakarta, and Manila. The association also includes in its membership one state that is essentially a mega-urban region in its own right, Singapore. This paper deals with two aspects of mega-urban regions: the challenges and opportunities facing the ASEAN mega-urban regions over the environment, and the roles and contributions of the private sector in the rational management of the environment. Let me deal with the environment first

Environment

Capital and Carrying Capacity
Most generations of humankind have assumed that the natural 'services' on which they have relied – the world's ecosystems, land, natural resources, and continuously renewed life-support systems in the forms of air, water, favourable temperature ranges, soil fertility, and so on – would always be available in infinite supply. This attitude persisted as a succession of societies evolved from small groups of hunter-gatherers to pastoralists, agriculturists, and on into industrial development. Some communities in marginal environments were forced to recognize limitations to the production of goods and services and to life itself. Others gradually but surely overexploited their environments so that communities or whole civilizations waned and expired. With the current growth of human populations, and the increasing demands placed upon the world's natural resources and systems, concern is growing that demands on the environment may exceed its capacity to supply them.

The discipline of economics is concerned with the production and distribution of 'wealth': the 'riches' or material possessions and capacities that are normally described in monetary terms. It has been known for some time, however, that conventional economics is an inadequate tool for valuing economies and their resources because it fails to include in its valuations stocks and flows of natural resources, environmental degradation (defor- estation, soil erosion, etc.), the capacity of the environment to render harmless and assimilate discharged wastes, and overarching life-support systems. These considerations are all vital for the achievement of sustain- able development, ensuring that future generations will have the same or better access to natural wealth as have all the present human populations.

The emerging science of ecological economics clarifies these relation- ships. It takes a holistic view of the environment-economy system; that is, the economy is considered a subset of the natural system of the earth and completely dependent upon it for living and non-living resources, life- support systems, and assimilation of wastes. Land, resources, and life-sup- port systems are represented by *natural capital* and are available in finite supply. The ability of humans to create not only material things but also complex social structures, cultural diversity, intellectual property, cooper- ative arrangements, and systems of ethics are all included in *cultural capi- tal* (Berkes 1992). Cultural capital interfaces between natural capital and manufactured capital, and it will largely determine how societies use nat- ural resources to manufacture capital. *Manufactured capital* is, of course, all the material things that humans make, from computer chips to container ships, books to space platforms, and plows to office towers. Since the pri- vate sector is intimately involved with all three types of capital, these rela- tionships and constraints are of fundamental importance in determining private-sector opportunities and contributions.

In the context of the supply of natural capital, all urban regions share a characteristic relative to land and resources that relates directly to supply and demand. The land and resource base required to support an urban region is usually at least an order of magnitude larger than that contained within its administrative boundaries or even within its associated built-up area (Rees 1992). Thus an urban area of, say, 50 km² will require an area of at least 500 km² to support it.

How is this relationship arrived at? Ecologists define the carrying capac- ity of a particular area as 'the population of a given species that can be supported indefinitely in a defined habitat without permanently damag- ing the ecosystem upon which it is dependent' (Rees 1992). For the human species, carrying capacity can be described as the maximum rate of resource consumption and waste discharge that can be sustained indef- initely in a defined area without progressively impairing the functional integrity and productivity of the ecosystems essential for its permanent maintenance. The relationship between sustainable production and per capita demand determines the size of the human population that can be sustained in that defined region. Rees (1992) observes that 'every city is an ecological black hole drawing on the material resources and productivity of a vast and scattered hinterland many times the size of the city itself. High density settlements "appropriate" carrying capacity from distant elsewheres.'

To illustrate this concept, Rees examined his own mega-urban region, Vancouver and the lower Fraser Valley of southern British Columbia in Canada. The population of the region is 1.7 million people. Considering present Canadian consumer demands in terms of only food, wood fibre, and fossil fuel, 8.3 million hectares (ha) of arable and forested land in continuous production is required. However, the lower Fraser Valley contains only 400,000 ha of such land. Thus the regional population 'imports' the productive capacity of a land area twenty-one times the size that it actually occupies to support these three types of demands. The sources are elsewhere in British Columbia, elsewhere in Canada, elsewhere in North America, and elsewhere in the world, defining the regional to global trading systems. The city and its associated population is a 'node of pure consumption' dependent on the resources, life-support systems, and assimilative capacities of natural systems for discharged wastes of an extensive land and resource base somewhere else. This dedicated resource base must grow if and as the city and its associated population grow.

It is no secret that Canadians rank high on the world's list of heavy consumers. Considering overall consumption patterns, let us say that, as a representative of a high-income country, Canadians' per capita consumption of the world's goods, services, and life-support systems is an order of magnitude greater than that of their developing-country neighbours. Using this as the basis for a very rough calculation, a developing-country population of the same size as that in the Lower Mainland of British Columbia might require a support area of 830,000 ha of land and resources in continuous production: one-tenth of the land and resources required to support the demands of their high-income, high-consumption global neighbours. This is an important basis for south-north tensions over the industrial northern countries' appropriation of much of the global resource base to support their economies and lifestyles and the equity issues that arise therefrom.

In common with others, ASEAN mega-urban regions exhibit this characteristic of drawing on lands, resources, and ecological life-support functions that vastly exceed the urban centres' respective administrative boundaries. The ASEAN mega-urban region examined here in some detail is Metro Manila, though it has much in common with Bangkok, Jakarta, and many other ASEAN cities.

Using a very unsophisticated analysis, Map 9.1 illustrates the mega-urban region of which Metro Manila is the centre. The criterion used for inclusion was a significant flow of produce, goods, and services to the

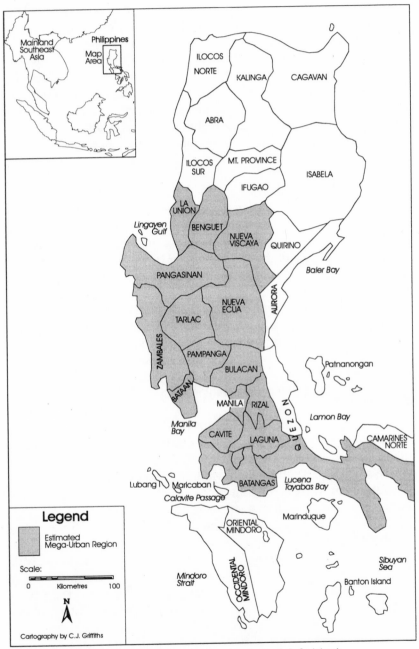

Map 9.1 **Metro Manila mega-urban region (ecological definition)**

Metro Manila urban centre from the outlying provinces (which have to support their resident populations as well). Access to adequate transportation infrastructure, specifically roads, seemed to determine the bounds of this mega-urban region. The map does not recognize the produce, goods, and services shipped in to Metro Manila from elsewhere in the Philippines and through international trade. The analysis in this chapter relating to private-sector activity will centre on just a portion of the region, as shown later. It will be evident from even this superficial analysis that Metro Manila draws on a vast hinterland to supply it with resources and services, confirming this characteristic of mega-urban regions.

The Total Environmental Management System

Carrying capacity was defined above as the maximum rate of resource consumption and waste discharge that can be sustained indefinitely in a defined area without progressively impairing the functional integrity and productivity of the ecosystems essential for its permanent maintenance. Easy to say, but much harder to do, especially as we are only beginning to learn what has to be done in a systematic way and at a scale sufficient to be effective. 'Environmental management' is the conscious direction of informed effort by people and agencies to maintain and sustain the carrying capacity of any given physical area, from a local field or stream to the global commons. The carrying capacity in question can be in terms of humans or of other species, or both. From a global perspective and in the world we all want, it will include millions of species, of which humankind is only one.

Who 'does' environmental management (one form of cultural capital)? The total environmental management system of any country or association of countries, such as ASEAN or the United Nations, is carried out by people working individually and within institutions and is divided into six mutually inclusive groups: the people, their governments, their private sector, their educational system, their non-governmental groups, and their communicators, including all forms of media by which they communicate (Figure 9.1). Rulers, leaders, and communicators are at the centre of the management system because these individuals tend to talk with each other, usually represent more than one group, and are an important means to develop and disseminate ideas, plans, and actions. The private sector plays an enormously important role in this environmental management and communications system.

My work and experience in both Southeast Asia and Canada have convinced me of an important point: that environmental management can and should be carried out at all levels of institutional organization and that environmental management ideas and initiatives can originate, and

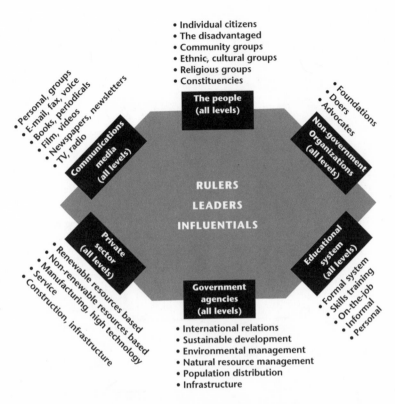

- Individual citizens
- The disadvantaged
- Community groups
- Ethnic, cultural groups
- Religious groups
- Constituencies

- Personal, groups
- E-mail, fax, voice
- Books, periodicals
- Film, videos
- Newspapers, newsletters
- TV, radio

Communications media (all levels)

The people (all levels)

- Foundations
- Doers
- Advocates

Non-government Organizations (all levels)

RULERS LEADERS INFLUENTIALS

Private sector (all levels)

- Renewable resources based
- Non-renewable resources based
- Manufacturing, high technology
- Service
- Construction, infrastructure

Educational system (all levels)

- Formal system
- Skills training
- On-the-job
- Informal
- Personal

Government agencies (all levels)

- International relations
- Sustainable development
- Environmental management
- Natural resource management
- Population distribution
- Infrastructure

Figure 9.1 **Generic environmental management and communications system**

must be applied, at *any* level, from systems of governance at the international level right down to and up from the grass roots. Figure 9.2 tries to illustrate this concept hydrologically, with a rain of ideas for understanding and action from the 'clouds' at the top supported equally by a rising flow of ideas from the 'ground water well' and exchanges at all points in between. The grouping is somewhat different here than in some models that separate developers, governments, and people and communities into three groups. Obviously, the boundaries between these three groups will be blurred in some situations. Equally obviously, mega-urban regions fit into this diagram from at least the provincial level on down and, in the case of the city-state of Singapore, from the country level down.

This figure also illustrates my belief that no single level of organization can 'do it all' in environmental management or in a host of other activities. Present moves on the parts of governments and other agencies to decentralize have many positive aspects, but the larger the system or area under consideration the greater will be the need for the rational involvement of higher levels of governance while maintaining good involvement

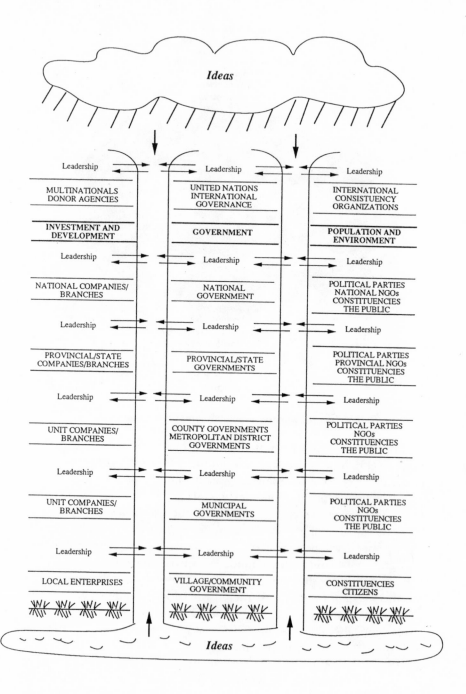

Figure 9.2 **Generic total environmental management system**

and integration of needs and concerns at lower levels. The needs and desires of individuals have to be balanced against the needs and desires of the relevant societies, raising important though often difficult questions of distribution and social equity.

Laguna Lake Basin, Philippines

The private sector of any country directs its efforts to a huge variety of resource extraction and manufacturing activities. In order to move this discussion from the general to the particular, let us examine a section of Metro Manila's mega-urban region, the Laguna Lake Basin. The following material is drawn from a study carried out by the Environment and Resource Management Project, Philippines, of Dalhousie University and the University of the Philippines at Los Banos, funded mainly by the Canadian International Development Agency (Sly 1992).

The Laguna Lake Basin covers an area of about 380,000 ha, of which about 90,000 ha is the lake surface. The outer boundary is the boundary of the basin's watershed. Important features are Metro Manila in the northwest, mountains of volcanic origin to the northeast and in the south, a significant area of flat agricultural land on the lakeshore being overtaken by urban sprawl and linear development, and extensive portions of irrigated land on the southeastern and southwestern lakeshore. Formerly heavily forested, forest cover has decreased from 53 per cent of the basin's area in the mid-1940s to about 8 per cent in the mid-1980s, and to less than 5 per cent at present. Mixed timber and agricultural plantations (agro-forestry) cover more extensive areas of the basin. Soil erosion is a major problem where forest cover has not been re-established on steep slopes, where soil conservation is not used to support cultivation, and on many construction sites in this rapidly developing region. The rainfall pattern includes a dry season and a wet season, with heavy rainfalls accompanying frequent typhoons (averaging twenty-one per annum), and these are heavy erosion events.

Conversion from rural to urban land use is proceeding at a rapid rate; between 1975 and 2000, urban areas could more than double in size, with a concomitant decline of rural populations from 11 to 8 per cent of the regional total in the same period. Overall, the population of the basin is expected to triple between 1975 and 2000.

Massive changes are occurring in the economic and social fabric of the basin, and stress is particularly severe in subsistence economies such as shifting agricultural cultivation and open-lake fishery, which used to provide up to 40 per cent of the protein supply to Manila. Forestry resources are depleted, and periodic collapses have occurred in both the cultured and the open-lake fisheries. On the other hand, improved agricultural practices are bringing about an estimated increase in overall apparent self-sufficiency from 12 per cent to over 40 per cent in key products such as pork, poultry, rice, fruits, and sugar. Nonetheless, self-sufficiencies in beef, corn, and vegetables will remain low and may even decline.

Water supply is becoming a major concern throughout the basin. By the year 2000, agricultural requirements are expected to take about half the available water capacity of the region. It is estimated that irrigation water in the Philippines is charged out to users at only 20 per cent of actual cost (World Bank 1992b), an example of distortions caused by subsidies. In addition, water use is growing in both urban and industrial areas. The Metropolitan Waterworks and Sewage System in Manila is expected to take a further 20 per cent of the basin capacity by the end of this century. Water imports from outside the basin's watershed are projected.

More then 10 per cent of the industrial capacity of the Philippines is located in Metro Manila. Industrial development is concentrated north of the city in the Marikina River valley and along the northwestern shore of Laguna Lake as far south as San Pedro. Industrial effluents and emissions are inadequately controlled; in the mid-1980s nearly one-quarter of the industries in the basin were without proper waste treatment facilities. Industrial development in the basin is estimated to have doubled since then.

The Napindan Hydraulic Control Structure was designed mainly to regulate the periodic flow of sea water from Manila Bay into the lake, caused by tidal exchanges during dry season low lake levels. The Mangahan Floodway is a partial diversion of the Marikina River and is designed to reduce the problems of severe flooding in Metro Manila. When the hydraulic control structure is open, polluted waters from the Pasig River and Manila Bay can back-flush into Laguna Lake, along with polluted waters entering from the Marikina River down the Mangahan Floodway. The completion of the control structure coincided with major crashes in the wild and cultured fish harvests. Many affected parties are convinced that the control structure is the culprit, even though the burden of proof suggests that the causes are much more complex, interconnected, and lie elsewhere.

Power generation facilities within the basin include both hydro-electric and oil-fired technologies. A geothermal power plant is also being considered as the Philippines is desperately short of power supplies in this region. A lube oil refinery and a large cement plant are other industrial operations on the lakeshore.

At least two large development plans are focused on the Laguna Lake Basin: the Southern Tagalog Plan for Region IV; and the Calabarzon Project, which includes five provinces in the Metro Manila mega-urban region. The objectives are to advance the economic and social well-being of the region, improve agricultural productivity, create industrial and urban growth centres away from Manila, and seek growth and development that is sustainable and compatible with the environment.

Proposed developments include construction of dikes and drainage channels to protect low-lying areas of Metro Manila near the out-flow of Laguna Lake; channelization of the Pasig River for pollution clean-up and raising and strengthening its banks to carry a greater volume of water and for flood control; a system of interceptor sewers to capture effluents being discharged from urban, industrial, and intensive agricultural areas, including a treatment plant or plants; the Paranaque Spillway for flood control and other water manipulation purposes; a circum-lake dike and roadway system; reclamation of 3,000 ha of land at the head of West Bay for urban and industrial use; shore and tributary clean-up and reclamation; solid waste and air quality management; additional municipal water supplies; road and rail connections; regional industrial parks; rural support programs; fisheries development; and additional tourism and recreation. Important tourist destinations at the moment include the Pagsanjan River Gorge, Mt. Makiling National Park and Botanical Garden, and Talim Island.

The Laguna Lake Basin lies within many overlapping jurisdictions. Availability and use of the resources of the basin are governed by public policy; by national, regional, provincial, and municipal development plans; and in operational terms by a number of agencies. As is common in such situations, a regional authority was created, the Laguna Lake Development Authority (LLDA), formed in 1966. While the overall intention of all these policies, programs, and agencies is desirable and sustainable development, rehabilitation of degraded areas, and conservation of essential resources, the structure of roles and responsibilities among the major agencies responsible for planning, enforcement, and standards for the basin is complex. The role of LLDA is central to the future of the basin, but helping it to become an effective coordinating agency as well as upgrading its analytical and management capabilities are major requirements. A number of recommendations for clarifying and enhancing its role and improving environmental management development in the basin are made in the Laguna Lake Basin report (Sly 1992) but these are not the subject of this chapter.

The Roles and Contributions of the Private Sector

As stated above, the private sector has an enormous, and enormously important, environmental management role to play in the rational development of mega-urban regions in ASEAN, as everywhere else in the world. This is especially evident now, when the problems and failures of central planning and government-owned and -operated corporations are sadly in evidence and there is a fairly universal move towards privatization, decentralization, and democratization. I should hasten to add that no system is without its problems and failures, including environmental management. Given the current direction of economic structuring, however, it is important to identify the means whereby the private sector can and will contribute positively and willingly to environmental management for sustainable development because, among other factors, it is to its advantage to do so.

In this analysis I wish to emphasize that the private sector, the major engine connecting consumers with that which they wish to consume, manifests itself at all levels of social organization, from exchanges of goods and services between individuals, through the informal sector, right up to national public utilities and multinational, or transnational, corporations. After all, all of us as individuals and families are consumers, the ultimate private-sector actors. All levels have to understand their roles in environmental management and sustainable development. It is important that systems of governance for mega-urban regions recognize this and not equate the 'private sector' with large and visible corporations only, concentrating their educative and regulatory efforts only there, as strategically important as it is to pay attention to those corporations.

Nonetheless, a focus on the obvious, larger industries is one important place to start (following the principle of 'worst first,' discussed in Bartone, Bernstein, and Leitman 1992). Visible improvements in this area can have a profound influence on other private-sector actors and yield positive political capital for those responsible for the systems of governance. This was the well-defined strategy of the government of Indonesia in instituting its Clean Rivers Program (PROKASIH), which has had a considerable degree of success.

As national to local environmental management systems develop and mature, private-sector environmental management systems develop in concert, often leading the way in certain aspects. In the United States, for example, the 1986 regulatory requirement for industries to fully characterize and publicly report their toxic chemical effluent and emissions discharges (USEPA Toxic Release Inventory) was found to be one of the most significant incentives to date in influencing industries to engage in self-examination and initiatives for pollution prevention and internalization (Howatson 1991; D. Wheeler, personal communication, 1992). Important results for private-sector actors were: increased profits due to improved technology efficiencies, reuse or recycling of what had formerly been considered wastes, and public approval and selection of the resulting products; peer pressure from within the particular industrial sector; promotion of mutual technical assistance and transfer of good practices within industrial sectors; increased contact with customers and suppliers; enlightened self-interest in wanting to be perceived as good corporate citizens; and fear of legal action by negatively affected individuals, groups (in class action suits), or other industries. Needless to say, these developments contributed significantly to the improvement of the total environmental management system.

Stages in Corporate Environmental Management
Three stages have been identified in the evolution of corporate environmental management: ad hoc management, management for compliance, and management for sustainable development (Howatson 1990, 1991; Schmidheiny with the Business Council for Sustainable Development 1992). These are clearly illustrated by the evolutionary history of pollution control and waste management but apply equally to resource extraction, construction, or any other phase of industrial processing with environment and sustainable development implications.

Stage 1 ad hoc responses to environmental issues and impacts are unsystematic, occur after the fact, often in response to violations or lawsuits, and are characterized as 'react and cure.'

Stage 2 occurs as the public gains environmental awareness and begins to exert pressures that result in tighter legislation and stronger legal sanctions. Corporations shift to the compliance mode in response to these pressures, institutionalizing environmental management functions, developing environmental policies, improving health and safety policies, sometimes instituting stricter corporate operational standards, initiating corporate environmental audits, and implementing systematic environmental impact management. Nevertheless, the compliance stage still operates in the mode of 'end of pipe' control.

Given ever increasing public environmental awareness and expectations, enlightened corporations recognize that they will never 'catch up' with increasingly stricter regulations and instead pass on to Stage 3, managing for sustainable development. Stage 3 is characterized by a proactive mode of operation. This includes: innovation, cradle-to-grave stewardship (designing products to include the effective management of their impact on the environment over their life cycle), 'anticipate-and-prevent' approaches, increased efficiency of operations, beneficial conservation practices, waste reduction and reuse, substitution of materials, manufacturing modifications, creative and committed management attitudes, minimizing the firm's environmental liabilities, and gaining competitive advantages through superior environmental performance. Common obstacles to attaining Stage 3 performance are initial perceived or real additional costs in time and money, inability or failure of key actors to gain access to relevant information and/or act on it, and non-supportive management attitudes at crucial locations within the firm.

The response of the best and most enlightened of the private-sector actors in recognizing that 'the carrying capacity of the planet – to absorb growing amounts of waste and to sustain burgeoning populations – must be the starting point for building a sustainable future' (Howatson 1991) is encouraging. It represents a fundamental change in corporate vision and resulting actions – in private-sector cultural capital – as firms move into Stage 3. The vision of sustainable development must be promoted and supported throughout private-sector development and operations. Governments and residents of mega-urban regions in ASEAN and worldwide should encourage and pressure resident and incoming industries to achieve Stage 3 performance levels quickly if they are not already there. Special efforts and strategies may be required to assist small-scale and cottage industries to operate in the desired manner, as their resources and access to information and services can be very limited (Schmidheiny with the Business Council for Sustainable Development 1992; World Bank 1992b).

Local, provincial, regional, national, and global trading systems are largely driven by the private sector. Returning to the Metro Manila mega-urban region example, I either know or can guess when the trading system may or will go outside national boundaries to the international private sector. Some details of this analysis are specific to the Laguna Lake Basin or the Philippines, but most can be generalized to ASEAN and elsewhere, and include forestry, agriculture, livestock, aquaculture, fishing, power generation, industrial development, irrigation development, potable water supplies, major infrastructure development including lakeshore reclamation projects, household domestic requirements, housing, and tourism.

The trend to globalization through trade in all sectors is clearly evident. This makes the process of assessing the long-term sustainability of private-sector decisions and actions very complex. It is a daunting task, but one which must be approached from as many angles as possible. Individuals, wherever and however they are operating within the trading systems, must be constantly thinking and acting in the context of environmental management for short-term and long-term sustainable development. Globalization also emphasizes the importance of full life-cycle environmental management thinking and actions.

Rio Principles
The environmental implications of the global trading system were recognized in several of the principles on general rights and obligations pro-

posed for the Rio Declaration on Environment and Development at the United Nations Conference on Environment and Development (1992). The most applicable of these to private-sector developments in ASEAN mega-urban regions are as follows:

Principle 3. The right to development must be fulfilled so as to equitably meet developmental and environmental needs of present and future generations.

Principle 4. In order to achieve sustainable development, environmental protection shall constitute an integral part of the development process and cannot be considered in isolation from it.

Principle 7. States shall cooperate in a spirit of global partnership to conserve, protect and restore the health and integrity of the Earth's ecosystem. In view of the different contributions to global environmental degradation, States have common but differentiated responsibilities. The developed countries acknowledge the responsibility that they bear in the international pursuit of sustainable development in view of the pressures their societies place on the global environment and of the technologies and financial resources they command.

Principle 9. States should cooperate to strengthen endogenous capacity-building for sustainable development by improving scientific understanding through exchanges of scientific and technological knowledge, and by enhancing the development, adaptation, diffusion and transfer of technologies, including new and innovative technologies.

Principle 12. States should cooperate to promote a supportive and open international economic system that would lead to economic growth and sustainable development in all countries, to better address the problems of environmental degradation. Trade policy measures for environmental purposes should not constitute a means of arbitrary or unjustifiable discrimination or a disguised restriction on international trade. Unilateral actions to deal with environmental challenges outside the jurisdiction of the importing country should be avoided. Environmental measures addressing transboundary or global environmental problems should, as far as possible, be based on an international consensus.

Principle 14. States should effectively cooperate to discourage or prevent the relocation and transfer to other States of any activities and substances that cause severe environmental degradation or are found to be harmful to human health.

Principle 16. National authorities should endeavor to promote the internalization of environmental costs and the use of economic instruments, taking into account the approach that the polluter should, in principle, bear the cost of pollution, with due regard to the public interest and without distorting international trade and investment (United Nations Conference on Environment and Development 1992, 389).

Application to Mega-Urban Regions

Evidence of understanding and conscientious application of these principles could be used by relevant decision makers in the ASEAN mega-urban regions as criteria by which to judge the acceptability of indigenous and international investment and development. It is relevant that a discussion group at the International Conference on Managing Mega-Urban Regions (on which this book is based) developed the following as one of its recommendations:

> It is important with new investments (in the ASEAN Mega-Urban Regions) to ensure the introduction of 'clean technologies.'
> a. An effort should be made to formulate an ASEAN regional policy on investments in clean technologies in order to protect the interests of all concerned and to prevent the (ASEAN) countries from being played off against one another.
> b. Developed country governments and international aid agencies should ensure that their commercial sectors invest in clean technologies (and other environmentally positive developments) in ASEAN.

The ASEAN countries may be able to bypass many of the environmental problems that accompanied industrialization in the developed countries by insisting on the introduction of newer, clean technologies, sustainable resource use, and effective use of environmental management tools such as environmental impact assessments and audits. When industrialized nations transfer environmentally appropriate technologies, the recipient countries may need to request assistance in developing the skills and physical, economic, and institutional infrastructure required to use them effectively (Howatson 1991).

Transnational corporations well into Stage 3 environmental management development can provide excellent pathways for transferring the skills and clean technologies required for sustainable development (Howatson 1991). In an analysis of the relationship between the introduction of effective pollution-control technology to developing countries and those countries' policies and regulations, it was found that countries that had open investment policies and welcomed the installation of the most modern industrial plants from the OECD nations (which have advanced environmental regulatory systems) had far better environmental results than those that excluded external investment in favour of local investors (Birdsall and Wheeler 1992; Hettige, Lucas, and Wheeler 1992; Wheeler and Martin 1991). The 'open' countries purchased the latest technology, which had been honed and refined by the industrialized country's environmentally sophisticated industrial sector and long-standing regulatory requirements. In the 'closed' countries,' local investors tended to purchase the cheapest facilities available, which often resulted in installation of technologies and actual plants that were no longer acceptable or economically viable in their countries of origin. This illustrates the dilemma between opening development to international trade and the desire of any country to develop its own economy for and with its own citizens. It also demonstrates a failure of ethics (cultural capital) in the industrial country private-sector actor that sells outmoded, 'dirty' technology to a developing country.

Two relatively new specialized developments reflect the widespread use of Stage 2 environmental management tools and requirements and some of the incentives moving the private sector to Stage 3. The first is the recent development of environmental auditing and 'green reporting' (Owen 1992). This started with individual industries doing performance audits on environmental aspects of their own operations, physical as well as financial. Characterization of pollution discharges is an example. The practice has taken on even greater urgency and importance in the field of investment. If an industry leaves behind a heavily and dangerously polluted set of premises, notably contaminated land or water resources, a potential purchaser and those who lend funds for the purchase can become liable for large and unexpected costs of clean-up and disposal. The banks and investors that lent the original company the funds, and the company's board of directors, may even be pursued retroactively to assume the costs of clean-up.

This is causing a related private-sector development in industrial countries. The Canadian banking system and chartered accountancy firms, for example, are developing this as a specialty service to protect investors interested in purchasing industrial lands and operations (Canadian Bankers Association 1991; Canadian Institute of Chartered Accountants 1992). The focus at present is on pollution issues, but it may not be long before other issues enter this arena. The clearly recognized connections between rapacious forestry operations in upland watersheds and downstream costs of sediment loading and flash floods on agricultural and urban centres, such as Ormoc and Metro Manila in the Philippines or valley towns in British Columbia in Canada, provide an example. Such service in the protection of investors and the public, or in establishing liabilities, requires clear-headed, highly informed, professional analysis.

The second development is closely related to the first. Legal systems, which have traditionally required the establishment of absolute cause and effect for conviction in environmental law – hard to prove in vastly interconnected ecological systems – are switching to the use of burden of evidence, which recognizes environmental complexity to a much better extent. The presence and activities of environmental specialists in the legal profession are another example of the privatization of environmental management.

For the legal system to function effectively in environmental management in any country, however, fair, reasonable, and uncorrupted legal and regulatory systems must be in place and fully functional. Industry environmental management units welcome such regulatory systems, which strengthen their ability to influence their own corporate senior management. In other words, there is a positive feedback loop between fair and honest regulatory systems and good private-sector environmental practices. Public demand for such systems, in the form of political pressure, is very influential on governments, the private sector, and legal practitioners, highlighting the importance of communication and public environmental education in the total environmental management system in mega-urban regions and elsewhere.

Cultural Capital

Obviously, the contributions of the private sector and the role it plays in rational development of mega-urban regions are numerous indeed, and there is not space to consider them all in detail. Before closing, however, the concept of cultural capital with respect to the private sector should be recognized. Larger, more developed industries have taken on responsibilities in environmental management, and in certain aspects, such as technological improvements, they lead the field. Concerned and responsible individuals within industry have also undertaken the task of influencing their own corporate structures. This is especially effective when the CEO leads the way (Schmidheiny with the Business Council for Sustainable Development 1992; Howatson 1990). The work of environmental units in corporate departments of policy, planning, and operations are very important, just as such units are in government agencies.

Two examples of the recent expression of private-sector cultural capital developed to promote Stage 3 performance are given below:

> An increasing number of corporate leaders are convinced that it makes good business sense to secure the future of their corporations by integrating the principles of sustainable development into all their operations in order to:
> - recognize that there can be no long-term economic growth unless it is environmentally sustainable;
> - confirm that products, services, and processes must all contribute to a sustainable world;
> - maintain credibility with society, which is necessary to sustain business operations;
> - create open dialogue with stakeholders, thereby identifying problems and opportunities as well as building credibility through their responses;

- provide meaning for employees beyond salaries, which results in the development of capabilities and growth productivity; and
- maintain entrepreneurial freedom through voluntary initiatives rather than regulatory coercion (Schmidheiny with the Business Council for Sustainable Development 1992).

Promotion of an environmental consciousness throughout an organization is fundamental for improved corporate environmental management. As organizations in the industrialized world consider the implications of 'sustainable development' for their policies and operations, businesses are increasingly realizing the need to integrate environmental factors into strategies, plans and decisions at all levels (Howatson 1990).

Highlights of recent findings include the following statements:

The support of top management is critical to the success of a corporation's environmental management efforts.

Management systems, including environmental audits, provide 'up and down' reporting and ensure that corporate practices comply with regulations and corporate standards.

Integrated planning is imperative to factor environmental considerations into major marketing, investment, production and human resource decisions.

Stakeholder consultation furthers the dialogue between a corporation's management, on the one hand, and government agencies, employees, investors, customers, suppliers and the general public, on the other (Howatson 1990).

Intracorporate environmental ways of thinking and initiatives spread quickly to the various industrial sector associations through peer pressure, and a variety of codes of ethics and good environmental practices have emerged as a result. The multinational oil industry was a leader in this field. A more recent example is the Responsible Care Initiative developed by the Canadian Chemical Producers' Association (CCPA), which has spread throughout the industry and the world and shows the way to responsible environmental management for this industry, with its high potential for creating serious, long-term, and intractable environmental problems. The Code of Ethics, the Definition of the Practice of Professional Engineering of the Canadian Engineering Qualifications Board (1992), and the Code of Consulting Engineering Practice (Association of Consulting Engineers of Canada 1992) are other examples.

Such commitments to professional behaviour and practice in environmental management, and the processes that led to them, should be transmitted along with technology. External investors and developers should be required to bring their codes of ethics and good practices – cultural capital

– with them when they engage in development in ASEAN countries. This must also be matched by similar codes and practices in the ASEAN countries themselves. Environment Minister Emil Salim of Indonesia has recently promoted the formation of a Business and Industry Council for Sustainable Development to marshall progress in environmental management among the most influential Indonesian corporate elites. This should have a positive effect on the mega-urban region of Jakarta, other developing urban and industrial areas in Indonesia, and elsewhere in ASEAN.

Good corporate environmental conduct is also good for industry and other private-sector actors. It produces favourable economics and competitive advantages, both strongly positive influences in leveraging private-sector behaviour in good environmental management. There is a desperate need for persuasive case studies to establish conclusively and with precise reference to costs and benefits that these advantages actually accrue in ASEAN and developing countries elsewhere, recognizing that good environmental conduct can at times put a company at a disadvantage until all competitors are operating under the same terms. An excellent start on such case studies has been made by the international Business Council for Sustainable Development (Schmidheiny with the Business Council for Sustainable Development 1992).

Publications, industry, business associations, and the personal interactions of influentials and decision makers all help to spread the message of the positive benefits of environmental planning and management for long-term sustainable development. A much harder task is to reach the lower and much more numerous groups and individuals at the more diffuse levels of small businesses, natural resource-based operations, and the informal sector (Figure 9.2). This is where communication, popular publications, environmental education, and the creation of favourable cultural capital are all important and essential. The total environmental management system must be made to function at all levels in mega-urban regions, as well as at all other levels of organization.

Recommendations

Many recommendations for present and future actions can be identified. Those that follow are fully applicable to ASEAN mega-urban regions and also to both smaller and larger geographic and administrative units:

- The natural resources and life-support systems of the world exist in finite and limited supply. Since the cultural capital of any country or region is the main determinant of how both natural and manufactured capital are developed, effort should be expended at all levels of society to instill understanding of, and commitment to, appropriate actions in support of sustainable development.

- The means to measure and monitor the carrying capacities of defined areas such as mega-urban regions should be established, and human behaviour and productive activity adjusted accordingly.
- Actions should be undertaken to activate all groups in the total environmental management system at all levels in any given region, including in the mega-urban regions of the ASEAN countries (Figure 9.2).
- Mega-urban regions are characterized by many types of development at several levels. The associated private sector expresses itself at all levels and in many ways. The appropriate mixes of education, incentives, disincentives, regulation, and peer pressure in support of environmental management and sustainable development should be applied to each of the many target groups, using the means most appropriate to that group.
- The results of environmental monitoring should be made publicly available, especially to potentially affected parties, as an important means of reinforcing good environmental management and responsible corporate behaviour and of reinforcing political will on behalf of sustainable development.
- Acceleration of the development of private-sector environmental management skills and practices should be encouraged in ASEAN mega-urban regions so that firms evolve rapidly from Stage 1 and 2 modes into the preferred Stage 3 mode. Investment from external sources should be required to operate in the preferred mode as well.
- When investing in industrial technology or resource development, clean technologies and practices that maximize environmental protection and resource sustainability should be preferred, both for the good of the environment and for the enhancement of long-term, national private-sector profitability and sustainability. In the context of ASEAN, if this is done under the Framework Agreement on Enhancing ASEAN Economic Cooperation (Private Investment and Trade Opportunities – Philippines 1992) or in the broader region under the Asia-Pacific Economic Cooperation (APEC) agreement, the decisions will have regional and international dimensions as well as local.
- Full cost-accounting economic analyses directly applicable to the private sectors of ASEAN countries should be developed to demonstrate that cost savings and enhanced short- and long-term profitability are gained by applying clean technologies and best environmental management practices. Such results should be publicized throughout the region and to relevant target groups worldwide.
- The principles of sustainable development as they pertain to the private sector, coupled with full life-cycle impact analysis and Stage 3 proactive performance, should be applied by all countries internally and through-

out the global trading system. This would benefit the development of the ASEAN mega-urban regions, ASEAN as a whole, and other countries worldwide.

- Consideration should be given to applying systems of environmental audits when making investment decisions in ASEAN countries in order to protect the investors, the investment, and the productive environment.
- Recognition should be given to the role of the private- and public-sector legal professions in environmental management. As well, the roles of fair and uncorrupted legal and regulatory systems, corporate environmental management units, and public opinion in reinforcing effective regulatory systems in the service of environmental management and sustainable development should all be recognized.
- Achieving sustainable development in the ASEAN mega-urban regions should be accelerated by applying visionary and proactive environmental management – private-sector cultural capital – and creating codes of ethics and good environmental practice to apply throughout a given commercial sector. Consideration may be given to the development and effective application of such instruments as candidates for technology transfer through such arrangements as APEC.

10
The Governance of Mega-Urban Regions
Aprodicio Laquian

As the world faces the prospect of becoming half-urban by the year 2000, there is renewed concern with the most visible manifestation of the so-called 'urban problem': the rapid growth of very large urban areas variously called 'megalopolis' (Gottmann 1961), 'city-centred regions' (Weissmann 1970), 'extended metropolitan regions' (McGee and Greenberg 1992), and 'mega-urban regions.' These regions typically have a densely populated city at the core and less densely populated towns, districts, and even smaller cities around them. In some cases, a metropolitan planning or governing structure exists but the urban sprawl goes beyond its boundaries, encompassing traditional villages and rural lands in the process. The sprawl, usually following ribbon development along major transportation corridors in what has been called a 'fingers' pattern, may join the sprawl of another urban area and through time the interstices between these settlements may be filled up with more physical structures and activities.

One of the major present challenges that will affect the future of the urban world is how to plan, manage, control, and govern the growth and development of these mega-urban regions. Traditional forms of urban governance such as municipal government, township administration, federal district authorities, special function authorities, and so on have proven inadequate to govern and manage these very large regions. Area-wide regional planning, sometimes encompassing natural regions such as river basins, has been very useful in a number of countries. Cooperative and coordinative devices – regional development councils, for example – have also been tried but results have not been very satisfactory.

The key problems in mega-region governance include the wide expanse of territory covered, the number and variety of local and national government entities involved, the complexity of functions involved in the region's development, and the outmoded legal and institutional structures currently in use in urban governance. The growth of mega-urban regions also varies because of differences in historical circumstances, socio-economic conditions, and national political cultures. Thus the search for generalizable approaches to urban governance is fraught with difficulties.

The problem of urban governance requires urgent attention because by the turn of the century, the world will have twenty-three urban agglomerations with populations of 8 million or more, and seventeen of these will be in developing countries (Table 10.1). They include a Mexico City of 25.6 million, a Sao Paulo of 22.1 million, and a Calcutta of 15.7 million. In Southeast Asia, Jakarta is expected to reach a population of 13.7 million, Manila 11.8 million, and Bangkok 10.3 million (United Nations, Department of International Economic and Social Affairs 1991). Because these statistics are based on formal institutional boundaries of urban units, the actual populations of expanded mega-urban regions are probably larger than the figures cited.

Demographic trends show that urban areas all over the world will continue to grow in the foreseeable future. Since 1950, the urban population of developing countries has grown from under 300 million to 1.3 billion persons. Demographic projections indicate that an additional 600 million people will be living in urban areas by the year 2000. By the year 2020, the UN Centre for Human Settlements (Habitat) predicts that 57 per cent of the world's population will be living in urban areas. Cities of all sizes, not just mega-urban regions, will be growing at annual rates in excess of 4 per cent. Intermediate cities like Bandung, Cebu, Chiang Mai, and Surabaya are growing at even faster rates (World Bank 1991).

Macro-economic factors are largely responsible for the rapid growth of cities. The World Bank has estimated that more than half of the GDP in most developing countries is generated in cities and towns. In Asia and Latin America, about 80 per cent of future economic growth will come from urban economies. Thailand is an excellent example of this: in the 1980s, Thailand grew at 11.2 per cent per year, and 50 per cent of GDP growth and 77 per cent of manufacturing output were accounted for by Bangkok. The global situation shows pretty much the same trends. With very few exceptions, per capita GDP levels and levels of urbanization in most countries are positively correlated.

Even as cities have become the engines of growth in national economies, however, they have been beset with serious problems of housing, traffic, crime, health, and environmental degradation. The World Bank has estimated that in 1988, 330 million people, about one-quarter of total urban populations, lived in poverty. More than one-third of the population of Metro Manila and more than one-quarter of those in Bangkok and Jakarta live in slum and squatter areas. Traffic in these cities is so congested that at rush hours the average travel speed is less than 8 kmh.

Table 10.1

Urban agglomerations with populations of 8 million or more, 1990 and 2000

	Country	1990	2000[b]
Mexico City[a]	Mexico	20.2	25.6
Sao Paulo	Brazil	17.4	22.1
Tokyo	Japan	18.1	19.0
Shanghai	China	13.4	17.0
New York	US	16.2	16.8
Calcutta	India	11.8	15.7
Bombay	India	11.2	15.4
Beijing	China	10.8	14.0
Los Angeles	US	11.9	13.9
Jakarta	Indonesia	9.3	13.7
Delhi	India	8.8	13.2
Buenos Aires	Argentina	11.5	12.9
Lagos	Nigeria	7.7	12.9
Tianjin	China	9.4	12.7
Seoul	South Korea	11.0	12.7
Rio de Janeiro	Brazil	10.7	12.5
Dhaka	Bangladesh	6.6	12.2
Cairo	Egypt	9.0	11.8
Metro Manila	Philippines	8.5	11.8
Karachi	Pakistan	7.7	11.7
Bangkok/Thonburi	Thailand	7.2	10.3
Istanbul	Turkey	6.7	9.5
Moscow	Russia	8.8	9.0
Paris	France	8.5	8.6
Osaka	Japan	8.5	8.6
Teheran	Iran	6.8	8.5
Lima	Peru	6.2	8.2
Bangalore	India	5.0	8.2

Notes:
a Urban agglomerations ranked in order of 2000 size
b Projected
Source: United Nations, Department of International Economic and Social Affairs (1991)

Heavy smog covers the cities most of the time; a 1989 study in Bangkok found that more than 10 per cent of residents of all ages suffered from chronic respiratory illnesses due to air pollution.

In Manila, energy needs so far outstrip supply that electricity 'brownouts' frequently occur. In June 1992, the Philippines Department of Trade and Industry announced that in an hour of electricity interruption, textile mills in Metro Manila lose Pesos 2.3 million. At least 20 per cent of total aggregate industry sales in Metro Manila was lost because of brownouts (*Newsday*, 23 June 1992).

A review of long-term goals of development plans in mega-urban regions usually reveals commitment to sustaining high rates of economic growth, coping with urban service problems, achieving socio-economic equity, and preserving the natural environment. Achieving these goals calls for effective, efficient, and equitable systems of urban governance. In the past, most developing countries have relied on the national government or local municipal governments to deal with urban issues. It has become increasingly evident, however, that traditional governance is inadequate to meet current and future needs. An important challenge to planners and policy makers, therefore, is the formulation and execution of effective processes for urban governance.

The remainder of this chapter will discuss the following: the governance problems facing large urban regions in both developed and developing countries and their reasons; the variety of governance forms established to plan, manage, control, and direct urban growth; the experience of different urban governance mechanisms in trying to achieve efficiency and equality; and their experience in trying to realize the objectives of economic development and sustainable environmental development, especially among the ASEAN mega-urban regions. It concludes with an outline of the important governance issues arising from attempts to achieve these goals.

Urban Governance and Mega-Urban Regions

Governance may be defined, quite simply, as the process by which authority structures are established and operated to carry out legitimate public functions in a polity that occupies a definite territory. It is concerned with the ways in which the polity sets policy goals, chooses its leaders, specifies and adopts various program options, raises and allocates resources, executes programs and projects, evaluates and monitors the effects and impact of those programs and projects, and then feeds back the findings of monitoring and evaluation to the policy setting and implementation processes.

This concept of urban governance is quite difficult to apply to rapidly changing mega-urban regions. To begin with, there may be quite a number of 'polities' within the urban region. At the core of the region is the central city with its municipal boundaries, mayor-council or commission forms of government, administrative departments, and so on. The core or central city, however, is usually in decline in most developing countries. The population of the city of Manila, for example, has been consistently declining in proportion to the metropolitan population because of out-migration to the suburbs. The outskirts of Bangkok and Jakarta are growing at rates in excess of 6 per cent per year due to migration and natural population growth.

Surrounding the central city are townships or districts, typically under the jurisdiction of other levels of government such as provinces or states. These jurisdictions have governmental structures of their own, especially in countries where a tradition of local government autonomy has been developed. While the central sections of these towns or districts may be quite urbanized, a significant portion of the population may live in small villages that lie within the town's jurisdiction. Despite the rapid penetration of urban lifestyles into these villages, their political structures and functions usually reflect traditional leadership patterns.

In many countries, the national government plays a dominant role in the mega-urban region. Since most large cities are also national capitals, it is quite common to have special districts, or regions run by special commissions, or authorities governing mega-urban regions. The Bangkok Metropolitan Administration (BMA), the Metropolitan Manila Authority (MMA), and the Special Capital Area of Jakarta (Daerah Khusus Ibukota, or DKI) are examples of central government efforts to govern mega-urban regions. Even more centralist efforts are seen in the case of Latin American capital cities such as the federal districts of Mexico, Caracas, and Bogota. The People's Republic of China exemplifies central government dominance in mega-urban region governance. In addition to the capital city of Beijing, two other mega-urban regions, Shanghai and Tianjin, fall under central government authority.

Aside from national government authorities with comprehensive powers, there are sections of central ministries exercising authority over mega-urban regions. Ministries of public works and construction, finance, health, education, transportation and communication, local governments, etc., have city-level bureaucratic branches at city, province, district, town, or even village levels in the mega-urban region. Of particular importance are special authorities charged with such functions as waterworks and sewerage, electricity, gas, telephone, rapid transit systems, ports and harbours, and airports. These usually have independent charters to exercise their functions. Many of the authorities are quasi-governmental corporations and some of them are even private-sector franchises with considerable public support and authority. While many manage to deliver urban services efficiently, they do compound the complex character of urban governance.

Formal central and local government structures do not complete the list of political actors in mega-urban regions. Other stakeholders' interests and political will find ample play in urban governance. The private business sector, both national and multinational, exercises an important role in urban affairs because its very survival often depends on the continued viability of the urban economy. In recent times, with the growing popularity of privatization of functions formerly carried out by governments, the private business sector has played an increasingly important role in urban regions.

Non-governmental organizations (NGOs) and community-based organizations (CBOs) have also become very important elements in urban polities. Forming around specific political and civic issues, such groups increasingly play decisive roles in urban decision making. They have been formed in response to the search for social equity and the championing of the causes of the urban poor, the underprivileged, minority groups, women and children, refugees, and newcomers to the cities. With their capacity to voice specific issues and to mobilize resources and political support (sometimes with the support of international NGOs, enabling local issues to be aired in a much wider arena), NGOs and CBOs have become the fastest growing elements in urban politics and government.

With so many different actors involved in mega-urban region governance, it is not surprising that formal efforts to develop the economy and to deliver urban services to regional inhabitants are mired in so much complexity. The stakes in metropolitics are very high, and the resources at play are plentiful and powerful. The rapidity of urban change has left formal governmental structures and processes way behind. The situation in Bangkok is instructive, as indicated in a recent study:

> The urban portion of the BMR, at about 1,600 square kilometres, has increased more than three-fold since 1974 ... Since 1988, roughly 3,100 buildings of six or more stories have been built or are under construction ... The haphazard urban development ... is directly related to the fact that the BMR may be the largest urban area in the world without an officially adopted plan ... There are over 50 local and national agencies involved in some aspect of urban management in the BMR, with no one agency having overall authority to act on a wide range of complex urban development issues. With so many actors, and overlapping mandates, it is virtually impossible to initiate efforts to address those issues, or even to enforce existing regulations (Setchell 1992).

Instituting Area-Wide Governance

The proliferation of governmental and non-governmental structures in urban regions, typified by Bangkok, has been a problem in the world for ages. In the West, the growth of urban regions, resulting in what Robert C. Wood has termed New York's '1400 Governments' (1959), called for metropolitan reforms. Numerous cases generated new ideas for area-wide governance: the expanding economies of urban areas in the North American eastern seaboard; the growth of municipalities and boroughs in such urban centres as Metropolitan Toronto, Dade County in the Miami area, and the San Francisco Bay area; the need for coordinating urban services in Greater London; and the search for a governing structure for the Paris metropolitan area. In India, the rapid growth of Calcutta, Delhi, Bombay, and Madras challenged the government to formulate expanded forms of urban governance. China, despite strong efforts to control the growth of large cities, had to expand the boundaries of Beijing, Shanghai, and Tianjin to accommodate urban expansion. Drawing from differing political philosophies, planning approaches, and governmental traditions, countries all over the world have searched for ways to plan and govern large urban regions.

Writing in the early 1960s, Jean Gottmann, who coined the term 'megalopolis,' saw the process of governmental evolution in the following way:

> What happens in [the] Megalopolis must be interpreted as a redistribution of what used to be city functions over a wider territory. The economic and social characteristics of administrative units in this territory and the relationships between them are being modified. The changes must occur in economic and social relationships first; then the legal and governmental framework can be redistributed from time to time to secure as far as possible a share to all participants. (Gottmann 1961, 764).

Historical hindsight enables us to see that the linear process envisioned by Gottmann in 1961 was not really followed in many regions. The sharp distinction between 'city functions' and other functions cannot really be made in many Asian urbanizing regions, where rural population densities are at levels higher than what would qualify for urban in other countries. Also, the rapid rate of socio-economic change in developing countries makes for reciprocal relationships. Even as 'city functions' permeate rural areas, 'village functions' persist in city cores, especially in communities inhabited mainly by squatters and migrant slum dwellers.

As shown by McGee (1991), and McGee and Greenberg (1992), so-called rural areas on a metropolitan area's periphery contain enclaves of manufacturing, industry, and production surrounded by rural villages and agricultural activities. Most mega-urban regions at present contain within their territories large tracts of primarily rural lands. The mixture of urban and rural characteristics within the same mega-urban region, of course, is not confined to Southeast Asia. In China and other parts of East Asia, the definition of city boundaries invariably includes huge sections of rural land, so much so that 'a distinction between the rural space and the urban space ... encompasses many difficulties and its relevance is now argued' (Rodrique 1992).

Pursuant to the Chinese slogan of 'leaving the land but not the village,' the growth of rural and urban small-scale enterprises is contributing to the rapid development of small towns and cities, in China, especially those located on the peripheries of metropolitan areas. The boundaries of metropolitan areas, therefore, are continually being expanded. The urbanized core of Shanghai now contains only 56.6 per cent of the metropolitan population (Laquian 1991). (The proportions are 60.4 per cent in Beijing and 66.2 per cent in Tianjin.) Efficient planning of Chinese cities specifically provides for urban agricultural activities to achieve the goal of food self-sufficiency (Yeung and Hu 1992).

Contrary to Gottmann's proposition, it is also not accurate to indicate that economic and social relationships in a growing megalopolis precede legal and governmental frameworks. In some instances, long-range plans have been formulated for basically rural regions, and governmental structures have been set up specifically to anticipate development. In the Philippines, for example, regional plans for the so-called Calabarzon area (composed of the provinces of Cavite, Laguna, Batangas, Rizal, and Quezon) have been formulated and coordinative mechanisms are currently being worked out (Ramos 1991). In Indonesia, the developmental impact of the Jakarta metropolitan region in the Jabotabek area (made up of the local units of Jakarta, Bogor, Tangerang, and Bekasi) is being anticipated. In fact, the rapid growth of the Bandung-centred region is being planned as a developmental strategy to anticipate Jakarta's expansion (Akbar and Pribadi 1992).

All over the world, there have been many efforts to institute area-wide governance to plan, manage, control, and redirect urban growth. The rapid growth of cities, metropolitan areas, and mega-urban regions has cast aside traditional forms of urban governance. These governmental forms, together with philosophies of governance, constitutional frameworks, statutory enactments, court decisions and jurisprudence, and various aspects of 'civil society' have not been able to keep up with societal changes in the rapidly changing urban regions. Administrative measures involving planning, urban management, and service delivery have also not been very successful. In both technologically advanced and developing countries, therefore, there is a widespread search for mechanisms for effective mega-urban region governance.

Typology of Urban Governance Forms
A review of governance arrangements for dealing with rapid mega-urban region growth yields four types of area-wide structures, based on such factors as: the political units in the territory; the allocation of functions among various units of government; the distribution of inherent and derived authority and power among the levels of government; and the extent of citizen or community participation in the process of governance. The typology of governance arrangements is as follows:

(1) *Autonomous local governments.* Authority and power in the mega-urban region is lodged in local governments (cities, towns, municipalities), which exercise considerable autonomy in planning, policy making, legislation, and execution of governmental functions. Governmental actions tend to be fragmented and uncoordinated. Constitutional provisions, legal traditions, and statutory law stress local autonomy and the inherent rights of local units to decide their own affairs. This was the situation, for example, in Metro Manila before 1965, when four cities with their own city charters and four towns in the province of Rizal deriving their powers from the *Revised Administrative Code of the Philippines* carried out their public functions without consultation or coordination with each other.

(2) *Confederated regional governments.* Several local government units enter into a cooperative arrangement wherein they agree that specific area-wide functions are to be carried out at a regional level, but they retain inherent local powers. In some cases, a special authority, commission, or council might be created to carry out the area-wide function, but the powers of such a body are carefully enumerated and delimited. Real authority and power, however, remain with the local governments. The situation in the Greater Vancouver Regional District is an example of this arrangement; policy making is lodged in a body composed of the chief executives of the participating local governments. The current situation in Metropolitan Manila also falls under this category. In 1991, upon abolition of the Metropolitan Manila Commission, power was vested in a Metropolitan Manila Council, composed of the mayors of four cities and thirteen municipalities.

(3) *Mixed systems of regional governance.* Higher levels of government (national, state, and provincial) share powers with local governments (cities, towns, and municipalities) in the performance of public functions. Some central government agencies might carry out particular functions through specialized authorities (administration of ports and harbours or water and sewerage systems). Quasi-public corporate bodies might also provide services of an area-wide nature (electricity, gas, telephone, and public transit). Municipal governments might carry out certain basic services (schools, health, police, and protective services), but they follow central government policies and standards. Various types of flexible arrangements may be set up in which functions are shared. Garbage collection might be a municipal function, for example, but garbage incineration, composting, or recycling might be given to a regional authority. The Bangkok Metropolitan Administration and the Special Area of Jakarta are examples of such mixed systems.

(4) *Unified regional governance.* The whole mega-urban region, made up

of urban and rural areas, is within one governing entity. The system of governance is dominated by the central government, although cities, municipalities, and towns might exist with authority to exercise enumerated powers. All systems of planning, plan implementation, and monitoring and evaluation are lodged in the regional body. Examples of this approach are the three cities in China under the jurisdiction of the national government (Beijing, Shanghai, and Tianjin).

The regional governance approach chosen in a particular country depends on the specific historical, cultural, and political characteristics of that country. In countries where the central government has traditionally been dominant, as in East Asia and Latin America, unified regional governance has been favoured. A country's legal tradition, usually heavily influenced by colonial experience, also plays an important role in the choice of urban governance forms. Thus, countries influenced by French, British, and American jurisprudence tend to stress local autonomy and municipal government.

In some instances, the evolution of forms of urban governance follows historical stages. In the Philippines, for example, strong commitment to local autonomy was inculcated during the American colonial period (1901-35). With the rapid expansion of the Manila metropolitan area, however, it was accepted after the Second World War that a broader, area-wide approach was needed to manage and coordinate problems of transportation, water, pollution, and so on. The Marcos dictatorship imposed centralist forms of governance throughout the whole metropolitan area from 1973 to 1986. With the Aquino government and the current Ramos government, there have been tendencies towards local autonomy and municipal governance once again, despite the realization by many that area-wide approaches are needed in Metro Manila because such problems as air and water pollution, epidemics, crime, traffic, and garbage collection and disposal do not respect local municipal boundaries. The passage of the Local Autonomy Law in 1992 has supported the swing towards more local government powers in the Metro Manila area. A bill in the Philippine Congress seeking the abolition of the Metro Manila Authority is currently being supported by municipal mayors and other local politicians.

With its monarchic traditions, Thailand has had a centralist view of urban management, and as the nation's capital, Bangkok has mainly been the concern of the national government. The city of Bangkok, and more recently, the municipalities of Bangkok and Thonburi, have been governed by central government authority. In fact, in terms of urban planning, the Town Planning Division of the Ministry of the Interior, which coordinates planning in local government units, did not originally have authority over the Bangkok area. This function was the responsibility of the Division of Public Works.

The rapid expansion of the Bangkok mega-urban region into outlying areas in the provinces of Samut Prakan, Nonthaburi, Pathum Thani, Nakhon Pathom, and other areas is engulfing many local government units. As a result, the public is clamouring for more local autonomy and public participation in planning and development of the region. A vibrant private business sector actively involved in housing, transportation, production, commerce, and industry has also been demanding greater democratization of the urban governance process. An important element in Bangkok's development is the rapid growth of NGOs and CBOs championing affordable housing, poverty alleviation, and environmental and other causes. All these developments, therefore, are exerting a very important influence on patterns of governance in the mega-urban region.

In general, it is instructive to analyze how particular approaches in mega-urban region governance have fared in terms of goals and expectations. In such an assessment, it may be useful to look at the specific objectives of urban governance. Usually, these are couched in terms of efficient delivery of urban services, effective economic development, equity among various groups and classes in the polity, and environmental sustainability of governmental interventions and private-sector actions in the mega-urban region. These goals, of course, are not consistent and can often be antagonistic to each other. The process of urban governance, after all, is basically a search for policy alternatives and trade-offs, as contending forces in an urban polity interact with one another.

Depending on the country's political culture, the specific values or objectives of governance might change from place to place, or from time to time in the same country. It is perhaps the unpredictability of urban governance outcomes that has enticed some people to look for urban management solutions to what are essentially political and conflict-resolution issues in urban governance. One of the most frequently tried approaches to making mega-urban regions effective, efficient, economically viable, and environmentally sensitive has been comprehensive planning.

Seeking Efficiency through Planning

A review of global experience reveals that many countries have tried to achieve efficiency through comprehensive planning. Planning, in the view of many, is a technocratic exercise that can be carried out by either central government bodies or those at the regional level. By going through the processes of defining urban problems, gathering data, and then coming up with 'technical' recommendations, planning efforts often attempt to skirt around the issues of governmental jurisdictions, financial resources, physical or political boundary changes, and conflicts among political parties and factions.

Most mega-urban regions have master plans that give, in ample detail, the objectives, conceptual framework, and land-use recommendations for specified areas. Most of these plans are rarely implemented. Most have never been formally adopted by national, regional, or local governments and they therefore have only an advisory or visionary function. Some plans have been prepared by external consultants, who might not even have consulted local authorities. In some mega-urban regions, master plans have been designed only to influence government actions, and because much urban development has been the result of private-sector activities, the plans have had very little influence on the shape of the region (see Chapter 4.)

Thailand

One serious difficulty in planning is that in most Asian countries, the exercise is seen primarily as a means of controlling urban construction and land use. In Thailand, for example, the Town and Country Planning Act (B.E. 2495, 1952) and the Town Planning Act (B.E. 2518, 1975) were meant as regulatory instruments 'to create the minimum order required to make cities workable' (Tapananont 1992). Although the Town Planning Act provides for the preparation of 'comprehensive plans' and 'project plans,' so far, only comprehensive plans have been prepared for Bangkok.

The Greater Bangkok Plan 1990 was prepared in the 1960s by the American consulting firm of Litchfield, Whiting, Bowne, and Associates. The plan anticipated a population of 4.5 million living within an urban area of 460 km^2 by 1990. It proposed 'finger-type' developments following six radial highways from the centre of the city. The plan was implemented through massive highway development, especially those linking Bangkok with the northeast, east, and southwest. Because these highways were constructed during the height of the war in Vietnam, there have been suggestions that their military significance was an important consideration in plan implementation.

In 1972, the Department of Town and Country Planning in the Ministry of the Interior prepared the first revised edition of the Metropolitan Plan, which anticipated a population of 6.5 million people living on 750 km^2 of land in the Bangkok metropolitan area. This plan advocated a 'monocentric form of development' instead of the 'finger-type' pattern. The emphasis, as in the old plan, was on the construction of highways: mainly circumferential roads to link up the 'fingers' or radial expressways.

The current plan for Bangkok is the Bangkok Metropolitan General Plan 2000, which anticipates a population of 9.5 million occupying 1,100 km^2 at the turn of the century. It follows the monocentric land-use patterns first laid out in 1972. Like the previous plans, this one has not been formally adopted, although some portions of it are being implemented, especially those on road construction (Peerapun and Silapacharanan 1992).

In a review of legislation and implementation of metropolitan plans in Bangkok, Tapananont (1992) gave the following reasons why comprehensive planning in Bangkok has not succeeded very well:

(1) The plans covered only general aspects of development, and detailed provisions for projects and other activities were left to other entities. This has resulted in a road pattern in which the arterial highways in the Bangkok region are provided for but the smaller roads, or *soi*, connected to them are developed haphazardly.

(2) The plans have not been able to stand by themselves because they have to be seen in the light of economic and social development plans such as those prepared by the NESDB. Since the so-called comprehensive plans deal primarily with infrastructure, housing, transportation, and so on, they sometimes do not fit in with economic development plans.

(3) The plans have not been formally adopted and have therefore lacked legal force. Enforcement of each aspect of the plan is effected by ministerial regulations, and such approvals are given piecemeal. The plans are given only five years before revision even though they serve mainly as guidelines. Because the approval process takes so long in Thailand, implementation is often delayed.

(4) Planning bodies, such as the Department of Town and Country Planning (DTCP), do not have adequately trained people to prepare the plans and coordinate their implementation. In any case, implementation is the responsibility of many different agencies and units at the central, city, and local levels. The private sector in Thailand is also very aggressive in implementing development activities and they disregard plans if these do not fit their schemes.

(5) Planning is basically 'top down.' Central government agencies prepare the plans with minimal consultation with local governments, civic groups, communities, NGOs, and CBOs. The standards used in planning, in any case, are derived from international, primarily Western, models and do not fit indigenous practices. The private business sector, with its control of ample resources, has a very strong role in the planning and implementation processes compared to the community and civic sectors.

Indonesia

Another example of efforts to achieve governmental efficiency through planning can be seen in Indonesia. Under the 1945 Constitution of the Republic of Indonesia, local units are divided into tiers: provinces (Tingkat

I), and municipalities, districts, towns, and subdistricts (Tingkat II). Indonesia has a republican government, so in accordance with the principle of decentralization the local units have autonomous governments. At the same time, Indonesia has a unitary form of government, so in accordance with the principle of deconcentration local governments are essentially agents of the central government, and administrative agents of central government agencies also run local affairs.

At the central government level, regional planning is carried out by the Ministry of Public Works (MOPW), Ministry of Home Affairs (MOHA), and the National Development Planning Board (BAPPENAS). The State Ministry of Population and the Environment and the Ministry of Finance are also involved in planning. Within the MOPW, the Directorate General for Human Settlements (Cipta Karya) is in charge of urban sector and infrastructure development. A complicating factor, however, is that within the MOHA, the Directorate General of Municipal Development, the Directorate General of Public Administration and Regional Autonomy, and the Directorate General of Regional Development are also charged with planning.

BAPPENAS, as the national socio-economic planning agency, is in charge of planning involving intersectoral and interagency activities. According to the prescribed procedure, all plans from local governments have to be submitted to BAPPENAS through relevant ministries since the agency is in charge of coordinating the allocation of funds.

The structures and functions involved in planning are supposed to be integrated at the regional level through the regional planning boards (BAPPEDAs). Each BAPPEDA, created by presidential instruction at the provincial, city, or regency level, is responsible for planning development projects financed by national and local government, in accordance with annual and multiyear development plans.

Implementation of plans in urban areas is the responsibility of the Office of Town Planning (Dinas Tata Kota). In addition to this office, however, there are also specialized agencies for planning specific aspects such as gardens and parks, historical heritage sites and buildings, and historical monuments.

One difficulty in the Indonesian case is that geographic jurisdictions of the various agencies tend to be confusing. The Bandung metropolitan area, for example, is divided into three administrative areas: Kotamadya Bandung, or municipality, which is an autonomous urban local government unit that also functions as the capital of West Java province; the Kabupaten Bandung, or regency, which is a large rural area on the outskirts of the city with its own capital town of Soreang, about 21 km from the city centre; and the Kabupaten Sumedang, another regency, which is largely rural. In addition to these three administrations in the Bandung metropolitan area, there is the *kecamatan* level, such as Kecamatan Cikeruh, a largely rural subdistrict where small towns are already emerging as development nodes.

Although the *kotamadya,* or city, of Bandung is headed by a mayor, it has no fewer than forty-one departmental offices that are administratively responsible to sectoral agencies at the central government level. Such sectoral agencies include important ones for planning, like census and statistics, land regulation, and taxation. While the mayor is supposed to 'coordinate' the activities of these departments, they are not responsible to the mayor.

Finally, there are separate planning departments at the city and regency levels. Under the 'bottom-up' concept of planning in Indonesia, local governments also have village community councils that prepare plans at the village level. These plans are aggregated and analyzed at the subdistrict level and then screened and amalgamated at the regency level. The final coordination of regional plans is supposed to be made at the provincial level, when urban and rural plans are integrated.

Trying to sort out the administrative lines of authority and coordination, linkage, and informal channels of command in Indonesia is an extremely complex exercise. In view of this complexity in formal and informal structures, most planning tends to be quite formalistic. Physical plans abound in Indonesian local government units and the preparation of maps and master plans is a full-time exercise. Urban planners attempt to freeze developmental reality in physical renderings despite the knowledge that shifting administrative and political realities will probably come up with different results. Despite efforts at bottom-up planning, most planning exercises continue to work from the top down. Essentially, therefore, the inherent conflict embodied in the nature of local governments – autonomous local governments function at the same time as field offices of the central government structure – is still being resolved. This lack of resolution directly influences the efficiency and effectiveness of regional planning.

The Philippines

The tug of war between national and local government planning efforts is also exemplified in the experience of Metro Manila. After the Second World War, when the Manila urban area was almost completely destroyed, Philippine planners attempted to plan the city and its environs rationally. Local municipalities and cities, however, exercising their autonomous powers, embarked on construction and development without waiting for formal city plans. Therefore, although there have been several plans for the Metro Manila area, not a single one has been formally adopted by either the national or local governments.

One of the most important functions given to the Metro Manila Commission (MMC) in the past was to produce area-wide development plans. An Office of the Commissioner of Planning was set up for this purpose. At the same time, however, the whole Philippine territory was divided into twelve regions under Regional Development Councils (RDCs) reporting to the National Economic and Development Authority (NEDA). With the weakening and eventual abolition of the MMC, the planning function in the National Capital Region (the thirteenth region) has been streamlined, with the office of the MMC Commissioner of Planning becoming the RDC for the Metro Manila area (Ocampo and Ocenar 1985).

The examples cited above reveal that seeking governmental efficiency through planning might have its uses, but real urban regional governance needs more than the preparation of plans. When comprehensive plans are well thought out, are based on accurate data, and reflect the various interests of sectors involved in a participative planning process, they actually influence the shape and functioning of mega-urban regions.

In fact, such well-developed plans need not even have formal adoption or statutory authority. The authority of ideas reflected in the plans is often enough to influence urban regional development patterns. Logic in the pattern of urban growth, proper analysis of developmental trends, and embodiment of correct conclusions in specific planned recommendations might sometimes have more influence than do statutory enactments.

The other side of the coin shows, however, that purely physical plans, even when they are formally adopted in legislative acts, may end up being changed and mangled during the implementation process. This happens when they do not reflect the alignment of political and economic forces at play in the urban regional political system or when they are based on faulty data, reasoning, or analysis.

Decentralization and Regional Governance

The key element in governance is the distribution and allocation of authority and power. Decentralization may be defined as the process by which authority and power, as well as responsibility for specific functions, are dispersed to lower levels of government. According to de Guzman (1989), decentralization may take on the following meanings:

- deconcentration or delegation of responsibility and authority by central government offices to regional and field units of such offices
- devolution or transfer of power and responsibility for the performance of certain functions from the central government to local governments
- privatization of certain functions that used to be carried out by the government
- transfer of responsibility and investment of authority from the govern-

ment to non-governmental organizations, community-based organizations, or other alternative channels of service delivery charged with specific functions.

Although the various forms of decentralization are very clear, their application to mega-urban regions is sometimes not easy. One source of problems is the multiplicity of governmental and non-governmental structures in mega-urban regions. Another problem is the duplication and overlapping of functions carried out by these various structures. Finally, it is a problem that an overly legalistic approach to decentralization assumes the presence of local units to which authority and power can be allocated. In some countries, the regional level of government does not have the same clarity of definition as do provinces, cities, and towns.

In the Philippines, for example, the 1987 constitution recognizes the regional level of government only by implication, mainly seen as a level of planning and implementation. While the constitution provided for RDCs, they were created 'to strengthen the autonomy of the units therein and to accelerate the economic and social growth and development of the units in the region' (de Guzman 1989). In other words, the RDCs were mainly instrumental in strengthening more intrinsic units of government; they were not expected to have autonomous status.

In the Manila mega-urban region, efforts to establish an area-wide body started as early as 1975 with the creation of the MMC by presidential decree 879. The MMC was to have a governor, a vice governor, and two commissioners, one for planning and another for finance. The MMC had jurisdiction over four cities and thirteen municipalities in the capital region. These local units, while required to allocate 15 per cent of their resources to the operations of the MMC, retained their city and municipal identities and continued to carry out functions not delegated to the MMC.

When the Marcos dictatorship was toppled in 1986, the metroregional approach associated with Imelda Marcos (who was the governor of the MMC) lost a great deal of credibility. In 1991, the Metro Manila Authority (MMA) was set up. Instead of a governor heading the body, policy making was embodied in a metropolitan council composed of the mayors of the cities and municipalities within the region. The chair of the council was selected from among the mayors every six months. The authority and power of the regional body has therefore been greatly undermined, and real power has swung back to the city and municipal units.

The recently approved Local Autonomy Law in the Philippines lends strong support to the swing towards more local government powers. In Metro Manila, however, this devolution of power might be coming at exactly the wrong time. Because of decades of neglect, most urban services in Metro Manila are run down. They need area-wide action to take advantage of economies of scale, managerial efficiencies, and financial viability. In the past, the Philippine government has paid lip service to the notion of devolving powers to local governments but continued to exercise its dominance by decentralizing authority to the lowest levels of government (the *barrio* and *barangay* levels), which had no financial powers to accomplish anything much. Now that real authority and power is being devolved through the Local Autonomy Law, the need for area-wide action in the national capital region might be adversely affected by the fragmentation of authority among the cities and municipalities.

The reluctance of national authorities to devolve powers to urban governments is also seen in Thailand. In 1972, the Bangkok Metropolitan Administration (BMA) was created as an autonomous local government led by an appointed governor. The post of governor was made elective in 1975, although, hierarchically, the governor was kept under the jurisdiction of the Ministry of the Interior. Central government dominance was also assured by the fact that many urban functions were carried out by central government agencies such as the National Housing Authority (NHA), the Expressway and Rapid Transit Authority, the State Railway of Thailand (SRT), and others.

Bangkok has a municipal council that is part of the BMA but it has extremely limited powers. The BMA can collect revenue, but proceeds from the land-development tax, the house and land tax, the tax on signboards, and the animal slaughter tax – the only taxes that the BMA collects – account for only 8 per cent of annual municipal income (United Nations 1987c). The BMA does not even have the authority to develop its own plans, as this function rests with the central government agencies.

The dominance of the national government is reflected in the current controversy over Bangkok's transportation system. To date, at least seven different systems have been proposed for Bangkok by central government agencies. Each of these is supported by a different agency. First, there is the 14 km two-route LRT system running down Sukhumvit and Silom Roads, the contract for which was awarded by the municipal government to the Bangkok Transit System (BTS). Second, there is the 36 km skytrain network sponsored by the Expressway and Rapid Transit Authority under the Ministry of the Interior. Third, there is the 60 km commuter and main rail line backed by the Ministry of Transport and Communications. All three contracts, so far, have been given the right to start building the systems. Yet there is practically no coordination among them, nor are they coordinated with the four road-based expressway systems, individually proposed with their respective backers. It should be noted that a consulting company hired by the NESDB to sort out all the schemes identified no less than thirty-three conflict points among the various proposals (*The Nation*, 18 December 1991; *Far Eastern Economic Review*, 30 April 1992).

In some countries, privatization of certain urban functions has been suggested as a means to achieve efficiency. Indeed, the capacity of the private sector has been proven many times in such fields as road construction, management, and maintenance; transportation; garbage collection and disposal; and electricity generation and distribution. Even such functions as public health, education, care for the elderly, and other social welfare activities have been privatized in some countries.

Decentralizing authority to the private sector has been particularly effective in the field of garbage collection and disposal and in public transportation. In some instances, a combined public-private approach has been tried. In Bandung, for example, solid waste disposal is carried out by a semi-private agency that combines the managerial flexibility and financial responsiveness of a private firm with the accountability of local government. The organization, named PDK, is a solid waste management agency created by the city. PDK is owned by the city but is granted complete financial autonomy to raise capital and operating funds from various sources. As an independent entity expected to be efficient and profitable, PDK pays salaries at market rates, constructs garbage transfer stations, sets up composting plants and landfills, carries on applied research on re-use of garbage, and pursues other entrepreneurial leads. The company has been so successful that it has expanded its services to cover most of Bandung's 2 million residents. PDK has also worked with non-governmental organizations, especially those representing the urban poor, who look after specific functions such as collection, sorting, and disposal. Local scavenger groups have formed the Integrated Resource Recovery (IRR) system, helping to make the city clean and at the same time providing employment to many people.

In Metro Manila and Jakarta Raya, the construction of expressways has been decentralized to the private sector. Tolls from expressway users are then collected by the entrepreneurs to recoup their investments. While there have been hints of overcharging from the travelling public, it is widely acknowledged that the privately built, operated, and managed expressways have eased traffic, that quality of construction is high, that the roads are well maintained, and that the traffic is efficiently managed.

Experience in decentralizing authority and power to local governments, the private sector, and NGOs has therefore had varying results. In many instances, decentralization to many local units has created fragmentation and lack of coordination, leading to poorer urban services in mega-urban regions. In other cases, the private sector has managed to deliver better and more efficient services, albeit at a price. To date, attempts to decentralize authority and power to achieve efficiency and effectiveness in mega-urban region governance have experienced extreme difficulty in finding the correct scale of governance. Tradition has favoured decentralizing to municipal governments and other units, but mega-urban regions often include many different levels of government.

Achieving Goals

In Search of Equity

A review of experiences with metropolitan governance and various types of area-wide jurisdictions in the past couple of decades reveals that not too many of them have lived up to the high expectations initially generated. The Greater London Council was abolished in 1991, the Greater Vancouver Regional District lost its planning and regulatory functions in 1983, the Metropolitan Manila Authority is a hollow shell, and the Bangkok Metropolitan Administration cannot even coordinate the region's transportation proposals. True, some metropolitan governments have come up with reasonable mega-urban region plans that have managed to guide economic and social development. In the effort to achieve social justice and equity, however, metropolitan governments have not been very successful.

One of the original misgivings about systems of metropolitan governance was that they might create distance between the citizens and the governmental structures set up to serve them. Because most metropolitan structures were created by national government initiatives and metropolitan officials tended to be appointed by central governments rather than elected by the people, their reputation for aloofness was often borne out by experience.

Objections have also been generated by the overly bureaucratic style of mega-urban region governance. Municipal governments often resented regional government's formulating master plans, passing zoning codes and building standards, imposing procedures, and passing detailed rules and regulations on urban administration. At the same time, these actions also did not endear mega-urban region entities to national agencies.

The Greater London Council (GLC), for example, was abolished partly because of the growth of active NGOs and special interest groups that pressed for more access to the processes of decision making. Area-wide concerns of the GLC were perceived as not responsive enough to the needs of NGOs and community-based organizations. At the same time, the confrontational behaviour of GLC leaders incurred the ire of the Thatcher government, which pursued a strong ideological commitment to privatization and reduction of governmental powers. Squeezed between small-group discontent and central government pressures, the GLC succumbed.

The same kind of forces have been at play in the Greater Vancouver area. After the Second World War, the economic boom in Vancouver generated a developmental boosterism that called for area-wide approaches. The Greater Vancouver Regional District (GVRD) was created in 1967 as a federation or partnership of eighteen municipalities and three electoral districts. The GVRD provided essential services of a regional nature, such as water, major parks, air pollution control, solid waste management, recycling promotion, sewage treatment and disposal, hospital planning and capital financing, regional housing, labour relations, and emergency services.

In their pursuit of economic development goals, however, the GVRD and the British Columbia provincial government that created it repeatedly failed to respond to local community demands. These took the form of active opposition to projects such as a freeway that would have cut through the Chinatown district in 1967, a proposal to tear down old downtown core housing in 1969, and the rapid loss of agricultural land to subdivisions and golf courses in the early 1980s. The fight for equity and popular participation by community groups since the 1970s eroded the powers of the GVRD to the point that, in 1983, the provincial government took away its planning and regulatory powers.

The GVRD is currently attempting to regain its former powers in the face of accelerating rates of environmental pollution and the resource demands of an economic boom on the west coast arising from Asian immigration. To this date, however, the strong voices and powers of local community groups and NGOs continue to influence Greater Vancouver governance. Still, the realization that confrontational debates along a left-right ideological spectrum is bad for development is dawning on political actors and stakeholders, and a more consultative and equitable process is evolving in planning and implementation of development programs.

As Asian cities continue to suffer from environmental degradation and as urban poverty continues to worsen, quite a number of NGOs and community-based groups have been formed to work for greater equity. In Metro Manila, for example, current goals of the National Capital Region Development Plan place high priority on poverty alleviation, social housing, and peace and order. Squatters and slum dwellers, frustrated by the repeatedly broken promises of government, have taken matters unto their own hands and invaded and settled vacant lands such as Reclamation, in the City of Manila adjacent to the Philippine Cultural Center. In Bangkok, the local affiliates of the Housing International Coalition have been putting pressure on government to make land and basic urban services more accessible to the urban poor.

These strong clamourings for equity on the part of poor and disadvantaged groups in the mega-urban region are becoming an integral part of decision making. To date, however, demands for equity have not succeeded in changing patterns of decision making significantly except during rare occasions, such as the explosion of 'people's power' in the Philippines that placed President Corazon Aquino in power. As shown by recent events, even these tendencies have been short-lived.

Economic Development

A mega-urban region grows because of its economic advantages: access to markets and ever increasing demand, the ability to transport goods, adequate sources of energy, a technical and professional workforce, and access to raw materials and other production inputs. The concentration of many people in a limited area creates economies of scale, locational advantages, and agglomeration economies. Mega-urban region governance has the role of harnessing all these advantages to optimize the region's economic and social development.

Because many mega-urban regions are national capitals, central governments often concentrate investments, government services, cultural facilities, and infrastructure in them. In the case of Indonesia, for example, both colonial policy and the stress on import-substitution economic policies after independence contributed to the rapid growth of the Greater Jakarta area. The dominance of oil in Indonesia's economy, the success of the rice production strategy rooted in the Green Revolution, and the growth of foreign investment also served to centralize most development in the Greater Jakarta-Bandung development corridor. By the advent of the 1980s, Jakarta and the surrounding areas in West Java accounted for 42 per cent of the total value added and two-thirds of the total employment in medium- and large-scale manufacturing in Indonesia. These trends have continued in recent years (Douglass 1991c).

The economic growth of a mega-urban region might arise from direct central government action or it might be influenced by the provision of physical infrastructure and social superstructure, which guides private investments and economic behaviour. Provision of physical infrastructure such as good transportation systems, reliable energy supply, potable water, and drainage and sewerage is the most important element in economic and social development. Conversely, allowing infrastructure to deteriorate and not providing enough resources for effective maintenance can adversely affect development in a critical way. Most of the problems of such mega-urban regions as Manila, Jakarta, and Bangkok in recent years are due mainly to inadequate construction and maintenance of infrastructure. Closely related to physical infrastructure are social superstructures such as educational institutions, job training and retraining programs, public health, housing, and welfare services. A mega-urban region must be able to attract the ablest and best people and hold them in the region by a high quality of life.

As important as the factors mentioned above are political processes that assure people's participation in governance of the mega-urban region. Such participation might be achieved through professional groups, community-based associations, and the activities of NGOs.

Towards Sustainable Environmental Development
One of the most critical problems faced by mega-urban regions is environmental degradation, which threatens the sustainability of continued urban development. All mega-urban regions in the world are faced with environmental problems. At current rates of development, most mega-urban regions cannot be sustained. They rely not only on their rural and urban hinterlands for continued development but many of them also exploit resources from far-off countries and regions to fuel their developmental needs.

The concentration of too many people in limited space is responsible for the severe shortages in resources that impinge on the environment. For example, only half of the Metro Manila area, containing about 70 per cent of the population, is served by piped water from bulk sources. Because of the limitations of the central water system, people have used deep wells, lowering the water table by up to 200 m below sea level in some areas. This has not only polluted the water supply but has also forced salt water to intrude into fresh water aquifers.

Similar water problems are faced by Bangkok. Despite recent improvements in Bangkok's water supply, only about 66 per cent of households in the city have access to piped water inside their homes. As in Manila, most people in Bangkok have drawn on groundwater, and more than 1,000 km^2 of land in the southern and eastern suburbs of Bangkok have been sinking by 5-10 cm per year. Even with current efforts – such as licensing the use of groundwater systems – it is estimated that it will take more than ten years before water supply systems in Bangkok can be implemented.

Water conditions in Jakarta are even worse than in Manila and Bangkok. As of the mid-1980s, less than one-quarter of the DKI Jakarta population had piped water inside their homes, with the result that 84 per cent of households in East Jakarta drew water from open wells and 74 per cent of those in North Jakarta had to purchase water from vendors. Lack of water exacerbates health problems because Jakarta does not have a waterborne sewerage system. The daily out-flow of sewage in Jakarta is about 700,000 m^3, and most of it is discharged into rivers and streams without any treatment.

As mega-urban regions like Manila, Bangkok, and Jakarta continue to expand, their consumption of scarce commodities such as water increases. To some extent, an area-wide approach that taps open and underground sources of water farther and farther away from the city might allow such mega-urban regions to continue growing. Improvements in water management – such as better maintenance of the water distribution system to prevent waste, price increases to encourage people to conserve water, and technical innovations in systems of impounding, purification, and distribution of water – might help to sustain water systems. Without proper water management and conservation techniques, however, indefinitely postponing the inevitable dwindling of water supplies might not be possible, thus imposing a real limit on sustainability.

One of the main reasons for the inability of mega-urban regions to conserve and protect the environment is the inability of mega-urban region governance to deal with environmental problems in an integrated and comprehensive way. The functional and geographical fragmentation of regional jurisdictions is hampering the ability of mega-urban regions to deal with environmental problems. In Jakarta, for example, environmental problems have been approached case by case by different government bodies. The following comments by Douglass are most instructive:

> The need for a regional approach managing environmental issues is particularly acute in the Jakarta metropolis. The rapid growth of this region and the already high degree of concentration of competing and often incompatible land uses in what is, in fact, a relatively small area, have created a number of problems that can no longer be solved on an ad hoc basis ... Jakarta is marked by high levels of air, river and sea pollution, water that can no longer be used for human consumption and a variety of problems associated with slum and squatter settlements, traffic congestion and waste disposal. It is also experiencing a rapid conversion of some of the nation's best irrigated agricultural land to nonagricultural uses and an expansion of agricultural production into ecologically sensitive upland areas and forests (1991c, 252).

Earlier reports on Jakarta by UN agencies pointed out the many environmental problems in the mega-urban region. They called on the Indonesian government to look at environmental degradation as a regional rather than a sectoral problem. Most important of all, they stressed the need for a strong agency capable of coordinating various programs on the environment in the Greater Jakarta area. Such an agency should have a jurisdiction much wider than the formal boundaries of the DKI and should encompass the whole mega-urban region. Using Indonesian acronyms, this means not only the Jabotabek area but also the Jabopunjur are (Jakarta-Bogor-Punjak-Cianjur), plus the city of Bandung and its environs.

Conclusions

This chapter has suggested that governance of mega-urban regions should strive to achieve four specific goals for a better quality of life for urban citizens: (1) efficiency in the delivery of urban services; (2) equity in the inter-relationships of groups and classes in the urban society; (3) economic development in the mega-urban region; and (4) environmental sustainability in the process of development.

In attempting to reach these goals, which might be antagonistic to each other under specific social, economic, and cultural conditions, a number of governance issues arise:

(1) To what extent is mega-urban region governance influenced by governmental policies of a macro-economic nature on the one hand and by spatial programs focused on rapidly growing extended metropolises on the other? In most countries, the rapid growth of mega-urban regions has come from a failure to recognize that so-called sectoral policies – import-substitution industries, self-sufficiency in rice – have significant implications for urbanization patterns. Better understanding of the spatial impact of sectoral policies should go hand in hand with more directly interventionist policies to locate specific activities in geographical space. Policies should be analyzed and applied to mega-urban region governance in an integrated way.

(2) What is the proper scope of area-wide jurisdiction in mega-urban region governance? A review of various approaches in many countries shows a tendency to limit regional jurisdictions to the built-up areas of mega-urban regions. Both local governments and national government agencies, not to mention special functional authorities and private-sector efforts, are often antagonistic to regional governance approaches that appear to carve too wide a territory or take over too many functions. Still, country experiences suggest the need for reasonably wider jurisdictions, encompassing both urbanized and rural areas and allowing more room for development. Such experiences also suggest the inherent logic in dealing with certain services in an area-wide manner, as the antecedents, effects, and impact of such services cannot be confined to narrowly delineated territories.

(3) What is the proper balance between central government and local government authority in mega-urban region governance? In most countries, central governments play a dominant role in mega-urban regions because of the sovereign powers that they exercise. This is especially the case where mega-urban regions are the national capitals. While most central government interventions might lead to efficient delivery of services, they are not so effective in eliciting popular participation and mobilizing community and local efforts. One of the challenges in mega-urban region

governance, therefore, is the proper allocation of various urban services and functions to all levels of government: central, provincial or state, regional, metropolitan, city, town, district, and urban neighbourhood. In some instances, it may also be possible to take one urban service and allocate its components to various levels of governance. The allocation of authority and responsibility over specific functions, of course, must be suited to the specific socio-economic and cultural conditions in each mega-urban region.

(4) How can the role of the private sector in mega-urban region governance be optimally harnessed for development? In many mega-urban regions, an active private sector has been found to provide urban services more efficiently, to respond more flexibly to changing conditions and needs, and to make urban services possible in a more regular and sustained way. At the same time, in political systems in which private entrepreneurship is heavily dependent on family ties, informal connections, and widespread corruption, the so-called private sector tends to neglect public service in favour of private gain. Bearing this caution in mind, it is an important function of mega-urban region governance to look more seriously into the possible role of the private sector in efforts to achieve socio-economic development, deliver basic urban services, and arrive at environmental sustainability. It might be wiser to be guided by actual experience than to be influenced by ideological leanings when searching for the proper place of the private sector in mega-urban region governance.

(5) How can civic, community-based, and non-governmental organizations be more thoroughly involved in mega-urban region governance? Disadvantaged groups need to gain access to public decision making. Although many arrangements for area-wide regional governance may achieve higher rates of development and more efficient delivery of urban services, they distance less privileged groups from decision-making centres. One major challenge in mega-urban region governance, therefore, is to establish participatory mechanisms. These may be supported by policies that explicitly assist disadvantaged groups in articulating their views and integrating these into the policy-making process. Such strategies, if they are to work, should not be based on a misguided sense of altruism and charity but on an appreciation that responding to the needs of the poor is an integral part of the decision-making process. This is a manifestation of the ideal that governance is rooted in an open political system, in which different ideas and interests compete, not in a hierarchical system of administration in which managers provide services and benefits to those who are governed.

(6) Finally, how economically and environmentally sustainable are mega-urban regions? Current levels of energy consumption, the types of

technology used for basic urban services, and the ever expanding populations of very large urban areas exert so much pressure on the environmental and resource bases of their regions that sustainability is out of the question. Reliance on non-renewable fossil fuels is increasing in mega-urban regions despite increased awareness of the pollution and other hazards attendant on such energy use. Although the private automobile has been shown to be the major cause of problems in most mega-urban regions in technologically advanced countries, types of land use favouring it are still being pursued in developing countries. Arrangements for mega-urban governance at present do not provide adequate incentives and disincentives to enhance sustainability, partly because such systems of governance reflect the dominant values of urban elites who measure their own living standards by those of technologically advanced countries and aspire to a lifestyle that is not in keeping with their immediate environments. Perhaps in future a wider global awareness of the environmental impact of urban lifestyles will change the attitudes and behaviour of the elites who govern mega-urban regions. Until that time comes, however, sustainability can only be a vague hope and an aspiration.

11
Developing Management Responses for Mega-Urban Regions
Ellen M. Brennan

Something must clearly be done about the management of ASEAN mega-urban regions, yet few countries know what to do or where to begin. In many mega-cities, metropolitan development and planning authorities have been established, but many of these tend to languish as weak institutions with nothing to do. This chapter examines a number of issues related to management of these large regions: whether or not city size is important; regional patterns, including desakota zones; the need for improved data; coordinated urban environmental management; land management; inadequate local administration; municipal finance; the desire for increased private-sector involvement; and various institutional arrangements.

Is Size the Issue?
According to information compiled by the United Nations, it is clear that the great majority of Third World governments are still of the opinion that mega-cities and large metropolitan regions adversely affect society and that mega-city growth should be slowed down if it cannot be halted.

Implicitly or explicitly, this belief relies heavily on 'optimal city size' theory. This theory, in and out of favour with planners over several decades, rests on the naïve but tempting idea that all the economic and social costs and benefits associated with different city sizes can be aggregated into two smooth functions, one representing costs and the other benefits, presumably expressed as real or imputed monetary values. Moreover, the theory usually goes much further by hypothesizing that the benefit function is S-shaped, eventually approaching some asymptotic limit, while the cost function is U-shaped. Under these assumptions, the marginal benefit and marginal cost functions are bound to intersect at some finite city size, ergo the optimal size (Richardson 1989a).

The old version of the theory was that the intersection point occurred at a relatively small city size, perhaps in the 100,000 to 250,000 range, reflecting some ideal concept of a 'livable' city free from congestion, pollution, and other externalities. Later, a modified version of the theory (Alonso 1971) suggested that, even if the intersection point occurred much further to the right, very large cities – and certainly mega-cities – would be far beyond the optimal size. This was also challenged. Wheaton and Shisedo (1981) argued that the optimum size would not be reached until the 20 million mark.

Surveying the top twenty mega-cities of the developing world, it is clear that size encompasses a very broad spectrum, from the traditional core city of 100 to 200 km^2 to mega-urban regions of 2,000 to 10,000 km^2 and more. Given these vast geographical differences, one has to question whether the absolute size of a city – whether it has 5 or 10 or 20 million inhabitants – contributes very much at all to an understanding of the issues and options, or whether emphasis on city size does little more than create an assumption of unmanageability. What exists, essentially, are polycentric clusters of identifiable and separate cities and towns that require both regional trunk infrastructure and effective local urban management, in much the same way that a province or a small country would – and would anyone be alarmed to hear that there are small countries or provinces with urban populations of 10-20 million (Hamer 1990)? Clearly, size per se is not the issue.

Developing-country mega-cities and mega-urban regions suffer to varying degrees from negative externalities such as poor air and water quality, chronic traffic congestion, inadequate solid waste disposal, sewerage deficiencies, and in a few cases high crime rates. These disamenities are often given more attention than agglomeration economies and other efficiency advantages, suggesting the concept of the 'big, bad city' (Richardson 1989b). Many of the most intractable urban problems have to do with factors other than size. It is clearly wrong to infer that intervention to control or influence city size would alleviate, if not remedy, these problems. It is always preferable to target the problem directly via specific policy measures rather than indirectly via city size manipulation. Even if air pollution was associated with city size and/or density, for example, a strategy for air pollution control such as imposing standards via regulation and pricing of emissions would be much more effective than attempting to change the future size or density of the metropolitan region (Brennan 1991).

Effective mega-city management is much more crucial than mega-city size, provided that management is not defined narrowly in terms of metropolitan finance. It must include coordination of macro, sectoral, and mega-city policies and strategies to deal with negative externalities directly (to control pollution and transportation demand, for example) and actions to improve distribution of public services among neighbourhoods and income groups to minimize risks of social unrest and political instability. These tasks are not easy to perform successfully, but they stand a much greater chance of success than mega-city size control policies.

The Growth of Mega-Urban Regions: Regional Patterns

Although size per se is not the problem, the complexity of the patterns of growth of mega-cities and mega-urban regions throughout the developing world poses a major challenge. In ASEAN countries, the growth of mega-urban regions and emergence of areas termed desakota zones (McGee 1990a) is only beginning to be understood. Whereas growth of these dynamic regions is largely fuelled by rapid economic growth, a very different pattern is occurring in Latin America. Many Latin American countries are experiencing historically atypical problems created largely by macro-economic mismanagement. Patterns of urbanization have undergone profound changes as a result of structural adjustment. In mega-cities such as Buenos Aires and Sao Paulo, for example, changes in spatial distribution reflect the deepening economic crisis rather than economic development. As many middle-class residents have experienced a decline in their standard of living and have moved to the less expensive periphery, many of the poor on the periphery have moved back into the city centre to live in substandard housing, and many of the poorest families have become homeless.

Even in Europe, profound and imperfectly understood changes have been taking place. A recent study of patterns of urbanization concluded that population redistribution tendencies in the 1980s were very different from those of earlier decades (Champion 1989). These patterns are not yet well documented or clearly understood, but essays in the study nevertheless speculated about a number of possibilities. They suggested that the counterurbanization tendency of the 1970s was possibly a temporary aberration and that the urban system is entering a new cycle of investment and 're-urbanization.' Alternatively, the processes possibly represented a temporary lull in the long-term process of population deconcentration, or a transitional stage in the large-scale reorganization of economic activity, marked by a massive decline in jobs in manufacturing and the emergence of jobs in information-processing sectors.

Data Needs

Clearly, it is imperative that existing and new sources of data provide a more adequate framework for monitoring and analyzing the profound changes taking place in the world's mega-cities and mega-urban regions. Even when data are available, the wide variation in national definitions, classification systems, and measurement complicates efforts to undertake comparative analyses. Countries also vary considerably, not only in how they define urban and rural places but also in how they delineate cities. Some include only the densely populated inner core of the city; others liberally overbound and incorporate populated suburban districts and rural areas tied to the city by one or more criteria, such as whether they provide residence for commuters, food for the city, or potential settlement areas for expansion (Goldstein, forthcoming). Depending on how extended the city boundaries are and how they have changed over time, both comparability with cities in other countries and comparability for any single city over time may be seriously impeded.

This argues for extreme caution in the use of all data on cities and towns and full awareness of the definitions employed and their comparability over time. It also argues strongly for coding and tabulating urban and rural data in small spatial or statistical units. These can then be used either aggregatively to construct larger units that are comparable over time or to remove data covering annexed areas from a city's total statistics in order to approximate the city as it was earlier (Goldstein, forthcoming). Such small-unit data would also facilitate international comparisons by allowing greater comparability in the criteria employed in establishing city boundaries. As well, it would allow development for analytical purposes of larger statistical areas, including mega-urban regions, which are not limited to political boundaries. Coding data for small areal units would serve still another useful purpose, even for mega-cities whose boundaries have remained stable for long periods. Such cities do not remain stable internally. Indeed, sub-metropolitan geographical data are of major importance for such cities, given their polycentric evolution and the fact that so many mega-cities and mega-urban regions encompass several political jurisdictions (Goldstein, forthcoming).

Efforts should also be made to compile, for the sub-areas of mega-cities and mega-urban regions, a comprehensive set of indicators on population characteristics, infrastructure, environmental and economic conditions, and other relevant variables for as many points in time as possible. This would fill a major knowledge gap. Currently, almost all hard research data on urban disamenities come from the developed countries, and conclusions about mega-cities in developing countries are thus based on inferences from this research reinforced with scraps of information about individual cities and the personal observations and experiences of visitors. Whereas most of the literature on Third World environmental problems focuses on deforestation, desertification, or the impact of large dams, environmental problems in urban areas of the developing world have received relatively little attention from Western environmental groups and international agencies. This distortion has sometimes been reproduced within Third World nations, where national environmental groups have become active to save endangered species but have given little attention to the acute public health hazards and pollution problems of their own cities (Lee Yok-shiu 1992).

Urban Environmental Management

A majority of the world's mega-cities and mega-urban regions suffer, to a greater or lesser extent, from severe negative externalities in the form of inadequate sewerage, poor drainage, insufficient solid waste disposal, and poor air and water quality. Municipal authorities responsible for these sectors are going to face very serious problems and challenges in the years ahead. These challenges will require radically new thinking about the future role of municipalities and of the private sector in managing these essential services.

Water Supply

Industrialized countries have reached standards of water supply and sanitation services that can only be described as profligate in terms of both consumption and capital investment. These luxury standards are clearly unattainable for the vast majority of the population in developing countries. Despite this clear evidence, the common approach in developing countries since colonial times has been to promote the adoption of standards from industrialized countries and systems to achieve them. Indeed, the methods used today around the world derive from those developed since the mid-1880s in the United States and Europe (Kalbermatten and Middleton 1991).

The serious problems of water supply, groundwater depletion, and consequent land subsidence in ASEAN nations are discussed in other chapters. Inadequate water supply also forces households to boil their water, thereby using energy, depleting dwindling supplies of fuel wood and contributing to air pollution. In Jakarta, for example, more than $50 million is spent each year by households for this purpose, an amount equal to 1 per cent of the city's GDP (Rietveld 1992).

In addition to the problems of bulk supply and overexploitation of resources, the water distribution systems of a majority of the world's mega-cities are obsolete and inadequate, mainly serving the core city originally inhabited by the colonial powers and new middle- and upper-income subdivisions. Jakarta's piped water distribution network, for example, was originally designed by the Dutch for a city of half a million inhabitants. Most cities have been unable to afford to extend their water distribution networks to the rapidly expanding settlements on the periphery.

One of the major problems affecting distribution systems are huge systems losses. Water that is unaccounted for – the difference between the amount delivered into the system and the amount paid for by consumers – is usually above 30 per cent of production in most developing-country mega-cities and may be above 50 per cent (Brennan 1992).

In most developing-country mega-cities and mega-urban regions, resources to expand systems are scarce because of a failure to introduce comprehensive cost-recovery schemes, often reflecting the principle that basic services such as water supply are social services for which users should not have to pay. This view is particularly strong in rural areas, where people have traditionally had access to rivers, ponds, or self-constructed wells and where there has been little government intervention in the sector until recently (Rietveld 1992). In towns and cities, where more complicated and costly systems were required, water supply and sanitation services came to be viewed as a government responsibility, again to be provided at little or no cost to the user.

Within this context, municipal authorities have generally been reluctant for political reasons to raise, tariffs and establish realistic prices for water and sewerage services sufficient to cover their true costs. The result has been heavy subsidization of these services in most developing countries, supplemented by borrowing to expand systems as demand grew. While some progress towards sounder pricing policies has been achieved during the past decade, urban water and sewerage continue to depend on large government subsidies in most countries. Indeed, a recent review of World Bank-financed projects showed that the effective price charged for water is only about 35 per cent of the average cost of supplying it (Rietveld 1992).

Given that in most developing-country mega-cities, external aid from higher levels of government or from bilateral and/or multilateral agencies abroad is not likely to increase, cost recovery becomes increasingly important. Surveys suggest that even low-income households can afford and will pay for basic services such as piped water if the alternative is doing without or paying more for an inferior substitute (e.g., water purchased from vendors). The managerial problems are to convince consumers that user fees will mean better services and to devise instalment financing schemes to make the capital costs of services – the house connection for water – affordable for low-income households (Brennan 1990).

Another key managerial issue is to give greater attention to operations and maintenance, repairing leaking standpipes and replacing damaged water meters, for example. It is also important to maximize the use of existing facilities – to take a 'systems management' approach – to relieve the burden on new capital investments. In the cities of developing countries, for example, it should be possible to repair systems quickly and easily when they fail. A water system that does not necessarily meet 'accepted' standards of reliability, but for which spare parts are available and which can be brought back into service within a short time by a community-based mechanic, is likely to be of far greater benefit to the community than a 'reliable' system that depends on imported parts and can stay out of commission for months if it fails (Kalbermatten and Middleton 1991).

Measures to address the water supply leakage problem are also crucial. It has generally been found that the cost of reducing systems losses to acceptable levels is rapidly recovered, usually within a year or two. Such actions are very simple, but they may be crucial to the realization of expected benefits from the original capital investment. Although the problems may be easy to handle technologically, however, they are more difficult from an organizational perspective, at least in mega-cities and mega-urban regions, because effective maintenance requires a spatial network of field engineers for monitoring, assessment, and upkeep (Brennan 1990).

Also needed is a firm commitment to water conservation at all times, not just during periods of drought. As was the case with energy twenty years ago, cities have tended to view demand for water as a given and to see their task as to increase supply to meet demand. Relatively little attention has been given to the need for demand management and water conservation, an omission with potentially harmful economic and environmental consequences. Whereas efforts to improve efficiency should ultimately consider multiple uses of water and work towards establishing a circular system, by which water is used repeatedly, rather than the present linear or single-use approach, in the short term the use of low water use devices (e.g., water efficient toilets and low flow faucets) and public education campaigns can make a major difference.

As for extending services to the vast numbers of squatters on the periphery, providing a conventional grid of large-diameter water mains in such areas is unrealistic, particularly considering that the marginal costs would probably not be met by the marginal revenues. To assist in planning for such areas, computer programs are now available that enable planners to design cost-effective distribution networks. Such programs enable designers to set parameters appropriate to the community being served rather than adopting standard criteria. There is no need, for example, to maintain high residual pressures in accordance with US insurance industry standards in areas where no house has more than a single storey (Kalbermatten and Middleton 1991).

Sanitation

In the mega-cities and mega-urban regions of developing countries, most municipally provided sanitation is based on conventional sewerage systems. Equipment and spare parts often have to be imported and there is a lack of skilled technicians. As a result, sewerage systems are typically in poor condition and sewage treatment plants discharge effluents that are little better than raw sewage. Because sanitation depends for its effectiveness on a very high level of consistent and reliable coverage, providing services to only a select minority, or providing intermittent service, will not produce the anticipated public health and environmental benefits and will not justify investments (Kalbermatten and Middleton 1991).

As with the water supply distribution networks in many mega-cities in developing countries, most sewerage systems were constructed to meet the needs of the colonial population of the core city. Metro Manila's primary sewerage network, for example, was built during 1904-11 to serve a population of only 500,000 inhabitants. Currently, only 11 per cent of Metro Manila's population has sewerage connections; in the large number of unsewered areas, sewage effluent is conveyed via road gutters, open ditches, and canals to water courses that overflow during the rainy season, and then is either pumped untreated into Manila Bay or allowed to flow into the bay via the tides (United Nations 1986a).

Because mega-cities and mega-urban regions in developing countries are growing so rapidly and in such an unregulated manner, their sewerage needs in the coming decades are likely to bear little resemblance to current needs. Conventional systems as presently constructed, with large interceptors discharging into centralized treatment plants, are extremely inflexible and require large front-end investments (Kalbermatten and Middleton 1991). Whereas the most economical and efficient way to provide urban water supply and sewerage services is with modern piped systems, because of the backlog of work and scarcity of investment funds, a large proportion of the urban population in these regions will not be served with in-home piped services for many years if this approach is followed. To reach all segments of the urban population, including the poor, the traditional utility approach needs to be complemented with middle- and low-cost technologies. Ideally, a full range of technical options should be considered and matched to the circumstances of each particular case.

On the one hand, cities need to use the most up-to-date management and technical tools available, including computer-based, least-cost design of systems and computerized billing and collection systems (Rietveld 1992). On the other hand, in most of the world's mega-cities and mega-regions, it is unlikely that a single solution can address the needs of the whole population. Some parts of the region may have a conventional sewer system, with an average per household investment ranging from $300 to $1,000. Other parts could be served by simplified or small-bore sewers, which cost about 30 per cent less, and others by pour-flush latrines, which cost about $100 to $200. Some low-income areas may be only able to afford incremental improvements upon traditional or informal means of night soil disposal (Brennan 1992; World Bank 1992b).

Clearly, to meet the needs and capacities of different areas of a mega-urban region, an alternative planning process is required to the conventional approach using master plans, which typically only considers completed sewerage. The multistandard, multitechnology approach described above needs to be matched by a new approach to sector institutional development. The needed large-scale applications of the above kinds of appropriate technologies will not take place until policy makers and engineers rethink their approach to urban water and sanitation sector planning (Rietveld 1992). Because the planning process generally operates from the assumption that the entire community will have a single service standard and be served by one central system, planners tend to focus mainly on issues affecting the rate at which the selected technology can be extended rather than on how to extend at least minimum services to the maximum number of inhabitants.

More informal CBOs need to be built up involving active user participation and cooperation in the design, operation, and maintenance of the kinds of non-conventional systems described above. As one World Bank expert notes, 'it is not a question of developing completely separate systems and institutional frameworks for the poorer and more affluent sections of a city; the need, rather, is for an imaginative and innovative mix of conventional and new approaches, and hi-tech, and low-tech solutions, based on a partnership between people, NGOs and utilities' (Rietveld 1992, 10).

Drainage

Inadequate stormwater drainage may, over the next decade, prove almost as great a threat to the quality of life in the world's mega-cities as inadequate water and sanitation have in the past. Because the growth of urban population has forced more and more people to occupy low-lying marginal land that is vulnerable to flooding, the population at risk throughout the world has been growing steadily.

In the past, stormwater drainage was regarded mainly as a local problem and tackled city by city. In general, there has been neither the widespread national and international concern that marked the International Drinking Water Supply and Sanitation Decade (1981-90) nor the commitment to devising alternative, sustainable solutions as the situation progressively worsens and planners come to appreciate the environmental and economic consequences of allowing this service to deteriorate (Kalbermatten and Middleton 1991).

Problems have been particularly severe in the great coastal cities in the tropics, such as Bangkok, Calcutta, Dhaka, Jakarta, and Metro Manila. In Bangkok, the problem of slow stormwater runoff during the early part of the monsoon season is compounded by overflows from the river, in-flooding from up-country areas, and high spring tides in the gulf. Because of the gradual obstruction of much of the city's natural drainage system, caused by converting irrigation and drainage canals to roads and filling in other canals as part of the malaria eradication program, the problem of seasonal flooding has worsened in recent years (United Nations 1987a). Flooding has also been a perennial problem in Jakarta, particularly in *kampung* in swampy areas. The common practice of dumping solid waste into the micro and macro drains has caused the system to overflow during the rainy season and hindered the water flow during the dry season (United Nations 1989). Metro Manila also has serious drainage and flooding problems, stemming partly from reliance on natural drainage channels, many of which have become blocked by siltation, weeds, and refuse, and partly from the construction of makeshift housing in the channels in squatter areas (United Nations 1986a).

In dealing with the problem of stormwater drainage, a number of new approaches are required, including catchment management, land-level controls, and improved management of other urban services. In many mega-cities of the developing countries, stormwater systems do not function at their full capacity because inlets and channels are blocked by garbage. Improved solid waste management is therefore an important contribution to better drainage. For maximum cost effectiveness and efficiency, the most appropriate institutional arrangement involves NGO or community self-help efforts combined with government staff for technical supervision or assistance. In Jakarta, for example, the government has encouraged community participation in unclogging drains.

Solid Waste

Throughout the developing world, cities are being inundated in their own wastes as a result of inadequate waste management policies and practices. A major problem regarding solid waste in the mega-cities of the developing countries is not one of disposal or recycling but of failure to collect garbage in the first place. Unaccounted-for garbage – the difference between the amount of waste generated and the amount collected – is usually over 30 per cent and may constitute more than 50 per cent of the total (Brennan 1992). Typically, it not only blocks the streets and creates a public health hazard but also, more seriously, contributes to the atmosphere of pervasive squalor, which discourages people from making any attempt to help themselves because the situation seems hopeless (Kalbermatten and Middleton 1991).

The problem varies considerably from city to city with the amount of waste generated tending to increase with the level of development. The technological solution most commonly adopted in the industrialized countries – having heavy compactor vehicles take all types of waste and crush it into a mixture that is then dumped into a landfill – does not serve as an appropriate model for the mega-cities of developing countries. For one thing, the waste generated in developing countries is typically much denser, with a high proportion of organic materials and a high moisture content, and the wet, dense material overloads both compactor trucks and the road structure (Kalbermatten and Middleton 1991). For another, so-called sanitary landfills in many developing countries are little more than open dumping sites and are major sources of groundwater pollution from infiltration of leachates. Modern sanitary landfills are expensive to build. It was recently estimated that cost of construction in the United States of an 80-acre landfill (which at present generation rates would serve a community of 500,000 for twenty years) would be about $33 million, and the cost of closing the landfill when it was filled would be another $8 million (Rathje and Murphy 1992).

In the mega-cities of developing countries, there should be much greater emphasis on resource recovery and recycling, with landfills being considered more as a last resort. Towards this end, the efforts of the informal private sector, including scavengers, should be encouraged and given assistance. In most of these mega-cities, there is considerable curbside salvaging and recycling, as well as recycling activity at landfills and dumpsites. Many Asian cities, for example, have extensive 'waste economies,' structured through itinerant waste buyers, waste pickers, small waste shops, second-hand markets, dealers, transporters, and a range of recycling industries (Furedy 1992). In many cities, however, the activities of scavengers, which are essentially economically driven informal recycling activities, have often been in conflict with efficient waste management practices. For many years, for example, Mexico City's large scavenger population of nearly 20,000, including dependents, was considered by the authorities to be something of a nuisance. Following negotiations with the scavenger's two powerful unions, the authorities took steps to begin to work with them. Likewise, Cairo's *zabbaleen,* a community that has earned its livelihood from scavenging and recycling for more than a century, were traditionally shunned and forced to live on the fringes of the city in squatter settlements. In an effort to improve solid waste collection, the authorities in Cairo issued a tender in 1986 for private companies to take over the collection and haulage of household waste, using motorized vehicles. Recognizing that, rather than abandon the waste collection business, they would have to find a way to institutionalize their activities, the *zabbaleen* submitted a bid emphasizing their traditional strengths – an experienced workforce and an efficient and inexpensive system – and were awarded the contract. In developing the project, which is considered to have been highly successful, attention was given to minimum disruption of the traditional *zabbaleen* roles, to securing credit to pay for the cost of mechanization, and to designing a system that would eventually extend service to the entire metropolitan region (United Nations 1990a). Similar projects are being developed in a number of Asian cities, including Jakarta, where the Institute for Development Studies is encouraging cooperatives of waste pickers and collectors in order to improve their bargaining power vis-à-vis the waste dealers.

In many developed countries, the popular image of what constitutes recycling – separating one's garbage into various categories, leaving it sorted neatly at curbside, and seeing it carted off by industrious sanitation workers to be stored in a warehouse – does not constitute recycling at all but only sorting and collecting. Recycling has not occurred until the loop is closed; that is, until someone buys or gets paid to take the sorted materials, manufactures them into something else, and sells that something back to the public (Rathje and Murphy 1992). In contrast, in many cities in the developing world actual recycling is occurring, in which waste is turned into usable materials. In Karachi, for example, newspapers, magazines, bottles, tin cans, and so forth are either sold directly to hawkers or are picked up by the city's scavengers; the recyclable material is then sold to wholesalers and reprocessors and is either reprocessed as is or mixed with new material and made into new products (United Nations 1988). Because of the subsistence character of the Dhaka economy, almost all industrial and household waste is recycled, and per capita solid waste production is one of the lowest in the world (United Nations 1987b). Rubber is made into shoes, glass into bangles, and so on. Clearly, in the developing countries, it is important to study ways of supporting small informal recycling industries, of raising the productivity of existing systems, of developing markets for recycled materials, and of removing technical, financial, and institutional obstacles (Pacheco 1992).

In mega-urban regions, future improvements in solid waste management should include a comprehensive policy framework and strategic plan that takes into account all the physical, technical, legal, institutional, financial, environmental, and sociocultural aspects of solid waste management in a jurisdiction. To cite an example of the need for overall management, in Sao Paulo, South America's largest city, collection is very efficient. Indeed, waste is collected from almost 95 per cent of households in the metropolitan area, and 70 per cent of household waste is put out for collection already packed in plastic bags (Leitmann 1991). Disposal, however, remains a different story. The entire waste disposal system is currently saturated; one sanitary landfill has an estimated lifespan of less than a year, and the other of less than four. The metropolitan area is currently operating several incineration plants, posing a serious problem for the future. A further problem arises from the fact that, because of growing environmental awareness, a number of municipalities have passed ordinances not only forbidding the construction of landfills but even prohibiting compactor vehicles from passing through their territory, a rather extreme example of NIMBY (not in my backyard).

Environmental Pollution
Quantification of the extent of water and air pollution in mega-cities in developing countries is difficult because monitoring stations are rare or non-existent. The World Health Organization recognizes that some mega-cities have serious pollution problems: air pollution in Mexico City, Sao Paulo, Bombay, Metro Manila, Bangkok, Calcutta, and Seoul; and water pollution in Dhaka, Delhi, Seoul, Karachi, Bangkok, Metro Manila, and Cairo. The sources of pollution vary from case to case. Air pollution is the result of automobile emissions in some cities and of polluting industries in others. Similarly, water pollution is the result of industrial contamination in some cities and of leaking sewage in others.

Water contamination comes from many sources: discharge of untreated industrial wastes into watercourses; leaching of liquids from industrial or municipal waste dumps into surface or ground water; inadequate treatment of municipal sewage; and hazardous and toxic materials flushed into watercourses during storms because of poor solid waste management. Many modern chemicals are so potent that trace contamination may make huge volumes of water unsuitable for drinking without special treatment. Most developing countries do not have the resources either to detect the trace chemicals or to establish facilities or sites to treat hazardous wastes. The impact of fecal contamination of water resources, however, is probably the most crucial water quality issue. In highly industrialized countries, the transition from traditional to modern types of environmental pollution took place over 100 years or more. The developing countries are faced increasingly with advanced pollution issues before control over traditional pollution sources has been successfully achieved (Bartone 1990).

Unfortunately, few countries have established comprehensive and realistic environmental protection legislation and regulations. Existing laws in most developing countries do not clearly assign jurisdiction and responsibility for monitoring and enforcement, nor do they specify mechanisms for enforcement and control (World Bank 1992b). In Mexico City, for example, full control of liquid and solid industrial waste disposal is limited by the lack of comprehensive legislation. The principal ordinance regulating industrial effluents dates back to 1941; whereas some modifications were introduced in the mid-1970s, the fines that can be legally imposed bear no relation to current monetary values (United Nations 1991).

As in the case of water supply, air pollution problems are specific to cities, reflecting differences in climate, topography, and so forth. Throughout the developing world, emissions from vehicles, industrial boilers, and domestic heating sources exceed the capacity of cities' natural ventilation systems to disperse and dilute emissions to non-harmful exposure levels (Bartone 1989).

Mexico City, which is usually regarded among the outlaws in terms of air pollution, has all the characteristics conducive to high air pollution. High altitude tends to increase significantly the emissions of fine particles, HC, and CO pollution from vehicles, and to make people more susceptible to certain of its effects. As a result of the city's elevation and the surrounding mountains, winds rarely blow with enough force to clear the air. The basin also has abundant sunlight, one of the key elements of photochemical smog. Moreover, thermal inversions that trap pollution are common, particularly during the winter months. Growing deforestation on the outskirts of the capital has led to frequent dust storms. The winds carry the deposited body wastes of about six million people and two million dogs. A partial list of the pathogenic organisms found in the air have included streptococcus, diplococcus, staphylococcus, salmonella, shigella, and amoeba (United Nations 1991).

In any discussion of environmental pollution, Mexico City provides an interesting example, for it has at least formulated if not necessarily implemented one of the developing world's strictest sets of environmental policies, including mandated emission control systems for automobiles manufactured after 1988, a ban on automobiles one working day a week ('Hoy no circula'), and inspection and retrofit of some older vehicles. Mexico City is also interesting because it illustrates the problem of trying to deal with air pollution at the level of a mega-urban region. It is governed by a number of authorities that separately control the emission levels of vehicles based in or passing through their part of the conurbation. To date, most remedial action has been taken in the Federal District. As a recent study noted, it is clearly not practical for one part of the conurbation to have an effective emission control policy without similar standards being set in the other parts.

Most mega-cities in developing countries have been less successful than have developed countries in avoiding negative externalities such as pollution. The main reason is too little intervention, in part from lack of public awareness of the problems and of political willingness to address them. In the absence of public pressure to improve environmental conditions, the easiest course of government action is no action. Where measures have been adopted, enforcement has generally been haphazard. Although many cities have adopted legislation requiring relocation of polluting industries, compliance generally has been slow, mainly because of high costs and the disruptive effects of such moves on employment and productivity. As a recent World Bank (1992b) report noted, industrial pollution control is greatly impeded by the fact that many of the large-scale pollution-intensive industries – paper and pulp chemicals, iron and steel – are typically owned and managed by the state or by the politically powerful, wealthy elite. Under these conditions, government officials have a difficult time finding the political will to impose strict regulations on the most polluting industries, particularly when those industries are viewed as vital to economic development.

Mexico City again illustrates the difficult trade-off between jobs and the environment. The government's politically courageous decision in April 1991 to close down the giant 18th of May oil refinery, which spewed as much as 88,000 tons of contaminants into the atmosphere each year, was widely heralded in the international news media. It is estimated, however, that shutting down the facility cost $500 million, required Mexico to import, at least temporarily, some refined petroleum, put up to 20,000 company workers and their dependants out of work, and in effect ruined an entire secondary economy that had served the local oil community (Brennan 1992).

Land Management

Considering the pace of urban growth in the developing countries over the past several decades, the extraordinarily adaptive nature of urban land markets under pressures without precedent in the history of the developed countries is perhaps surprising. This situation is now rapidly changing. Many options previously available to low-income urban populations, such as available unused public land and low-density central city neighbourhoods, are rapidly disappearing. As the shortage of serviced land and the competition for that land have priced the urban poor out of the legal land market, many low-income populations have been forced to occupy illegal settlements on low-lying lands, steep hillsides, floodplains, or other hazard-prone areas.

While the demand for land is growing – indeed, it has been calculated that rapid urbanization is likely to double the size of built-up areas in most developing countries over the next fifteen to twenty years – the supply in most of these cities is both genuinely and artificially limited. It is interesting to note that the problem is generally independent of the type of ownership. It is as severe in cities where much of the land is publicly owned, such as Karachi and Delhi, as in cities where most of it is privately owned, such as Bangkok, Metro Manila, and Seoul (Brennan and Richardson 1989). In all cases, the price of land has increased much faster than the consumer price index, exacerbating the difficulty of acquiring land for low-income housing. In some cities, this is partially explained by special circumstances, such as the absolute scarcity of land not subject to flooding (Dhaka), mountainous terrain (Rio de Janeiro), or the existence of a large green belt (Seoul).

Since land is the essential ingredient in all urban growth, devising equitable and efficient land-development policies is one of the major challenges facing planners and policy makers in Third World cities. Because land is not homogeneous – indeed, each parcel of land is unique – basic assumptions of perfectly competitive markets routinely fail to apply to land markets (Mayo, Malpezzi, and Gross 1986). Because market mechanisms alone are unlikely to allocate land uses efficiently in cities, physical, financial, legislative, or administrative interventions are required to increase efficiency, distribute benefits more equitably across income groups, and reduce the negative effects of inappropriate land development, such as congestion and pollution (United Nations Centre for Human Settlements 1989b). Thus, even the most capitalistic, free-enterprise-oriented societies have increasingly imposed some measure of public control over the use of urban land.

The degree of intervention has varied among developing countries. In a number of cities (e.g., Bangkok, Dhaka, Metro Manila), there have been virtually no effective measures to influence or control land development. Seoul, one of the few cities in the world to have experimented widely with a broad range of metropolitan development strategies, probably represents the opposite extreme. Independent of the degree of intervention are a number of similarities. Many cities in developing countries have formulated master plans that include some prescriptions for future directions of urban growth. These master plans have rarely, if ever, been realized and have languished in metropolitan planning offices as irrelevant documents (Brennan and Richardson 1989). The reasons are simple. The population projections underpinning the master plans were often widely off the mark, and on-the-ground uses therefore soon differed widely from land-use patterns in the master plan. Moreover, most plans were formulated in too rigid and inflexible a manner and did not allow for readjustments in the light of changing conditions.

Land-use controls, which generally were the primary means designated to implement these master plans, have been mainly ineffective. They have often reflected an engineering or planning concern with order and with the clear delineation of land uses common in town-planning ideals for developing countries (United Nations Centre for Human Settlements 1989b). Plot size, infrastructure requirements, and so forth were typically set higher than could be afforded by the majority of low-income residents. Indeed, a recent World Bank study noted that the area per house serviced by roads was up to four times greater in the typical Malaysian low-income subdivision than in comparable projects in North America or Western Europe (Bartone, Bernstein, and Leitman 1992). Moreover, there was little or no recognition of the limited powers of enforcement available to planning departments in most cities in developing countries, where most land development has taken place outside the formal, regulated sector.

Inadequate Local Administration

There is growing recognition that a major reason why local administrations in most cities in developing countries have not coped successfully with urban population growth is because they are 'flying blind'; they simply do not know what is going on in their local land markets (United Nations Centre for Human Settlements 1989a). The information base in many of these cities is improving, particularly with the aid of aerial photography which eliminates much labour-intensive data gathering. By and large, however, most cities lack sufficient accurate and current data on patterns of land conversion, the number of formal and informal housing units built during the past year, infrastructure deployment patterns, land subdivision patterns, and so forth. Frequently, urban maps are twenty to thirty years old and lack any description of entire sections of cities, particularly of the burgeoning peri-urban areas. Without adequate information, planners and policy makers have been operating on assumptions or using often inappropriate standards from other countries to develop land policies.

For under $10,000, a complete computer installation can now be used for conducting a land and housing market assessment. By employing two aerial surveys that closely correspond with the time interval of the assembled demographic data, the assessment can estimate the current and future supply of land that can be developed and determine the rate and pattern of land conversion attributable to housing demand (United Nations Centre for Human Settlements 1989a).

Unclear property rights contribute to the degradation of land and natural resources. Land registration has traditionally been a serious problem in most cities in developing countries. Information about who owns what is typically poor. Squatter settlements increase uncertainty about property rights, and legal and administrative systems for establishing, recording, and transferring title are typically inadequate (Mayo, Malpezzi, and Gross 1986). If land markets are to work properly, transactions need to be registered. Once facts are recorded, land can be bought and sold with fewer obstacles, which helps the pace of development (World Bank 1989). Improved land registers, besides being associated with improved property tax systems, can also bring in substantial transaction fees, since approximately 10 per cent of property in urban areas worldwide changes ownership each year.

Bangkok provides a good example of a successful land titling project. The city's growing fiscal capacity had not tapped property values. Although substantial increases in land and property values in recent years resulted in many instances from public investments – such as highway construction and flood control projects – this 'betterment' was not even partially recaptured. To remedy the problem, the government, with financial assistance from the World Bank, undertook a $76 million land titling project. The project aimed at producing up-to-date maps on a scale of 1:1,000 (the Bangkok Metropolitan Administration had been using cadastral maps that were some forty to fifty years old), introducing new surveying technology, strengthening the Central Valuation Authority through technical assistance, and eliminating leakages in the current valuation system (United Nations 1987a). The photo maps were sufficiently detailed so that few parcels of land escaped identification for taxation purposes. Before the titling project, it was estimated that one-third to one-half of the one million land parcels in Bangkok were not linked to a property tax record. In 1988 alone, Bangkok's land titling project brought in $200 million in fees (World Bank 1989).

Municipal Finance

The inability of mega-cities and mega-urban regions throughout the developing world to provide adequate social and physical infrastructure is only to be expected. For one thing, many of the cities are continuing to grow very rapidly. It is difficult from both a resource and a management point of view to resolve problems relating to water resource depletion, lack of basic sanitation services, solid waste collection, and so forth at a pace equal to the rate of metropolitan population growth, and deficits thus tend to become larger. As well, all the mega-cities in developing countries have capital resource constraints and competing claims on scarce public investment, so that the resources available for extending public services, and particularly for resolving environmental problems, are inevitably limited. Efforts to improve revenue generation have been very mixed, with little across-the-board implementation of cost-recovery mechanisms except within the narrow context of internationally supervised (World Bank) projects.

Numerous researchers have argued that more responsibilities have to be delegated to municipalities and a better correspondence needs to be established between local expenditure and revenue authority, in order to improve provision of social and physical infrastructure. Several arguments have been advanced in support of fiscal decentralization. If expenditure and tax rates are determined by those who run the city rather than by those who run the country, local preferences will be better addressed, local services will improve, and local residents will be more satisfied. Also, local revenue mobilization will be increased because local governments are more aware of the parts of the local economic base that are growing quickly and can tax them more easily than can the central government (Linn and Wetzel 1990).

Based on a series of empirical case studies, Bahl and Linn (1992) have set out a framework to pinpoint the sources of revenue appropriate to finance particular types of urban expenditures. First, for publicly provided goods and services of measurable benefit to readily identifiable users within a jurisdiction, user charges are the most efficient means of financing the service. Such services include water supply, sewerage, power, telephones, public transit, and housing. Second, local services such as administration, traffic control, street lighting, and security, which are public goods of benefit to the general public within the urban areas, are most appropriately financed by taxes on local governments. Third, the costs of services for which significant spillovers to neighbouring jurisdictions occur, such as health, education, and welfare, should be borne by substantial state or national intergovernmental transfers. Finally, borrowing is an appropriate source of financing capital outlays on infrastructural services, particularly public utilities and roads.

Extended metropolitan regions – particularly those in which persons live and work in different jurisdictions – may pose particularly difficult problems in regard to municipal finance. The Rio de Janeiro Metropolitan Region is only one example. Within the region, there are several municipalities with relatively little economic activity but with large residential populations that usually work in Rio but live on the periphery. These municipalities have to provide their residents with public services but have limited administrative capacity to collect local taxes. Moreover, they are discriminated against by the national tax sharing and transfer system, which actually works as a disincentive to local fiscal efforts. Despite the large populations of these municipalities, federal transfers to them are proportionally small. Because their economic activities are scarce, their state transfers – which are based on a share of the value-added tax – are also meagre. Thus, in effect, the tax system actually enhances the poverty belt on the periphery of Rio and other large Brazilian cities (United Nations, forthcoming a and b).

Increasing Private-Sector Involvement

Municipalities throughout the developing world can no longer meet the water, sanitation, and other infrastructure needs of their populations by continuing to serve as sole direct providers of those services. Needs have grown too large, and municipalities are too weak financially to cope with rising demand while maintaining the systems already built. Clearly, it is necessary to rethink the institutional and management arrangements, moving away from excessive dependence on public revenues and government subsidies and progressively drawing upon the financial and technical expertise available in the private sector (Rietveld 1992). By allowing private enterprises to compete with public entities on a level playing field – with no differential subsidies or regulatory advantages accorded to public entities – the availability of urban services can be significantly increased, while costs to users can be lowered and the burden on public finances reduced.

BOT projects – those that would normally be considered as public-sector activities but are temporarily placed in the hands of the private sector – represent one way of involving private investors in large-scale infrastructure projects. In such projects, a consortium of companies or individual companies typically form a 'project company' specifically for the purpose of financing, building, operating, and eventually transferring infrastructure to the sponsoring government jurisdiction. Successful BOT projects have been conducted to date in a number of ASEAN countries: two toll road projects and a water treatment plant in Malaysia, a gas turbine plant in Metro Manila, and the Second State Expressway and preliminary work for the construction of 'Stage One, Phase One' of the Bangkok metro (Linn and Wetzel 1990).

On the positive side, privatization enables municipal governments to provide services or build structure that they couldn't otherwise provide; to inject new technology into the area of municipal services; to work with business leaders on municipal long-range planning; and to introduce competition into the provision of government services (Lillywhite 1992). However, the experience with BOT projects to date indicates that they involve a delicate and complicated balancing of public and private interests and involvement. As Linn and Wetzel (1990) have noted, the host government must be able to provide powerful bureaucratic support and a legal environment in which the various regulatory and other issues that arise may be addressed. Moreover, the government must be able to ensure a revenue stream. This is essential in persuading investors and lenders to commit their funds for the long term.

This will not be easy. As Rietveld (1992) notes, several things will be necessary to attract private capital into the sector. For one thing, financial mechanisms and instruments will have to be established capable of mobilizing private savings in sufficient amounts and channelling them to the public utility sector. In countries where well-established capital markets do not yet exist, alternative institutional arrangements will have to be developed as an interim measure. A more rational pricing policy for water and sanitation services will also be necessary. Private investors in the sector will require a fair and competitive rate of return in comparison with competing investment opportunities, and the old concept of water as a free or nearly free good will clearly have to be abandoned once and for all. An additional requirement is careful and continuing attention to operational procedures, maintenance, and timely repair of facilities, all of which in turn require adequately trained and motivated staff. Finally, it is not enough to implement these reforms; municipal authorities must be able to provide convincing evidence to potential investors that they have in fact been implemented and that the utilities in which people are asked to invest are in fact operating efficiently and providing a satisfactory product at a reasonable rate of return. This will require the introduction of honest and effective accounting and auditing procedures to generate financial reports capable of gaining investors' confidence. Studies show that more than seventy developing countries have no modern accounting standards and that few countries have uniform training standards (Rietveld 1992).

Institutional Arrangements

Mega-cities typically experience rapid population growth and an expansion of economic activities, both of which have strong locational impacts that spill over the boundaries of the core city into an ever expanding metropolitan region. Mexico City is a case in point. Within a few years, more than half of the population of the Mexico City Metropolitan Zone will be located outside of the Federal District in the State of Mexico. There is no single metropolitan region authority with responsibility for implementing a comprehensive and integrated strategy of metropolitan development. Events occurring outside the Federal District affect both it and the metropolitan area at large, yet the Federal District is currently powerless to respond (Ward 1990).

This situation is true in many other mega-urban regions in the developing world. In some mega-cities and mega-urban regions, particularly in Latin America, the situation is made more difficult because the residents of the outlying municipalities are relatively powerless since they are usually from the lower socio-economic strata and may support opposition political parties.

Developing the appropriate institutional framework is a problem in managing the growth of mega-cities and mega-urban regions. Municipal administrations cannot perform this task well because their jurisdictions are underbounded, and they are usually fully occupied with the day-to-day problems of routine administration, service provision, and finance. Moreover, as a recent World Bank report has noted, the ability of local governments to solve urban problems is weaker than ever before (Parker 1992). Indeed, throughout the developing world, the institutional capacity of city governments has declined over the last two decades in response to centralization at the national level and inadequate maintenance of essential infrastructure.

Although something must clearly be done, few countries know what to do or where to begin. Metropolitan development and planning authorities have been established in many mega-cities, and these have frequently served as conduits for international assistance in the urban sector. Many authorities have tended to languish as weak institutions, however, with nothing to do and little to say. The Dhaka Improvement Trust, Bombay Metropolitan Development Authority, Karachi Development Authority, Metro Manila Commission (about to be disbanded), and Bangkok Metropolitan Administration are examples. Others have evolved into public works agencies, such as the Calcutta Metropolitan Development Authority and the Delhi Development Authority. Other mega-cities, such as Cairo, Mexico City, Jakarta, Seoul, Buenos Aires, Rio de Janeiro, and Sao Paulo, do not have a metropolitan development authority. In certain cases, key urban services and/or major metropolitan investments are the responsibility of the central or provincial governments instead of a metropolitan authority, as in Seoul, Metro Manila, Bangkok, and Jakarta. In other cases, conflicts have arisen between a metropolitan planning authority and the municipality and, as in Bombay and Karachi, the latter often turns out to be the stronger.

A metropolitan development authority may be an effective mechanism for managing mega-cities, provided that its role is clearly defined. Limited territorial control of existing municipalities and extensive jurisdictional fragmentation usually mean that metropolitan problems cannot be handled at the sub-metropolitan level. It is nonetheless very important that the metropolitan development authorities do not usurp the functions of other agencies. Instead, they should perform functions that other bodies cannot do, such as identifying and promoting an appropriate spatial strategy (but not via heavy-handed government intervention), coordinating a capital investment budget for the metropolitan region, promoting economic development (e.g., giving strong political support for major economic infrastructure programs that could increase metropolitan economic efficiency), seeking consensus among existing bodies and agencies for regional approaches to problems, and finding mechanisms to increase public participation and access.

Conclusions

It is counterproductive to talk about urban size or how to 'control' the growth of cities. Even if all in-migration were stopped, all of the world's large cities and mega-urban regions would still have to absorb huge population increments as a result of natural increase. Despite the abounding rhetoric, size per se is not a critical policy variable. The size of a mega-city or mega-urban region is generally not closely correlated with the severity of its negative externalities. Even the growth rate of a mega-city or a mega-urban region need not be a problem unless it is so high that it impedes economic growth, fiscal stability, and so forth. Currently, no mega-cities are in the dangerous range.

Spatially disaggregated data are needed to enable policy makers and planners to begin to understand the complex processes taking place in mega-cities and mega-urban regions throughout the developing world. In addition, research is required on the successful application of new technologies (e.g., computers to design cost-effective water supply and sanitation systems, remote sensing), new informational approaches (e.g., geographic information systems), land information systems, land market assessments, and public education programs.

Giving greater attention to operations and maintenance and maximizing the use of existing facilities to relieve the burden on new capital investment is a key managerial issue. Clearly, it is absurd to have water supply systems with unaccounted-for water rates of 30 to 50 per cent. Moreover, a crucial requirement for better management is a predictable, growing level of revenues. The structure of various local fees should be reviewed and simplified, and should be subject to vigorous collection efforts. User fees should be fully explored.

New approaches, free from the preconceptions of the past, are also required. Because the only certain aspect of urban growth is that its rate, direction, and nature are highly unpredictable, plans need to incorporate as much flexibility as possible. As cities grow larger, the logistics of providing services become more complex. Because of resource constraints, it is not possible to provide all segments of the population of a mega-urban region with piped water, full internal plumbing, conventional waterborne sewerage, and so forth. Much greater attention should therefore be paid to using a multistandard, multitechnology approach, with large-scale applications of various kinds of appropriate technologies.

Unfortunately, planners continue to adopt the solutions of the past rather than learning from its lessons. For one thing, facilities, once constructed, tend to preclude a change in approach even if new evidence indicates that one may be desirable, mainly because the sunk investment is considered, often wrongly, too great to be abandoned (Kalbermatten and Middleton 1991). Too frequently, as well, the approaches of developed countries are transplanted. With some notable exceptions, university curricula in public-health engineering still tend to concentrate on conventional solutions, so that professional engineers responsible for planning urban utility systems are not in the habit of thinking about viable alternatives. It is conventional wisdom that donor agencies and consultants from developed countries encourage the use of costly imported equipment and materials produced in their countries of origin (Lee Yok-shiu 1992). Gakenheimer and Brando (1987) argue, moreover, that there is an unintentional conspiracy in the developing countries – which includes politicians who wish to avoid being accused of 'demodernizing' services – to insist on maintaining unnecessarily high standards.

Much greater attention needs to be paid to environmental management and planning at the local level. Government agencies have tended to concentrate on environmental degradation on a grand scale, ignoring the micro-scale neighbourhood and community levels on which it must actually be handled (Parker 1992). Most attempts to deal with environmental issues in mega-urban regions have been partial, fragmented, and compartmentalized. Municipal authorities tend, for example, to pay attention to environmental concerns when they are voiced by local communities and to ignore responsibilities that spill over into adjacent municipalities or downstream cities. Waste collection is an example of the former and waste disposal of the latter. The planning efforts of local authorities also fail to incorporate appropriate technologies, community involvement, and, where feasible, formal and informal private-sector participation (World Bank 1992b).

Part 3
Case Studies of ASEAN Mega-Urban Regions

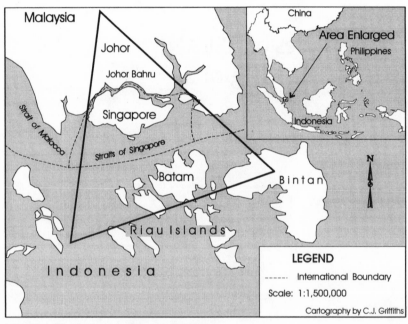

Map 12.1 **The Singapore Growth Triangle**

12

The Johor-Singapore-Riau Growth Triangle: The Effect of Economic Integration

Lee Tsao Yuan

In the economic development literature, the concept of growth poles and spillovers is not a new one. In fact, it is about thirty years old (Hirshmann 1960). It explains such phenomena as the extension of economic activity from major urban industrial areas into their respective surrounding hinterlands and postulates this as a means of economic development of the country. What has captured international attention in recent years is that the growth pole-spillover phenomenon has occurred across national boundaries, resulting in cross-border economic integration of contiguous border areas and not entire countries. In the Asia-Pacific, the largest and best known of these is the Southern East Asian Pacific Rim, comprising the more developed Asian newly industrializing economies of Hong Kong and Taiwan on the one hand and the less developed southern China coastal provinces of Guangdong and Fujian on the other. In Southeast Asia, a smaller version of such cross-border economic integration exists in the Johor-Singapore-Riau (JSR) Growth Triangle, also known as the Singapore Growth Triangle, the Southern Growth Triangle, or Sijori (see Map 12.1).

There is a new but growing literature on the JSR Growth Triangle, and its genesis and rationale are by now well established (*Business Times,* 26 February 1991, 15 April 1992; Kumar and Lee 1991; Ng and Wong 1991; Perry 1991). The key success factors have also been analyzed (Lee Tsao Yuan 1992): economic complementarity among the subregions in terms of factor endowments and prices; geographical proximity, which lowers transportation, communication, cultural, and informational transaction costs; infrastructural development, such as industrial infrastructure; cooperation in customs and immigration procedures; joint investment promotion as a marketing tool; and private-sector participation as the engine of growth.[1] Various authors (Ahmad 1992; Kamil, Pangestu, and Fredricks 1991; MacLeod and McGee 1992) have discussed the economic, sociological, environmental, and political problems associated with the cross-border economic integration. The literature includes a discussion on the future of the growth triangle concept, in terms of its possible extension and replication, and a comparative perspective vis-à-vis other subregional economic zones in the Asia-Pacific (Chia and Lee 1992; Kamil, Pangestu, and Fredricks 1991; Kumar and Lee 1991; Lee 1992a; Wong 1992).

One of the main issues in the JSR Growth Triangle that needs further analysis is the effect of economic integration on each of the three subregions, in terms of the extent and nature of the benefits of such integration, the extent and nature of the structural adjustments entailed, and the ensuing costs. This chapter attempts to contribute to the discussion by examining the effect of economic integration within the growth triangle with regard to Johor, Batam/Riau, and Singapore. In the remainder of the chapter, the growth triangle is defined, its effects on Johor, Riau, and Singapore are discussed, and some policy issues are examined.

The Johor-Singapore-Riau Growth Triangle[2]

The best way to think about the growth triangle is as an extension both of the levels of economic development in each of the three areas and of economic relations between Singapore and Malaysia and Singapore and Indonesia. It is essentially a cross-border spillover of economic activity from labour- and land-scarce Singapore into the southernmost state of Johor in peninsular Malaysia on the one hand and the nearby Riau islands of Indonesia, principally Batam, on the other, where labour and land are in more plentiful and inexpensive supply.

Such extension of economic activity makes sound business sense. Manufacturing companies can engage in vertical specialization, locating labour-intensive processes in Johor/Batam, and more skill- and knowledge-intensive activities in Singapore, in line with each area's comparative advantage. Thus, headquarter operations – finance, marketing and distribution, and legal and administrative operations – are located in Singapore, as are newer and more sophisticated product lines. Geographical proximity and ease of communication tie the various activities together. At the same time, there are attractive opportunities to develop tourist and leisure activities in Johor/Riau, to cater not only to the domestic Singapore market but also to the 5 million or so annual throughput of tourists who visit Singapore. In short, the growth triangle offers opportunities to take advantage of economies of scale and scope (as a result of specialization) and economies of agglomeration (as a result of external economies).

The growth triangle, although acknowledged in ASEAN as a means to achieve more rapid economic integration, is not a formal form of economic integration in the sense that a free-trade area is. The Indonesian, Malaysian, and Singapore governments do not have a trilateral agreement as such, but the informal arrangement has been endorsed at the highest levels.[3] One reason why this is the case is that economic integration within the growth triangle is facilitated by the general process of economic liberalization in Malaysia and Indonesia. Major economic reforms undertaken by both economies in the 1980s were instrumental in reducing barriers to trade, capital, and labour flows. In particular, Malaysia relaxed its guidelines for foreign equity participation in the manufacturing sector in 1986 to allow 100 per cent foreign ownership, provided that 50 per cent of production is exported or at least 350 Malaysian workers are employed full time (Bank Negara Malaysia 1990, 67). Indonesia in 1989 also relaxed its foreign investment regulations to allow 100 per cent foreign equity ownership for the first five years and 5 per cent divestment thereafter for the Batam Economic Zone. Both Johor and Batam provide duty-free status for export-oriented production, so that the growth triangle can be conceived of as a transnational export processing zone.

The term 'triangle of growth,' first coined by the then Singapore deputy prime minister Goh Chok Tong in December 1989, has been subject to a certain degree of misinterpretation. Some are of the view that there should be three dynamic and more or less equally vibrant bilateral relationships between Singapore, Johor, and Riau. At the moment, however, the more or less similar levels of economic development of Johor and Riau do not warrant significant flows of trade or investment.[4] Instead, economic integration is directed in two channels: Singapore with Johor and Singapore with Riau. A more realistic interpretation of the term triangle is therefore merely that three areas are involved in a subregional economic zone.

The growth triangle is an interesting mix of government initiative and market-driven investment and offers a useful case study of the respective roles of government and the private sector. The Singapore-Johor and Singapore-Riau links are different in this regard. The Singapore-Johor connection is much more a response to market forces and occurred earlier than the other, in part because Johor by the late 1970s already had in place fairly good industrial infrastructure and transparent rules and regulations. Companies in Singapore began to relocate their labour-intensive manufacturing activities in Johor and other states in Malaysia in that period, long before the official pronouncement of a growth triangle. Thomson Consumer Electronics, for example, established a factory in Muar, Johor, in 1979 (Lee 1992b). Such investments accelerated after the liberalization of foreign investment regulations in 1986.

On the other hand, the Singapore-Riau link would probably not have occurred if it were not for government initiative and facilitation. As mentioned previously, new rulings in 1989 enabled private-sector development of infrastructure and 100 per cent foreign ownership on Batam for the first five years. Moreover, the first industrial park to operate in

Batam, the Batam Industrial Park, is a joint venture between the Indonesian Salim conglomerate and two Singapore government-linked companies. Government endorsement is also formalized in four agreements between Indonesia and Singapore: an agreement to cooperate in the development of Riau province, an investment guarantee agreement, and two agreements to develop water reservoirs in Riau and Bintan respectively for eventual water supply to Singapore. Two joint Indonesia-Singapore missions were also organized to promote investment opportunities in Riau.

In light of the above, it is appropriate to analyze the Singapore-Johor and Singapore-Batam linkages separately, as the subsequent discussion does.

The Singapore-Johor Link

How has the Singapore-Johor link contributed to economic development in Johor? In order to answer this question, Johor's economic development has to be seen in the context of the economic development of Malaysia as a whole, and the Singapore-Johor link should be viewed in the overall context of Singapore-Malaysia economic relations.

Johor in Malaysia

Johor is an important state to Malaysia, comprising 12.4 per cent of the total population and 10 per cent of the total GDP in 1990 (Kamil, Pangestu, and Fredricks 1991, 50). Economic development in Johor is therefore an integral part of Malaysian economic development as a whole. Johor is regarded in Malaysia as a middle-income state, with a per capita GDP slightly below the national average. It is significant that although its per capita GDP was 0.91 times the national average in both 1970 and 1990 (Malaysia 1991c, 51), Johor grew as fast as the national average, 7 per cent, over that period. Johor, like all the other Malaysian states, has seen important reductions in the incidence of poverty, from 29 per cent in 1976 to 10.1 per cent in 1990, the fifth lowest of the eleven states in peninsular Malaysia (p. 52).

National government emphasis on continued growth in Johor incorporates an explicit recognition of spillover effects from growth poles to less developed states (p. 123). Three such growth poles are mentioned in the Sixth Malaysia Plan (Malaysia 1991b, 37, 39): (1) Kuala Lumpur/Selangor, with spillover to the states of Melaka, Negeri Sembilan, and Perak; (2) Singapore, with spillover to Johor; and (3) Pulau Pinang, with spillover to the Kulim-Sungai Petani areas in the state of Kedah. The link with Singapore is thus viewed as a positive factor for Johor's economic development. Due to this boost, it is expected that Johor's per capita GDP, relative to the national average, will increase substantially by 2000 (Malaysia

1991c, 125). In other words, Johor is expected to grow faster than the planned national average of 7 per cent in the 1990s because of its links with Singapore.

Malaysia-Singapore Economic Relations

Malaysia and Singapore have historically been economically integrated and culturally close. In fact, a border did not exist until the formation of independent Malaya (later Malaysia) in 1957 and Singapore in 1965. Bilateral trade, investment, and tourism flows have been intensive. While it is to be expected that Johor, as the state geographically closest, will have the most intensive interaction with Singapore, it is almost impossible to distinguish between Singapore's links with Johor and with other states.

Singapore continues to be Malaysia's largest trading partner, and its importance has increased. About a quarter of Malaysia's imports and exports originated or passed through Singapore in 1980, and this figure increased to well over 40 per cent in 1991 (Malaysia, Department of Statistics, various years and months). Not only does Malaysia use Singapore's port facilities (Singapore has a traditional function as an entrepôt), but intra-company trade between Singapore and Malaysia has probably increased as a result of spatial vertical specialization of processes. There are no statistics on the destination and origin of such trade by state in Malaysia, so it is impossible to determine Singapore-Johor trade.

Statistics on foreign investment approvals for 1985-90, excluding hotels and tourist complexes, show that Singapore was the third largest investor in Malaysia after Taiwan and Japan (Malaysia 1991c, 135). Approval data for Johor state show the same pattern (Chia and Lee 1992, Table 4). There is, of course, the remote possibility that the majority of Singapore's investments in Malaysia are located in Johor but this is highly unlikely as all foreign investment approvals for Johor did not constitute more than 23 per cent of the total for Malaysia for 1985-90. In fact, Selangor was the top destination for foreign investment (Malaysian Industrial Development Authority 1990).[5]

Tourism deserves special mention. Singaporeans constitute by far the largest group of tourists in Malaysia: nearly 60 per cent in 1991. It is worthy of note that, while the absolute number of Singaporean tourists visiting Malaysia steadily increased from 1.3 million in 1980 to 3.23 million in 1990, the number of non-Singaporean tourists has increased even faster since 1986, so that by 1990 the number of Singaporean tourists as a percentage of the total had fallen below the 1980 figure. Unfortunately, no further details are available regarding the possibly multiple destinations of these visitors or their expenditure pattern and average length of stay. We do know that the majority of Singaporeans (87 per cent in the first quarter of 1992) enter Malaysia via the causeway linking the two countries, with Johor Bahru, the capital city of Johor, as their point of entry (Malaysia, Tourism Promotion Board 1992). There is also anecdotal evidence that many of these tourists are day trippers to Johor Bahru, for shopping, dining, and entertainment because of the exchange rate and relatively lower prices.

The conclusion, therefore, is that Johor, as the closest Malaysian state to Singapore, arguably benefits the most from economic spillovers, although Singapore and Malaysia as a whole are relatively closely economically integrated. Singapore, and hence the growth triangle, does play an important role in Johor's economic development, although Johor's dynamism derives mainly from being an integral part of a larger, rapidly growing, Malaysian economy.

The Singapore-Riau Link

The Indonesian province of Riau comprises part of Sumatra as well as a number of islands such as Batam, Bintan, Karimun, and Bulan. It has 4.9 per cent (94,561 km²) of the total Indonesian land area, 1.8 per cent (3.3 million) of the total population in 1990, and 6.4 per cent of the Indonesian GDP in 1988.[6] Riau is known in particular for its oil resources.[7] Although the cooperation agreements between Indonesia and Singapore pertain to Riau province as a whole, our immediate interest is with specific islands in Riau that already have joint developmental efforts underway. These are: Batam Island, 415 km² and 40 minutes by ferry from Singapore; Bintan Island, 1,100 km² and 60 minutes by ferry from Singapore, where an integrated development project spearheaded by a consortium of major Indonesian and Singapore companies is under construction, comprising a resort and an industrial estate; Karimun Island, 40 km southwest of Singapore, where there are plans to construct a multimillion dollar shipyard and petroleum processing centre; and Bulan Island, which has orchid and pig farms and is earmarked for agro-business (Kumar and Lee 1991). The ensuing discussion will focus on Batam as statistical evidence is most readily available for that island.

The economic development of Batam has had a rather long history (Ahmad 1992; Pangestu 1991). Batam was designated as a logistical base for oil industries in 1970 as part of Indonesia's offshore petroleum exploration effort, which began in 1968. The development of Batam as an industrial area started in 1973, and it became a duty free zone in 1978. The basic infrastructure on Batam, such as the road system and port, were also built well before the mid-1980s.

All indicators point towards rapid increases in economic activity on Batam only since the mid-1980s (Tables 12.1 and 12.2). Batam's population doubled between 1985 and 1991, for example, and the workforce nearly quadrupled within the same period. Exports from Batam increased tenfold from $20.9 million in 1986 to $210.3 million in 1991, with corresponding increases in the number of ships' calls and cargo loaded and unloaded. Foreign investment in-flows (on an approval basis) have also increased dramatically since 1988.

Table 12.1

Batam main economic indicators, 1973-91

	Population growth	%	Workforce growth	%	Exports growth ($US millions)	%	Approved foreign investment ($US millions)
1973	6,000	–	–	–	–	–	–
1978	31,800	–	–	–	–	–	–
1983	43,000	–	–	–	–	–	148.0
1985	58,000	–	6,389	–	–	–	7.0
1986	–	–	7,013	9.8	20.9	–	1.0
1987	–	–	8,935	27.4	26.8	28.2	0.0
1988	79,400	–	9,631	7.8	44.2	64.9	65.4
1989	90,500	14.0	11,181	16.1	53.0	19.9	139.3
1990	95,751	5.8	16,336	46.1	148.4	180.0	295.6
1991	107,564	12.3	23,237	42.2	210.3	41.7	–

Table 12.2

Batam total investments, December 1991

	($US millions)	(%) share	(%) share
Total investments	3,280.0	**100.0**	
Source of investments			
Government	628.8	**19.2**	
Private	2,652.0	**80.8**	
Domestic	599.5	18.3	
Non-facility	997.5	30.4	
Foreign	1,054.8	32.2	**100.0**
Singapore	531.8	16.2	**50.4**
US	159.0	4.8	**15.1**
Japan	119.8	3.7	**11.4**
Other	244.2	7.4	**23.2**
Destination sectors of private investment		**100.0**	
Industry		**48.6**	
Trade		**0.9**	
Tourism/hotel		**17.1**	
Developer		**18.5**	
Agro-business		**3.3**	
Other		**11.6**	

Likewise, tourism is a relatively new economic activity in Batam. Batam has only been listed separately in Indonesian statistics on visitor arrivals since 1983, with 21,000 arrivals, 3.4 per cent of the Indonesian total. This rapidly increased to over 145,000 arrivals by 1987, and over 600,000 by 1991, 24 per cent of the Indonesian total. In fact, Batam has become the second most important port of entry in Indonesia after Jakarta, having overtaken Bali in 1990. The evidence therefore suggests that the Batam boom began in the mid-1980s. Ahmad (1992) goes further to pinpoint it in 1988.

What led to the exponential growth in economic activity on Batam? One factor was a notable increase in investment since 1984, particularly in the oil mining equipment industry before 1988 (Ahmad 1992). The two policy changes in 1989, mentioned previously, were instrumental in encouraging investments in other sectors, undoubtedly causing the jump in foreign investment in-flows in 1988-90 (Table 12.2).

The role of Singapore is quite significant in the recent economic boom on Batam. Although joint development of the island was first proposed in 1979 by the Indonesian minister of state for research and technology, Dr. Habibie, to the then Singapore prime minister, Lee Kuan Yew, it only took off ten years later when Singapore, like a balloon, had reached bursting point and needed another outlet (Habibie 1992). As a result of the policy changes, a joint venture between Indonesia's Salim group and two Singapore government-linked companies was formed to own and manage Batam Industrial Park, a self-contained industrial estate with its own utility centre, telecommunications facilities, commercial centre, and workers' living quarters. Work began on the industrial estate at the end of 1989, and the first factory, Thomson, began operations in January 1991.[8]

In addition to Singapore's joint ownership and management of the industrial estate, Singapore-based investment and tourism in Batam are substantial. Singaporean tourists alone account for more than two-thirds of visitor arrivals in Batam, and this does not include the foreign tourists who travel to Batam via Singapore. Singapore investments made up 50.5 per cent of the $1 billion total foreign investment on Batam at the end of 1991, with US and Japanese investments a distant second and third at 15.2 and 11.4 per cent respectively (Table 12.2). Foreign investment in turn constitutes 20 per cent of total private investment on Batam, considered as the sum of foreign, domestic, and non-facility investments. Many foreign companies in operation at the end of 1991 were located at the Batam Industrial Park.

How does Singapore's involvement in Batam compare with its involvement in Indonesia as a whole? Comparisons can be made with regard to exports, investments, and tourism.

Indonesian exports to Singapore were $1,238.9 million and $2,409.4

million in 1986 and 1991 respectively (*Indonesia Financial Statistics,* various years). Suppose that all exports from Batam were destined for Singapore, which, although an overestimation, may not be grossly off the mark. These exports were \$20.9 million in 1986 and \$210.3 million in 1991. In other words, from a negligible 0.9 per cent in 1986, exports from Batam as a proportion of total Indonesian exports to Singapore increased to 8.7 per cent in 1991.[9]

The main locations for foreign investment in Indonesia are Jakarta and West Java. Since 1988, however, the share of foreign investments located in Riau province has increased, so that in terms of the cumulative total (1967-91), Riau is fourth after West Java, Jakarta, and East Java. Although there could be difficulties of data comparability between foreign investment flows into Riau and into Batam, it does appear as if the latter account for a major share of foreign investment in-flows into Riau. For Indonesia as a whole, foreign investment in-flows from Singapore-based companies have been lower than investments from Northeast Asian economies, particularly Japan and Taiwan, but a significant increase has been noted since 1988.[10] This is in stark contrast to Batam, where Singapore-based companies constitute the largest source of foreign investments on Batam.

Finally, since 1989, Singaporeans have constituted the largest group of tourists in Indonesia. Batam remains the most popular port of entry (61 per cent of all tourists in 1991).[11]

In short, available statistics point to a significant Singaporean contribution to the current economic boom of Batam in terms of industrial infrastructure, investments, exports, and tourism. Even in the context of Singapore-Indonesian economic relations, the Singapore-Batam link is fairly significant. This could no doubt be explained by the proximity of Batam to Singapore, and the convenience of 'neighbourhood' investment and travel.

In conclusion, a comparison of Singapore's roles in the development of Johor and Batam is in order. It can be seen that, where Johor is concerned, the link with Singapore, although important, is but one of the many causes of its rapid economic growth. In particular, the general pro-growth policy environment of Malaysia, characterized by economic pragmatism and openness to foreign investment, has resulted in large in-flows of Taiwanese and Japanese multinational corporations (MNCs) into Johor. Singapore investments are by no means the largest. It is only in tourism that Singapore is the lead nationality, but even this in relative terms has declined. Moreover, it is natural for contiguous border areas to experience continuous cross-border movement of people.[12] This has been occurring for decades and certainly predates the formation of the growth triangle.

Singapore has had a much more direct role in the development of Batam, however, participating in the establishment of the first operational industrial park, foreign investment, and tourism.

The Effect on Singapore

The macro-statistics do not, as yet, show significant evidence of a 'growth triangle' effect on the Singapore economy (Lee Tsao Yuan 1992). Unlike Hong Kong – where outward processing has resulted not only in considerable downsizing of the manufacturing sector in relative and absolute terms but also in alteration of the trade pattern and composition towards China – in Singapore the newness of the growth triangle and its relatively small population may account for its still undetectable effect on aggregate statistics. Company surveys reveal, however, that the extent of redistribution of labour-intensive activities is by no means insignificant.[13] In addition, a September 1992 survey by the Singapore Manufacturers' Association covered 352 manufacturers in Singapore, 22 per cent of whom have invested in the growth triangle, mainly in Johor (*Business Times*, 5 October 1992). Of these, nearly one-third were from the electronics and electrical industry, 12.3 per cent from the metal and machinery sector, 9 per cent from rubber and plastics, and 6.2 per cent from food and beverages. Although 60 per cent of the manufacturers were large companies, 39 per cent were small and medium enterprises, an increase from the 32 per cent of a similar survey conducted in January 1992. Of the local manufacturers who invested in Batam and Johor, 46 per cent indicated that they had become more competitive by lowering their production costs, about one in four indicated that they had not gained, and the rest indicated that it was premature to make conclusions.

One point to bear in mind is that both Malaysia and Indonesia have historically been, and still are, close economic partners of Singapore. Malaysia is Singapore's third largest trading partner after the US and Japan. More recently, as shown in both Malaysian and Indonesian statistics, Singapore and Singapore-based companies have been moving offshore, although not to Johor and Riau alone. The growth triangle is in many ways an extension of these close economic relationships.

Challenges and Policy Solutions

Some Problems

Writers on the growth triangle have discussed the problems and challenges associated with the cross-border spillover phenomenon (Ahmad 1992; Kumar and Lee 1991; Lee Tsao Yuan 1991; MacLeod and McGee 1992; Pangestu 1991). These can be broadly categorized as follows: problems of excess demand, in particular, labour shortages and lack of physical and industrial infrastructure, resulting in traffic congestion, housing shortages, and escalation in the cost of living; sociological problems associated with rapid urbanization; interministry administrative problems leading to inconsistencies in policy formulation and implementation; and political problems associated with cross-border economic integration.

The dissatisfaction summarized above at times gives the impression that the growth triangle entails more costs than benefits for Johor and Riau. Rapid growth and structural adjustment have resulted in unequal gains for different groups, and those who gain relatively little have been more vocal in their complaints than those who have benefited have been in their praise for the arrangement.

Some Solutions

Policy solutions fall into two broad categories: economic and political. On the economic front, infrastructural and human resource development should be clear priorities. Six new townships costing a total of Ringgit $9 billion, for example, will be built in Johor Bahru to overcome the shortage in low- and medium-cost housing (*Straits Times,* 26 September 1992). There are also plans to ease the traffic congestion in Johor Baru. The proposed second link between Singapore and Johor is already well into the planning stage, and this is expected to reduce congestion at the causeway. A further measure is restriction of purchases by foreigners. The Johor state government is planning to introduce limitations on the sale of land to non-citizens (*Straits Times,* 2 October 1992), and the Johor Consumers' Association is planning to establish a low-price consumer cooperative for locals only, to help keep living costs down (*Straits Times,* 6 September 1992).

On the political front, it is important that the growth triangle be recognized as having net benefits for all three parties involved. It is not so clear-cut who gains more from the arrangement, especially if both the short and long runs are taken into account, and nor is this particularly important. It is perhaps with this in mind that the heads of state of all three countries have endorsed the growth triangle.

It is also important for political leaders to downplay parochial sentiments that counter what Malaysian minister for international trade and industry, Datuk Rafidah Aziz, calls 'economic pragmatism' (*Business Times,* 30 September 1992). Recognizing the business potential of the growth triangle, she suggested that three-way joint ventures involving Malaysian, Singaporean, and Indonesian companies be formed for the purpose of investing in the growth triangle and in third-country markets such as Vietnam or Europe. She also said that Singapore and Malaysia would be jointly promoting the growth triangle as a single investment entity and a tourist destination.

Conclusion

In the end, the ASEAN nations must realize that economic competition comes from without. There are, for example, real concerns that the rapidly growing Greater South China Economic Zone could attract investments away from ASEAN, on two counts. The zone is not only driven by the entrepreneurial dynamism of both Hong Kong and Taiwan and by the sheer size and resources of South China but in addition holds the lure of the potentially huge Chinese market, an attraction that the growth triangle does not possess to the same degree.[14] Deng Xiao Peng's endorsement of the economic reform process in southern China in early 1992 has created an even more upbeat mood among investors regarding China's potential. More recently, there has been talk that foreign-funded ventures could be allowed greater access to the China market (*Straits Times,* 6 October 1992). Further afield is the North American Free Trade Agreement and the competitiveness of Mexico as a location for labour-intensive investments aimed at the US market. The growth triangle, seen in this context, is ASEAN's immediate answer to these other regional and subregional arrangements, before the materialization of an ASEAN free trade area.

Notes

1 See Wong (1992) for a neat tabular presentation of the key competitive business advantages of the growth triangle.

2 Since a brief literature review has already been outlined in the introduction, references are excluded from this section.

3 There are, however, several agreements signed between Indonesia and Singapore, as will be mentioned later. See also Pangestu (1991) and Lee (1992a).

4 A leisure development project was proposed at Gunong Ledang in Johor, but to date it has not materialized.

5 It would be ideal to obtain data by state and home country, but those are available only from each state's economic development board.

6 The percentage is of the total of twenty-seven provinces, which is less than that of the total Indonesian GDP, and had statistical discrepancies amounting to 3.7 per cent in 1988 (Indonesia 1990, Tables 1.1, 3.11, and 11.9).

7 For example, Riau's gross regional domestic product in 1983 constant prices with and without oil and gas in 1988 were Rupiah 8105 and 1877 billion respectively (Indonesia 1990, Tables 11.10 and 11.11).

8 There are, in addition, two other industrial parks in various stages of completion: Kabil Industrial Park and Suar International Development.

9 Again, this could be an overestimate, as exports from Batam could be destined for countries other than Singapore. There may well also be entrepôt exports in both the Indonesian and Batam export statistics.

10 It would be ideal if foreign investment data for Indonesia were available by region and home country, but this is not published.

11 Data since 1988 show that although Singapore residents constituted the largest group of tourists (28.5 per cent in 1990), estimated revenue from this group was only 13.7 per cent (Indonesia n.d.).

12 Incidentally, of the 16.8 million outgoing Malaysians in 1991, 76 per cent departed via Johor Baru; that is, to and via Singapore (Malaysia, Tourism Promotion Board 1992).

13 A 270-respondent survey conducted by the Singapore Manufacturers' Association in January 1992 shows that two out of five manufacturers have either moved or intend to relocate part of their business to neighbouring countries to cope with rising labour costs. In a mail questionnaire survey to which 310 manufacturing companies responded, 148 indicated that they already had production facilities outside Singapore: 45.9 per cent in Johor, 10.8 per cent in Batam, and 50.7 per cent elsewhere (Yeoh, Lau, and Funkhouser 1992).

14 For example, Batam is a bonded zone; goods produced on Batam are not automatically allowed into Indonesia.

13

The Metro Manila Mega-Region

Romeo B. Ocampo

Metro Manila, comprising four cities and thirteen towns in what is otherwise known as the National Capital Region (NCR) of the Philippines, has been growing rapidly during the past few decades. But population and urban growth has been faster in some towns just outside Metro Manila, especially in the provinces immediately to the south and east. Apparently, Metro Manila has been spilling over into a wider region beyond its official borders (Map 13.1).

This expansion of Metro Manila into a mega-region has been acknowledged since at least the early 1970s.[1] It is hard not to notice, because it has aggravated the manifold problems of urban sprawl and primacy. Many of these processes and problems are attributed to market forces, but some are also traceable to government initiatives. Certain current responses, including the Calabarzon project, may provide a better solution to mega-urbanization. But new problems and pressures, in the region and elsewhere, may also help to shape this process and to show up inadequacies in the policy and institutional framework for development planning and urban management.

The Growth of Metro Manila

Metro Manila's population has been increasing rapidly since at least the end of the Second World War. Its growth rate peaked at an annual average of 4.9 per cent during 1960-70, and then declined to 3.6 per cent during 1975-80. During 1980-90, its population grew from 5.9 to 7.9 million, or by nearly 33 per cent, a growth rate much higher than the national rate of 2.3 per cent. At this rate, the NCR population is expected to grow by another 1.25 million by 1995. This will mean corresponding increases in population densities over the 636 km^2 area.

Urban uses have intensified within the NCR, with residential uses increasing their share of total land from 37 per cent in 1980 to 45 per cent in 1990. Meanwhile, open spaces have shrunk from 47.8 to 39.6 per cent,

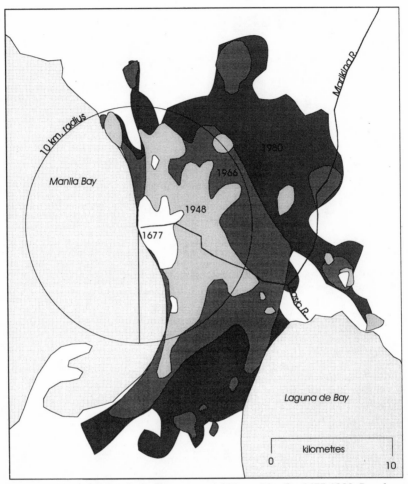

Map 13.1 **Growth of main built-up areas of Metro Manila, 1677-1980.** Based on Manila Metropolitan Authority (1992, 25)

and authorities no longer provide separate data on agriculture and other primary uses (which now account for only 1.5 per cent of employment in the NCR). Moreover, for the first time, two localities within Metro Manila (Manila and neighbouring San Juan) experienced net losses in population during the 1980s, albeit of less than 1 per cent (see Table 13.1).

Adjacent towns, especially in Bulacan province just north of the NCR, Rizal to the east, and Laguna and Cavite to the south, have been growing faster than Metro Manila since 1960-70, when their average annual growth rate (5.2 per cent) overtook that of the NCR (4.9 per cent). This rate peaked at 6.3 per cent during 1975-80 and then declined to an average of 4.3 per cent a year in 1980-90 (United Nations 1986c). Despite this

Table 13.1

Population size and growth rate, land area and density of Philippines National Capital Region and adjacent towns, 1980, 1990, and 1995

	Population (thousands)		Growth rate (%)	Projected population (thousands) 1995	Land (km^2)	Persons/hectare	
	1980	1990				1980	1990
Manila	1,630	1,601	-0.18	1,587	38.3	426	418
Kaloocan	468	763	5.02	975	55.8	84	137
Quezon City	1,166	1,670	3.66	1,999	166.2	70	100
Pasay	288	368	2.50	417	13.9	207	265
Las Pinas	137	297	8.09	438	41.5	33	72
Makati	373	453	1.98	500	29.9	125	152
Malabon	191	280	3.90	339	23.4	82	120
Mandaluyong	205	248	1.92	273	26.0	79	95
Marikina	212	310	3.90	376	38.9	54	80
Muntinglupa	137	278	7.37	397	46.7	29	60
Navotas	126	187	4.04	229	2.6	485	721
Paranaque	209	308	3.98	375	38.3	54	80
Pasig	269	398	4.00	484	13.0	207	306
Pateros	40	51	2.47	58	10.4	125	122
San Juan	130	127	-0.25	125	10.4	125	122
Taguig	134	266	7.11	376	33.7	40	79
Valenzuela	212	340	4.82	431	47.0	45	72
Total	5,927	7,945	2.98	9,379	636.0	93	125
35 adjacent municipalities	1,426	2,180	4.33	2,695	1,681.8	8	13

Sources: Demographic Research and Development Foundation and Commission on Population – NCR (1992); Metro Manila Commission (1985)

decline, some of these towns registered over 6 per cent annual growth rates during the intercensal decade 1980-90. The net losses of the city of Manila and the municipality of San Juan during 1980-90 probably resulted from such trends (Table 13.1).

According to a UN study, the faster growth rates just outside Metro Manila indicated a significant shift in the direction of migration: 'In recent years, there have been marked spillover effects from Metro Manila into the adjacent provinces' (United Nations 1986c, 15). (See Table 13.2.)

Table 13.2

Population, growth rate, and density of Metro Manila and nearby regions, 1980 and 1990

	Population (thousands)		Growth rate (%)	Persons per km²
	1980	1990		1990
Metro Manila (NCR)	5,926	7,929	3.0	12,467
Central Luzon	4,802	6,199	2.5	340
Bulacan	1,096	1,505	3.2	573
Pampanga	1,182	1,533	2.6	703
Tarlac	688	860	2.2	282
Nueva Ecija	1,069	1,313	2.1	248
Bataan	323	425	2.8	309
Zambales	444	563	2.4	152
Southern Tagalog (IV)	6,118	8,265	3.0	176
Calabarzon	4,603	6,351	3.3	609
Cavite	771	1,152	4.0	895
Laguna	973	1,370	3.5	778
Batangas	1,174	1,477	2.3	466
Rizal	556	980	5.8	749
Quezon	1,129	1,372	2.0	158
Aurora	107	140	2.6	43
Marinduque	174	186	0.7	194
Occidental Mindoro	222	282	2.4	48
Oriental Mindoro	447	550	2.1	126
Palawan	372	528	3.5	35
Romblon	193	228	1.6	168
Philippines	48,098	60,685	2.3	202

Source: Philippines, National Statistics Office (1992)

Migration data for earlier years (1975 and 1980) indicate that while some provinces and regions close to Metro Manila continued to send people into the NCR, the number of in-migrants from these areas was offset by out-migrants. This was especially true for the five neighbouring provinces collectively called Calabarzon.[2] When combined with Metro Manila, they created an extended metropolitan region of 14.2 million people in 1990. According to the planning report (Ramos 1991), these five contributed 15.6 per cent to in-migration into the NCR but drew 41.6 per cent of out-migrants from the metropolitan area. While two of the provinces (Batangas and Quezon) continued to be net senders to Metro Manila, the other three (Cavite,[3] Rizal, and Laguna) were net receivers of migrants from the NCR (see Tables 13.3 and 13.4).

Table 13.3

In-migration and out-migration of Calabarzon provinces, 1975-80

	In-migration total rate (%)*		Out-migration total rate (%)*		Net migration
Cavite	53,045	8.4	15,150	2.4	37,895
Laguna	43,638	5.4	21,369	2.7	22,269
Batangas	18,165	1.8	28,464	2.8	-10,299
Rizal	54,795	13.2	26,493	6.4	28,302
Quezon	22,718	2.2	32,951	3.2	-10,233

* Total in- or out-migration divided by 1975 population
Source: Japan International Cooperation Agency (1990b) and (1991)

Table 13.4

Migration into and out of the National Capital Region from/to Calabarzon and other regions, 1975-80

Origin/ destination	Migration into NCR		Migration out of NCR		Net number of migrants into NCR
	Share in total (%)	Rate (%)*	Share in total (%)	Rate (%)*	
Cavite	2.1	1.29	15.9	5.18	-24,406
Laguna	2.7	1.28	7.9	2.00	-5,785
Batangas	3.8	1.39	1.7	0.34	10,901
Rizal	3.3	3.00	14.2	7.01	-16,609
Quezon	3.7	1.37	1.9	0.38	10,185
Other Region IV provinces	4.2	1.22	2.8	0.44	10,283
Region III	13.5	1.22	20.7	1.01	8,853
Region V	13.6	1.61	7.8	0.50	35,616
Northern regions	15.6	1.14	8.5	0.33	41,956
Southern regions	37.4	0.74	18.7	0.20	103,701

* Total migration divided by 1975 population
Source: Japan International Cooperation Agency (1991)

Problems of Expansion

Metropolitan expansion in the mega-region has tended to exacerbate the problems of urban sprawl and primacy that have accompanied growth within the NCR. Urbanization had been typified by leapfrogging 'ribbon developments' along major roadways. This earlier tendency has been mitigated by the filling-in of vacant areas, the preference of subdivision developers to locate their projects in towns closest to Metro Manila, and the development of large, planned residential, commercial, and industrial development projects, including the 'mega malls' and condominiums built in the NCR in recent years. In the widening frontiers of the metropolis, however, the urbanization process has skipped considerable spaces, and the larger commercial and industrial projects have created new suburban centres of activity. Thus, according to a recent government report,

> the trend of spatial development in the NCR during the last 10 years is characterized by the following: (a) urban sprawl in the fringes of Metro Manila towards the provinces of Region 3 [Central Luzon] and IV [Southern Tagalog] and conversion of agricultural lands to urban uses; (b) increased density and location of high intensity commercial centers along major transportation routes particularly along and outside Epifanio delos Santos Avenue (EDSA); (c) development of large-scale residential subdivisions; and (d) location of new industries in the metropolis (Philippines 1992, 7).

The sprawl has strained public utilities and services to the limit, stretched travel distances and time, and resulted in social disparities and conflicts of various kinds. Commuting, which has become interprovincial for many workers, has become harder and more expensive. The number of person-trips in Metro Manila grew by 6.7 per cent a year to 17.65 million in 1990, which meant vehicular traffic congestion was 'becoming inevitable' (Manila Metropolitan Authority 1992). During peak periods, traffic flows on one side of major roads become so thick that they are allowed to spill over the median and 'counterflow' along one lane on the other side. Gridlock often occurs, especially when it rains hard or the traffic lights go off with brown-outs and the legion of 'traffic enforcers' leave their stations.

The NCR continues to dominate its national hinterland as the economic, sociocultural, and political centre of the country. But it also has a substantial share of national problems, including unemployment, depth of poverty, and law and order problems. In 1986, for example, the unemployment rate in the NCR was 28.6 per cent, more than twice the national rate of 11.1 per cent. The latter declined to 9.0 per cent in 1991 but the rate in the NCR was still 15.4 per cent. The percentage of NCR families falling below the poverty line was lower than the national rate – 49.5 per cent compared to 59.0 per cent in 1980 – and declined from 43.9 to 31.5 per cent between 1985 and 1988 (Philippines 1992, 10).

Despite the decline, poverty may have deepened in terms of lack of such

Regional Development Framework Plan, but the funds were used more to coordinate public projects than to encourage private investments (United Nations 1986c, 18, 21-2).

Current Regional Plans

The expansion of Metro Manila beyond its official borders has been recognized since at least 1971, when the University of the Philippines Institute of Planning proposed a plan for a 'Manila Bay Region' of eight provinces plus Manila, with a metropolitan core of five cities and thirty-five towns. The MMC, organized in 1975, initially adopted a large planning area, with the NCR and thirty-five other towns as the metro area (Manila Metropolitan Commission 1985). This was later reduced to the NCR and twenty-five other towns for the 1985-94 metropolitan framework plan.

Several metropolitan plans for the medium term have been confined to the NCR. Within Metro Manila, key urban-forming infrastructure projects have focused on transportation rather than land use. Several 'flyovers' have been built at major intersections to ease traffic congestion. New segments of the highway network in Metro Manila are under construction. An eastward line of the light-rapid transit (LRT) system, which has thus far been viewed as successful despite rising fare rates, has been proposed. An old proposal to ban 'jeepneys' from the main roads in the NCR has also been dusted off, with the government thinking of buying them for resale to provincial operators.

The larger regional context of NCR plans has been considered in other ways. Proposals for the NCR have been incorporated in a comprehensive plan for five regions, the Luzon Area Development and Strategic Investment Program (National Economic and Development Authority, Republic of the Philippines 1990, 10-14). The Calabarzon project represents another major development plan that takes Metro Manila into account as its point of origin and departure.

The Luzon program reiterates the spatial strategy of industry and population dispersal from the NCR to other regions, but especially to two nearby Central Luzon provinces and to Calabarzon. While keeping its 'primacy' as the centre for government, education, trade, finance, and commerce, Metro Manila would shift manufacturing and population to these places. Calabarzon would receive population and heavy and light industries from the NCR and semi-processed products from elsewhere for final processing and export (National Economic and Development Authority, Republic of the Philippines 1990, 10-13).

The Calabarzon project, or 'master plan study,' prepared by the Japan International Cooperation Agency (1990b) under Philippines government auspices (especially the Department of Trade and Industry), is a more detailed document with a number of supporting studies. It proposes a 'high industrialization' strategy involving rapid growth and high rates of spillover from Metro Manila into adjacent areas, as against an 'agro-based' approach with slower growth, less spillover from the NCR, and a more decentralized spatial pattern. A summary of the plan opted for a third, intermediate course, 'with more decentralized growth and with moderate spillover' from Metro Manila. Although rural areas would be affected in different ways by these alternative strategies, agriculture is expected to improve in any case, and rural communities would be better connected to the rest of the region (Japan International Cooperation Agency 1991, ch. 3).

The Calabarzon plan has received high-level support with the prospect of Japanese financing. Some ongoing infrastructure and industrial projects have been identified already. But the plan has also raised a wide range of issues and vocal protests about its economic and physical goals, social priorities, environmental impact, and institutional framework.[6] Despite reviews and revisions, there remain ambiguities. 'High industrialization' does not seem to include 'high tech' industries. The plan would split the Calabarzon area into two, one to absorb spillovers close to the border and the other to encourage decentralization from Manila. It is not clear which spatial development scheme this would support.

One of the most hotly disputed issues about the Calabarzon project is the proposed conversion of a 230 ha agrarian land parcel in Cavite province, intended for redistribution to farmers, into an industrial estate for foreign and domestic investors. Cavite is the location of a number of large industrial projects. The land in question is known as the NDC-Marubeni industrial site. The Comprehensive Agrarian Reform Law is supposed to cover all agricultural lands and prohibits conversion to avoid the distribution of a piece of land, but the law has many loopholes. If farm land had been designated for non-agricultural uses in a land-use plan approved by 15 June 1988, then it is not protected by the program. In this particular case, critics claimed that the NDC-Marubeni project was in an approved town plan, not in a land-use plan. The Calabarzon plan itself says that most cities and municipalities in the area had not prepared land-use plans (Japan International Cooperation Agency 1991, 3-14), but the legal opinion of the Department of Justice has clinched the case for the government, sacrificing the appointment of a new, pro-people secretary of agrarian reform in the process, and the industrial estate has gone ahead.

For the spatial development of the mega-region, the question is whether the Calabarzon is more likely to contain urban expansion close to the borders of Metro Manila or to allow a decentralized pattern independent of NCR influence. The former may aid centripetal forces and intensify congestion problems in and around the NCR. On the other hand, it offers opportunities for a more compact and economical development, if existing fragmentation and negative externalities could be overcome. The more decentralized scheme should mitigate metropolitan giantism, urban-rural conflicts, and environmental hazards, assuming that local governments, with their newfound powers under the 1991 Local Government Code, would play along. This scheme would require a more determined effort to limit NCR expansion and to disperse growth to other regions beyond Calabarzon and the provinces adjoining Metro Manila to the north.

The Institutional Framework

Another issue is the institutional framework for the mega-region. Existing organizations do not have responsibility for the growing region, although efforts to catch up have not been lacking. The idea of a metropolitan body for greater Manila goes back to 1927, but it did not materialize then. As Laquian (1993) recalls, postwar attempts at loose confederations of a few localities also came up short of effectively encompassing the metropolis. In 1975, the three-member MMC was formed over a larger jurisdiction. With Imelda Marcos as governor and, concurrently, human settlements minister, the MMC gained power at the cost of the constituent localities. The MMC also showed proficiency and vision in planning, with its commissioner for planning in the lead.

Nonetheless, as a vestige of the Marcos regime, the MMC was abolished shortly after the 1986 revolt. It was replaced by the Metropolitan Manila Authority, led by a council composed of the local mayors but having powers, functions, and resources reduced from those of the MMC. The council is chaired by one of the mayors, who is elected by the council for a six-month term, reflecting the MMA's weakened and transient character. Metropolitan planning has apparently declined in status and output as well as scope: the plan for 1993-8 was still in draft form as of 1992. MMA leaders have bickered over who should finance and perform the functions of garbage collection and disposal. Recently, traffic management has been decentralized to local units, though traffic enforcers with various powers still participate in it.

Proposals to replace the MMA have been put forward. The organization is mandated by its basic charter to have jurisdiction over delivery of basic services requiring coordination, including: land use, planning, and zoning; traffic management; public safety; urban development and renewal; disaster management; and sanitation and waste management. The council was to be assisted by a professional metropolitan general manager and three deputy general managers appointed by the president of the Philippines.

Two pending bills in Congress, introduced by Senator Jose Lina and Representatives Rolando Tinga and Renato Yap (Senate Bill no. 302 and House Bill no. 1291), would simply ratify the creation of the MMA with the same seventeen-locality jurisdiction and some of the same functions. These bills, however, would modify the council by including private-sector representatives as well as mayors. (The Lina bill also includes representatives of city and municipal councils.) The chair would have an elective term of one year, and plebiscites would be held to determine if voters in each locality wanted to remain in the jurisdiction of the MMA.

A third bill, introduced by Senator Vicente Sotto III (Senate Bill no. 636), would replace the MMA with a National Capital Region Planning Authority (NCRPA), with no political functions and structure and no implementing powers. It would have jurisdiction over regional land-use planning, the planning of intercity/municipal urban functions and services, and the coordination, funding, and technologies required to realize NCRPA plans. However, the programs and projects called for by the plans would be implemented by the local governments affected. Another function of the NCRPA would be to monitor and evaluate plan implementation. It would be directed by a council composed of the local mayors and the heads of specified national and regional agencies. The council would elect a chair and co-chair from among the members. The NCRPA would have an executive director appointed by the president.

The MMA has submitted its own draft bill. This would also replace the interim agency with a regular one performing the same functions but also having charge of health and infrastructure development and maintenance. The council would have selected department secretaries as well as the local mayors, and would elect one of the mayor for a three-year term. There would be a metropolitan manager and four deputy managers for planning, operations, finance, and administration. Other, more detailed provisions are included in the MMA draft.

These proposals offer prospects of 'institutionalization' for the MMA, but some of them may also be destabilizing, particularly where plebiscites are prescribed. Nonetheless, they would only partially respond to the institutional needs of the mega-region by providing national agency representatives on the council. In this connection, another proposal of the MMA seems relevant. This is a draft executive order that would create a Regional Development Council (RDC) for Metropolitan Manila. RDCs are the governing bodies for the thirteen standard regions into which the Philippines has been subdivided for purposes of coordinating planning and administration among regional offices and local governments. Although the MMC and MMA regional plans have borne the National Economic and Development Authority imprimatur, an RDC would, in effect, be superimposed on the existing authority for the first time.

The RDC proposal would require the MMA to perform the range of planning, programming, and budgeting that other RDCs are usually called upon to do according to a common schedule and set of procedures. In this way, it would get linked and coordinated with the larger system. But the RDC would also increase the kinds and number of representatives to the MMA and thus complicate its governing body far more than any of the legislative bills would. If past experience with RDCs is any guide, such complications could be paralyzing as well as 'democratizing.' The MMA's attempt to reach up and out may instead drag it down by the sheer weight of the RDC superstructure.

Conclusion

The expansion of Metro Manila into a mega-region has intensified various problems of urban growth and structure. One consolation is that, by showing up the deficiencies of existing public planning and policies, it has also offered opportunities to consider more radical departures from past strategies and to re-examine the basic institutional framework. These opportunities are represented by the Calabarzon project, but the Philippine government is still in search of an appropriate framework for implementing and managing its plans and programs. Since its planning has been sponsored mainly by a single department assisted by the Japan International Cooperation Agency, the Calabarzon has a chance to design and propose a simpler and yet more effective administrative organization. Yet there are also pitfalls in oversimplifying a complex situation, as reflected in the idea that organizational strength means getting the president to head the project governing body. The project planners of Calabarzon have fortunately been more circumspect and provided alternative organizational designs. Whether any of them can comprehend the larger dimensions of the project area, however, is uncertain.

Notes

I wish to thank the Metro Manila Authority Planning staff, and the library and research staff for helping me prepare this paper.
1 Pernia (1977) outlines this pattern of urbanization. See also McAndrew (1994)
2 Calabarzon is the acronym for the five provinces of Cavite, Laguna, Batangas, Rizal, and Quezon. It is also the region designated under the Calabarzon Master Plan, a long range plan (1991-2000) intended to accelerate agro-industrial growth. The Plan was designated by then president Corazon Aquino as one of five special projects under the Philippine Assistance Program in 1990.
3 One town in Cavite, Carmona, lost more than half its population between 1980 and 1990. Most of Carmona's population had been resettled earlier from Manila by the government. Many were said to have left this relocation site to return to a reclamation area in Manila Bay.

4   For a further discussion of these developments see Paderanga (1992) and Laquian (1993).
5   From their survey of the locational preferences of private, foreign, and local firms, Herrin and Pernia (1987) concluded that public policies influenced locational decisions only indirectly. Implicit macro-economic policies were far more influential than explicit dispersal policies. As well, Metro Manila's long-developed central-place functions kept it attractive.
6   For an excellent summary of these issues see Ramos (1991) and McAndrew (1994).

14
Problems and Challenges of Mega-Urban Regions in Indonesia: The Case of Jabotabek and the Bandung Metropolitan Area

Ida Ayu Indira Dharmapatni and Tommy Firman

The Jakarta Metropolitan Region, known as Jabotabek, and the Bandung Metropolitan Area are among the fastest growing urban regions in Indonesia (see Map 14.1). Regional road and railway networks connecting these two regions have induced their almost continuous physical growth, now extending about 200 km, so that they are rapidly becoming a single, integrated mega-urban region. This massive corridor of urban growth is a unique phenomenon in Indonesia, since other fast expanding metropolitan areas, such as Medan (in Sumatra) and Surabaya (in East Java), have grown as single metropolitan areas in their respective regions.

Jabotabek consists of seven administrative units: the capital city of Jakarta, the municipalities of Bogor, Tangerang, and Bekasi, and the *kabupaten* (districts) of Bogor, Tangerang, and Bekasi. The acronym Jabotabek is taken from Jakarta plus Botabek (comprising the three *kabupaten* surrounding Jakarta: *Bo*gor, *Ta*ngerang, and *Bek*asi). The Bandung Metropolitan Area consists of two administrative units: the municipality of Bandung and the *kabupaten* of Bandung (Map 14.1). In 1990, the total population of Jabotabek was 17.1 million persons, 13.1 million of whom were urban and 4.0 million rural. The Bandung Metropolitan Area's total population was 5.26 million people, of whom 3.3 million were urban and the rest rural. The merged physical growth of Jabotabek and the Bandung Metropolitan Area becomes more obvious as the area around Kabupaten Cianjur – located along the Bandung-Jakarta regional road and administratively and physically separate (see Map 14.2) – is squeezed from both ends by the two metropolitan regions.

During the last two decades, Jabotabek and the Bandung Metropolitan Area have experienced changing patterns of urbanization, changes in the types of socio-economic activities, and increased pressures on the environment. A number of factors have contributed to these changes: rapid economic growth, new towns, industrial estates, toll road development, and population mobility within and into these regions. Change has

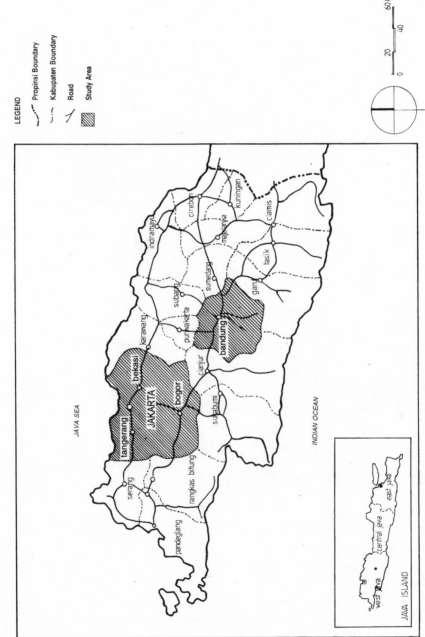

Map 14.1 **Jabotabek region and Bandung Metropolitan Area**

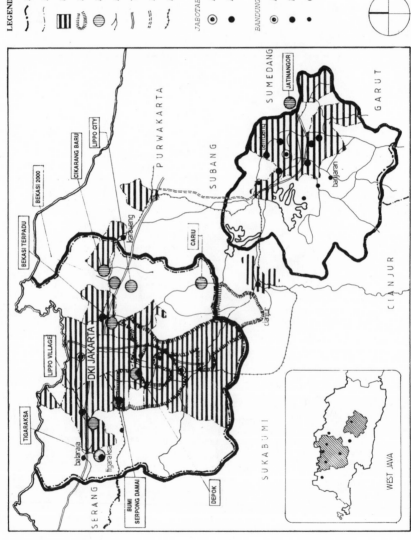

LEGEND

⟨ Kabupaten Boundary
⟨ Kecamatan Boundary
▦ Urban Area
𝄜 Bopunjur Corridor
◯ New Town
⌒ Road
⫽ Toll Road
⇢ Planned Toll Road
〰 Railway

JABOTABEK BOUNDARY
◉ Main Regional Sub-Center
● Main Sub-Center

BANDUNG BOUNDARY
◉ Main City
● Nearby Town
• Counter Magnet Town

Map 14.2 **Urban development and new towns**

brought about unique problems and challenges, as well as opportunities for governments, the private sector, and local communities. New approaches and responses in the form of policies, strategies, and actions are needed to direct future development in these regions.

Within this context, the purpose of this chapter is, first, to identify the characteristics of the existing situation in Jabotabek and the Bandung Metropolitan Area and, second, to examine current responses by the development actors to identified problems, challenges, and opportunities. Finally, the chapter outlines future policy actions and research agendas needed to deal with problems and challenges and to take advantage of the opportunities.

Socio-Economic and Spatial Growth in Jabotabek and Bandung Metropolitan Area

The Spatial Pattern of Population

The geographical pattern of the urban populations in Jabotabek and the Bandung Metropolitan Area (Map 14.2) reveals that they are becoming spatially unified. In other words, urban population is largely concentrated in areas adjoining the 200 km long arterial road connecting Jakarta-Bogor and Bandung. In addition, another major corridor of urban development is emerging from Jakarta on an east-west axis approximately 120 km long. A basic feature of these corridors is their mixture of socio-economic activities, including agriculture, industries, residences, and retail trade. This has created intense rural-urban linkages, blurring the rural-urban distinction and making for a distinctive settlement pattern. Overall, these characteristics manifest themselves in the form of a single mega-urban region, or what McGee and other scholars have previously defined as an extended metropolitan region (Greenberg 1992, 1994; McGee 1991; McGee and Greenberg 1992).

The trend of unified physical growth between Jabotabek and the Bandung Metropolitan Area is also reflected in the increasing functional relationship between Jakarta and Bandung. During 1983-7, it is estimated that as many as 3.3 million people took annual trips between the two cities (Rosmiyati 1990).

During the last ten years, the amount of land approved by the National Land Agency for housing development in the surrounding areas of Bandung reached 1,100 ha. Despite this, people who live in the fringe areas of Bandung city are still largely dependent on the facilities and employment available in the city centre. A study revealed that, in 1985, 48 per cent of the go-to-work trips originating from the immediately surrounding areas (before the city's administrative expansion) were to Bandung city (Simamora 1991, 20). Likewise, about 70 and 80 per cent of shopping and recreation trips, respectively, were to Bandung city.

The trip patterns within the Bandung Metropolitan Area show a strong orientation to the city and along the east-west and south axis of Bandung, where expansion of industrial activities is taking place. Of the daily 248,486 trips using public road transport recorded in 1988, one-quarter and one-third were between Bandung-Cimahi (west) and Bandung-Cileunyi (east), respectively (Simamora 1991, 35). The second highest number of trips occurred between Bandung and the southern towns of Soreang (11.2 per cent) and Banjaran (19.6 per cent). The third highest occurred between Bandung and the eastern towns, such as Cicalengka. Yet many trips also occurred among the small towns located in the eastern parts of Bandung, where most of the textile industries are located: Cileunyi-Cicalengka, Cileunyi-Majalaya, Cicalengka-Majalaya, and Ciparay-Majalaya.

The plans for Jabotabek and the Bandung Metropolitan Area have designated countermagnet towns intended to reduce migration to the core cities. The existing spatial development pattern in Jabotabek and the Bandung area to a certain degree follows the development plans. Nevertheless, in a major difference, the east-west axis of Jabotabek has been growing faster than planned. The north-south axis of Jabotabek, which was planned to grow as a limited urban corridor, has also been growing much faster than planned. In fact, the presidential decree (*keppres*) launched to preserve this corridor as an aquifer recharge area has failed to protect it from further development.

The east-west and north-south physical developments in Jabotabek have been accelerated by the operation of toll roads connecting Jakarta and Tangerang, Jakarta and Bekasi, and Cikampek and Jakarta-Bogor. These toll roads have a great impact on decentralization of development towards the surrounding areas of Jakarta, where large-scale housing areas, new towns, and industrial estates are located. A recent study reveals that housing sales increased after the operation of the Jakarta-Tangerang toll road (Puslitbang PT Jasa Marga and Institut Technologi Bandung 1992, V-15). The study also found that a toll road increases incentives for housing development even in areas located far away from the core city and that these incentives work more strongly if accompanied by industrial estate development. In fact, private investors consider the toll road as a guarantee for reliable infrastructure for the development of industrial estates.

Besides the new town developments mentioned, it is expected that some of the existing *kecamatan* (subdistrict) towns will grow rapidly in the future, induced to do so by the planned industrial estates. This includes the towns of Cikupa, Jatiuwung, and Pasar Kemis in Kabupaten Tangerang, Cileungsi in Kabupaten Bogor, and Cibitung, Lemah Abang, and Serang in Kabupaten Bekasi (West Java Provincial Government [DTKTD] 1992, V-21).

Adapting to the distribution of medium-income segments of the population, which are considered a potential market, big retail supermarkets tend to locate in the surrounding areas of the main cities. This has been the case in Jabotabek region, where the well-known big supermarket, Hero, for instance, built its 'one stop service' shopping centres in Ciledug, Tangerang, and in Bekasi. Another company awaits a permit to locate its commercial stores in the Botabek area. It is reported that this development is threatening the traditional, small-scale retail shops (*Kompas*, 23 January 1991).

The Growth and Spatial Pattern of Industrial Activities

During the last two decades, Indonesia's urban development has been largely influenced by new forces emerging from the internationalization of the country's economic activities. Responses to this phenomenon, such as liberalization of foreign investment, international trade, and the finance sector, have propelled the growth of metropolitan cities, particularly the Jakarta and Bandung metropolitan areas (West Java) and Surabaya (East Java), through the expansion of industrial and commercial activities.

Jakarta and the Bandung Metropolitan Area have been the major areas of foreign and domestic investment in the country for the last twenty-five years. In fact, about two-thirds of the total approved foreign investment projects during 1967-91 in Indonesia was located in Jakarta and West Java, notably in the Jabotabek and Bandung regions, as were about 45 per cent of approved domestic investment projects (*Prospek*, 2 May 1992, 10; 11 July 1992, 82). Financially, Jakarta's and West Java's shares of foreign and domestic investment during the same period were 49.6 and 47.4 per cent of the national total, respectively. Looking at West Java in more detail, during 1967-89 about four-fifths of foreign investment and half of domestic investment in the industrial sector were located in the *kabupaten* of Botabek and Bandung (Bandung Institute of Technology 1991, 17).

Jabotabek and the Bandung Metropolitan Area are major industrial regions in Indonesia. In terms of large and medium manufacturing value added per capita, the regions are considered as having a 'moderate to heavy' industrial development, comparable to the Surabaya Metropolitan Area in the eastern part of Java (Hill 1990, 110). Major industries in Jabotabek include textiles, electrical equipment, cement, plastics, metal and glass products, transport equipment, printing, publishing, and other chemical industries. The Bandung area is dominated by textiles and electrical equipment (Hill 1990, 119). In terms of large and medium-sized manufacturing firms' output (excluding oil and gas), around 35 per cent of the total national output was produced by this region in 1985 (Hill 1990, calculated from Table 11, p. 107). About 84 per cent of the total output of

Jabotabek and the Bandung Metropolitan Area came from industries located in Jabotabek.

The role of industrial development in West Java, notably in Botabek and the Bandung Metropolitan Area, has been substantially increasing, particularly in terms of output and employment in non-oil large- and medium-scale manufacturing. During 1974-85 for example, the share of employment for West Java increased from 18.7 to 21.2 per cent, and the share in output increased from 19.2 to 26 per cent (Hill 1990, 104). In the same period, the share of output in Jakarta declined from 19.3 to 18.7 per cent. These figures reveal that manufacturing activities have spilled across the administrative boundaries of Jakarta and Bandung. In fact, spillover of industrial development in Jabotabek has currently reached as far as Karawang and Serang, both in West Java. This phenomenon is likely to continue in the future as urban land prices in the city centres of Jakarta and Bandung increase and markets, capital, skilled labour, and entrepreneurs continue to be concentrated in Jakarta and Bandung.

In the near future, it is likely that manufacturing and commercial activities in Jabotabek and the Bandung Metropolitan Area will still grow at an accelerated pace through new investments and reinvestments in these sectors, as 80 per cent of the national money is accumulated in Jakarta (*Kompas,* 7 April 1988). Moreover, about 28 per cent of the gross domestic product of twenty-six out of twenty-seven provinces in the country flowed back to Jakarta in 1988 as net funds ('Pulang Mudik dan Peranan Ekonomi Jakarta,' *Kompas,* 13 April 1992). These potential sources of investment, on the one hand, and increasing urban land prices and agglomeration advantages, on the other, will intensify the spillover of manufacturing and commercial activities to the areas surrounding Jakarta and Bandung.

As a result of these developments, demand for land for industrial activities in Jabotabek and the Bandung Metropolitan Area has also increased during the last decade, particularly since Keppres 53/1989 was launched. This decree allows the private sector to manage or own an industrial estate. As a response to the decree, many foreign companies have shifted their operations from foreign countries: 119 private companies have applied during the last three years for permits to develop industrial estates covering an area of 33,249 ha all over Indonesia (*Kompas,* 18 July 1992, 57). About 20,817 ha (62.6 per cent) are located in West Java, particularly in the areas surrounding Jakarta and Bandung, of which 3,083 ha (9.3 per cent) are in Jakarta, involving a total of seventy-six private investors.

In addition, development of factories in non-industrial estate areas has been substantial, particularly in the areas adjacent to the regional roads connecting Tangerang-Jakarta-Bekasi, Jakarta-Bogor, Bandung-Padalarang,

Bandung-Banjaran, Bandung-Majalaya, and Bandung-Sumedang. For instance, in Kabupaten Bekasi alone, about 2,400 ha of land was already occupied by industrial activities in 1991 (Puslitbang PT Jasa Marga and Institut Technologi Bandung 1992, II-3). In response to the rising land demand for industrial development, the government of West Java province has allocated 18,000 ha of land for industrial estates development distributed in nine *kabupaten,* almost 40 per cent of which (7,000 ha) is located in the Jabotabek and Bandung regions: 3,000 ha each in Kabupaten Bekasi and Kabupaten Tangerang, 500 ha in Kabupaten Bogor, and 500 ha in Kabupaten Bandung.

Very recently, as part of the effort to promote non-oil export products, the government has encouraged the private sector to participate in development of so-called 'industrial bonded estates,' where one can process all the needed permits under one roof and avoid import taxes if at least 85 per cent of products is for export (*Warta Ekonomi,* 18 November 1991, 36). Fourteen private companies have applied for permission to develop this kind of industrial estate (*Warta Ekonomi,* 24 February 1992, 43), two of which are located in Bekasi and Tangerang and will soon be operating.

The Growth and Spatial Pattern of Large-Scale Housing Areas

During the last ten years, housing development in Jabotabek and the Bandung Metropolitan Area has increased tremendously, particularly in the areas surrounding the cities of Jakarta and Bandung. The spillover of residential settlements across the administrative boundaries of Jakarta and Bandung has several reasons: high urban land and housing prices and high living costs in the city centre; increasing numbers in the medium-income group who cannot afford to live in the main cities; increasing employment opportunities in the areas surrounding Jakarta and Bandung; good transportation facilities connecting the surrounding areas with the two main cities; and the better social and economic facilities provided by real estate developments located outside the main cities.

Housing in the Jabotabek and Bandung regions is developed in the form not only of large-scale subdivisions but also of new town developments (Table 14.1). In Kabupaten Bekasi since 1991, for instance, more than 235 developers have applied for permits to develop housing covering an area of 8,122 ha, and 487,320 houses have been built (*Kompas,* 25 July 1992). In addition, new town developments funded by both the government and private developers have become popular lately. Depok (Kabupaten Bogor) and Jatinangor (East Bandung), for example, are new towns in which the basic infrastructure is developed by government and which serve as educational centres as well as housing settlements.

Bumi Serpong Damai and Tigaraksa, both in Kabupaten Tangerang;

Bekasi 2,000 in Kabupaten Bekasi; and Cariu in Kabupaten Bogor (Map 14.2) are among the new towns currently being developed by private investors. Another new town, Bekasi Terpadu, is being developed by the state-owned National Housing Corporation, Perumnas, in cooperation with three private developers. Each of these new towns is planned to become a 'self-contained,' middle-to-high-income settlement, equipped in some cases with complete and modern social and modern economic facilities.

Table 14.1

Selected new town developments in Jabotabek and Bandung Metropolitan Area

	Area (ha)	Location	Developer
Bumi Serpong Damai	6,000	Tangerang	Private
Tigaraksa	3,000	Tangerang	Private
Cariu	–	Bogor	Private
Bekasi 2000	2,000	Bekasi	Private
Bekasi Terpadu	1,500	Bekasi	Private and government
Cikarang Baru	500-2,000	Bekasi	Private
Lippo City	450	Bekasi	Private
Depok	–	Bogor	Government
Jatinangor	–	Bandung*	Government
Lippo Village	500	Tangerang	Private

* Administratively is located in Kabupaten Sumedang

Another kind of new town, at present still in the planning stage, is to be integrated with industrial estate development. The idea behind this is to provide livable and self-sufficient settlements for people not only in terms of social and economic amenities but also in terms of employment. The new towns are to be located near industrial estates and financed by the companies that operate the estates. Cikarang Baru and Lippo City in Kabupaten Bekasi, which are going to be developed as one package with the Cikarang Industrial Estate and Bekasi Terpadu Industrial Estate, respectively, are examples of this type of new town (Map 14.2). Both of them will have modern facilities: Cikarang will be equipped with a golf course, and Lippo City will have hotels and office complexes in addition to the standard urban amenities.

Land-Use Changes and the Environment
Rapid housing and industrial developments in the surrounding areas of Jabotabek and the Bandung Metropolitan Area have dramatically transformed the prime agricultural land. Although the data presented in Tables 14.2 and 14.3 could be misleading, as they only reveal land-use changes

on the basis of permits granted, at least they give a general picture of the transformation pattern of agricultural land. The tables show that during 1980-9, housing development in Botabek took up 15,900 ha of former rice fields, constituting three-quarters of total land needed for housing development. Four-fifths of the total land needed for industrial development was taken from wet and dry rice fields. In the same period, about 70 per cent of land for housing development in Kabupaten Bandung was from wet rice land, and about three-quarters of the total land for industrial development was from dry rice fields. However, as one might suspect, the actual amount of agricultural land transformed into housing and industrial uses could be much greater than recorded.

Other data based on permit applications show that during 1983-92, about 45,500 ha of land in the *kabupaten* of Botabek and Bandung were transformed into settlements and 3,000 ha into industrial activities. This constitutes about 95 per cent of land for housing development and about 80 per cent of land for industrial activities in West Java province.

Although the local government since 1986 has required investors to replace converted agricultural land, Kabupaten Bekasi has lost about 200 ha annually of its prime agricultural land and Kabupaten Bogor about 8.4 per cent annually (*Media Indonesia*, 29 September 1991). Uncontrolled conversion of prime agricultural land has been exacerbated by the reluctance of farmers to retain their land as land prices increase (*Kompas*, 13 April 1991). Pressures on prime agricultural land in other places such as Teluk Naga, Tangerang, have continued, as a consortium of seven private developers is presently applying for 4,500 ha to be developed as a 'modern tourism city.'

Besides the rapid transformation of prime agricultural land, another important environmental issue that needs to be addressed is the condition and use of water resources. As housing and tourism developments have encroached on the uplands of Bopunjur (Bogor-Puncak-Cianjur) and on Bandung, the water supply for the rest of the Botabek area and for Jakarta and Bandung has become critical, particularly during the dry season. In fact, it is anticipated that beyond the year 2005 the present dams of Jatiluhur, Cirata, and Saguling will no longer be adequate to provide water for industrial and domestic needs in Jakarta and the northern part of West Java (*Suara Pembaruan*, 13 May 1991).

Groundwater and surface water are also in critically short supply in both Jabotabek and the Bandung Metropolitan Area. As a consequence of the inability of the limited water systems to supply adequate water, groundwater has been withdrawn at an alarming rate. This has resulted in seawater intrusion as far as 12 km inland of Jakarta and the decline of deep groundwater at a rate of 2 to 6 m annually in Bandung. Rivers in

Table 14.2

Recorded land-use changes in Botabek (in hectares), 1980-9

Changes to	Settlement	Wet rice field	Dry rice field	Rubber plantation	Mixed farm	Alang bushes	Forest	Mining	Total
Bogor									
Industry	46.60	70.32	47.88	12.98	67.25	2.13	–	–	247.00
%	18.80	28.50	19.40	5.20	27.20	0.90	–	–	100.00
Housing	222.14	372.73	1,177.26	539.97	1,023.18	112.88	1.50	19.51	3,469.00
%	6.40	10.70	33.90	15.60	29.50	3.30	0.00	0.60	100.00
Tangerang									
Industry	–	78.67	228.17	–	–	–	–	–	306.00
%	–	25.64	74.36	–	–	–	–	–	100.00
Housing	–	8,273.25	4,312.01	–	3,066.10	–	–	–	15,651.00
%	–	52.86	27.55	–	19.59	–	–	–	100.00
Bekasi									
Industry	–	27.47	1.37	–	0.20	–	–	–	29.00
%	94.59	4.72	–	–	0.69	–	–	–	100.00
Housing	–	1,664.49	95.94	–	–	–	–	–	1,760.00
%	–	94.55	5.45	–	–	–	–	–	100.00
Botabek									
Industry	46.6	176.46	277.42	12.98	67.45	2.13	–	–	583.00
%	7.99	30.26	47.58	2.23	11.57	0.36	–	–	100.00
Housing	222.14	10,310.47	5,585.21	539.97	4,089.28	112.88	1.50	19.51	20,880.00
%	1.06	45.38	26.75	2.58	19.58	0.00	5.00	0.09	100.00

Column group heading: Original use

Source: National Land Agency, Directorate of Land Use, in Soegijoko (1989), Tables 10, 11, 12

Table 14.3

Recorded land-use changes in Kabupaten Bandung (in hectares), 1979-80 to 1988-9

Changes to	Original use		
	Wet rice field	Dry rice field	Total
Housing	1,081.26	448.98	1,530.24
%	70.66	29.44	100.00
Industry	43.51	140.56	184.07
%	23.64	76.36	100.00
Fisheries	0.87	–	0.87
%	100.00	–	100.00
Others	3,396.82	3,482.42	6,879.24
%	49.38	50.62	100.00
Total	4,522.46	4,071.96	8,594.42
%	52.62	47.38	100.00

Source: Soegijoko (1989), Table 19

Jabotabek are highly polluted, particularly the Ciliwung and the Bekasi. Likewise, many rivers in Bandung are polluted by textile industries.

Another recent serious threat to the environment is the conversion of the mangrove forest in the coastal area of Jakarta into a modern, self-contained housing complex. This is in addition to the conversion of another mangrove forest into commercial shrimp ponds in Teluknaga, Tangerang. Currently, about 830 ha of mangrove and swampy areas, which have been the habitat of protected birds and monkeys, are being planned for hotels, condominiums, a golf course, and medium- to high-income housing by private investors (*Tempo*, 12 September 1992, 105). Recently, however, local communities and some government officials have expressed many concerns about and objections to these developments, but they are proceeding.

The Pattern of Population Mobility

The past two decades have witnessed a gradual change in the migration pattern in the Jabotabek region. Permanent movement from West Java (including Botabek) and other parts of Indonesia into Jakarta city declined during 1975-90 and was accompanied by a reverse movement of permanent migrants from Jakarta city to the Botabek area (Ida Ayu Indira Dharmapatni 1991, 7). It is estimated that since 1989 about 1.5 million Jakarta residents have moved to the Botabek region (*Kompas*, 15 January 1991). In fact, about 100,000 of the population of Depok still held Jakarta residency cards in 1990 (*Kompas*, 15 January 1991) and in 1992 about 400,000 people in Bekasi did the same (*Kompas*, 30 July 1992). The reluctance to give up their Jakarta residence identity cards indicates that to a certain degree Jakarta is still an attractive place to work for most residents.

Besides receiving migrants from Jakarta city, Botabek has been increasingly targeted as the destination of migrants from all over Indonesia, mainly from Java. Migrants have chosen Botabek instead of Jakarta because of its lower living costs, its increasing employment opportunities resulting from the spillover of industrial growth from Jakarta, and its high accessibility to Jakarta via a well-developed transportation system (Ida Ayu Indira Dharmapatni 1991, 9). It is estimated that 60 to 70 per cent of the industrial labourers working in Bekasi, for instance, are migrants from Central and East Java and other parts of West Java (*Pikiran Rakyat,* 15 April 1991). The role of Botabek in receiving increasing numbers of migrants from Jakarta and from outside the Jabotabek region is reflected in the high population growth of Kabupaten Bogor, Tangerang, and Bekasi during 1980-90. While the rate of population growth in Jakarta decreased from 4.1 per cent in the period 1971-1980 to 2.4 per cent in 1980-90, the population of Kabupaten Bogor, Tangerang, and Bekasi during 1980-90 was growing at annual rates of 4.1, 6.1, and 6.3 per cent, respectively (see Table 14.4). As a result, Jakarta's population share in the Jabotabek region decreased from 54.5 to 48.1 per cent from 1980 to 1990.

Only about 10 per cent of the Botabek population works in Jakarta and only 4 per cent studies there but commuting is substantial in Jabotabek (Biro Kota Statistik Pusat, Jabotabek 1992, appendix p. 20). In 1992, as many as 1.2 million people commuted daily, of whom 34, 21, and 45 per cent originated from the *kabupaten* of Bogor, Tangerang, and Bekasi, respectively.

Population movements in the Bandung Metropolitan Area are similar to those in Jabotabek, although they have occurred at a much slower pace. The phenomenon is reflected in the increasing amount of housing being built in the south and east fringe areas of Bandung city.

Jabotabek and the Bandung Metropolitan Area are facing not only the spatial movement of population but also vertical movement in terms of job changes. This has several aspects. First, farmers whose land is being given up for housing or industrial development are being displaced. In Bekasi alone, for example, if we assume a person-land ratio of four persons per hectare, the 3,000 ha of industrial estate development will have to displace 12,000 farmers. If this assumption is valid for the whole of Botabek, then the 6,500 ha planned for industrial development will have to displace about 26,000 farmers. This figure could be much higher if we include farm labourers and families of farmers.

Second, those working in the brick and roof-tile small-scale industries are also being displaced. The industrial estate of Bekasi, for example, will have to relocate 16,500 people who have made bricks for decades in that area (*Kompas,* 30 December 1990). Some of them have been pushed south,

Table 14.4

Urban and rural population of Jabotabek region and Bandung Metropolitan Area, 1980 and 1990

City/district	Urban population 1980	Urban population 1990	Average annual growth(%) 1980-90	Rural population 1980	Rural population 1990	Total population 1980	Total population 1990	Total annual rate (%) 1980-90
Jabotabek region	7,366,207	13,122,962	7.82	4,520,372	4,008,394	11,886,579	17,131,356	4.41
Botabek	1,294,459	4,868,927	27.61	4,111,466	4,008,394	5,405,925	8,877,321	6.42
DKI Jakarta	6,071,748	8,254,035	3.03	408,906	–	6,480,654	8,254,035	2.70
City of Bogor	246,946	271,341	0.98	–	–	246,946	271,341	0.98
Bogor	625,911	1,923,866	20.73	1,855,814	1,812,734	2,481,725	3,736,600	5.05
Tangerang[a]	232,934	1,520,837	55.29	1,300,857	1,244,151	1,533,791	2,764,988	8.02
Bekasi[a]	188,668	1,152,883	51.11	954,795	951,509	1,143,463	2,104,392	8.40
Bandung								
Metropolitan Area	2,099,854	3,318,791	5.80	2,030,753	1,941,215	4,130,607	5,260,006	2.34
City of Bandung[b]	1,461,407	2,026,893	3.87	–	31,756	1,461,407	2,058,649	4.08
Bandung Kabupaten	638,447	1,291,898	10.23	2,030,753	1,909,459	2,669,200	3,201,357	1.99

a Including the City of Tangerang and Bekasi
b City expansion in 1989
Source: Biro Pusat Statistik (1990)

and many have begun to work in small-scale retail shops and services.

Third, there has been a spillover of *becak* vehicles from Jakarta, where they have been banned since 1990, into Tangerang and Bekasi, creating new problems for these cities. It is estimated that there were 10,000 in Tangerang in 1991, for instance, but that the city needed only 4,000. (*Kompas*, 31 January 1991). In Bekasi, there are about 9,000 but only 2,500 are needed (*Kompas*, 13 August 1992). The governments of Tangerang and Bekasi *kabupaten* are currently banning the excess *becak* vehicles by destroying them.

Current Problems, Opportunities, and Responses

Discussion in the previous sections of this chapter suggests that economic and market forces have been, and will be, central in shaping the development of the urban system within the Jabotabek-Bandung mega-urban region. The two major issues to emerge from the new wave of economic development in this mega-urban region – physical and institutional developments – appear as if they will persist in the future, as the government tends to let market forces, especially internationalization of the economy, work themselves out freely.

Current socio-economic development has substantially decentralized growth from the core cities of Jakarta and Bandung to the surrounding regions. Growth centres are proliferating; in fact, they exceed the number estimated in the *Jabotabek Metropolitan Development Plan* (Jabotabek Advisory Team 1981). In the future, besides Bogor, Bekasi, and Tangerang, there will be several other growth centres in Jabotabek, constituting new, self-sufficient settlements and industrial towns. Meanwhile, planned growth centres in the Bandung Metropolitan Area such as Majalaya, Banjaran, and Cicalengka are also growing as industrial centres, and most migrants will make them their destinations. As a matter of fact, decentralization of development is even taking place in areas further away, reaching to Serang in the west and Karawang in the east. Displacements of local people are becoming a serious problem in Jabotabek and the Bandung area. It is estimated that during 1980-9 about 24,000 people were displaced by housing and non-housing developments in Botabek alone. This does not include unrecorded displacements.

As a consequence of the changing pattern of urbanization and the increasing types of socio-economic activities, pressures on the ecosystem have been increasing from the upland areas of Bopunjur to the coastal zone of Jakarta. The Jakarta-Bogor-Ciawi toll road, for instance, has induced the growth of the Bopunjur corridor, which should have been protected as an aquifer recharge area. The failure of a presidential decree to stop further growth is indicated by rapid population growth, reaching as high as 3.9

per cent annually during the last decade, higher than Jabotabek's growth of 3.7 per cent. The district government of Cianjur, where most of the Bopunjur corridor is located, has the dilemma of either preventing further physical growth or maintaining the approximately 80 per cent of local revenues that are levied from tourist-related activities in this area.

In other areas, physical development has also deviated from the *Jabotabek Metropolitan Development Plan*. Some manufacturing activities in Tangerang, for instance, are located on irrigated land. Similarly, large-scale housing developments built in the southern part of Tangerang are located in erosion-prone areas.

The government is facing several problems and challenges. How can the emerging mega-urban region of Jabotabek-Bandung be managed? To what extent can the loss of agricultural land be tolerated, if rice self-sufficiency is to be maintained? How can adequate infrastructure be provided to promote growth but at the same time direct the locations of industrial activities and new-town developments in line with the Jabotabek and Bandung Metropolitan Area plans?

The private sector and the communities are also up against several problems. Private investors have been faced with lack of infrastructure (particularly electricity and telecommunication) and difficulty acquiring land, increasing the costs of investment. Farmers, farm labourers, and workers in traditional industries have been displaced, and only a small proportion of them have been absorbed by the new manufacturing activities in the region. The local communities appear to have been disadvantaged the most by the new waves of development. They are the last to be told what will happen in their areas and to their assets but the first to be displaced. Although recently they have become more aware of their rights, their power to defend themselves is far behind that of market forces.

Despite all the problems, the new pattern of urbanization and the increasing variety of socio-economic activities in the Jabotabek-Bandung mega-urban region bring about opportunities for further economic development. Both the national and local governments may generate more tax income, derived from a wider range of social-economic activities. The new urbanization also greatly enhances agglomeration economies, allowing the private sector to work more efficiently. In turn, this allows investment turnover in a shorter time.

So far, the region's governments have responded inadequately to the problems and opportunities discussed above. Integrated policies and actions to deal with the emerging mega-urban region have not yet been formulated. In an attempt to fulfil infrastructure needs, however, the national government has allowed privatization of electricity, water, and toll roads. The Jababeka Industrial Estate in Bekasi has a privatized electricity supply. Toll roads have been built in Jakarta and are planned for the Jakarta-Serpong connection.

To avoid overexploitation of the environment, every large-scale development is now required to undergo environmental impact analysis before obtaining permits. The local governments of Tangerang and Bekasi have also required developers to build irrigation systems in other locations as compensation for loss of prime agricultural land. This measure has not met great success, however, as the government control is inadequate.

Institutional aspects of the new wave of economic development in the Jabotabek-Bandung mega-urban region constitute another major issue, with three key areas of concern: the changing roles of government and the private sector; the increasing conflicts of interest among the governments, private sector, and communities; and the inability of conventional mechanisms and measures to control such a dynamic development.

The role of the private sector in large-scale housing, new towns, industrial estates, and infrastructure developments has been increasing, creating new forces that affect the pattern of spatial development. At the same time, the government role is declining, especially in directing and controlling the growth of a wider range of socio-economic activities. This is part of the reason why environmental degradation, prime agricultural land encroachment, and displacement of local people are still occurring. In addition, public-private partnership in large-scale housing and toll road developments is on the rise. The development of Bekasi Terpadu and the toll road connecting Jakarta and Serpong are examples of cooperation between government and the private sector.

Conflicts have not only occurred among the governments, private sector, and communities but also among the government agencies themselves. The management of Jabotabek involves three levels of autonomous entities: the provincial level (the Jakarta Special District and West Java); the *kabupaten* and *kotamadya* levels (Tangerang, Bekasi, and Bogor), and the village level. Management of the Bandung Metropolitan Area, on the other hand, involves only the municipality and *kabupaten* levels. In 1976, the national government established the Biro Kota Statistik Pusat (BKSP) Jabotabek, an agency whose task is to coordinate activities of different agencies operating in the Jabotabek region. The BKSP is a non-structural agency, however, and has not been given legal authority by the government. It therefore lacks the power to implement the Jabotabek Plan.

Other conflicts have arisen. For instance, the communities of Teluknaga, in Tangerang, have persistently opposed modern tourism elements in the new-town development plan for the area (*Kompas*, 2 October 1992). The local communities have been given very little information about the plan, making them feel threatened.

Four questions face the various governments with respect to the management of the Jabotabek-Bandung mega-urban region. First, to what extent can the private sector be used to promote regional economic development while government capacity to mobilize funds becomes more limited? Second, how can new management approaches be developed that are able to anticipate and accommodate the dynamics of economic growth in the region? Third, what kind of administrative cooperation should be developed for governments, the private sector, and communities in order to minimize conflicts among the interested parties? Finally, what forms of decentralization should be adopted by the *kabupaten* governments to increase their capacity to cope with the growing urban areas in the region?

The dynamic development of housing and socio-economic activities in the Jabotabek-Bandung mega-urban region obviously requires a new form of management plan for the region as a whole. Conventional approaches adopted by the Jabotabek Plan, Bandung Raya Plan, and other plans for cities located in this mega-urban region fail to cope with the new urbanization process. This is clearly reflected in the inconsistencies between the plans and reality. The authorities and capacities assigned to the *kabupaten* governments are no longer suitable to deal with the many problems caused by the new pattern of development. The urban *desa* have to be managed by *kabupaten* governments, which are particularly equipped to manage rural areas but have very little capacity to deal with urban problems.

In sum, government responses have been generally too little and too late. In fact, only the central government responds actively, reflecting the limited institutional capacity of local governments. In other words, the local governments simply have to adopt policies set by the central government.

Future Policy Actions and Research Agendas

Future policy actions and research agendas for development in the region should deal with the following areas of concern:

- New management arrangements are needed to cope with the emerging Jabotabek-Bandung mega-urban region or beyond, as far as Serang and Cikampek, particularly in response to changing patterns of urbanization, environmental pressures, and growing socio-economic activities. Such arrangements should involve mechanisms for coordinating development of the Jabotabek-Bandung region as a whole and also include analysis of the authority and capacities of the existing coordinating agency (BKSP) for Jabotabek.
- Legal authority and facilities should be decentralized to the local, *kabupaten* governments to enable them to respond efficiently and effectively

to rapid urban development in their areas.

- New policies and strategies are required to deal with the rapid transformation of prime agricultural land, including measures to increase the efficiency and productivity of both urban and agricultural land.
- New strategies of infrastructure provision should be introduced to promote socio-economic growth and direct the location of socio-economic activities. Division of responsibilities between governments and the private sector in infrastructure provision should be clearly formulated.
- New strategies are needed to increase local government income by expanding tax bases and levying user charges on socio-economic activities.
- New policies, strategies, and measures are needed to take advantage of the increasing role of the private sector in urban development.
- New policies, strategies, and measures are needed to cope with the rapidly deteriorating regional environment. These should take into account the responsibilities not only of government at all levels but also of the private sector and local communities. It is vital that the private sector recognize its responsibilities in alleviating the negative consequences of development resulting from its activities.
- New approaches and mechanisms are needed to develop suitable but flexible spatial plans to plan and manage the new pattern of urbanization and population mobility.
- New mechanisms of public, private, and community partnerships should be developed that are appropriate for and conducive to the rapid changes.
- Information systems are needed that can accommodate rapid change in the field and are accessible to government agencies, the private sector, and communities.
- Educational programs should be implemented to increase the skills of the labour force so that it can take advantage of the rapid socio-economic changes in the region.

15
Challenges of Superinduced Development: The Mega-Urban Region of Kuala Lumpur-Klang Valley
Lee Boon Thong

At the time of independence in 1957, Malaysia was quintessentially rural in nature, with an economy based on rubber and tin. Today, however, the world of tranquil villages has been transformed into a world of urban agglomerations that are being propelled by new sets of forces. Malaysia is rapidly urbanizing; 43 per cent of the population already live in towns and cities. A vexing trend is the predilection of rural-urban migrants in favour of the major metropolitan areas. In 1957, 45.1 per cent of the urban population was in metropolitan areas, but in 1980, almost three-quarters of it was living in the fourteen metropolitan centres (Lee 1985). In the 1991 census, almost 20 per cent of the 17,566,982 people in the country were located in the nodal region of Selangor, where the mega-urban region of Kuala Lumpur is located, making it the most densely pop-ulated state in Malaysia.

This chapter analyzes the policies and actions that have led to the development of the mega-urban region of Kuala Lumpur and argues that palliative measures to overcome problems must give due cognizance to forces that are projected from the international arena. This is because the existing mega-urban regions in Malaysia (whether in Kuala Lumpur, Johor Bahru, or Penang) exhibit growth brought about largely from outside forces, in other words, a superinduced development.

Economic Growth and Structural Change
Malaysia was undoubtedly one of the world's fastest growing economies in the last five years. In 1991, for instance, the growth of the Malaysian economy was 8.7 per cent, compared to Thailand (7.5 per cent) and Japan (4.4 per cent). This ultimately puts Malaysia on the fast lane of success, largely because of the market- and growth-oriented policies pursued by the government since the mid-1980s. Policies undertaken to adjust to changing global conditions in the 1980s have been successful, for instance, in enhancing the private sector's role in generating economic

growth, in privatizing government agencies and selected services, in placing greater emphasis on the development of the export-oriented industries and urban growth centres, and in establishing many new industrial estates.

These policies, however, have led to continuing population concentration and growth in urban areas, especially in the major metropolitan centres. Nevertheless, this is not just a recent phenomenon. Though initially slow, such a transformation has been taking place for the last three decades. In the 1960s, the beginnings of import substitution had started to stir movements of people from rural areas to urban centres. The process intensified in the 1970s, when export-oriented industrial policy was introduced and led to rapid growth of labour-intensive industries such as textiles and electronics. Even at that time, when primary commodities were subjected to international shocks, the national economy had begun to realign itself with international activities such as the transnational flows of goods, services, capital, labour, and technology. These expanded quickly.

An obvious change in the nature of the Malaysian economy in the mid-1980s can be detected. In 1987, the agricultural sector's share in the GDP was superseded by that of the manufacturing sector. By 1990, the agricultural share was 19.4 per cent, compared with 26.6 per cent in the manufacturing sector. Thus, the structure of the Malaysian economy switched from an agricultural to a manufacturing base. This indeed marks a milestone in the national transition to an industrializing economy (Malaysia 1991b). Table 15.1 shows the sectoral distribution of employment for 1970-88. It is evident from the table that there has been a major structural shift of employment from the primary to the secondary sector, particularly to manufacturing and construction from 1970s onwards (Salih and Young 1987). While agriculture, fishing, and forestry accounted for more than half of the total workforce in 1970, it was only about 35 per cent in 1988. The secondary sector grew from almost 12 per cent in 1970 to 22 per cent in 1985. Manufacturing created the most jobs in the secondary sector, especially in the 1970s. Its share of total employment increased from 9 per cent in 1970 to 15.6 per cent in 1980, primarily in the electronics and textile industries.

The Manufacturing Sector in Economic Growth and the Urban Spatial Configuration

In the 1980s, the main catalyst in Malaysian economic growth was the expansion of the industrial sector resulting from an outward-looking industrialization strategy and the encouragement of export-platform industries (Ahmad 1988). After the limited success of the import-substitution strategy from 1957 to the late 1960s, it was only logical that industrial development be geared towards exports. The new phase was marked

Table 15.1

Sectoral distribution of employment, 1970-88

	1970	1975	1980	1985	1988
Agriculture, forest and fishing	53.1	47.6	39.7	34.8	35.3
Mining	2.6	2.2	1.7	1.1	1.0
Primary sector	55.7	49.8	41.4	35.9	36.3
Manufacturing	9.0	11.1	15.6	15.1	14.5
Construction	2.7	4.0	5.6	6.9	6.1
Secondary sector	11.7	15.1	21.2	22.0	20.6
Transport and Communication	4.0	4.5	4.1	4.8	4.8
Commerce	16.6	17.6	19.0	22.2	23.6
Service sector	20.6	22.1	23.1	27.0	28.4
Government services	12.0	13.0	14.4	15.0	14.6

Source: Salih and Young (1987)

by rapid industrialization, which was encouraged through free trade zones and other incentives. The manufacturing sector was not only the leading growth quarter but also the largest generator of employment. In 1990, the manufacturing sector contributed 79,900 new jobs, accounting for 31.6 per cent of the total new jobs created in the country (Malaysia 1991a).

The advancement of a large export sector usually requires the presence of multinational corporations that can provide the capital, technology, and access to foreign distribution networks. As Malaysia began to ease its control of direct foreign investment, the number of approved foreign projects, from more than forty-five countries, increased almost tenfold between 1981 and 1990. Almost half of the total capital investments in the manufacturing sector were foreign. The major sources were Japan, Taiwan, Singapore, the UK, the US, Hong Kong, Indonesia, and South Korea. Thus, it is very clear that foreign investments in the manufacturing sector have played a very significant role in the economic buoyancy of the country in the last decade or so and have had implicit consequences on mega-urban development because of the locational predilection of manufacturing activities.

Although urban migration had taken place earlier, during the time of independence, it is clear that it responded to the pull of the informal and government service sectors. The growth of manufacturing has had a more tangible impact on urbanization, however, as it has generated urban employment. This has certainly been true from the 1970s onwards (Chi and Taylor 1986; Lee Boon Thong 1991, 1992a; McGee 1986; Young 1987).

The surge in manufacturing has had important spatial results on the urban system. The incorporation of the 'western corridor' concept in the *Medium and Long Term Industrial Master Plan Malaysia 1986-1995* (Malaysia 1985) is evidence of these developments. The nation's industrial activities have been spread along the western part of Peninsular Malaysia, following existing highways, railroad systems, and port facilities in order to minimize infrastructural expenses. Subsequently, the states of Selangor, Johor, and Penang have become magnets for industrial projects, attracting some 63 per cent of the total projects approved in 1990 alone. The plan has thus had the primary influence on the process of urbanization. Given the impetus of the international dimension of economic activities described earlier, it is inevitable that greater agglomeration will result in the major nodal regions, especially in the Kuala Lumpur extended mega-urban region (EMR).

Urban Transformation in Kuala Lumpur: From Bullock Cart Tracks to Superhighways

The development of Kuala Lumpur and surrounding areas began with the discovery of tin cassiterite in Kanching and Ampang. Early penetration into these areas was accomplished primarily by going up the Klang River until its confluence with the Gombak River, where in 1859 early traders established the first settlement (Tsou 1967). The trading post prospered because of its strategic location, and the population rose to 2,600 by 1879 (Gullick 1955). Roads built at that time were narrow as they were meant for horse and bullock carts. Soon, with the expansion of mining operations and the cultivation of coffee and rubber, rail transport came on the scene, and increasing numbers of commercial and residential brick shophouses were erected between 1905 and 1915 (Concannon 1955). After the Second World War, there was an influx of some 100,000 persons, resulting in a disproportionate growth of squatter settlements and slums (Ruddick 1956).

Increasing squatterization motivated construction of the first new town of Petaling Jaya in the mid-1950s. Subsequently, however, the objective of resettling squatters and slum dwellers was superseded by growing demand from the rapidly burgeoning middle class for better-quality houses (Lee Boon Thong 1976; McGee and McTaggart 1967). Since then, the growth of Petaling Jaya has been phenomenal. It has gone from one of the least populated towns in the country in 1957 to the fifth largest in 1980, with a population of 218,300. Nonetheless, Petaling Jaya alone could not siphon off the excess population building up in the inner areas of Kuala Lumpur. From the mid-1960s onwards, the supply of housing for the growing population took the form of urban scatter around the fringes of the growing metropolis, in extensive medium-density housing estates built by the private sector (Lee Boon Thong 1974). By 1970, more than a quarter of a million people were located in the fringe areas (Malaysia, Department of Statistics 1971).

In the mid-1960s, another new town was built to absorb the Klang

Valley expansion – Shah Alam. While construction of Petaling Jaya sparked development towards the coast, the location of Shah Alam right in the middle of the Klang Valley expedited formation of the primary corridor, the nexus of the 20 km corridor development from Kuala Lumpur to Port Klang (Lee Boon Thong 1992b). The excellent highway built at this time and running parallel to the railway line and the Klang River continues to attract substantial state and private housing and industrial development. Subang Jaya, an adjacent town built in the early 1970s adjoining Petaling Jaya, now provides housing for 30,000 population. Shah Alam has an industrial area of 1,661 acres, which is currently the fastest growing in the country (Lee Boon Thong 1983; Malaysia 1977). In Port Klang, an industrial area of some 3,000 acres is being developed.

In retrospect, development along the corridor can be seen as a logical extension from the dominant metropolitan core to form an elongated polycentric region. By the mid-1970s it was also necessary to attract population away from the Klang Valley corridor, and Bangi, a university town, was conceived in 1975, just 30 km south of Kuala Lumpur in the direction of Seremban (Lee Boon Thong 1987; Sulong and Katiman 1984). Demand for industrial land in Bangi remains high because of its propinquity to the highway. However, population totals were initially below target until the provision of low-cost housing and facilities attracted more population to the new town.

What has been briefly described is a pattern of extended metropolitan growth, in which the physical and economic limitations of a supersaturate inner core coerce development onto fringes and, in particular, along the macro-axis of transportation routes. Figure 15.1A shows the initial infilling of the interstices of the stellated urban shape of the 1950s and the early 1960s. Macroaxial development began from the 1960s in the direction of Port Klang through Petaling Jaya and Shah Alam (Figure 15.1B). In the 1970s, some development occurred in the direction of Seremban but the major focus was still in the Klang Valley, which established itself as the primary corridor. In the 1980s, the corridor was further perpetuated, and the northern and southern sectors were beginning to respond to development. All in all, the areas outside inner Kuala Lumpur began to experience development on a much larger scale than before. According to the 1991 census report, the outer periphery of Kuala Lumpur registered a very substantial increase of population with an average annual growth rate of 4.3 per cent, compared to only 1.99 per cent in the inner areas of Kuala Lumpur. In fact, between 1981 and 1990, about one-third of all approved industrial projects, employment opportunities, and total industrial investments spilled over to areas immediately outside the primary corridor (Lee Boon Thong 1992b). Map 15.1 shows the extent of urban

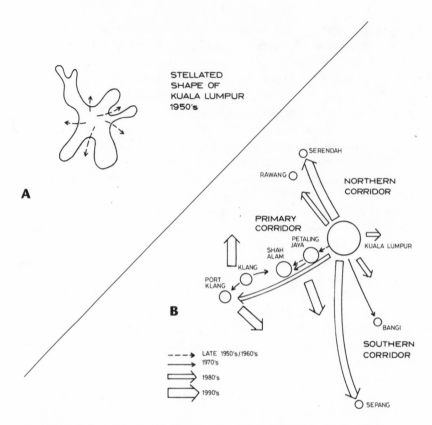

Figure 15.1 **Schematic representation of growth of Kuala Lumpur, 1950s and 1990s**

development in the mega-urban region of Kuala Lumpur, traced from a 1991 satellite photograph.

The megacephalic tendency will be further perpetuated in the 1990s, given government policies and the current economic scenario. The manufacturing sector, for example, which currently contributes some 54 per cent of the GNP of Selangor state, will reach 61 per cent by the turn of the century. Up to 1992, twenty-six state and private industrial estates had been developed, as far from the city core as Bangi, Banting, Cheras, and Sungai Besar. By the mid-1990s, another 10,000 ha had been developed for industrial purposes. Of course, all these developments will be facilitated by the completion of four major expressways within the Klang Valley: the Kuala Lumpur-Shah Alam Expressway; the South Klang Valley Expressway; the New Klang Valley Expressway (already completed); and the North-South Link connecting the three expressways to the North-South Highway. Through these developments, Selangor state – in which

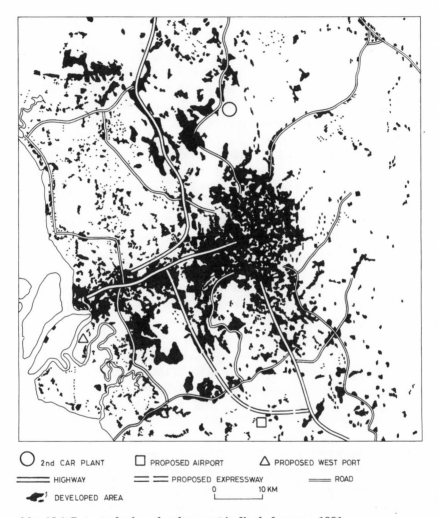

Map 15.1 **Extent of urban development in Kuala Lumpur, 1991**

the Kuala Lumpur mega-region is located – is expected to achieve industrialized status by the year 2005.

Two major factors are likely to affect the directional growth of the EMR in the 1990s. The first is the Selangor government's decision to encourage industrial development away from the primary corridor. A 640 ha site in Serendah about 35 km to the north of Kuala Lumpur in the northern corridor has been identified as the location for the second national car plant. As this will contribute some 2,000 jobs in small- and medium-scale factories and related support activities, the northern sector is geared for intensive growth in the 1990s, which will swing the spatial configuration northwards.

In fact, private developers have already started development here in the form of golf resorts, housing estates, and industrial parks (Goh 1992).

The second factor is related to the development of two major infrastructural projects, namely the West Port development project in Port Klang to the west and the new international airport in Sepang to the south. In 1991, Port Klang handled more than 26 million tonnes of cargo and there are plans to increase that capacity three times by 2010 to make it the leading port not only in Malaysia but also in Southeast Asia. Besides the M$1.2 billion West Port, there are also proposals for a marine industrial park along the coast from North Port to Kapar. Enhancement of port facilities in Port Klang will further intensify the primary corridor and cause growth to invade the coastal areas towards Kapar, Meru, and Sungai Besar. The second major infrastructural project is the M$20 billion Kuala Lumpur International Airport at Sepang on a 10,000 ha site, to be operational by 1997. This airport – the largest international airport in Southeast Asia – has, of course, triggered substantial spin-offs, especially in the form of potential projects in the 50 km southern corridor, including the construction of M$10 billion rail and road links between the airport and Kuala Lumpur and the other surrounding major towns. New townships are expected to mushroom, especially along highways linking the airport with Kuala Lumpur. The Puchong Jaya Commercial Centre and the proposed M$1 billion township near Bangi just 7 km northeast of the airport are examples. Also planned is a miniature economic triangle linking Shah Alam, Klang, and Sepang with proposals for commercial and other economic ventures.

A Restatement of Growth: Superinduced Development

The overall growth scenario may be restated from another perspective. Urbanization and its nascent concentration in the EMR of Kuala Lumpur occurred immediately after the Second World War, even before a strong industrial base was developed. The shift from an agricultural base to an industrial one through the strategy of import-substitution industrialization hastened this process after independence. Much of the concretized urban form up to the early 1970s was due to this shift. From the 1970s onwards, however, the transition to an export-based economy meant greater globalization of economic activities and resulted in the structural transformation of the economy noted earlier.

The consequence of this economic transformation is vigorous enlargement of the major city regions such as Penang, Johor Bahru, and, especially, Kuala Lumpur, simply because economic development favours urban agglomerations. The engine of economic growth is the manufacturing sector, to a large extent comprising foreign investments. Of course, other sectors such as tourism, merchant banking, and other professional services are also increasingly global in nature. These globalized activities place a renewed and heightened emphasis on existing large urban centres, which possess developed infrastructure and serve as export channels.

In the Kuala Lumpur EMR over the last ten years or so, physical development has been so rapid that it is tantamount to a new city built over the existing city. Interestingly, the stimulating force behind these new structures is directly or indirectly external in nature. Therefore, a 'superinduced' arrangement develops; physical and functional development within the region is brought in through forces from without and superimposed on existing structures.

This pattern of EMR growth will continue, given the impetus of current industrial development. More than 35 per cent of the country's total investments in the manufacturing sector are located in the mega-urban region of Kuala Lumpur in the 1990s, and more than M$40 billion worth of investments will be poured into this region alone. In 1990, the region received M$4.85 billion in investments for 237 projects, of which M$1.2 billion came from high-tech industries such as semi-conductors and computers. This is enormous compared to other emerging mega-urban regions in Malaysia, such as Johor Bahru (204 projects worth M$2.7 billion) and Penang (132 projects worth M$1.8 billion).

The Characteristics of the Kuala Lumpur SMR: New Wine in an Old Wineskin

The superinduced metropolitan region (SMR) of Kuala Lumpur is almost inevitably the result of market- and growth-oriented policies, in the form of active strategies to attract foreign investments. Like the proverbial fish on a line, big or small might take the bait. In this case, the big bites came from Taiwan, Singapore, the US, and Japan, and these were translated into spatial processes in the mega-urban region of Kuala Lumpur, especially in the late 1980s, leading to substantial private and state industrial land development and its concomitant residential, infrastructural, and ancillary demands. 'Intelligent' buildings, high-rise buildings, and condominiums are sprouting all over the SMR, and the inner areas are becoming gentrified.

Because the spatial transformation was not planned, traffic snarls and congestion have resulted. The existing infrastructure cannot accommodate the added functions and activities; it is putting new wine into an old wineskin, so to speak. It is obvious that the internal constraints of the existing road systems are causing major blockages. It is estimated that about 400 new cars are registered daily and there are 359,243 more vehicles clogging the roads of Kuala Lumpur today than ten years ago. The number of vehicles is projected to reach 1.4 million by the year 2000.

Because of this large volume of traffic, Kuala Lumpur is also experiencing the highest number of road accidents in the country. The government response to this has been more road upgradings, bypass roads, flyovers, and expressways, such as the Kuala Lumpur-Shah Alam Expressway, South Klang Valley Expressway, and so on. About M$105.5 million have been set aside by the state government of Selangor to construct and maintain roads outside the inner core area of Kuala Lumpur under the Sixth Malaysian Plan.

Nonetheless, infrastructural bottlenecks and mounting land prices will further disperse residential and manufacturing activities to the peripheral areas, initially in macro-axial development along major transportation lines. This movement to the periphery and the nearby rural areas may also be abetted by the difficulties of finding female labour in the EMR core. By moving outwards, factory enterprises are able to recruit female labour in the outlying areas without additional expenses in accommodation and transportation. Paradoxically, any winds of change in the intensity and direction of foreign investments will affect these outermost areas first. In the Klang Valley, for instance, a slow start in the first quarter of 1992 in terms of foreign investments resulted in a drop of more than 50 per cent in sales of industrial land immediately outside the Klang Valley.

The excellent economic climate has also encouraged the growth of many small- and medium-scale support factories filling essential needs for major industries. As many as 1,500 of these are illegal, however, operating on unconverted agricultural and residential lands. Their existence may be due to the fact that demand from foreign investors for industrial lands have forced local manufacturers into the sidelines as land prices have been jacked up from $14 to about $25 per square foot, far beyond their means. The location of these factories in non-designated areas, of course, contributes to the traffic crunch. Relocation to the urban fringe is a massive task but will be a significant feature of the SMR. The demands for relocation to traditional rural areas will mean the steady conversion of rural land to non-agricultural use at an unprecedented rate and further blurring of the distinction between rural and urban.

The SMR of Kuala Lumpur is also marked by the proliferation of medium- and high-cost apartments and condominiums, which are sprouting up everywhere and often juxtaposed with the traditional *kampung* and squatter landscapes. In 1989, 4,307 medium-cost and 1,595 high-cost condominiums were approved for construction. The figures rose to 15,203 medium-cost units and 10,403 high-cost units in 1990. About 20 to 30 per cent of these were sold to foreigners. In terms of affordable housing for the lower income group, another 478,000 housing units are required to cope with accommodation needs in inner Kuala Lumpur in the next ten years. On the periphery in the Petaling, Hulu Langat, Gombak, and Klang districts, there are some 50,000 squatter families. Thus it is clear that the EMR is in dire need of housing for the expanding population.

To cope with increased population, new townships and growth centres are being developed by the government as well as the private sector. The M$1 billion Bandar Bukit Beruntung, for example, is a self-contained township about 25 km to the north of Kuala Lumpur and is expected to transform 2,200 ha of oil palm and rubber plantations into a business, commercial, industrial, and residential complex beside a golf course. About 15,000 medium- and low-cost homes will be built for a population of 100,000. Another example is Bandar Tun Hussein Onn in Cheras, where it will cost M$800 million to build 7,000 houses for some 35,000 people.

The SMR of Kuala Lumpur, with its imposition of new structures upon old, has inevitably left pockets of traditional life as squatter communities continue to grow at a rate of 5.7 per cent per annum. In addition, the traditional Malay reservation areas such as Kampung Baru, Kampung Datuk Keramat, and Kampung Kerunchi remain, where the pace of development is perceptively slower. These areas consist of low-rise, village-style housing and contrast dramatically with the high-rise condominiums and apartments. Moreover, the traditional areas are highly congested. Kampung Kerunchi, for instance, was a mere village of farmers in the 1950s, but today it has a population of some 35,000.

In the wake of rapid development in other parts of the mega-urban area, many such traditional areas are facing identity crises. Sandwiched as they are between prime commercial areas, the cost of redevelopment for such vicinities is extremely high and not financially feasible. Attempts to redevelop Kampung Bahru, located in the heart of Kuala Lumpur, and Kampung Padang Jawa in Shah Alam, for example, had to be shelved because of the high cost of land and the haphazard development that had already taken place. Some form of action – perhaps a linkage policy similar to that of Boston – may have to be implemented in order to bring about a spatially balanced mega-urban region.

It needs to be mentioned also that with the rapid development of the mega-urban region, environmental pollution is becoming more serious. Air pollution is an example; in many urban centres, ozone presence has been recorded at 70 to 95 parts per billion in the lower atmosphere, much higher than the World Health Organization standard of 60 parts per billion. Besides that, the rivers in the region are badly polluted by industrial and household wastes. In 1990, three out of the seven river basins in the Kuala Lumpur EMR were reported to be Malaysia's most polluted rivers, the pollution being largely from rubber product factories, chemical product factories, and the food and beverage industries.

Some Implications of SMR Development in Kuala Lumpur

It is apparent that superinduced development in Kuala Lumpur is highly dependent on a well-developed infrastructural network and will continue to evolve and converge around the mega-urban region because it offers the best comparative advantage. The momentum is self-perpetuating because as activities become more global, investments in infrastructure become necessary to make the city more supportive and to maintain its competitiveness. This, in turn, attracts more investors. The pattern probably explains why industrial dispersion and decentralization is not taking place rapidly enough to the eastern industrial corridor comprising other states such as Pahang, Trengganu, and Kelantan, or to Sabah and Sarawak. It is therefore pertinent to note that growth of the Kuala Lumpur SMR in the 1990s is being driven by these external forces resulting from internationalization.

Nonetheless, as the mega-urban region of Kuala Lumpur becomes more and more saturated, neighbouring states will feel spillover effects. Negri Sembilan state, for instance, located just south of the new airport, has braced itself for greater developments. The next five years will see ten new industrial areas, requiring about 72,000 industrial workers. There will be some 570 factories in the state by 1998, and new townships will be developed in Panchor, Senawang, Tasik Jaya, Bukit Kepayang, and so on. The western end of Negri Sembilan in particular, which borders the new airport, will receive substantial benefits from the growth of Kuala Lumpur. North of Kuala Lumpur, Selangor and Perak states have agreed to set up industrial estates jointly in the border areas in Tanjung Malim and Sabak Bernam, where some 2,400 ha of agricultural lands have been converted to industrial status waiting to absorb the likely spillover of industrial investments.

Conclusion

Clearly, the development of an urban spatial configuration that is largely based on factors beyond government control is likely to be bogged down by problems that will slow industrialization and especially the in-flow of direct foreign investment (DFI). A number of external and internal factors may decelerate the country's industrialization process. It is estimated that to maintain the targeted growth rate of the manufacturing sector would require M$80 million investment up to 1995, of which more than 40 per cent would have to come from outside sources. New policies and strategies would be necessary as other countries scramble for scarce capital and investments as a result of the liberalization of Eastern European socialist economies. Further, emerging developing countries such as China, Vietnam, the Philippines, Indonesia, and Thailand are in a strong position to compete for DFI because of their vast domestic markets and cheaper land and labour costs. Because Malaysia is highly dependent on manufacturing exports, the persistent slowdown of the economies of developed countries will affect its economy. In addition, alliances between countries and trading blocs can change the pattern of capital and investment flows. NAFTA, for instance, may redirect North American companies to Mexico instead of Asia and Malaysia.

Of great concern among internal factors is the current shortage of about 80,000 skilled workers in the manufacturing sector. Over the next five years, another 250,000 skilled and semi-skilled workers will be needed. Whether in terms of a relative shortage of unskilled and skilled labour or of high labour turnover, the economy is confronted by a possible labour market crunch and a human resource development constraint (Salih and Young 1987). The government has proceeded to ease the labour shortage by allowing the import of foreign labour in the plantation, construction, and domestic sectors. Finally, not only the level of technology and skills for small manufacturing industries but also the quality of infrastructure such as roads, airports, ports, transportation, and water and electricity supplies is crucial in determining whether investors will stay long in the country.

It is clear that the rate of economic growth has put the country on the fast lane of success, but this brings dangers, especially in the dysfunctionality of the Kuala Lumpur SMR. It is irrefutable that major surgery will be needed to ensure flows and remove structures that are not in consonance with the functions of the global economy. This will be the most serious challenge for the 1990s and beyond: how to decongest and realign the dynamics of urban growth in Kuala Lumpur. As the inner areas become more congested and more exorbitantly expensive, a massive and dramatic intensification of urban investments in the outer fringes will be the dominant pattern of growth. New wine will require a new wineskin of planning and organization. Consequently, planning for the SMR of Kuala Lumpur can no longer be confined to old political boundaries. Holistic thinking on a regional and even a global scale becomes essential. The myopic view of city planning has to be broadened to focus on an approach encompassing the forces, principles, and processes by which large urban regions can be managed successfully.

16
The Bangkok Metropolitan Region: Policies and Issues in the Seventh Plan

Utis Kaothien

As the world's economy develops, trade competition among nations has intensified. Fortunately for Thailand, its economic base has continued to diversify, not only by utilizing its rich natural resources and labour-intensive activities but also by widening the import-export of raw materials and finished products. The improved production management that makes use of efficient regional and intercontinental transportation networks helped establish Thailand in the forefront of the Southeast Asian economy.

The Seventh National Economic and Social Development Plan (1992-6) supports this idea of Thailand 'at the forefront of the Southeast Asian economic center' by recognizing the 'metropolitan region development scheme.'[1] The region consists of the area covering Bangkok metropolis and its vicinity towns, the country's Eastern Seaboard subregion, and the newly proposed Industrial Zone of the Upper Central Region. The entire area is expected to become an integrated urban conglomeration, large enough to serve the nation's economic base and countries bordering Thailand.

The Existing Situation[2]

In general, urbanization in Thailand has never been limited by a city's administrative boundaries, so that the built-up area in a number of big cities in Thailand has grown beyond administrative boundaries. It is estimated that at least 32 per cent of the national population (about 18.3 million) lives in urban areas and is still increasing at the rate of about 3.4 per cent per year. If this trend continues, within the next two decades urban population will account for one-half of the total.

It is also known that in 1991 about 42 per cent (7.7 million) of the total urban population was concentrated in the Bangkok metropolis and towns in the vicinity. The trend is less severe in the metropolis than in the surrounding areas. Studies suggest that by the year 2010, the urban population of Bangkok metropolis will decrease from the present 34 per cent to about 24 per cent of the total national urban population but urban population in the vicinity towns will increase from 8 to 11 per cent.

Most urban areas known to have outgrown their administrative boundaries are to be found along the major transportation network. In the case of the Bangkok Metropolitan Region, extension corridors link the metropolis, via existing industrial sprawl in the northern part, to the neighbouring Saraburi province and to the Eastern Seaboard in the southeast (see Map 16.1). Presently this area has an estimated 9 million people but projections suggest that within the next two decades the population will increase to about 16 million.

Although the metropolis and its vicinity will have comparatively less significance in terms of primacy in the future, the area's role as the national economic base will continue to increase. The GDP of the metropolis and vicinity increased from 46 per cent of the gross national domestic product to 49 per cent in the Sixth Plan period (1988-92). It should be noted that although the metropolis and vicinity have only 16 per cent of the total national population, the area contributes up to 70 per cent of the national industrial product, with 53 per cent of the service sector and 60 per cent of foreign investment, especially in the non-agricultural sector. Thus it is not surprising that the average income in the metropolis is ten times higher than the average in the Northeast Region, considered the poorest and most depressed region in Thailand.

For the same reasons, the metropolis and its vicinity continue to be the major job generator, drawing migrants in large numbers. The economic efficiency of the metropolis has also made it the economic catalyst of the nation. Its growth affects the national well-being as its economic conglomeration creates advantages for competition in the world market. Naturally, such rapid growth has both positive and negative effects. The problem that causes grave concern is that the public sector, especially the local administration, can no longer provide adequate services for the rapidly expanding newly urbanized areas.

Changes and Problems in the Metropolitan Region[3]

The Problem of Land Use and Management

Land-use and management problems are at the root of many other urban problems. The rapid expansion of urban land use, characteristically misused and sprawling along the main infrastructure networks, unduly concentrates activities in one region of the country and leaves much waste land. It is thus difficult to provide systematic and interconnected service networks. The present town and country planning law emphasizes strict land-use control, which does not function very well with the existing weak enforcement and cannot fit in with the present dynamic urban land market. The limited administrative capacity of local authorities further complicates infrastructure investment coordination, resulting in traffic

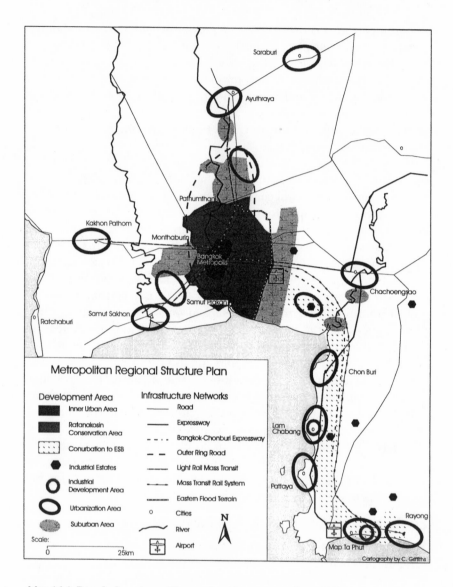

Map 16.1 **Bangkok metropolitan regional structure plan, 1990**

congestion, shortages in urban amenities, increases in unserviced land, and deterioration of the urban environment.

In 1991 alone, there was a considerable increase in the number of high-rise buildings (about 180 new projects) in the core area of the metropolis. It was estimated that the increase of building space totalled 54 million m^2, with about 2.5 million m^2 for office space. These buildings demand far more public utilities and services than the local government can provide.

The demand for land, especially in areas where infrastructure and services are available, has increased rapidly. The limited supply of serviced land has pushed prices to unbelievable heights. Land prices in the city have increased by about 22 per cent annually – and no less than 30 per cent in the recently built suburban areas – during the last few years.

Industrialization of the metropolis has spread into the surrounding agricultural areas at the rate of 28,000 rai annually. This has occurred along the major roads in an uncontrolled fashion, leaving areas of agricultural land in the interstices between the major roads.

To this day, the Bangkok metropolis still lacks an effective land-use plan, one acceptable to all government departments and practical enough to be used as a guideline and coordinating tool. The existing land-use plan seems to rely on strict legal measures that are difficult to implement as they do not provide room for objective bargaining between developers and the local government. It would serve both the populace and the local government to adopt land-use measures that allow room for dynamic bargaining as long as developers can find technical solutions to problems that otherwise prevent such developments in specific areas.

The Problem of Traffic Congestion

Traffic congestion is one of the most obvious problems of the metropolis. Many areas in the metropolis are 'superblocks,' where real estate is booming. Patches of empty land can be found in between major developments because of speculation. Also, the existing mass transit system is inadequate, forcing those who can afford it to use private cars, thereby increasing traffic congestion and the demand for road use. A few hours of congestion and traffic jams each day and loose concern for safer fuel consumption can cause serious air pollution.

Public bus service is very poor and negligent control in granting licences to an increasing number of private vehicles is going to worsen the problem of traffic jams. The rate of increase of vehicles in the metropolis is estimated at about 5.7 per cent annually and if allowed to continue, by the next decade the number of vehicles will have doubled.

Although a number of subdivisions in the suburbs have built their own road networks, there is no integrated master plan to guide and link one subdivision to the next. The result is a patchwork of fragmented and disconnected roads that could otherwise serve as diversion roads. At present a number of gigantic projects have been identified in order to cope with the problem, especially expressways and a mass rapid transit system. However, these mega-projects could be underused if there are not enough secondary and feeder road networks to link them. It is believed that land acquisition is the main constraint.

Construction of the mass rapid transit system has been delayed, leaving only the inadequate bus service of the Bangkok Mass Transit Authority to meet transportation needs in the metropolis. At the same time, ongoing road repairs and construction works at many significant points in the city have caused heavy traffic jams. On bad days, traffic jams have been known to stand still for hours.

The Problem of Environmental Deterioration

There is much concern about the waste water and sewerage system in the metropolis. About 1.4 million m^3 of waste water per year is discharged into canals and rivers. Of this, 75 per cent is from urban residential areas and the remaining 25 per cent from factories. About 1,000 tons of garbage per day and 1.9 million tons of toxic waste per year find their way to canals and rivers. It is now illegal to dump toxic waste or garbage into the waterways, and factories are required to have their own waste water treatment plants. However, weak enforcement continues to allow factories to operate without such plants, and as a result only 2 per cent of industrial waste gets proper treatment. If nothing is done to prevent waste water and garbage dumping into the Chao Phraya, it is expected that within the next decade contamination will reach the northern part of the metropolis.

Several plans and programs for waste water treatment and garbage disposal plants have been identified but so far the operation is thought to be too costly for the local government. The Bangkok Metropolitan Administration has invited a number of private firms to initiate a turnkey project but no contract has been signed. Slow implementation has caused considerable damage to the main canals and even to the Chao Phraya river, on which a significant number of residents depend for their water supply.

The Problem of Lack of Potable Water

Lack of potable water in the rapidly growing suburban areas is another cause for concern. Inadequate water supply in the metropolis has led factories and subdivisions in the suburbs to resort to using underground water. This causes land subsidence, which in turn causes serious flooding during the rainy season. Land subsidence in these areas was found by government research areas to be anywhere from 5 to 15 cm per year.

Of the daily 3.2 million m^3 total requirement for potable water in the metropolis, the Metropolitan Waterwork Authority (MWA) can produce only 2.8 million m^3, serving only 85 per cent of the 6.2 million people in the metropolis and covering an area of about 580 km^2. The rest of the population is supplied by smaller municipalities and by the Provincial Waterworks Authority (PWA).

The Problem of the Urban Poor

The influx of rural migrants into the metropolis in search of better job opportunities has exacerbated the problems of the urban poor. These problems include housing security, limited opportunities for education, low-level working skills, and unstable income, as the prospect of obtaining employment in either the formal or the informal sector is rather low. It should be noted that while the national incidence of poverty has declined over the last few years because of general economic recovery, poverty in municipal areas, especially in the metropolis, has actually risen.

At present, the metropolis and its vicinity towns have at least 230,000 urban poor. There are approximately 1,700 slum areas all over the metropolis, with a high concentration in the core area. Most slum residents do not have legal status and are thus unlikely to obtain public services. Also, they face the ever present problem of relocation, as most often they illegally squat on other people's land.

The Problem of Local Government's Absorptive Capacity

Although the overall economy has increased local revenue to allow more investment in urban service infrastructure, the increase cannot keep up with demand, especially during the Seventh Plan period. Dramatic changes can be observed as the central government provides less and less investment in infrastructure and services.

During the Fifth Plan (1982-7), the central government's share was 48 per cent of the total investment. This was then reduced to 15 per cent during the Sixth Plan (1987-91). At the same time, the fiscal responsibility of the local government for provision of infrastructure decreased from 12 to 7 per cent. Thus the main responsibility for providing urban infrastructure investment during the Sixth Plan fell on state enterprises – which are equivalent to crown corporations – increasing their share from 40 per cent during the Fifth Plan to 60 per cent during the Sixth Plan, while private-sector participation during the Sixth Plan was about 12 per cent, mainly in housing and transportation.

Although the responsibility of providing urban services and infrastructure falls most heavily on state enterprises, the government does not allow them to charge for services based on actual market rate. Many planners see this as sheer shortsightedness, depriving the enterprises of income that could otherwise help them to enlarge and diversify their services. Regulations currently enforced by the government are not flexible enough to attract the private sector to provision of urban infrastructure. Also, local governments are not legally allowed to take direct loans from any international financial institutions except through the relevant ministries, and this makes it more difficult to meet the demand for urban infrastructure investment.

It is estimated that during the Seventh Plan, demand for urban infrastructure investment in traffic and transportation, waste water treatment and garbage collection, flood protection, water supply expansion, and housing will cost about Baht 300 billion. Half of this will be spent to ameliorate the worsening traffic problem in the metropolis. Unless the budget is properly managed, however, the problem of inadequate urban services will remain and can be expected to intensify.

The Problem of Institutional Organization and Coordination
More than fifty agencies share the responsibility for planning, financing, and managing the various development programs, especially in areas relating to traffic and transportation, water supply, and housing for the metropolis. There is still plenty of room for improved coordination in planning, budgeting, and operating these major projects. The classic bureaucratic system, with its emphasis on input and processing rather than on output, is not conducive to fulfilling the immediate needs of the metropolis.

During the Sixth Plan, a national committee was established to look after development in the metropolis and vicinity. The committee was assigned the task of organizing the direction and formulation of the various investment programs of the related agencies, and has had considerable success. Nevertheless, ad hoc committees cannot conduct their work on a continuing basis, as they have to be abolished when the government changes. They are therefore of limited use in coordinating long-term projects.

It can be concluded that the Bangkok metropolis and its vicinity towns have certain problems that impede their existing economic roles. These impediments will continue and perhaps intensify as the metropolis expands its built-up core area into the metropolitan region. They affect not only the economic role of the metropolis but also the urban poor, more than anyone else. How much the metropolitan region will benefit the nation in the future will depend on the policies that deal with such problems.

Metropolitan Regional Development Policies
The problems of the metropolis did not stop Bangkok from growing. Perhaps the economic benefit and the trade and business advantage offset

the costs derived from these problems. The metropolis continues to contribute the largest proportion of gross regional product (GRP). In fact, Bangkok and the central region together produced more than 50 per cent of the total national product in 1989. It is noticeable that the main non-agricultural sectors contributing to the GRP growth of the metropolis are manufacturing and services. These growing sectors fuel national growth, and the growth of the metropolis contributes significantly to national growth.

Although the performance of the metropolis allows the country to compete successfully in the world market, it can be argued that growth has not spread to other regions as it should and that regional disparities have not been reduced. Such disparities have in fact grown in Thailand, because although the outer regions have grown, they have done so at a slower rate than has the metropolis. To be fair, there is no evidence to suggest that the primacy of Bangkok causes the growth rate to decline in other regions.

One of the viable ways of solving regional disparity is to emphasize measures that increase growth and efficiency in the outer regions rather than to control the growth of the metropolis or to disturb its growth-generating characteristics. Consequently, the Seventh Plan has devised guidelines for the development of the metropolitan region that are intended to maintain the role of the metropolis. The plan allows the metropolis not only to act as a major economic centre in facilitating structural transformation and socio-economic growth in Thailand but also to enlarge its role and spatial coverage to compete with neighbouring countries and accomplish closer integration into the international economic system. Accordingly, urban development policies for the metropolitan region in the Seventh Plan can be grouped into four areas, to be discussed next.

Targeting the Metropolitan Region for Development
The Seventh Plan recommends studying how to target the metropolitan region for development by using the Bangkok Metropolitan Region Structural Plan to provide the region with a proper plan of orderly growth. The Bangkok Metropolitan Region Structural Plan emphasizes growth to the northern and southeastern parts of the metropolis, to link Bangkok with the Saraburi Industrial Complex and the Eastern Seaboard. The clear direction offered for regional growth in the plan will assist the alignment of major infrastructural investments rather than allowing growth to sprawl in every conceivable direction. When directed to desired locations, growth is cost effective. The private sector also benefits from the information the plan provides and the guarantee that targeted areas will be served properly, subsequently improving the efficiency of urban land use.

The Bangkok Metropolitan Region Structural Plan also formulates measures to relieve congestion in the metropolis through construction of satellite cities and new towns, controls on building construction in the city core, and prevention of housing sprawl along the main highways. The following strategies are laid out in the plan:

- Empty and unused lands in the suburban areas will be used efficiently by providing access roads to link them with existing main roads.
- Promotion zones will be established, with proper controls on high-rise buildings, especially in areas directly served by rapid mass transit. The high standard of services that these areas need could be met by requiring relevant private entrepreneurs to participate in investment projects to solve traffic problems, water supply and waste water treatment, and other environmental issues. In fact, a master plan for waste water treatment and a garbage disposal system has been jointly undertaken by the Bangkok Metropolitan Administration and a number of private firms (playing a part in both investment and operation) and could eventually serve the entire metropolitan area.
- Urban communities will be improved and rehabilitated, provision of more recreation areas will be encouraged, and historically and culturally significant areas will be conserved. This last point applies particularly to Rattanakosin Island, where it would also benefit tourism.

As part of the metropolitan region, the Eastern Seaboard will serve as the country's major industrial base and a new gateway to industrial growth. The seaboard is seen as a countermagnet, providing alternative investment locations to reduce congestion in the Bangkok metropolis and its vicinity towns. It is envisaged that the seaboard will be served with a regionally integrated transportation network of a high standard, which would link the metropolis with the inner parts of the country. Communication networks and the new deep-sea port in the Eastern Seaboard development will increase international contacts for the metropolitan region.

To accomplish these development schemes, it is necessary to speed up expansion of major infrastructure in the seaboard, especially roads, rail, and communication systems connecting the major ports to industrial estates at Laem Chabang and Map-Ta-Phut. All the major urban centres of the seaboard must be well equipped with standard social services and infrastructure, community environmental improvement programs, and upgraded administrative bodies. The seaboard must be connected to the rest of the nation via new transportation and communication networks, and an improved international communication network will be needed to maximize its role as a new economic zone.

The northern part of the metropolitan region is envisaged as the industrial zone for the Upper Central Region, the centre for industrial activities relocated from the Bangkok metropolis. The regional network of roads and rail will directly link the industrial zone with the seaboard for transporting export commodities without having to go through Bangkok. This direct network is important not only because it will save time but because it could help reduce congestion in Bangkok.

This industrial zone can be divided into three areas: (1) Saraburi as the main urban centre and economic base of the Upper Central Region in trade, transportation, and support services; (2) Kaeng Koi as the centre for cement and construction industry and other industries relocated from Bangkok and its vicinity towns; and (3) Tha Rua/Tha Luang as an agro-processing centre for exports. To make the zone function effectively and attract industrial relocation and new factories, it is important to provide incentives beyond the speedy provision of necessary infrastructure services. The creation of export promotion zones is an example.

Strengthening the Role of the Metropolitan Region

In Thailand, major infrastructure is believed to be crucial for successful urbanization. Effective infrastructure shapes not only the development pattern but also types of activities. On the other hand, it also leads to environmental deterioration if not adequately served or managed.

Manageable levels of urban and metropolitan growth could be achieved by providing links between Bangkok and the rest of the metropolitan region. An example is the development of the second international airport at Nong Ngu Hao. The project will require transportation links with the first airport at Don Muang and regional rail links throughout the metropolitan region. The area surrounding the airport will need well-planned and -managed land use to avoid problems like those in Bangkok.

It is necessary to emphasize that existing problems in the metropolitan area need to be addressed by infrastructure investment schemes. Foremost in the hierarchy of problems that need special attention is the chronic traffic problem in Bangkok. To ease traffic congestion to an acceptable level, the public transportation system should be developed to reduce traffic congestion in densely populated areas. In particular, this will involve construction of a mass transit and rail system, improvement of bus service, and promotion of water transport service. The expressway system must be coordinated with local road networks. Construction of ring roads, main roads, secondary roads, and suburban truck depots should be speeded up to reduce urban traffic jams and interurban expressway systems developed to guide urban growth according to the metropolitan regional structural plan.

Other infrastructure development projects, however, such as intranational and international communication networks, are just as important as major transportation networks. As well, flood protection plans within the Bangkok metropolis and its vicinity towns should be speeded up by establishing a permanent agency responsible for maintaining the flood protection system, conserving flood terrain, and preserving low-lying lands for temporary water storage. The rapidly growing suburbs of the metropolis need expanded water supply services and control over the exploitation of underground water.

Supporting the Urban Poor in the Metropolitan Region

The urban poor represent potential labour power, giving Bangkok a competitive production base. This labour pool should be encouraged by providing training in new skills and promoting small-scale enterprise and self-employment development skills in order to upgrade its production capability. In fact, a credit scheme has been established to provide loans to slum people. The objective of this loan is to promote urban poor occupational development and subsequently to create stable incomes and enable self-help financing for housing improvements.

The slum community's basic demand focuses on their housing rights. Accordingly, the Seventh Plan recommends a policy to enact specific legislation to protect the housing rights of these communities. The plan also includes upgrading the quality of existing slum communities and providing new housing for those who have been forced to relocate. Each relocated family is subsidized from the central budget at the cost of about Baht 18,000.

A joint investment developed by the central government, the local authorities (BMA), slum communities, land owners, and the National Housing Authority will make loans available for housing improvement or initial investment in small-scale or service-oriented businesses. In addition, the government will provide public subsidies for investment in construction of higher standard public utility systems such as roads, pavements, and drainage systems.

A more effective way of improving the quality of life and security in slum communities is through community-based organizations. Thus the Seventh Plan emphasizes the promotion of community-based organizations to look after the slum dweller's well-being.

Improving Urban Management and Institutional Capability

The effectiveness of all the aforementioned policies will depend largely on urban management and institutional capability. The metropolitan region consists of different levels of local government, most with a weak financial base. Accordingly, the Seventh Plan emphasizes increased efficiency of local revenue collection efforts and enlargement of the local tax base.

The plan recognizes and promotes a greater role for the private sector in both investment in and operation of major urban infrastructure and services. The bylaws and regulations governing operational procedures and conditions need to be clearly spelled out or revised as necessary to effect greater private-sector participation. It is also necessary to implement cost recovery measures and programs to attract private investment to urban services and development projects. As well, there is a need to increase direct charges on those who benefit directly from investments in public infrastructure and services.

During the Seventh Plan period, local authorities have been asked to try so-called 'positive town and country measures,' such as the 'urban land readjustment scheme,' which can be used to formulate effective land-development programs with adequate provision for infrastructure and services. Investment in infrastructure and services will have to be shared by the land owners and government agencies concerned and even the developers.

The plan also emphasizes improving and strengthening the planning capability of local organizations by persuading them to set up their own town planning office, financial administration, and management. Certain laws and regulations need to be adjusted and some new ones enacted for such a decentralization scheme, not only to achieve economic goals but also to make the metropolis a more humane place in which to live. Laws involving urban land readjustment and improvement and rehabilitation of cities within the metropolitan region are examples.

In short, the policies in the Seventh Plan appear to cover all aspects of maintaining the economic role of the metropolitan region. The plan emphasizes the use of the Bangkok Metropolitan Region Structural Plan as a guideline for spatial and infrastructural development. An infrastructure investment program has been established for the purpose of implementing guidelines for the region and creating more effective urban areas, as well as preventing further environmental deterioration. It is believed that infrastructure projects can aid the development pattern of the metropolitan region, as existing town planning measures alone – the land-use plan – are no longer sufficient.

The Seventh Plan also prepares the administrative system for decentralization, as development of the metropolitan region requires both support from central and local development authorities and joint ventures with the private sector in the future.

Conclusion

Thailand realizes that it has to keep up with the rapid growth of Bangkok. The national economy has come to depend on the continued growth of the metropolis, which is rapidly transforming into a metropolitan region with a variety of functions and able to serve not only the surrounding regions but also the neighbouring countries. The recent national development plan envisages this process taking place soon. The Bangkok Metropolitan Region Structural Plan has therefore been devised as a set of development guidelines to prepare the metropolitan region for this new role.

Development policies for the metropolis have emphasized maintaining its economic functions and solving problems caused by congestion in the city. However, the plan requires investment in a number of gigantic programs, too large for the public sector to handle alone, taking into account its weak administrative capability. And although certain central ad hoc committees have been established to provide better ongoing implementation of some projects with political priority, too much reliance on such committees could weaken the local administration and fragment the urban institutional structure.

Thus, urban management issues, especially organization of a practical body to coordinate the concerned agencies, is the first area of concern that needs to be explored. This can be done either through administrative and political consensus or through action-oriented studies that focus on ways to strengthen local administrative bodies in the metropolitan region and to encourage private-sector investment in various infrastructure projects in the metropolitan region.

The policies in the Seventh Plan aim to enhance the positive functions of the metropolitan region to create a centre that can provide opportunities for higher incomes and better services and living standards. The future of the metropolis not only involves problems of economic function, land use, public services, traffic, housing, and community facilities but also is affected by criminal, social welfare, and even social conflicts, which influence the quality of life and social security.

We also cannot ignore important social issues concerned with regional rehabilitation. Further exploration of two areas is needed: (1) social strategies to create a liveable metropolis, and (2) an understanding of social change in the metropolitan region on which to base the new strategies.

Notes

1   See National Economic and Social Development Board (1992).
2   Much of the data for this section are taken from National Economic and Social Development Board (1991c).
3   For a further elaboration of these problems see National Economic and Social Development Board (1991a).

Part 4
Conclusions and Policy Implications

17
ASEAN Mega-Urbanization: A Synthesis
T.G. McGee and Ira M. Robinson

The conference and the essays from it that have been produced in this book represent the most comprehensive review available at present of the growth of large urban regions in ASEAN.[1] The purpose of this concluding chapter is not to summarize those findings but rather to draw out underlying questions concerning the urbanization process in ASEAN countries and to summarize the implications of these findings for future policy formation.

Five intriguing questions emerge from this review. First, in a global context, are certain features of the urbanization process unique to ASEAN experience? Second, is it possible to develop appropriate research paradigms for ASEAN urbanization? Third, in what way is this process contributing to the development process? Fourth, what paths of urbanization are most likely in ASEAN in the next two decades? And, fifth, what are the policy implications of these findings?

Five Questions on the Urbanization Process in ASEAN

Is the ASEAN Urbanization Experience Unique?
There is general scholarly agreement that the history of Southeast Asian urbanization is different from that of North American and European countries. The distinctive history of colonial incorporation and dependent development within the world system has created an urban settlement pattern dominated by primate cities such as Bangkok, Manila, and Jakarta. Singapore occupied a similar primate position with respect to Malaya in the colonial period.

It is also generally agreed that the pattern of population growth during the nineteenth and early twentieth centuries encouraged international migration to these countries, particularly by Chinese and Indians, who came to occupy a major role in the commerce of these cities alongside the colonial companies and agency houses. These colonial relationships also structured the functions of these cities, emphasizing ports, military centres, and service and administrative centres. Thus, the Southeast Asian states, and ASEAN in particular, inherited a common historical experience of urbanization (Drakakis-Smith and Dixon 1991; Fisher 1966; McGee 1967; Rigg 1991; and Yeung and Lo 1976).

Four general features of ASEAN have reinforced these patterns. First, it must be emphasized that ASEAN is a political grouping of nation states and that urbanization is occurring at a national level. As yet the agreement among ASEAN countries to lower tariffs and become more economically integrated is just beginning, and therefore regional integrative forces are not nearly as advanced as, for example, those at work in the European Union. Thus the process of urbanization is primarily affected by a mixture of global and national processes rather than regional ones. Emerging cross-border urban phenomena such as the Singapore Growth Triangle, however, represent incipient trends that will become more powerful in the future.

Second, the ASEAN region is geographically and ethnically very fragmented. It includes part of mainland Southeast Asia and part of archipelagic Southeast Asia. Historically, it has always been a 'cultural shatterbelt,' subject to outside influences from the larger regions of China and South Asia, and this was accentuated in the period of colonial domination from 1600 to the end of the Japanese war (Furnivall 1939). This has created an extraordinary mixture of ethnic, cultural, and religious diversity, which the newly independent states of ASEAN had to accommodate as they embarked upon development of their respective countries. As urbanization levels have increased in these countries, this diversity has continued, particularly in the largest urban regions with which this volume deals.

Third, although population size in the ASEAN countries is diverse, ranging from 185 million in Indonesia to 3 million in Singapore, the population is continuing to agglomerate in the major mega-urban regions, seeming to follow an inexorable global trend. For the majority of ASEAN countries, however – Indonesia being the exception – smaller total populations suggest that the size of mega-urban regions will not reach those of China or India.

Fourth, the ASEAN countries have generally been well positioned in the global economy. While their roles as primary commodity suppliers have continued, they have also received the wave of investment in global manufacturing that followed investment in the first group of NICs, including South Korea, Taiwan, and Hong Kong. This certainly places them in a much more advantageous position than most of the African and Latin American countries. Rapid economic growth rates in the 1990s, significant structural shifts from agriculture to manufacturing and services, and rapid urbanization have been the result. It is therefore important to realize that most of the ASEAN countries are firmly embarked upon the road to NIC status.[2]

At present, intense debates are going on over whether these directions can be sustained, but there is no lack of agreement that much of this economic growth is a direct consequence of strong state intervention and encouragement. At times it seems as if these policies have been paradoxical. On the one hand, the ASEAN governments have made a strong commitment to rural development, as is evident in recurring statements in various five-year plans. On the other hand, efforts to encourage industrial growth have led to the growth of the major urban regions. For instance, in most ASEAN countries, industrial estates have been located within the main urban regions.[3] Weak implementation of land-use regulations has also encouraged mega-urbanization, as land developers and theme park and other recreational operators have multiplied their investments in the urban region. State policy in ASEAN has therefore explicitly and implicitly encouraged mega-urbanization.

Finally, this surge of economic growth in ASEAN, besides fostering rapid growth of mega-urban regions, is also fuelling the growth of household income, particularly in these large urban areas. The landscapes of the urban regions now reflect a revolution of mass consumption. New housing developments proliferate, and shopping malls, golf courses, and theme parks are scattered throughout the urban peripheries. Often, they are juxtaposed with industrial estates and old rural villages, reflecting the historical layering of the landscape. These regions form networks of various forms of transport, in which motorized traffic prevails. Car ownership soars within the middle class but even the poorer families own two-stroke motorbikes. The region is networked by telephones as well, and geographical proximity is no longer a dominating criterion of location.

On the face of it, this description of mega-urbanization in ASEAN seems similar to Gottmann's (1961) description of the northeastern seaboard of the United States or Soja's (1989) of Los Angeles, suggesting that underlying processes are the same in the US and the ASEAN region. Whether this is indeed the case has been the subject of other debates about the manner in which the morphology and function of these mega-urban regions will evolve. Evidence from this text points to various models in the broader context of Asia, ranging from the emergence of giant corridors stretching between major city cores, of which the Tokyo-Osaka (Tokkaido) corridor is the prototype (Chapter 7), to world systems dominated by world cities (Chapter 3), transborder regions (Chapter 12), and finally to national urban systems dominated by one large urban region, such as Bangkok.

To some extent, these varying models reflect different disciplinary and theoretical perspectives. Nevertheless, it may also be argued that they respond to the present state of research on urbanization, which is grappling with ways to study the complex processes of urbanization in the contemporary period. As Bourne (1995) has pointed out, four broad research paradigms prevail at this time: the world system paradigm; the world city hypothesis; industrial restructuring; and the growth of service-led information- and knowledge-based global economies. Among researchers working in each of these paradigms – researching, for example, the role of world cities in international finance – there is no lack of agreement over the underlying processes of urbanization at a global level, but the complexities of the process encourage them to carry out research from particular perspectives.

There are strong indicators that the processes fuelling the emergence of these mega-urban regions are different only in degree from those leading to the emergence of mega-urban regions elsewhere, such as Tokyo. Since they have been discussed in considerable detail earlier, in chapters 1 to 4, they are not spelled out here, but it is necessary to summarize them in order to determine the uniqueness of ASEAN mega-urbanization. These processes are described below.

Globalism

Globalism refers to various aspects of the development of the global economy in the last thirty years: capital movement, technological change, and changes in the industrial location of certain types of manufacturing, often falling under the rubric of the international division of labour. As Rimmer, Douglass, and others in this volume point out, Southeast Asia and ASEAN have benefited by comparison with other parts of the developing world in the 1980s by achieving an important share of global investment. Increasingly, a significant part of this investment is coming from other parts of East Asia, such as South Korea and Taiwan. It is also strongly argued that locational effects have been focused on the mega-urban regions.

Transactional Revolution

While the transactional revolution is less generally treated in this volume, Chapter 7 in particular focuses on the locational impact of technological changes in transportation on the growing centralization of distribution nodes. Other chapters at least implicitly accept the collapse of time and space. Developments in transportation and information flows have paradoxically increased centralization in a number of nodes – or global cities – at a global level while permitting economic activity to be located in 'diffuse' patterns within mega-urban regions. This trend is further facilitated by the development of just-in-time distribution systems, which permit the dispersal of warehouses and the direct transfer of commodities from the point of production to the point of sale.

The Role of the National State

This volume does not concentrate heavily on the role of the national state in the growth of the mega-urban regions. A careful review of the chapters, however, reveals that through a variety of implicit and explicit policies, national states have encouraged the development of these mega-urban regions.

The Role of the Private Sector[4]

Persuasive arguments can be put forth that the private sector, made up of a number of land-development companies, industrial investors, retailers, and so on, are the main agents of development in the mega-urban regions of ASEAN. Certainly the evidence of the landscape supports this assertion. A strong argument can also be made that the activities of the private sector have been carried out in a very permissive environment, in that the local administration has rarely enforced regulations that would limit the private sector. Indeed quasi-state/private institutions have often been allowed to operate in a virtually unregulated environment. In this respect, it is salutary to look at the case studies of Bangkok, Manila, and Jakarta, as opposed to Singapore and Kuala Lumpur. In the first three cities, the private and private/state groups have been able to invest almost at will in the mega-urban regions; in Kuala Lumpur and Singapore, this process has been much more controlled.

It should be emphasized that this argument does not rest upon some view of the Machiavellian goals of the state but rather on the fact that there was, and still is, an inadequate regulatory environment. McGee's argument concerning the 'grey zone' of administrative responsibility in the periphery of these urban regions is a major explanatory factor, supported by Laquian in Chapter 10.

The Timing and Rapidity of the Urban Transition

While it is not unique to the region, some attention must be paid to the rapidity of ASEAN's economic and urbanizational change. Most ASEAN countries have embarked upon a process of change that will see a decline of agriculture, a domination of manufacturing and services, and a doubling of urbanization levels in twenty years. Economic transformation is being telescoped at a time during which institutional change is much slower. As a consequence, the economic and technological processes that have driven the growth of mega-urban regions have had ascendency over any institutional capacity to respond to them. This is perhaps the most challenging aspect of the ASEAN urbanization process and certainly the most challenging for policy response, as described below.

Can Appropriate Research Paradigms Be Developed for ASEAN Urbanization?

While it would be rash to argue that there is only one appropriate research paradigm for ASEAN urbanization, it is certainly possible to suggest that the processes of urbanization may be grouped into four broad categories. First are the economic, social, and political processes responsible for the *composition* of the cities' economies, labour markets, and so on. Second are the processes that lead to *construction* of the cities' built form, including public-sector investment in transportation infrastructure and housing and private-sector investment in development schemes. Third are the processes of *competition* among the cities, particularly at a global level, to establish themselves as major international nodes in global networks of transactions. Fourth, the three preceding processes all have a *configuring role* in the morphology and spatial structure of these cities. It is generally agreed that the growth of mega-urban regions is the product of these processes.

From a research point of view, the presentation of such a multidimensional paradigm is very challenging because it makes no effort to disentangle the relative importance of these processes and the manner in which they interact. On the other hand, so much unidimensional research on urbanization proves inadequate for policy formation. For example, the assumption that improvements in transportation systems will resolve major urban problems has been proven incorrect. What is more, research studies are complicated by specific features of national urbanization history and patterns. Nonetheless, it can certainly be argued that there are enough commonalities in the experience of urbanization in ASEAN countries that all can benefit from comparing their experiences and attempting to develop policy responses together.

What Are the Major Challenges of ASEAN Mega-Urbanization?

It would scarcely be likely that ASEAN mega-urban regions could grow as rapidly as they have without encountering a variety of problems and challenges. This book has catalogued the various dimensions of these problems but has paid less attention to the human dimensions: the effect of long commuting times on family life; the growing inequality of household incomes; the conditions of work for young women in many of the new factories; the ill health caused by pollution and other environmental problems; and the increasing violence in mega-urban regions. These characteristics are similar to what one finds in Tokyo, Los Angeles, or New York, and are certainly some of the more deleterious aspects of urbanization. The chapters of this book concentrate on the macro-dimensions of urban change and largely ignore the local level: the farmer who can no longer grow rice because of industrial pollution; the workers who perish in a factory fire, and the local areas that are transformed by land appropriation. It would be false and blind to argue that the process of mega-urbanization occurs without social and human costs.

On the whole, the chapters of this volume are informed by the belief that analysis of the problems and policy intervention will alleviate social and human costs. In this sense, the challenges that urbanization raises are centred on the issue of how to make the urban region more liveable and ultimately more sustainable. An important thrust of the book is that the present problems of incompatible land uses, inadequate housing, inefficient transportation systems, environmental degradation, and weak government can indeed be resolved.

There is no doubt, for example, that the rapid growth of the population is leading to an immense challenge to provide adequate housing. Chapters 5 and 6 document the diversity of responses to this situation in the ASEAN context. Singapore is the wealthiest of the urban regions and has provided for a major part of its housing needs through the public sector, but in other ASEAN urban regions the response is more diverse, including private-sector, middle-class housing and a significant proportion of illegal squatter dwellings. One of the attractions of the periphery in these regions has been that land is more available to squatters than in the city core, where it has become much too valuable for them to be permitted to occupy it. In the mega-urban regions of Bangkok, Manila, and Jakarta squatter housing will continue to be of importance. Researchers take different positions over this form of housing. In Chapter 5, Angel and Mayo argue that the growing housing demand necessitates an increase in both public- and private-sector involvement as well as toleration of the 'informal' or 'popular' sector in the short term.

With respect to transportation, Chapter 8 is a vigorous plea for controlling the private car. Pendakur's documentation of the costs of congestion, highway construction, and pollution catch the mood of governments and residents of these urban regions alike. But as he and others recognize, there is an inevitability about this situation, as there is about mega-urbanization itself. Thus the solutions of mass transit and more efficient public transportation systems cannot be avoided. Like Angel and Mayo, Pendakur sees a role for the informal sector and various forms of paratransit, emphasizing the need for a flexible response not only to transportation but to other problems of the mega-urban region.

Another set of problems involves the environment, captured in the microcosm of the Manila metropolitan area described by Conover in Chapter 9. If there is one message that this chapter delivers, and implicitly it emerges in all the case studies, it is that the physical environments in which many of the mega-urban regions are located are ecologically fragile. In the expansion of Manila to the south, the whole hydraulic system is being modified. Similar situations in Bangkok and Jakarta are described by Robinson (Chapter 4) and Ida Ayu Indira Dharmapatni and Firman (Chapter 14) respectively.

Of all the problems posed by mega-urbanization, environmental degradation is perhaps the most challenging because it is the most difficult to predict. It assumes even more importance if the chaotic tapestry of landscape in the outer rings of the mega-urban regions is to continue for any time. The ability of this mixture of agricultural and non-agricultural activity to persist depends on adequate water supply and refuse removal. This type of urban form thus poses much greater challenges than the compact city, although, as is becoming obvious, retrofitting these services in the compact cities in Western countries is far more expensive than providing them for the outer peripheries.

Less attention is paid to the issue of employment in the ASEAN mega-urban regions.[5] The gloomy predictions of an inability to create productive employment that prevailed in the 1960s are no longer valid. The surge of industrialization has created growing employment opportunities but there are still lags in the absorptive capacity of labour markets in the ASEAN mega-urban regions. Informal-sector employment in street vending, transportation, and service occupations plays an important economic role in these urban regions. In the inner cities, the informal sector is largely an historical persistence of small-scale retailing and service industries, but informal-sector employment serves a major function in the integration of the outer rings. The motorcycle 'soiboys' of Bangkok, the 'jeepneys' of Manila, and the 'oplets' of Jakarta have the flexibility of routes and time to move people throughout these regions. Food vendors are ubiquitous. Most labour force data suggest that the informal sector is beginning to decline, but it still plays an important role in providing both employment and services for these mega-urban regions.

The final challenge dealt with in this book is the need to develop an adequate governmental, administrative response to the challenges of the region. Robinson, Brennan, Laquian, and Ida Ayu Indira Dharmapatni and Firman all give this message. There are severe difficulties in developing an adequate institutional response to the problems facing the emerging mega-urban regions. The existing system of governance is a patchwork of local, provincial, and national administrative units with overlapping responsibilities. As a result, virtually every aspect of what might be thought of as 'conventional municipal administration' is inadequate for these large regions. Thus, local administration and other governing bodies in the periphery whose responsibilities have been almost entirely devoted to dealing with rural and semi-rural matters, now have to cope with the influx of industry, housing, retailing, leisure, and other urban-like activities. The intermediate levels of adminstration, such as provinces, also have limited experience with this phenomenon. As Laquian points out, national governments and planning agencies are trying to develop more comprehensive plans for the regions but the difficulties of implementation are immense. So rapid are the changes that planning intervention is often too late to solve the problem.

What Are the Future Scenarios for ASEAN Urbanization?

The dominating fact concerning the emergence of the ASEAN mega-urban regions is the rapidity of their growth. What has occurred there in the space of thirty years took sixty to one hundred years in the West. The most intriguing question arising from this volume is therefore whether the present chaotic pattern of land use is likely, to use Webster's words, to 'stall or solidify based on present form, function and characteristics' or develop into a more cohesive system of specialized urban centres functionally integrated by telecommunications and transportation networks, as is the case in Los Angeles.

Within the context of ASEAN, there is a tendency among some planners and politicians to see the Singapore example of a high-density, multinodal urban region as an option for other ASEAN cities. As has already been shown, however, the expansion of economic activity into the Singapore Growth Triangle is creating the same kind of mega-urban landscape as in Bangkok or Jakarta, though some would argue it is more planned. Certainly the Kuala Lumpur mega-urban region is showing a more controlled form of development than either Bangkok and Jakarta with the creation of new towns in the surrounding urban region. This, it can be argued, has been greatly aided by the fact that large blocks of land can be alienated for large-scale residential and town development. This is not impossible but is far more difficult in Jakarta, Manila, and Bangkok.

One other aspect of the future scenario of ASEAN mega-urban regions needs to be considered: their size and importance in the urban system. Currently there is a prevailing view among ASEAN governments, supported by many planners and researchers, that the physical growth of these regions is inimical to national economic growth and undermines strong cultural and national values.[6] As a consequence, regional and urban development policies are proposed, and in some instances implemented, to disperse population and economic activity from the mega-urban regions into secondary cities, small centres, or new towns. As has been argued elsewhere, there is little evidence that such policies are successful, at least at this phase of rapid mega-urban growth, and at the very least they will only serve to reduce the growth of mega-urban regions to a small extent.[7] Undoubtedly this negative view of mega-urban regions is enhanced by the perception that their population size makes them unmanageable. But various chapters in this book (see, in particular, Chapters 1 and 11) argue that the issue of size is a mirage; that, in fact, these regions are made up of myriad different communities and it is at this local level that most management issues have to be carried out.

Of course, another scenario might be considered: that ASEAN governments would be willing to adopt various strategies designed to produce a form of urbanization that relies more upon sustainability. Certainly current concerns about urban environmental pollution and water contamination are major considerations in the growth model of ASEAN urbanization that relies upon industrialization focused on the mega-urban regions. It is generally argued that policies emphasizing sustainability will have to incorporate greater efforts to hold population in rural areas, to decentralize economic activities in the urban hierarchy, and to toughen government environmental policies. While the majority of ASEAN governments are certainly well aware of these needs, there is only limited evidence that they will introduce comprehensive sustainable policies. For this reason we believe that the present patterns of urbanization are unlikely to change radically.

Several strong arguments seem to suggest that the present characteristics of ASEAN mega-urban regions will continue: the vigorous position of ASEAN in the East Asian and global economies; the fact that the process of structural change, particularly the shift from agriculture, is already well advanced; the fact that urbanization is occurring rapidly; and, finally, the fact that in the longer term, regional integration in the style of the European Union will strengthen the growth of mega-urban regions. These changes also favour the emergence of a multifunctional, polycentric settlement pattern in the mega-urban region, as Robinson recommends in Chapter 4. Central to this process will be the development of transactional space in the form of transportation and telecommunications, and the development of effective forms of urban management. Thus, land uses will still characteristically be mixed, but increasingly they will be incorporated in a more integrated framework.

What Are the Policy Implications of Emerging ASEAN Mega-Urban Regions?[8]

Assuming the scenario projected in the preceding section, there are important policy implications to be considered. These are dealt with in the various chapters and may be broadly characterized as: governmental, fiscal (i.e., tax base, infrastructure), environmental, and human resource development. The emerging ASEAN mega-urban regions epitomize both problems and challenges to development, but all the writers in this volume are committed to the idea that better planning and policy formation strategies can be developed and implemented for the regions.

The first policy issue facing the mega-urban regions concerns the major challenges for data collection and information gathering posed by rapid growth. It is clear that efforts should be made to develop systems of rapid data collection. In this respect, the use of aerial photographs for information on changing land use, within the framework of a suitable geographic information database, is important. Data can be checked using a system of rapid ground appraisal, already well developed in the methodology of 'rapid rural appraisal.' In addition, every effort should be made to gather demographic and economic data at the smallest spatial unit of analysis possible. This enables data to be aggregated at larger scales and helps identify emerging areas of rapid change. In view of the need to collect the information quickly, it may be necessary to use private or quasi-government research agencies that can move with speed to collect and analyze data. Furthermore, there is a need to evaluate carefully data that will be used for policy purposes.

The second major policy issue concerns the relationship between urban policy and general development policy. At the most macro levels of planning, there is a general view that urban policy should be embedded in general development policy and that the role of national governments is to promote a pattern of development in their mega-urban regions based on diversity and services as a means of maintaining a national competitive edge, assuring continuing economic development, and improving the quality of life for all inhabitants. While the development of rural areas should not be neglected, this investment should not be seen primarily as a means of preventing rural-urban migration. Within the mega-urban regions, governments should be encouraged to adopt policies that improve transportation networks and promote the polycentric spatial structure that is already emerging.

The third policy issue concerns the pressing need to improve infrastructure, housing, and transportation systems. The major issues surrounding the provision of adequate infrastructure are threefold: the financial requirements of such development; the need for effective land-pricing policies that could be used to fund infrastructure developments; and the need to determine which agencies would best deliver and administer infrastructure. While accepting that strong national leadership is needed, most of the authors in this volume thought that infrastructure services should be designed to recover costs and can in many cases be administered by agencies outside the government sector.

The fourth policy issue involves environmental problems resulting from rapid growth. Environmental regulations are clearly necessary to prevent water pollution. In fact, most ASEAN mega-urban regions have environmental regulations, but these have been continually avoided or circumvented. There is therefore a need to develop effective regulatory agencies with trained personnel. Calculating a polluter's monetary responsibility for damages, for example, is very complex and difficult to implement. It was also generally agreed within this book that this is an area in which sharing research and information among ASEAN countries would be very beneficial.

The fifth policy issue concerns the management, administrative, and governmental mechanisms for planning and managing mega-urban regions. There was general agreement in this text that these are inadequate. That there is no clear delineation of responsibility among national, metropolitan, city, and district governments and the private sector presents a serious problem. While there was no consensus among the authors represented here on how the responsibilities of each of these sectors could be organized, there was strong agreement that an administrative authority is needed on the mega-urban scale. The power of such an authority could range from coordination to clear responsibility for adminstration. Whatever the relationships among the various sectors, there should be flexibility, decentralization, and local involvement. The establishment of systems of mega-urban regional governance relies also upon adequate sources of financing, and the need for effective fiscal management of taxes was stressed. In order to accomplish these changes, priority must be given to a strategic planning and management approach. Change is so rapid in these extended metropolitan regions that 'top-down' comprehensive plans of the master plan variety are probably insufficiently flexible. Planning for the future of these areas involves indicative flexible planning, which can mould the future quality of life in the regions.

It is very clear that the emergence of mega-urban regions is posing major problems for the ASEAN national governments in terms of planning, adminstration, fiscal management, environmental degradation, and infrastructure provision. These developments also create a real challenge in human resource training. With the exception of Singapore, most ASEAN mega-urban regions lack trained personnel to undertake research and management. Although these needs can be met in part by local responses such as informal-sector garbage collectors and by private companies, the dimensions of these regions and their need for water, sewage removal, adequate housing, and suitable transportation networks, among other things, demand some form of administrative, governmental mechanism for planning and implementation at the regional level.

Conclusion

Fundamentally, policies for the mega-urban region must be based on a view of the region as a system and this involves developing a new 'mindset' with respect to urban development in ASEAN countries. Decision makers are still caught in a web of outmoded thought: the rural-urban dichotomy; small towns versus large urban centres; mega-urban regions as 'cancers' rather than catalysts in the process of economic growth. A sin qua non for making any progress in these regions is, above all, to get rid of these myths.

Developing this new mindset does involve careful generation of information based upon qualitative research designs that recognize the complexity of the urbanization process. Much of this volume is devoted to the pursuit of this objective. Its contributors are on the whole optimistic for the future of mega-urban centres. They are mostly wedded to the idea that planning interventions can make mega-urban regions more liveable. This makes imperative the need for greater understanding of the processes creating this growth and of the features of mega-urbanization. If this volume can stir the process of understanding, the inevitable mega-urban future of ASEAN will certainly see more sustainable and viable societies.

Notes

1 Several other volumes on urbanization have touched on this theme in the earlier 1980s but the rapidity of social and economic change in this decade makes their conclusions somewhat dated. See Hauser, Suits, and Ogawa (1985) and Fuchs, Jones, and Pernia (1987).

2 Not all commentators agreed that this path of development would necessarily lead to overall improvements in the quality of life of ASEAN's inhabitants. See Robinson, Hewison, and Higgott (1987).

3 It is interesting that proponents of industrial dispersal have often seen this locational policy as some evidence of strong state commitment to industrial relocation to peripheral regions. Location of industry outside the city core boundaries but within the functioning mega-urban region is defined as decentralization, however, not dispersal. See Chapter 4 for definitions of these terms.

4 Investigation of the various private-sector groups involved in the development of mega-urban regions could provide an important academic research follow-up to this volume. It would also have to include quasi-state/private agencies that have played a major role in urban development such as the Urban Development Authority in Malaysia.

5 See McGee (1990a) for a discussion of the employment situation in Third World cities.

6 This is despite overwhelming evidence that these mega-urban regions produce 40 to 60 per cent of gross national product in their countries.

7 The most frequently cited study arguing that the lower order of the urban centres will fill out as the urban transition occurs is Richardson's U-turn theory. However, it can be shown that this study is methodologically weak in that it takes rapidly growing urban centres occurring in mega-urban regions outside city boundaries as evidence of a shift away from larger urban centres, when in fact they are functionally part of the mega-urban region.

8 This section incorporates the results of the small-group discussions and recommendations made by participants in the International Conference on Managing the Mega-Urban Regions in ASEAN Countries: Policy Challenges and Responses, held in Bangkok, Thailand in 1992.

References

Ahmad, Mubariq. 1992. Economic Cooperation in the Southern Growth Triangle, An Indonesian Perspective. Paper presented at the International Symposium on Regional Cooperation and Growth Triangles in ASEAN, National University of Singapore, 23-4 April

Ahmad Sarji Bin Abdul Hamid. 1988. The Industrial Master Plan: Incentives for Manufacturing Activities. Professional Lecture Series, no. 5, Universiti Utara Malaysia

Aiken, S. 1981. Squatters and Squatter Settlements in Kuala Lumpur. *Geographical Review* 71:158-750

Akatsuka, Y., M. Kunishima, and M. Kitauchi. 1989. *Development and Management Profile of Transport Infrastructure in Asia and the Pacific.* Tokyo: Institute for International Cooperation (IIC), Japan International Cooperation Agency

Akbar, Roos, and Krishna Noor Pribadi. 1992. Bandung and Its Region. Paper presented at the Workshop on Metropolitan and Regional Planning and Development, Bangkok, Thailand, 29 June-4 July

Alonso, William. 1971. The Economics of Urban Size. *Papers and Proceedings of the Regional Science Association* 26:67-83

Andersson, A. 1990. The Emerging Global Network of C-regions. In *Cosmo Creative '90: International Forum on Logistical Development and Its Regional Cooperation in Osaka – Towards a Cosmo Creative City*, 57-61. Osaka: Osaka Prefectural Government

Angel S., and P. Amtapunth. 1987. The Low-Cost Rental Housing Market in Bangkok, 1987. In *The Land and Housing Markets in Bangkok: Strategies for Public Sector Participation*, by PADCO/NHA/ADB. Vol. 2, pp. 4.1-4.26. Manila: Asian Development Bank

Angel, S., and S. Chuated. 1990. The Down-Market Trend in Housing Production in Bangkok, 1980-1987. *Third World Planning Review* 12:1-20

Angel S., and S. Pornchokchai. 1987. The Informal Land Subdivision Market in Bangkok. In *The Land and Housing Markets in Bangkok: Strategies for Public Sector Participation*, by PADCO/NHA/ADB. Vol. 2, pp. 4.1-4.26. Manila: Asian Development Bank

Archer, R.W. 1987. The Possible Use of Urban Land Pooling/ Readjustment for the Planned Development of Bangkok. *Third World Planning Review* 9(3):235-44

Ard-Am, Orathai. 1991. City Background Paper: Bangkok. Presented at the International Meeting and Workshop on Urban Community-Based Environmental Management in Asia, Institute for Population and Social Research, Mahidol University Bangkok, 22-5 October

Armstrong, W., and T.G. McGee. 1985. *Theatres of Accumulation.* London: Methuen

Arnold, F., and Suwanlee Piampiti. 1984. Female Migration in Thailand. In *Women in the Cities of Asia: Migration and Urban Adaptation*, edited by J.T. Fawcett, Siew-Ean Khoo, and P.C. Smith, 143-64. Boulder, CO: Westview Press

Ashakul, Teera. 1990. Interim Report on Urban Population, Employment Distribution and Settlement Patterns. Unpublished report, Thailand Development Research Institute, Bangkok

Ashakul, Teera, and Charuna Ashakul. 1988. Economic Analysis of Decentralization and Urbanization in Thailand. Unpublished report, Thailand Development Research Institute, Bangkok

Asian Development Bank. 1986. *Statistical Indicators*. Manila: Asian Development Bank

–. 1991. *Asian Development Outlook*. Manila: Asian Development Bank

–. 1992. *Southeast Asian Regional Transport Survey*. 3 vols. Prepared by Arthur D. Little Inc. and Associated Consultants. Singapore: Asian Development Bank

Asian Development Bank and Economic Development Institute. 1991. *The Urban Poor and Basic Infrastructure Services in Asia and the Pacific*. Manila: Asian Development Bank

Asian Institute of Technology, Urban Planning Workshop. 1991. *Proposed Development Plan for Nava Nakorn: An Academic Exercise*, Course no. HS 12. Bangkok: Asian Institute of Technology, Human Settlements Development Division

Association of Consulting Engineers of Canada. 1992. *Code of Consulting Engineering Practice*. Toronto: Association of Consulting Engineers of Canada

Bahl, Roy W., and Johannes F. Linn. 1992. *Urban Finance in Developing Countries*. New York: Oxford University Press

Bandung Institute of Technology. 1991. Peranan Pusat-Pusat Perkenbangan Wilayah Dalam Persebaren Penduduk. Unpublished report

–. 1992. Rencana Pengembangan Lippo City. Unpublished report

Bangkok Post. 1991. *1991 Mid-Year Economic Review*. Bangkok: Bangkok Post

Bank Negara Malaysia. 1990. *Annual Report 1990*. Kuala Lumpur: Dicetak Oleh Percetaken Kum San Bhd

Bank Indonesia. Selected years. *Financial Statistics*, Jakarta

Bartone, Carl R. 1989. Urban Management and the Environment in Developing Country Cities: Priorities for Action. Paper presented at the meeting on Cities, the Mainspring of Economic Development in Developing Countries, Lille, France, 6-10 November

–. 1990. Water Quality and Urbanization in Latin America. *Water International* 15:3-14

Bartone, Carl R., J. Bernstein, and J. Leitman. 1992. *Managing the Environmental Challenge of Mega-Urban Regions*. Washington, DC: Urban Development Division, World Bank

Batten, D.F. 1990. Network Cities versus Central Places: Building a Creative Cosmo-creative Constellation. In *Cosmo Creative '90: International Forum on Logistical Development and its Regional Cooperation in Osaka – Towards a Cosmo Creative City*, 83-5. Osaka: Osaka Prefectural Government

Bello, Walden, and Stephanie Rosenfeld. 1990. Dragons in Distress: The Crisis of the NICs. *World Policy Journal* (summer):431-67

Berkes, Fikret. 1992. Application of Environmental Economics to Development: The Institutional Dimension. Presented at the Workshop on Ecological Economics, Sustainable Development and Southeast Asia, Institute for Research on the Environment and the Economy, University of Ottawa, 7-10 November

Biggs, T., P. Brimble, D. Snodgrass, and M. Murray. 1990. *Rural Industry and Employment Study: A Synthesis Report*. Bangkok: Thailand Development Research Institute

Birdsall, Nancy, and David Wheeler. 1992. Trade Policy and Industrial Pollution in Latin America: Where Are the Pollution Havens? Unpublished ms for the World Bank, Washington, DC

Biro Kota Statistik Pusat (BKSP), Jabotabek. 1992. The City Management in Jabotabek Region. Paper presented to the Seminar on Metropolitan Management Based on Development Cooperation, Surabaya, 5-7 November

Biro Pusat Statistik. 1990. *Statistical Yearbook of Indonesia 1990*. Jakarta: Government of Indonesia

–. Various years. *Indonesia Financial Statistics*. Jakarta: Government of Indonesia

–. Various years. *Statistical Report on Visitor Arrivals to Indonesia*. Jakarta: Government of Indonesia

Black, J., and P. Rimmer. 1992. *Sydney's Transport: Contemporary Issues, 1988-1992*. Current Issues Background Paper. Sydney: New South Wales Parliamentary Library

Bourne, L.S. 1989. Are New Urban Forms Emerging? Empirical Tests. *Canadian Geographer*

33(4):312-28

–. 1991. Recycling Urban Systems. *Economic Geography* 67(3):185-209

–. 1995. Urban Systems in an Era of Global Restructuring: Expanding the Research Agenda. Unpublished paper

Brennan, E.M. 1990. Mega-City Management and Innovation Strategies: Regional Views. Paper presented at the Symposium on the Mega-City and the Future: Population Growth and Policy Responses, Tokyo, 22-5 October

–. 1991. The Issue of Mega-Scale. Paper presented at Mega-Cities Project 1991 coordinators' meeting, Delhi, 28 October-1 November

–. 1992. The Mega-Cities: Environmental Issues. Paper presented at 1992 annual meeting of the American Association of the Advancement of Science, Chicago, 8-12 February

–. Forthcoming. Urban Land and Housing Issues Facing the Third World. In *Third World Urbanization and Development Policies,* edited by John D. Kasarda and Allan M. Parnell. Newbury Park, CA: Sage Publications

Brennan, E.M., and H.W. Richardson. 1989. Megacity Characteristics, Problems and Policies. *International Regional Science Review* 12(2):117-29

Bronger, Dirk. 1985. Metropolitanization as a Development Problem of Third World Countries: A Contribution towards a Definition of the Concept. *Applied Geography and Development* 26:71-97

Brotchie, John, Peter Newton, Peter Hall, and Peter Nijkamp. 1985. *The Future of Urban Form.* London: Croom Helm

Brunn, Stanley D., and Jack F. Williams. 1983. *Cities of the World: World Regional Urban Development.* New York: Harper and Row

Camp, Sharon. 1991. *Cities: Life in the 100 Largest Metropolitan Areas.* Washington, DC: Population Crisis Committee

Canadian Bankers Association. 1991. *Sustainable Capital: The Effect of Environmental Liability in Canada on Borrowers, Lenders and Investors.* Ottawa: Canadian Bankers Association

Canadian Chemical Producers' Association (CCPA). 1985. *The Canadian Chemical Producers' Association's Responsible Care Initiative.* Ottawa: CCPA

Canadian Engineering Qualifications Board. 1992. *Code of Ethics, and Definition of Practice of Professional Engineering.* Ottawa: Canadian Engineering Qualifications Board

Canadian Institute of Chartered Accountants (CICA). 1992. *The Environmental Handbook for Business and Professionals.* Toronto: CICA

Castells, M. 1989. Social Dimension of Industrialization in ASEAN Countries. Nagoya: United Nations Centre for Regional Development

Champion, Anthony G., ed. 1989. *Counterurbanization: The Changing Pace and Nature of Population Deconcentration.* London: Edward Arnold

Chandler, Tertius, and G. Fox. 1974. *3,000 Years of Urban Growth.* New York and London: Academic Press

Changani, A.S. 1976. Industrial Workers Housing: A Case Study of Industrial Sites in Bangkok, Thailand. MSc thesis, Asian Institute of Technology, Bangkok

Cheema, Shabbir. 1986. *Reaching the Urban Poor.* Boulder, CO: Westview Press

Cherunilam, Francis. 1984. *Urbanization in Developing Countries.* Bombay: Himalaya Publishing House

Chi Seck Choo, and M. Taylor. 1986. Business Organizations, Labour Demand and Industrialization in Malaysia. In *Industrialization and Labour Force Processes: A Case Study of Peninsular Malaysia,* edited by T.G. McGee, 141-77. Canberra: Australian National University

Chia Siow Yue and Lee Tsao Yuan. 1992. Subregional Economic Zones: A New Motive Force in Asia-Pacific Development. Paper presented at the 20th Pacific Trade and Development Conference, Washington, DC, 10-12 September

Chng Meng Khg. 1989. Singapore and Johor State, Malaysia: A Case of Cross Border Regional Development. Nagoya: United Nations Centre for Regional Development

Clark, Giles. 1991. Urban Management in Developing Countries. *Cities* (May):79

Clausen, A.W. 1984. *Population Growth and Social and Economic Development.* Washington, DC: World Bank

Cohen, M., J. English, and H. Brookfield. 1977. Functional Diversity at the Base of the Urban System in Peninsular Malaysia. *Journal of Tropical Geography* 45:12-25

Concannon, T.A.L. 1955. A New Town in Malaya: Petaling Jaya, Kuala Lumpur. *Malayan Journal of Tropical Geography* 5:39-43

Culpin Planning. 1993. *Jabotabek Development Plan (Revision).* Jakarta: Culpin

Dapice, David, and Frank Flatters. 1989. Thailand: Prospects and Perils in the Global Economy. Paper presented at the 1989 Thailand Development Research Institute Year-end Conference on Thailand in the International Economic Community, Ambassador City Jomtien, Thailand, 16-17 December

David, Cristina C. 1983. Economic Policies and Philippine Agriculture. Philippine Institute of Development Studies Working Paper Series, no. 83-02, Manila

Davidson, F. 1991. Gearing up for Effective Management of Urban Development. *Cities* (May):121-33

de Guzman, Raul. 1989. Decentralization as a Strategy for Redemocratization in the Philippine Political System. Unpublished paper, University of Philippines, Manila

Demographic Research and Development Foundation and Commission on Population-NCR. 1992. *Metropolitan Manila Profiles.* Manila: Demographic Research and Development Foundation

Douglass, Mike. 1984. National Urban Development Strategy Scenarios. National Urban Development Strategy Project 1, Jakarta. Mimeographed

–. 1988a. The Future of the Cities of the Pacific Rim. In Vol. 2 of *Pacific Rim Cities in the World Economy: Comparative Urban and Community Research,* edited by M.P. Smith, 9-66. New Brunswick: Transaction Publications

–. 1988b. Transnational Capital and Urbanization of the Pacific Rim: An Introduction. *International Journal of Urban and Regional Research* 12(3):343-55

–. 1989a. The Future of Cities on the Pacific Rim. Discussion Paper no. 3, Department of Urban and Regional Planning, University of Hawaii, Honolulu

–. 1989b. The Environmental Sustainability of Development: Coordination, Incentives and Political Will in Land Use Planning of the Jakarta Metropolitan Region. Working paper no. 12, Department of Urban and Regional Planning, University of Hawaii, Honolulu

–. 1990. Regional Inequalities and Regional Policy in Thailand: An International Comparative Perspective. Unpublished paper, Thailand Development Research Institute and National Economic and Social Development Board, Bangkok

–. 1991a. *Urban and Regional Development Policy for the 7th Five-Year National Plan in Thailand; Final Report for TDRI/NESDB Bangkok.* Bangkok: Thailand Development Research Institute and National Economic and Social Development Board

–. 1991b. Transnational Capital and the Social Construction of Comparative Advantage in Southeast Asia. *Southeast Asian Journal of Social Science* 19(1 and 2):14-43

–. 1991c. Planning for Environmental Sustainability in the Extended Jakarta Metropolitan Region. In *The Extended Metropolis: Settlement Transition in Asia,* edited by N. Ginsburg, B. Koppel, and T.G. McGee, 239-74. Honolulu: University of Hawaii Press

–. 1992a. The 'New' Tokyo Story. In *Japanese Cities in the World Economy,* edited by K. Fujita and R.C. Hill, 83-119. Philadelphia: Temple University Press

–. 1992b. Global Opportunities and Local Challenges for Regional Economics. *Regional Development Dialogue* 13(2):3-21

–. 1993a. Urban Poverty and Policy Alternatives in Asia. In *State of Urbanization in Asia and the Pacific 1993,* 4.1-4.87. Bangkok: United Nations Economic Commission for Asia and the Pacific

–. 1993b. Socio-political and Spatial Dimensions of Korean Industrial Transformation. *Journal of Contemporary Asia* 23(2):149-72

Dowall, D.E. 1992. A Second Look at the Bangkok Land and Housing Market. *Urban Studies* 29(1):25-38

Dowall, E. David, and Ballobh Kritayanavaj. 1987. Northern Corridor Land-and-Housing Project Feasibility Study. In *The Land and Housing Markets of Bangkok,* by PADCO/NHA/ADB. Vol. 2, pp. 8.1-8.8. Manila: Asian Development Bank

Dowall, David, and P. Alan Treffeisen. 1991. Spatial Transformation in Cities of the Developing World: Multinucleation and Land-Capital Substitution in Bogata, Colombia. *Regional Science and Urban Economics* 21:201-24

Drakakis-Smith, David, and Chris Dixon. 1991. *Growth and Development in Pacific Asia.* London: Routledge

Duncan, Otis Dudley. 1967. *Metropolis and Region.* Baltimore: John Hopkins Press

Edwards, J.L., and J.L. Schofer. 1975. *Relationships between Transportation Energy Consumption and Urban Structure: Results of Simulation Studies.* Minneapolis, MN: Department of Civil and Mineral Engineering

Erickson, Rodney A. 1986. Multinucleation in Metropolitan Economics. *Annals of the Association of American Geographers* 76(3):331-46

Esho Hideki. 1985. A Comparison of Foreign Direct Investment for India, S. Korea, and Taiwan by Size, Region and Industry. *Journal of International Economic Studies* 1(March):1-32

Eskelund, Gunnar. 1992. *Demand Management in Environmental Protection: Fuel Taxes and Air Pollution in Mexico City.* Washington, DC: World Bank, Country Economics Department

Ex Corporation. 1993a. *Japan's Experience in Urban Environmental Management.* Tokyo: Ex Corporation

–. 1993b. *Case Study Report of the Three Subject Cities: Yokohama, Osaka, Kitakyushu.* Tokyo: Ex Corporation

Fairclough, Gordon. 1992. Fields to Factories: Changing Employment Patterns Help Unions. *Far Eastern Economic Review* 5(November):22-4

Firman, Tommy. 1992. The Spatial Pattern of Urban Population Growth in Java, 1980-1990. *Bulletin of Indonesian Economic Studies* 28(2):95-109

Fisher, C.A. 1966. *South-east Asia, A Social, Political and Economic Geography.* 2nd ed. London: Methuen

Foo Tuan Seik. 1992a. The Provision of Low-Cost Housing by Private Developers in Bangkok: The Result of an Efficient Market? *Urban Studies* 29(7):1137-46

–. 1992b. *Low-Cost Condominiums: A Viable Alternative for Housing the Urban Poor? A Case Study in the Northern Corridor of Bangkok.* Bangkok: Asian Institute of Technology

Forstall, Richard, and Victor Jones. 1970. Selected Demographic, Economic and Governmental Aspects of the Contemporary Metropolis. In *Metropolitan Problems: International Perspectives and a Search for Comprehensive Solutions,* edited by Simon Miles, 3-69. Metropolitan Studies Series. Toronto, London and Sydney: Methuen

Friedmann, John. 1986. The World City Hypothesis. *Development and Change* 17:69-83

Frisbie, W. Parker, and John Kasarda. 1988. Spatial Processes and Change. In *Handbook of Sociology,* edited by N. Smelser, 629-66. Newbury Park, CA: Sage Publications

Fuchs, R.J., E. Brennan, J. Chamie, F.C. Lo, and J.I. Uitto, eds. 1994. *Mega-City Growth and the Future.* Tokyo, New York, and London: United Nations University Press

Fuchs, R.J., G.W. Jones, and E.M. Pernia, eds. 1987. *Urbanization and Urban Policies in Pacific Asia.* Boulder, CO, and London, UK: Westview Press

Furedy, Christine. 1992. Garbage: Exploring Non-Conventional Options in Asian Cities. *Environment and Urbanization* 4(2):42-61

Furnivall, J.S. 1939. *Netherlands India, A Study of the Plural Economy.* Cambridge: Cambridge University Press

Gakenheimer, Ralph, and Carlos H.J. Brando. 1987. Infrastructure Standards. In *Shelter, Settlement and Development,* edited by Lloyd Rodwin, 132-50. Boston: Allen and Unwin

Ganesan, N. 1992. Conceptualizing Regional Economic Cooperation: Perspectives from Political Science. Paper presented at the Conference on Regional Cooperation and Growth Triangles in ASEAN, National University of Singapore, 23-4 April

Gardiner, Peter. 1990. Urban Population in Indonesia: Future Trends. Paper presented at the Workshop on Spatial Development in Indonesia: Reviews and Prospects, sponsored by the Ministry of Education and Culture, Republic of Indonesia, and the University of Indonesia

Gibb, A. 1984. Tertiary Urbanization: The Agriculture Market Center as a Consumption-Related Phenomenon. *Regional Development Dialogue* 5(1):110-39

Gilbert, A. Third World Cities: Housing, Infrastructure and Servicing. *Urban Studies* 29(3/4):435-60

Ginsburg, N. 1991a. Extended Metropolitan Regions in Asia: A New Spatial Paradigm. In *The Extended Metropolis: Settlement Transition in Asia,* edited by N. Ginsburg, B. Koppel, and T.G. McGee, 26-45. Honolulu: University of Hawaii Press

–. 1991b. Preface to *The Extended Metropolis: Settlement Transition in Asia,* edited by N. Ginsburg, B. Koppel, and T.G. McGee, xiii-xviii. Honolulu: University of Hawaii Press.

Ginsburg, Norton, Bruce Koppel, and T.G. McGee. 1991. *The Extended Metropolis: Settlement Transition in Asia.* Honolulu: University of Hawaii Press

Goh Tian Sui. 1992. Kuala Lumpur/Klang Valley Development Scene. Paper presented at the Malaysian Property Seminar, Johor Bahru

Goldstein, Sidney. Forthcoming. Demographic Issues and Data: Needs for Mega-City Research. *Third World Urbanization and Development Policies,* edited by John D. Kasarda and Allan Parnell. Newbury Park, CA: Sage Publications

Gordon, P., A. Kumar, and H.W. Richardson. 1989. The Influence of Metropolitan Spatial Structure on Commuting Time. *Journal of Urban Economics* 26:138-51

Gordon, P., H.W. Richardson, and H.L. Wong. 1986. The Distribution of Population and Employment in a Polycentric City: The Case of Los Angeles. *Environment and Planning A* 18:161-73

Gorynski, J., and Z. Rybicki. 1970. The Function Metropolis and Systems of Government. In *Metropolitan Problems: A Search for Comparative Solutions*, edited by Simon Miles, 291-317. Toronto: Methuen Publications

Gottmann, Jean. 1961. *Megalopolis: The Urbanized Northeastern Seaboard of the United States.* New York: Twentieth Century Fund, Kraus International Publications

–. 1976. Megalopolitan Systems around the World. *Ekistics* 41(243):109-13

Grandstaff, Somluckrat. 1990. The Role of Demand in Provincial Industrialization. Bangkok: Thailand Development Research Institute

Gras, N.S.B. 1926. The Rise of the Metropolitan Community. In *The Urban Community,* edited by E.W. Burgess, 183-91. Chicago: University of Chicago Press

Greenberg, Charles. 1992. Angelic Scatter: The Outer Cities of Los Angeles and Bangkok. Unpublished paper

–. 1994. Region Based Urbanization in Bangkok's Extended Periphery. PhD dissertation, University of British Columbia

Gullick, J.M. 1955. Kuala Lumpur, 1880-1895. *Journal of the Malayan Branch of the Royal Asiatic Society* 28:7-172

Habibie, B.J. 1992. Technology and the Singapore-Johor-Riau Growth Triangle. Dinner address presented at the Tripartite Meeting and Seminar on Economic Development on the Growth Triangle and Its Environmental Impact, organized by the Institution of Engineers, Turi Beach Hotel, Batam Island, Indonesia, 8 May

Hackenberg, Robert, and Kua Wangboonsin. 1990. Labour Force Shortages in Thailand and Surpluses in Neighbouring Countries: Recent Trends and Implications for the Future. Paper presented at the Seminar on Population and Labour Force of the Suwannaphum Region, Institute of Population Studies, Chulalongkorn University, Bangkok, 18 September

Haines, Valerie A. 1986. Energy and Urban Form: A Human Ecological Critique. *Urban Affairs Quarterly* 21(3):337-53

Hamer, Andrew. 1990. Economic Impacts of Third World Mega Cites: Is Size the Issue? Paper presented at the Symposium on the Mega-City and the Future Population Growth and Policy Response, United Nations University, Tokyo, 22-5 October

Harvey, D. 1989. *The Condition of Postmodernity.* Oxford: Basil Blackwell

Hauser, Philip M., and Robert Gardner. 1982. *Population and the Urban Future*. Albany: State University of New York Press, in cooperation with the United Nations Fund for Population Activities

Hauser, Philip M., Daniel B. Suits, and Naohiro Ogawa, eds. 1985. *Urbanization and Migration in ASEAN Development*. Tokyo: National Institute for Research Advancement

Herrin, A.N., and E.M. Pernia. 1987. Factors Influencing the Choice of Location, Local and Foreign Firms in the Philippines. *Regional Studies* 21(6):531-41

Herzog, L. 1991. Cross-National Urban Structure in the Era of Global Cities: The US-Mexico Transfrontier Metropolis. *Urban Studies* 28(4):519-33

Hettige, Hemanala, Robert E.G. Lucas, and David Wheeler. 1992. The Toxic Intensity of Industrial Production: Global Patterns, Trends, and Trade Policy. Unpublished ms for the World Bank, Washington, DC

Hill, Hal. 1990. Indonesia's Industrial Transformation: Part I. *Bulletin of Indonesian Economic Studies* 26(2):79-120

Hirshmann, A. 1960. *The Strategy of Economic Development*. New Haven, CT: Yale University Press

House, W.J. 1984. Nairobi's Informal Sector: Dynamic Entrepreneurs or Surplus Labour? *Economic Development and Cultural Change* 32(2):276-302

Howatson, A.C. 1990. *Toward Proactive Environmental Management: Lessons from Canadian Corporate Experience*. Report 65-90. Ottawa: Conference Board of Canada

–. 1991. *Managing Corporate Change for Sustainable Development*. Ottawa: Conference Board of Canada

Hoyt, Homer, and Jerome P. Pickard. 1969. The World's Million-Population Metropolises. In *The City in Newly Developing Countries: Readings on Urbanism and Urbanization*, edited by Gerald Breese, 198-204. Engelwood Cliffs, NJ: Prentice-Hall

Hoyt, J.G. 1990. A 2040 Airport – One Fifty Year Conjecture. In *Airports into the 21st Century: Proceedings*, 231-41. Hong Kong: University of Engineers

Hymer, Stephen. 1972. The Multinational Corporation and the Law of Uneven Development. In *Economics and World Order from the 1970s to 1990s*, edited by J. Bhagwati, 113-40. New York and London: Collier Macmillan. Reprinted in *International Firms and Modern Imperialism*, edited by Hugo Radice, 37-62. Harmondsworth, UK: Penguin 1979

Ida Ayu Indira Dharmapatni. 1991. Jakarta Metropolitan Region: Issues, Problems and Policies for Population Distribution and Environmental Management. Paper presented to the Twenty-second Summer Seminar on Population, East-West Population Institute, East-West Center, Honolulu, 3 June-5 July

Imran, Bulkin. 1992. The Dynamics of Urbanization in Indonesia from 1971-1990. MA thesis, Cornell University

International Civil Aviation Organization (ICAO). 1984. *On Flight Origin and Destination Year and Quarter Ending 31 March 1983, No. 301*. Montreal: ICAO

–. 1991. *On Flight Origin and Destination Year and Quarter Ending 31 March 1990, No. 378*. Montreal: ICAO

International Labour Organization. n.d. The Urban Informal Sector in Metro Manila: A Macroperspective. Unpublished report

International Urban Research. 1959. *The World's Metropolitan Areas*. Berkeley, CA: Institute of International Studies, University of California

Iqbal, Javaid. 1990. Verification of the Desakota Concept, Assessment of Land Use and Environmental Problems and Related Policy Implications: Case Study of the Northern Corridor, Bangkok, Thailand. Unpublished paper

Isarankura, Watana. 1990. Emerging Urban Rural Linkages: The Bangkok Metropolitan Region. *Regional Development Dialogue* 11(2):56-82

Jabotabek Advisory Team. 1981. *Jabotabek Metropolitan Development Plan. Executive Summary*. Implementation report no 1/1. Jakarta: Directorate General of Cipta Karya Ministry of Public Works

Jacobs, Jane. 1961. *The Death and Life of Great American Cities*. New York: Random House

Jacobson, Leo, and Ved Prakash, eds. 1974. *Metropolitan Growth: Public Policy for South and Southeast Asia*. New York: Sage Publications and John Wiley and Sons

Japan International Cooperation Agency (JICA). 1990a. *Upper Central Region Study*. Bangkok: National Economic and Social Development Board

–. 1990b. *The Master Plan Study on the Project Calabarzon*. Manila: Department of Trade and Industry

–. 1991. *The Master Plan Study on the Project Calabarzon Interim Report 2*. Manila: Department of Trade and Industry

Jitsuchon, Somchai, and Chalongphob Sussangkarn. 1990. Thailand's Medium-Term Growth Opportunities and Their Distributional Impacts. Unpublished report, Thailand Development Research Institute, Bangkok

Kalbermatten, John M., and Richard N. Middleton. 1991. Future Directions in Water Supply and Waste Disposal. Kalbermatten Associates

Kamil Yuhanis, Mari Pangestu, and Christina Fredricks. 1991. A Malaysian Perspective. In *Growth Triangle: The Johor-Singapore-Riau Experience*, edited by Lee Tsao Yuan, 39-74. Singapore: Institute of Southeast Asian Studies

Kammeier, H. Detlef. 1984. A Review of the Development and Land Use Problems in Bangkok. Working Paper no. 13, Human Settlements Development Division, Asian Institute of Technology, Bangkok

Kaothien, Utis, and Witit Rachatatanun. 1991. *Urban Poverty in Thailand: Review of Past Trends and Policy Formation, Bangkok*. Bangkok: Government of Thailand, National Economic and Social Development Board, Urban Planning Division

Kellerman, Aharon. 1993. *Telecommunications and Geography*. London: Belhaven Press

Kelley, Allen C., and J.G. Williamson. 1984. *What Drives Third World City Growth? A Dynamic General Equilibrium Approach*. Princeton: Princeton University Press

Kim Ji Hong and Park Eul Yong. 1991. Foreign Direct Investment for Industrial Restructuring. Unpublished report, Korean Development Institute, Seoul

Kitauchi, M., and Y. Akatsuka. 1989. *Development and Management Profile of Transport Infrastructure in Asia and the Pacific (Supplement)*. Tokyo: Japan International Cooperation Agency

Kobayashi, K., and N. Okada. 1989. Technological Substitution between Telecom-munications and Transportation in Production. In *Transport Policy, Management and Technology towards 2001: Selected Proceedings of the Fifth World Conference on Transport Research, Yokohama 1989*. Vol. 2, pp. 241-55. Ventura: Western Periodicals

Korea, Republic of. 1991. *Korea Statistical Yearbook 1976-1990*. Seoul: Bureau of Statistics, Economic Planning Board

Krongkaew, Medhi. 1991. Review of Investment Expenditures on Infrastructure during the 6th Plan Period, 1987-1991. Background Report no. 4-2. Bangkok: Thailand Development Research Institute

Kumar, Sree, and Lee Tsao Yuan. 1991. A Singapore Perspective. In *Growth Triangle: The Johor-Singapore-Riau Experience*, edited by Lee Tsao Yuan, 3-36. Singapore: Institute of Southeast Asia Studies and Institute of Policy Studies

Kung, Shiann-Far. 1986. Growth Relation between the Urban Center and Its Hinterland: A Case Study of Surat Thani in Southern Thailand. Bangkok: Asian Institute of Technology, Human Settlements Division

Ladavalya, Bhansoon, and Vasant Siripool. 1988. The Impact of the Regional City Development Project upon Outlying Areas: The Chiang Mai Case. Social Research Institute, Chiang Mai University, Chiang Mai

Laquian, Aprodicio A. 1991. Urbanization in China. In *Population and Development Planning in China*, edited by Wang Jiye and Terence Hull, 235-63. Sydney: Allen and Unwin

–. 1993. Metro Manila, The Exceptional City. Unpublished paper, Centre for Human Settlements, University of British Columbia

Lee Boon Thong. 1974. Urban Growth and the Development of Residential Areas. *Geographical Bulletin* (Malaysian Geographical Association) 1(1):9-27

–. 1976. Patterns of Urban Residential Segregation. *Malayan Journal of Tropical Geography* 43:41-8

–. 1983. Planning and the Kuala Lumpur Metropolis. *Asian Journal of Public Admin-istration* 5:76-86

–. 1985. The Urbanization Process in Malaysia: Intervention Strategies and Neglected Issues. Paper presented at the International Conference on Asian Urbanization: Processes, Problems and Prospects, Akron, OH, March

–. 1987. New Towns in Malaysia: Development and Planning Issues. In *New Towns in East and South-East Asia: Planning and Development,* edited by D.R. Phillips and A.G.O. Yeh, 153-69. Kuala Lumpur: Oxford University Press

–. 1991. Industrialization and Its Implications on Urban Growth and Development. Paper presented at the World Town Planning Day seminar, Vision 2020: Innovative Planning and Development of Urban Centres, Kuala Lumpur

–. 1992a. Globalization and the Urban System in Malaysia. Paper presented at the workshop The Asian Pacific Urban System: Towards 21st Century, Chinese University of Hong Kong, 11-13 February

–. 1992b. The Growth of the Kuala Lumpur Region, 1960-1990. Paper presented at the workshop The Asia-Pacific Urban System: Towards the 21st Century, Chinese University of Hong Kong, 11-13 February

Lee Kyu Sik. 1988. Infrastructure Constraints on Industrial Growth in Thailand. International Urban Development Working Paper, WP#88-2, Urban Development Division, Planning and Research Staff, World Bank

Lee Tsao Yuan, ed. 1991. *Growth Triangle: The Johor-Singapore-Riau Experience.* Singapore: Institute of Southeast Asia Studies and Institute of Policy Studies

–. 1992. *Growth Triangles in ASEAN: Private Investment and Trade Opportunities Economic Brief.* Honolulu: Institute for Economic Development and Policy, East-West Center

Lee Yok-shiu F. 1992. Myths of Environmental Management and the Urban Poor. Unpublished paper, Environment and Policy Institute, Population Institute, East-West Center, Honolulu

Leinbach, T.R. 1989. Road and Rail Transport Systems. In *South-East Asian Transport: Issues in Development,* edited by T.R. Leinbach and Chia Lin Sien, 60-96. Singapore: Oxford University Press

Leinbach, T.R., and Chia Lin Sien, eds. 1989. *South-East Asian Transport: Issues in Development.* Singapore: Oxford University Press

Leitmann, Joseph. 1991. *Environmental Profile of Sao Paulo.* Washington, DC: World Bank

Lemon Group, Industrial Consultants. 1993. *Metropolitan Regional Structure Study.* Main Report and Interim Reports, Vol. 1, Sector studies 1 and 2. Bangkok: Office of the National Economical Social Development Board

Lewis, W.A. 1954. Economic Development and Unlimited Supplies of Labour. *Manchester School of Economic and Social Studies* 22(2):139-91

Lillywhite, Jack W. 1992. Infrastructure Privatization: A Viable Option for Improving Municipal Service. Paper presented for 13th Pacific Asian Congress of Municipalities, 19-22 July

Linn, Johannes F. 1979. Policies for Efficient and Equitable Growth of Cities in Developing Countries. World Bank Staff Working Paper no. 3, World Bank, Washington

–. 1983. *Cities in the Developing World: Policies for Their Equitable and Efficient Growth.* New York: Oxford University Press for the World Bank

Linn, Johannes F., and Deborah Wetzel. 1990. Financing Infrastructure in Developing Countries Mega-Cities. Paper presented at the Symposium on the Mega-City and the Future Population Growth and Policy Response, United Nations University, Tokyo, 22-5 October

Linnemann, P.D., and I.F. Megbolugbe. 1992. Housing Affordability: Myth or Reality. *Urban Studies* 29(3/4):369-92

Lipton, Michael. 1977. *Why Poor People Stay Poor: Urban Bias in Third World Development.* London: Temple Smith

McAndrew, John P. 1994. *Urban Usurpation from Friar Estates to Industrial Estates in a Philippine Hinterland.* Manila: Ateneo de Manila University Press

McGee, T.G. 1967. *The Southeast Asian City.* London: G. Bell and Son

–. 1982. Proletarianization, Industrialization and Urbanization in Asia: A Case Study of Malaysia. Flinders Asian Studies Lecture no. 13, Flinders University, Adelaide

–. 1986. Joining the Global Assembly Line: Malaysia's Role in the International Semi-Conductor Industry. In *Industrialization and Labour Force Processes: A Case Study of Peninsular Malaysia,* edited by T.G. McGee, 35-67. Canberra: Research School of Pacific Studies, Australian National University

–. 1987. The Urban Transition in Asia: The Emergence of New Regions of Economic Interaction in Asia. Paper prepared for the Only One Earth Forum, New York

–. 1988. Industrial Capital, Labour Force Formation and the Urbanization Process in Malaysia. *International Journal of Urban and Regional Research* 12(3):356-74

–. 1989a. Urbanisasi or Kotadesasi: The Emergence of New Regions of Economic Integration in Asia. In *Urbanization in Asia: Spatial Dimensions and Policy Issues,* edited by L. Ma, A. Noble, and A. Dutt, 93-110. Honolulu: University of Hawaii Press

–. 1989b. New Regions of Emerging Rural-Urban Mix in Asia: Implications for National and Regional Policy. Paper presented at the Seminar on Emerging Urban-Regional Linkages: Challenges for Industrialization, Employment and Regional Development, Bangkok, Thailand, 15-20 August

–. 1990a. Labour Force Change and Mobility in the Extended Metropolitan Regions of Asia. Paper prepared for the Symposium on the Mega-City and the Future: Population Growth and Policy Responses, Tokyo, 22-5 October

–. 1990b. Guest Editor's Introduction. *Regional Development Dialogue* 11(2):iii-ix

–. 1991. The Emergence of Desakota Regions in Asia: Expanding a Hypothesis. In *The Extended Metropolis: Settlement Transition in Asia,* edited by N. Ginsburg, B. Koppel, and T.G. McGee, 3-25. Honolulu: University of Hawaii Press

–. Forthcoming. The Urban Future of Vietnam. *Third World Planning Review*

McGee, T.G., and C. Greenberg. 1992. The Emergence of Extended Metropolitan Regions in ASEAN, 1960-1980: An Exploratory Outline. In *Regional Development and Change in Southeast Asia in the 1990's,* edited by Amara Pongsapich, Michael C. Howard, and Jacques Amyot, 133-62. Bangkok: Social Research Institute, Chulalongkorn University

McGee, T.G., and Lin Chusheng. 1991. Footprints in Space: The Production of Space in the Asian NICs 1950-1990. In *Growth and Development in Pacific Asia,* edited by David Drakakis-Smith and Chris Dixon, 128-51. London: Routledge

McGee, T.G., and W.D. McTaggart. 1967. *Petaling Jaya: A Socio-Economic Survey of a New Town in Selangor, Malaysia.* Pacific Viewpoint Monograph no. 2. Wellington, NZ: Victoria University of Wellington

McGee, T.G., and Om Mathur. 1993. Urbanization Trends: Patterns and Impacts. In *State of Urbanization in Asia and the Pacific 1993,* 1-66. New York: United Nations Economic and Social Commission for Asia and the Pacific

McGee, T.G., Kamal Salih, and Mei Ling Young. 1991. Silicon Island: Household Change in Penang State, Malaysia. Draft manuscript

McGee, T.G., and Y.M. Yeung. 1993. Urban Futures for Pacific Asia: Towards the 21st Century. In *Pacific Asia in the 21st Century,* edited by Yeung Yue-man, 47-67. Hong Kong: Chinese University Press

MacLeod, Scott, and T.G. McGee. 1992. Emerging Extended Metropolitan Regions in the Asia-Pacific Urban System: A Case Study of the Singapore-Johor-Riau Growth Triangle. Paper presented at the workshop The Asia-Pacific Urban System: Towards the 21st Century, Chinese University of Hong Kong, 11-13 February

Malaysia. 1985. *Medium and Long Term Industrial Master Plan Malaysia 1986-1995.* Malaysian Industrial Development Authority/United Nations Development Organization. Kuala Lumpur: Government of Malaysia

–. 1991a. Report on the Performance of the Manufacturing Sector in Malaysia, 1990. Unpublished report, Malaysian Industrial Development Authority, Kuala Lumpur

–. 1991b. *The Sixth Malaysia Plan 1991-1995*. Kuala Lumpur: Government Press

–. 1991c. *Second Outline Perspective Plan, 1991-2000*. Kuala Lumpur: National Printing Department

Malaysia, Department of Statistics. 1971. *Urban Conurbations – Population and Households in Ten Gazetted Towns and Their Adjoining Built-Up Areas*. Kuala Lumpur: Department of Statistics

–. Various years. *Monthly Statistical Bulletin*. Kuala Lumpur

–. Various months. *Malaysia Monthly Statistical Bulletin*. Kuala Lumpur

Malaysia, Tourism Promotion Board. 1992. *Malaysian Tourism Statistics Update, First Quarter 1992*. Kuala Lumpur: Pempena Consult Sdn Bnd

Malaysian Industrial Development Authority. 1990. *Statistics on the Manufacturing Sector in Malaysia 1985-1990*. Kuala Lumpur: Inventra Print Sdn Bnd

Malaysian Institute of Economic Research. 1989. *Johor Economic Plan 1990-2005 Final Report*. Kuala Lumpur: Malaysian Institute of Economic Research

Malpezzi, S., and S. Mayo. 1987. The Demand for Housing in Developing Countries. *Economic Development and Cultural Change* 35 (4):687-722

Manila Metropolitan Authority. 1992. *Draft Regional Development Plan*. Manila: Manila Metropolitan Authority

Manila Metropolitan Commission. 1985. *Development Trends*. Technical Paper no. 3. Manila: Manila Metropolitan Commission

–. Various dates. *Development Technical Papers*. Manila: Manila Metropolitan Commission

Marcussen, Lars. 1990. *Third World Housing in Social and Spatial Development: The Case of Jakarta*. Hampshire, UK: Gower Publishing Group

Mayo, S., A. Malpezzi, and D.J. Gross. 1986. Shelter Strategies for the Urban Poor in Developing Countries. Paper prepared for the annual meeting of the American Real Estate and Urban Economics Association, New York

Mayo, S., et al. 1989. Malaysia: The Housing Sector, Getting the Incentives Right. Report no. 7292-MA, Infrastructure Division, World Bank, Washington, DC

Midgeley, Peter. 1991. Transportation and Urban Development in the Pacific Rim. Paper presented at the 1991 congress of the Pacific Region Council on Urban Development, Vancouver, 6-9 October

Mitsui Research Institute (MRI). 1989. *PECC Triple T Project: JANPEC Study Group Report*. Vol. 1, *Transportation*. Prepared for the Japan National Committee for Pacific Economic Cooperation. Tokyo: Centre for Pacific Business Studies, MRI

Mutlu, S. 1990. Regional Disparities, Industry and Government Policy in Japan. Mimeograph

Narayanan, S., and L. Kimura. 1992. On Thai Women in the International Division of Labour. *Development and Change* 23(2):141-48

National Capital Planning Board. 1988. *Regional Plan: 2001, National Capital Region*. Delhi: National Capital Region Planning Board, Ministry of Urban Development, Government of India

National Economic and Development Authority (NEDA), Republic of the Philippines. 1990. *The Luzon Area Development Framework and Strategic Investment Program*. Manila: NEDA

National Economic and Social Development Board (NESDB). 1977. *Fourth National Economic and Social Development Plan 1977-1981*. Bangkok: NESDB

–. 1982. *Fifth National Economic and Social Development Plan 1982-1986*. Bangkok: NESDB

–. 1987. *Sixth National Economic and Social Development Plan 1987-1991. Summary*. Bangkok: NESDB

–. 1988. *National Income of Thailand*. Bangkok: NESDB

–. 1989. The Outlook for the Thai Economy. Unpublished report, Thailand Development Research Institute and National Economic and Social Development Board, Bangkok

–. 1991a. Problems and Urban Development Guideline. Paper presented at the Seminar on Urban Development Policies, Pattaya, 4 May. (In Thai)

–. 1991b. *The Southern Seaboard Development Project: Inception Report, March 1991*. Bangkok: Office of the Southern Seaboard Development Committee

–. 1991c. *National Urban Development Policy Framework*. Final Report, Vol. 1-2. Bangkok: National Economic and Social Development Board

–. 1992. *The Seventh National Economic and Social Development Plan 1992-1996*. Bangkok: National Economic and Social Development Board, Office of the Prime Minister

National Statistical Office. 1970. *1970 Population and Housing Census*. Bangkok: National Statistical Office

–. 1978-88. *Statistical Yearbook of Thailand*. Bangkok: National Statistical Office

–. 1988. *Report on the 1988 Household Socio-Economic Survey, Bangkok Metropolis, Nonthaburi, Pathum Thani and Samut Prakan*. Bangkok: National Statistical Office

–. 1990. *Preliminary Report 1990 Population and Housing Census*. Bangkok: National Statistical Office

National Urban Development Strategy Project (NUDS). 1985. *NUDS Final Report*. Report T2 3/3. Jakarta: Directorate of City and Regional Planning, Department of Public Works

Ng Chee Yuen and Wong Poh Kam. 1991. The Growth Triangle: A Market Driven Response. *Asia Club Papers 2*, 123-152. Tokyo: Asia Club

Ocampo, Romeo B., and Remigio D. Ocenar. 1985. Local Planning in the Philippines. *Local Government Bulletin* 18-20:12-19

Odlund, John. 1978. The Conditions for Multi-Center Cities. *Economic Geography* 54:234-44

Owen, D. 1992. *Green Reporting: Accounting and the Challenge of the Nineties*. London: Chapman and Hall, University and Professional Division

Owens, Susan. 1986. *Energy, Planning and Urban Form*. London: Pion

Pacheco, Margarita. 1992. Recycling in Bogata: Developing a Culture for Urban Sustainability. *Environment and Urbanization* 4(2):74-9

PADCO-LIF. 1990. Bangkok Land Market Assessment. Unpublished report, Bangkok

Paderanga, Cayetano. 1992. Emerging Mega Urban Regions in Asia: The Case of Metro Manila. Paper presented at the International Conference on Managing Mega-Urban Regions of ASEAN Countries: Challenges and Responses, Asian Institute of Technology, Bangkok, 30 November-3 December

–. 1988. *Leading Issues in Thailand's Development Transformation 1960-1990*. Bangkok: National Economic and Social Development Board.

Panayatou, Theodore, and Dhira Phantumvanit. 1991. *Environment and Development*. Bangkok: Thailand Development Research Institute

Pangestu, Mari. 1991. An Indonesian Perspective. In *Growth Triangle: The Johor-Singapore-Riau Experience*, edited by Lee Tsao Yuen, 75-115. Singapore: Institute of Southeast Asian Studies

Parker, Ronald Stephen. 1992. Vulnerability and Resiliency: Environmental Degradation in Major Metropolitan Areas of Developing Countries. In *Environmental Management and Urban Vulnerability*, edited by Alcira Kreimer and Mohan Munasinghe. Washington, DC: World Bank

Peerapun Wannasilpa and Siriwan Silapacharanan. 1992. The Patterns and Problems of Urban Development in Bangkok. Unpublished paper, Department of Urban and Regional Planning, Chulalongkorn University, Bangkok, June

Pendakur, V. Setty. 1986. *Urban Growth, Urban Poor and Urban Transport*. Vancouver: Centre for Human Settlements, University of British Columbia

–. 1989. The Elaboration of the Transportation System: The Why and How of Success. In *Management of Success: The Moulding of Modern Singapore*, edited by K. Sandhu and P. Wheatley. Singapore: Oxford University Press

–. 1992. Congestion Management, Non-Motorized Transport and Sustainable Cities. Paper presented at the Non-Motorized Transport Seminar, Washington, DC, 12 May.

Pendakur, V. Setty, R. Behbehani, and A. Armstrong-Wright. 1984. *Case Study of Singapore*. Document no. ENV/TE/84.11, July. Paris: Organization for European Community Development, Transport and Environment Directorate

Perlman, Janice K. 1990. Introduction: A Dual Strategy for Deliberate Social Change in Cities. *Cities* (February):4-15

Pernia, E.M. 1977. *Urbanization, Population Growth and Economic Development in the Philippines.* Westport, CT, and London, UK: Greenwood Press

–. 1992. Southeast Asia. In *Sustainable Cities: Urbanization and the Environment in International Perspective,* edited by R. Stren, R. White, and J. Whitney. Boulder, CO: Westview Press

Perry, Martin. 1991. The Singapore Growth Triangle: State, Capital and Labour at a New Frontier in the World Economy. *Singapore Journal of Tropical Geography* 12(2):139-51

Phantumvanit, Dhira, and Winai Liengcharernsit. 1989. Coming to Terms with Bangkok's Environmental Problems. Unpublished report, Thailand Development Research Institute, Bangkok

Philippines. 1992. *Report on Manila Metropolitan Authority.* Manila: Government of the Philippines

Philippines, Department of Trade and Industry/Japanese International Cooperation Agency. 1991. *The Master Plan: Study of the Project.* Calabarzon, Interim Report 2. Manila: Government of the Philippines

Philippines, National Statistics Office. 1992. *1990 Census of Population and Housing.* Various reports. Manila: Republic of the Philippines

Phisit Pakkasem. 1987. Thailand Country Paper. In *Urban Policy Issues,* edited by Asian Development Bank (ADB), 774-823. Manila: ADB

Porpora, D.V., M.H. Lim, and U. Prommas. 1989. The Role of Women in the International Division of Labour: The Case of Thailand. *Development and Change* 20(2):269-94

–. 1992. Reply to Narayanan and Kimura. *Development and Change* 23(2):149-53

Private Investment and Trade Opportunities – Philippines (PITO – P). 1992. *Framework Agreement on Enhancing ASEAN Economic Cooperation.* Manila: PITO – P.

Public Works Department (PWD). 1991. *Electronic Road Pricing.* Singapore: Ministry of National Development

Puslitbang PT Jasa Marga and Institut Technologi Bandung. 1992. Penelitian Manfaat Jalan Tol Ditinjau Dari Aspek Sosial Ekonomi Pada Ruas-Ruas Jakarta-Tangerang dan Jakarta-Cikampek. Draft final report

Ramos, Carlos P. 1991. *Calabarzon Master Plan: Issues and Implications.* Manila: Ramon Magsaysay Award Foundation

Rathje, William, and Cullen Murphy. 1992. *Rubbish: Archaeology of Garbage.* New York: Harper Collins

Rees, William E. 1992. Natural Capital in Relation to Regional/Global Concepts of Carrying Capacity. Paper presented at the Workshop on Ecological Economics, Sustainable Development and Southeast Asia, Institute for Research on the Environment and the Economy, University of Ottawa

Richardson, H.W. 1984. Towards a National Urban Development Strategy for Thailand. In *Equity with Growth? Planning Perspectives for Small Towns in Developing Countries,* edited by H. Detlef Kammeier and Peter J. Swan, 110-13. Bangkok: Asian Institute of Technology

–. 1988. Monocentric vs. Polycentric Models: The Future of Urban Economics in Regional Science. *Annals of Regional Science* 22(2):1-12

–. 1989a. Managing Metropolitan Growth and Development in Asia. *Review of Urban and Regional Development Studies* 1(2):3-17

–. 1989b. The Big, Bad City: Megacity Myth? In *Third World Planning Review* 11(4):355-72

–. 1990. Urban Development Issues in the Pacific Rim. *Review of Urban and Regional Development Studies* 2(January):44-63

Rietveld, J. Carlo. 1992. Municipal Water Supply and Sanitation: the Need for Innovation. Paper prepared for 13th PACOM Congress, 19-23 July

Rietveld, P. 1988. Urban Development Patterns in Indonesia. *Bulletin of Indonesian Economic Studies* 24(1):73-95

Rigg, J. 1991. *Southeast Asia: A Region in Transition.* London: Unwin, Hyman

Rimmer, P.J. 1986a. 'Look East!' The Relevance of Japanese Urban Planning and Technology to Southeast Asian Cities. *Transportation and Technology and Planning* 11:47-67

–. 1986b. *Rikisha to Rapid Rail Transit: Urban Public Transport Systems.* Sydney: Pergamon

–. 1988. Buses in Southeast Asian Cities: Privatisation without Deregulation. *Bus Deregulation and Privatisation: An International Perspective,* edited by J.S. Dodgson and N. Topham, 185-208. Aldershot: Avebury

–. 1990. Restructuring Transport Parastatals: Case Studies from Southeast Asia. In *Deregulation and Transport: Market Forces in the Modern World,* edited by P. Bell and P. Cloke, 156-82. London: David Fulton Publishers

–. 1991a. The Internationalisation of the Japanese Freight Forwarding Industry. *Asian Geographer* 10(1):17-38

–. 1991b. A Tale of Four Cities: Competition and Bus Ownership in Bangkok, Jakarta, Manila and Singapore. *Transportation and Technological Change* 15:231-52

–. 1991c. The Emerging Infrastructural Arena in Pacific Asia since the Early 1970s. *Proceedings of the Japan Society of Civil Engineers* No. 431/IV-15, pp.1-17

–. 1991d. Megacities, Multilayered Networks and Development Changes in the Pacific Economic Zone: The Japanese Ascendancy. Keynote address at the Third Annual Conference on Transport and Development in the Pacific Rim, Vancouver, 6-10 October

–. Forthcoming. *International Transport and Communications between Pacific Asia's Emerging World Cities.* Tokyo: United Nations University

–, ed. 1987. *The ASEAN-Australian Transport Interchange.* Canberra: National Centre for Development Studies, Australian National University

Rimmer, P.J., and G.C. Cho. 1989. Locational Stress on Kuala Lumpur's Urban Fringe. In *Transport Policy, Management and Technology towards 2001: Selected Proceedings of the Fifth World Conference on Transport Research, Yokohama 1989,* 4 vols. Vol. 1, pp. 407-21. Venture: Western Publications

Rimmer, P.J., with Abdul Rahim Osman and H. Dick. 1989. Priming the Parastatals: Improving the Efficiency of State-Owned Transport Enterprises in the Asian-Pacific Region. In *Transport Policy.* Vol. 1, Regional seminar, pp. 133-83. Manila: Asian Development Bank and Economic Development Institute of the World Bank

Robinson, Ira M. 1985. Energy and Urban Form: Relationships between Energy Conservation, Transportation and Spatial Structure. In *Energy and Cities: Energy Policy Studies,* Vol. 2, edited by John Byrne and Daniel Rich, 7-50. New Brunswick: Transaction Books

–. 1991. The Emerging Mega-Urban Regions of Asia: Problems and Issues. Paper prepared for the International Congress of City and Regional Planning Schools/Departments of Asian Universities, University of Tokyo, Tokyo

Robinson, R. 1991. *The Changing Patterns of Commercial Shipping and Port Concentration in Asia.* Paper presented at the first ASEAN port meeting on Privatisation, New Technology and Deregulation, Kuala Lumpur, September

Robinson, R., K. Hewison, and R. Higgott, eds. 1987. *Southeast Asia in the 1980s: The Politics of Economic Crisis.* Sydney, London, and Boston: Allen and Unwin

Rodan, Gary. 1989. *The Political Economy of Singapore's Industrialization: National State and International Capital.* Basington: Macmillan

–. 1993. Regionalism and Sub-Regional Economies in the Asia-Pacific: Singapore and the Growth Triangle Concept. In *Pacific Economic Relations in the 1990s: Cooperation or Conflict?* Edited by R. Higgott, J. Ravenhill, and R. Leaver. Boulder, CO: Lynne Rienner Publishers

Rodrique, Jean-Paul. 1992. The Role of Transportation in the Emergence of Mega-Urban Regions in East Asia: The Case of Shanghai, Hong Kong and Singapore. Paper presented at the 1992 annual meeting of the Canadian Association of Geographers, Vancouver, 20-4 May

Romanos, M.C. 1978. Energy-Price Effects on Metropolitan Spatial Structure and Form. *Environment and Planning A* 10:93-104

Rondinelli, Dennis A. 1986. Metropolitan Growth and Secondary Cities, Development Policy. *Habitat International* 10(1/2):263-71

–. 1987. National Objectives and Strategies for Urban Development in Asia. In *Urban Policy Issues,* 61-88. Manila: Asian Development Bank

Rosmiyati, Rina. 1990. Perilaku Pelaku Perjalanan Bisnis Dinas Antar Kota Jakarta Dan Bandung. Undergraduate thesis, Department of City and Regional Planning, Institute of Technology, Bandung

Ruddick, G. 1956. *Town Planning in Kuala Lumpur.* Kuala Lumpur: C. Grenier

Ruland, Jurgen. 1988. *Urban Government in Southeast Asian Regional Cities: Issues and Problems in Dispersing Urban Growth.* Bangkok: Asian Institute of Technology

Salih, Kamal, and Mei Ling Young. 1987. Structural Adjustment, Employment Policy and Unemployment in Malaysia. Malaysian Institute of Economic Research Discussion Paper no. 14, Kuala Lumpur

Sassen, Saskia. 1991. *The Global City: New York, Tokyo and London.* Princeton: Princeton University

Schmidheiny, Stephan, with the Business Council for Sustainable Development. 1992. *Changing Course.* Cambridge, MA: MIT Press

Schwartz, P. 1991. *The Art of the Long View.* New York: Doubleday

Setchell, Charles A. 1991. Urban Transportation in Thailand: A Review and Evaluation of Policy and Research Needs. Unpublished report to the International Development Research Centre and the Chulalongkorn University Social Research Institute, Bangkok

–. 1992. Urban Management in Bangkok: Muddle amidst a Model? *Interplan* 39(spring):1

Sheikh, Ayub T. 1991. Study of Low-Income Housing Market in Bangkhan Area, Unpublished paper, Asian Institute of Technology, Bangkok

Simamora, Hot Asi. 1991. Kereta Api Sebagai Moda Angkutan Perkotaan: Kasus Studi Bagian Barat-Timur Wilayah Bandung Raya. Undergraduate thesis, Department of City and Regional Planning, Institute of Technology, Bandung

Singapore. 1991a. *The Next Lap.* Singapore: Government Press

–. 1991b. *The Strategic Economic Plan.* Singapore: Economic Planning Committee, Ministry of Trade and Industry

–. 1991c. *Singapore Statistics 1990.* Singapore: Department of Statistics

Sivarmakrichnan, K.C., and Leslie Green. 1986. *Metropolitan Management: The Asian Experience.* London: Oxford University Press, published for the Economic Development Institute of the World Bank

Sklair, Leslie. 1989. *Assembling for Development: The Maquila Industry in Mexico and the US.* London: Unwin Hyman

Sly, Peter G., ed. 1992. *Laguna Lake Basin Problems and Opportunities.* Institute of Environmental Science and Management, University of the Philippines at Los Banos, Philippines, and School of Resource and Environmental Studies, Dalhousie University, Halifax, Canada

Smith, David, and Bruce London. 1990. Convergence in World Urbanization? A Quantitative Assessment. *Urban Affairs Quarterly* 25(4):574-90

Soegijoko, Sugijanto. 1989. The Ordering of Land Use in the Suburbs of Urban Areas: The Cases of Botabek, Bopunjur and Bandung Raya. Undergraduate thesis, Department of City and Regional Planning, Institute of Technology, Bandung

Soja, E. 1989. *Postmodern Geographies: The Reassertion of Space in Critical Social Theory.* London: Verso

South Coast Air Quality Management District (SCAQMD). 1991. *Managing Air Quality.* Los Angeles: SCAQMD

Staple, G.C. 1990. *The Global Telecommunications Traffic Boom, A Quantitative Brief on Cross-Border Markets and Regulation, An IIC Research Report.* London: International Institute of Communications

Stopford, J., and J. Dunning. 1983. *Multinationals: Global Performances and Global Trends.* London: Macmillan

Strassmann, P., Blunt, A., and R. Tomas. 1992. Land, Incomes, and Housing: The Case of Metro-Manila. Unpublished manuscript

Struyk, J.R., M.L. Hoffman, and H.M. Katrusa. 1990. *The Market for Shelter in Indonesian*

Cities. Washington, DC: Urban Institute

Sulong Mohamad, and Katiman Rostam. 1984. Matlamat Dan Arah Pembangunan Bandar Baru Di Malaysia: Pengalaman Bandar Baru Bangi, Selangor. Paper presented at the National Conference on Development in Malaysia: Planning, Implementation and Performance, Bangi

Sussangkarn, C. 1987. The Thai Labour Market: A Study of Seasonality and Segmentation. Draft research report, Thailand Development Research Institute, Bangkok

Tamburnlertchai, Somsak. 1990. A Profile of Provincial Industries. Unpublished report, Thailand Development Research Institute, Bangkok

Tapananont, Nopanant. 1992. The Legislation and Implementation of Bangkok Metropolitan Development Plans. Paper presented at the International Workshop on Research and Planning Methodologies for Metropolitan/Regional Development, Chulalongkorn University, Bangkok, 29 June-3 July 1992

Thailand, National Statistical Office. 1971. *Population and Housing Census, 1970.* Bangkok: Office of the Prime Minister

–. 1980. *Statistical Reports by Changwat.* Bangkok: Office of the Prime Minister

–. 1978-88. *Statistical Yearbook of Thailand.* Bangkok: Office of the Prime Minister

Thomson, J.A. 1983. *Toward Better Urban Transport Planning in Developing Countries.* World Bank Staff Working Paper no. 600. Washington, DC: World Bank

Toffler, A. 1990. *Power Shift: Knowledge, Wealth and Violence at the Edge of the 21st Century.* New York: Bantam

Tsou Pao-chun. 1967. *Urban Landscape of Kuala Lumpur: A Geographical Survey.* Singapore: Nanyang University

United Nations. 1984. *Population Distribution, Migration and Development.* Proceedings of the Expert Group Population Distribution, Migration and Development, Hammamet, Tunisia, 21-5 March 1983

–. 1985. *Estimates and Projections of Urban, Rural and City Populations, 1950-2025: The 1982 Assessment.* Department of International Economic and Social Affairs, Report no. St/ESA/SER.R/58. New York: United Nations

–. 1986a. *Population Growth and Policies in Mega-Cities: Calcutta.* Department of International Economic and Social Affairs (DIESA) Population Policy Paper 1. New York: United Nations

–. 1986b. *Population Growth and Policies in Mega-Cities: Seoul.* DIESA Population Policy Paper 4. New York: United Nations

–. 1986c. *Population Growth and Policies in Mega-Cities: Metro Manila.* DIESA Population Policy Paper 5. New York: United Nations

–. 1986d. *Population Growth and Policies in Mega-Cities: Bombay.* DIESA Population Policy Paper 6. New York: United Nations

–. 1986e. *Population Growth and Policies in Mega-Cities: Delhi.* DIESA Population Policy Paper 7. New York: United Nations

–. 1987a. *Population Growth and Policies in Mega-Cities: Dhaka.* DIESA Population Policy Paper 8. New York: United Nations

–. 1987b. *Population Growth and Policies in Mega-Cities: Bangkok.* DIESA Population Policy Paper 10. New York: United Nations

–. 1987c. *Population Growth and Policies in Mega-Cities: Madras.* DIESA Population Policy Paper 12. New York: United Nations

–. 1988. *Population Growth and Policies in Mega-Cities: Karachi.* DIESA Population Policy Paper 13. New York: United Nations

–. 1989. *Population Growth and Policies in Mega-Cities: Jakarta.* DIESA Population Policy Paper 18. New York: United Nations

–. 1990a. *Population Growth and Policies in Mega-Cities: Cairo.* DIESA Population Policy Paper 33. New York: United Nations

–. 1990b. *World Population Policies.* 3 vols. New York: United Nations

–. 1991. *Population Growth and Policies in Mega-Cities: Mexico City.* DIESA Population Policy Paper 32. New York: United Nations

–. 1992a. *World Investment Report 1992: Transnational Corporations as Engines of Growth.* New York: United Nations

–. 1992b. *World Population Monitoring 1991.* Sales no. E.92.XIII.2. New York: United Nations

–. Forthcoming, a. *Population Growth and Policies in Mega-Cities: Rio de Janeiro.* New York: United Nations

–. Forthcoming, b. *Population Growth and Policies in Mega-Cities: Sao Paulo.* New York: United Nations

United Nations Centre for Human Settlements. 1987. *Global Report on Human Settlements.* London: Oxford University Press

–. 1989a. *Analysis of Land Markets: Analysis and Synthesis Report.* Nairobi: United Nations Centre for Human Settlements

–. 1989b. *Analysis of Land Markets: Analysis and Synthesis Report. Revised draft.* Nairobi: United Nations Centre for Human Settlements

United Nations Centre on Transnational Corporations (UNCTC). 1988. *Transnational Corporations and World Development.* New York: United Nations

United Nations Conference on Environment and Development. 1992. *Report of the United Nations Conference on Environment and Development: Rio de Janeiro, 13-14 June 1992.* Rio de Janeiro: United Nations

United Nations, Department of International Economic and Social Affairs (DIESA). 1989. *Prospects for World Urbanization 1988.* Population Studies No. 112. New York: United Nations

–. 1991. *World Urbanization Prospects 1990.* New York: United Nations

United Nations Development Program (UNDP). 1985. *National Urban Development Strategy Final Report.* Jakarta: National Urban Development Strategy Project

United Nations, Economic and Social Commission for Asia and the Pacific. 1993a. *1993 ESCAP Population Data Sheet.* Bangkok: United Nations

–. 1993b. *State of Urbanization in Asia and the Pacific.* New York: United Nations

United Nations Environment Program (UNEP). 1988. *Assessment of Urban Air Quality and Consequences.* Paris: United Nations

United Nations, UNICEF. 1990. *Children and the Environment.* New York: United Nations

University of the Philippines, Institute of Planning. 1971. Proposed Plan for Manila Bay Region. Unpublished report, Manila

Unkulvasapaul, M., and H.F. Seidel. 1991. *Thailand: Urban Sewage and Wastewater Management.* Washington, DC: World Bank

Van Til, Jan. 1979. Spatial Form and Structure in a Possible Future: Some Implications of Energy Shortfall for Urban Planning. *Journal of the American Planning Association* (July):318-29

Vining, D.R. 1986. Population Redistribution towards Core Areas of Less Developed Countries, 1950-1980. *International Regional Science Review* 10(1):1-45

Von Eckardt, Wolf. 1964. *The Challenge of Megalopolis: A Graphic Presentation of the Urbanized Northeastern Seaboard of the United States.* A Twentieth Century Fund Report, based on the original study of Jean Gottmann. New York: MacMillan

Ward, Peter M. 1990. Mexico City. Paper prepared for the Mega-Cities of the Americas conference, State University of New York at Albany, 5-7 April

Webster, D. 1992. Generating Political Support for Improvements to Urban Environments in ASEAN. Paper prepared for the International Workshop on Planning for Sustainable Urban Development – Cities and Natural Resource Systems in Developing Countries, Cardiff, Wales, 13-17 July

Weissmann, Ernest. 1970. Planning and Development of the Metropolitan Environment. In *Metropolitan Problems: International Perspectives, A Search for Comprehensive Solutions,* edited by Simon Miles, 411-50. Toronto: Methuen

West Java Provincial Government (DTKTD). 1992. Rencana Struktur Tata Ruang Propinsi Jawa Barat. Unpublished report

Wheaton, W., and H. Shisedo. 1981. Urban Concentration, Agglomeration Economies and the Level of Economic Development. *Economic Development and Cultural Change* 30(1):17-30

Wheeler, David, and Paul Martin. 1991. Prices, Policies, and the International Diffusion of Clean Technology: The Case of Wood Pulp Production. Paper presented at the Symposium on International Trade and the Environment, World Bank, 21-2 November

Wong Poh Kam. 1992. Economic Cooperation in the Southern Growth Triangle: A Long Term Perspective. Paper presented at the International Symposium on Regional Cooperation and Growth Triangles in ASEAN, organized by the Centre for Business Research and Development and Centre for Advanced Studies, National University of Singapore, 23-4 April

Wood, Robert C. 1959. *New York's 1400 Governments*. Boston: Houghton Mifflin

World Bank. 1986. *World Development Report 1986*. New York: Oxford University Press

–. 1989. Debate over Land Registration Persists. *The Urban Edge* 13(7)

–. 1990. *World Development Report 1990*. New York: Oxford University Press

–. 1991a. *Urban Policy and Economic Development, An Agenda for the 1990s*. World Bank policy paper. Washington, DC: International Bank for Reconstruction and Development

–. 1991b. *Housing Indicators Program Extensive Survey Part II: Indicators Modules and Worksheets*. Washington, DC: World Bank

–. 1992a. *World Development Report 1992*. New York: Oxford University Press

–. 1992b. Environmental Strategies for Cities: A Framework for Urban Environmental Management in Developing Countries. Strategy framework paper, working draft, World Bank, Washington, DC

–. 1993. *Housing: Enabling Markets to Work*. Washington, DC: World Bank

World Health Organization (WHO). 1991. *Urbanization and Health in Developing Countries*. Geneva: WHO

Yap Kioe Sheng. 1989. Some Low-Income Delivery Subsystems in Bangkok, Thailand. *Environment and Urbanization* 1(2):27-37

–. 1992. The Slums. In *Low-Income Housing in Bangkok: A Review of Some Housing Sub-Markets*, 31-48. Bangkok: Asian Institute of Technology

Yap, K.S., K. De Wandeler, and A. Khanaiklang. In preparation. *Low-Income Rental Housing in Bangkok*

Yap Soon Heng. 1991. Town Planning Law in Malaysia: Politics, Rights and Jealousies. *Habitat International* 15(4):105-14

Yeoh, Caroline, Lau Geok Theng, and G. Funkhouser. 1992. Summary Report: Business Trends in the Growth Triangle. Faculty of Business Administration, National University of Singapore. Mimeographed

Yeung Yue-Man. 1992. China and Hong Kong. In *Sustainable Cities: Urbanization and the Environment in International Perspective*, edited by R.E. Stren, R. White, and J.B. Whitney. Boulder, CO: Westview Press

Yeung Yue-Man and C.P. Lo, eds. 1976. *Changing South-East Asian Cities: Readings on Urbanization*. Singapore: Oxford University Press

Yeung Yue-Man, and Xu-wei Hu. 1992. *Chinese Coastal Cities: Catalysts for Modernization*. Honolulu: University of Hawaii Press

Young Mei Ling. 1987. Industrialization and Its Impact on Labour Migration. Malaysian Institute of Economic Research Discussion Paper no. 6, Kuala Lumpur

Zhou Yixing. 1991. The Metropolitan Interlocking Region in China: A Preliminary Hypothesis. In *The Extended Metropolis: Settlement Transition in Asia*, edited by N. Ginsburg, B. Koppel, and T.G. McGee, 89-112. Honolulu: University of Hawaii Press

Contributors

Shlomo Angel was for many years a faculty member of the Human Settlements Development Program at the Asian Institute of Technology. He has concentrated his research work on the study of low-income settlements and is currently a consultant to the World Bank on low-income housing.

Ellen M. Brennan is chief of the Population Policy Section of the United Nations Population Division. She developed the United Nations project, 'Population Growth and Policies in Mega-Cities' in the developing world, under which rubric she authored more than a dozen profiles on selected mega-cities. Her special area of interest is urban environmental problems.

Shirley A.M. Conover is Leslie Pearson Senior Fellow in the School for Resource and Environmental Studies, Dalhousie University. She is currently the director of two CIDA-funded projects based at Dalhousie University. The first is the Environmental Management and Development in Indonesia (EMDI) Project, with the Indonesian Ministry of State for Population and Environment. The second is the Environment and Resource Management Project, with the University of the Philippines at Los Banos.

Mike Douglass is chair of the Department of Urban and Regional Planning at the University of Hawaii at Manoa. He is the author of several major studies of urbanization in East and Southeast Asia and has also acted as a consultant for the urban strategy plans developed in Indonesia and Thailand.

Tommy Firman is a former dean of graduate studies at the Bandung Institute of Technology. A graduate of the University of Hawaii at Manoa, he has ongoing research interests in the development of urban labour markets in Indonesia.

Ida Ayu Indira Dharmapatni is a research associate in the Department of Planning at the Bandung Institute of Technology, Indonesia. She has been actively involved in urban planning and policy formation in Indonesia.

Utis Kaothien is the director of the Urban Development Coordination Division in the National Economic and Social Development Board, Bangkok, Thailand. He also serves as secretary to and a member of a number of national policy committees. He headed a special task force in charge of formulating the national urban development policies for the Seventh Plan (1992-6) of Thailand.

Aprodicio Laquian is the director of the Centre for Human Settlements and a professor of Community and Regional Planning at the University of British Columbia. Prior to joining UBC in 1991, Dr. Laquian was chief of the Evaluation Branch and deputy director of the Technical and Evaluation Division of the United Nations Population Fund. He has written extensively on low-cost housing policies and practices, self-help efforts, the adjustment of rural-urban migrants to life in large cities, and the planning and management of metropolitan areas.

Lee Boon Thong is a professor in the Department of Geography at the University of Malaya. He has researched and written on, among many topics, urbanization, the role of small towns and intermediate cities, urban interethnic relations, and settlement patterns in frontier areas. He is currently involved in a study of out-migration of tribal groups in Sarawak and a regional study of urban development and urbanization in Johor.

Lee Tsao Yuan is the deputy director of the Institute of Policy Studies (IPS) in Singapore, an independent think-tank established in 1987 to study issues of policy interest to Singapore. Prior to joining IPS, she was a senior lecturer in the Department of Economics and Statistics at the National University of Singapore. Dr. Lee has written extensively on the Singapore economy, ASEAN, and the Asian NICs. Her current research interests centre on ASEAN and Singapore's external economic relations.

T.G. McGee is a professor in the Department of Geography and director of the Institute of Asian Research at the University of British Columbia in Vancouver, Canada. He has spent more than thirty years researching urbanization in Southeast Asia and has written extensively on the subject. He served as co-chair of the International Conference on Managing the Mega-Urban Regions in ASEAN Countries: Policy Challenges and Responses, held at the Asian Institute of Technology in December 1992.

Stephen K. Mayo has worked in the Urban Development Division of the World Bank.

Romeo B. Ocampo is a professor in the Department of Political Science at the University of the Philippines. He is one of the Philippines' leading political scientists and has been closely involved with policy formation in the Manila Metropolitan Region for many years.

V. Setty Pendakur is a professor in the School of Community and Regional Planning at the University of British Columbia. He is an expert on transportation planning and acts as a consultant for the World Bank on transportation projects.

Aminur Rahman is an architect by early training, prior to obtaining his master's degree in human settlements planning at the Asian Institute of Technology in 1992. Part of the research he undertook for his thesis formed the basis for Chapter 6 of this book, undertaken with Dr. Yap Kioe Sheng.

Peter J. Rimmer is currently head of the Department of Human Geography at Australian National University, Canberra. He is the author of several books on transportation in Asia and of studies of the development process in this region. He has acted as a consultant for various Australian and international assistance agencies.

Ira M. Robinson is professor emeritus of urban and planning and former chair of the Graduate Program in Urban and Regional Planning at the University of Calgary. Prior to joining the University of Calgary, he taught at the University of Southern California in Los Angeles and the University of British Columbia. Since 1989, he has also served as a visiting faculty member in the Human Settlements Development Program at the Asian Institute of Technology. With Dr. McGee, he served as co-chair of the International Conference on Managing the Mega-Urban Regions in ASEAN Countries: Policy Challenges and Responses.

Douglas Webster is a professor of Development Planning at the University of Calgary and has taught at the University of British Columbia. While on sabbatical, he is now serving as senior urban planning adviser to the Urban Development Coordination Division of the National Social and Economic Development Board in Bangkok, Thailand.

Yap Kioe Sheng is an associate professor in the Human Settlements Development Program at the Asian Institute of Technology in Bangkok, Thailand. Previously he served as a consultant to the United Nations Center for Housing Settlements. He has also been a consultant to various international aid agencies, focusing on the problems of housing and infrastructure provision for the poor in Asian cities.

Index